Beginner's Korean

WITH ONLINE AUDIO

Beginner's
Korean
WITH ONLINE AUDIO

JEYSEON LEE & KANGJIN LEE

Hippocrene Books, Inc.
New York

Audio files available for download at:
http://www.hippocrenebooks.com/beginners-online-audio.html

Online audio edition, 2019.
Text & audio copyright © 2007 Jeyseon Lee and Kangjin Lee.

For information, address:
HIPPOCRENE BOOKS, INC.
171 Madison Avenue
New York, NY 10016
www.hippocrenebooks.com

Previous edition ISBN: 978-0-7818-1092-0

Cataloging-in-publication data available from the Library of Congress.

ISBN 978-0-7818-1377-8

Table of Contents

Introduction:
About the Korean Language

Korean is the native language of 67 million people living on the Korean peninsula, as well as the heritage language of 5.6 million Diaspora Koreans.

The Korean language consists of seven geographically based dialects. Despite the differences in dialects, Korean is relatively homogeneous, with strong mutual intelligibility among speakers from different areas. This is because the mass media and formal education are based on standard speech and strongly contribute to the standardization of the language.

The closest sister language of Korean is Japanese. However, they are not mutually intelligible and their relationship is very weak. Some scholars claim that Korean and Japanese are remotely related to the Altaic languages, such as native Manchu, Mongolian, and the Turkic languages.

Although Korean and Japanese are geographically, historically, and culturally close to China, Korean and Japanese are not part of the same language family as Chinese, and therefore are not grammatically similar to Chinese. However, both Korean and Japanese have borrowed a large number of Chinese words and characters throughout the course of their long historical contact with various Chinese dynasties, and those borrowed Chinese words and characters have become an integral part of the Korean and Japanese vocabularies.

Since the end of World War II, Korean people have been in contact with many foreign countries and have borrowed thousands of words, the majority from English. During the 35-year occupation of Korea by Japan, a considerable number of Japanese words were also borrowed.

The Korean vocabulary has three components: native words and affixes (approximately 35 percent), Sino-Korean words (approximately 60 percent), and loanwords (approximately 5 percent). Native words denote daily necessities (food, clothing, and shelter), locations, basic actions, activities, states of being, lower-level numbers, body parts, natural objects, animals, and so forth.

Due to their ideographic and monosyllabic nature, Chinese characters are easily combined and recombined to coin new terms as new cultural objects and concepts are created. Most institutional terms, traditional cultural terms, personal names, and place names are Sino-Korean words. There are 14,000 loanwords in Korean, almost 9 percent from English. Most of those loanwords are commonly used, facilitating, to a certain extent, cross-cultural communication.

Korean is often called a situation-oriented language in that contextually or situationally understood elements, including subject and object, are omitted more frequently than not. Therefore, inserting the pronoun "you" or "I" in expressions such as 안녕하세요? (an-nyeong-ha-se-yo?) / How are you?, or 고맙습니다 (go-map-sum-ni-da) / thank you, would sound awkward in normal contexts.

Korean is a "macro-to-micro" language. The larger context of something is presented first, followed by gradually smaller contexts, ending with the individual context. For example, when referring to someone by name, Koreans say or write the family name first and the given name second, which may be followed by a title. An address is given by first indicating the country, followed by, in descending order, the province, city, street, house number, and, finally, the name of the addressee. Koreans indicate a date with the year first, the month second, and the day last.

Korean may be called an honorific language, in that one uses different words and phrases depending on the status of the person being discussed or to whom one is speaking. Differences such as age, family relationship, and social status are systematically encoded in the structure and use of Korean. A small number of commonly used words have two forms, one plain and one honorific. The honorific forms are used with an adult of equal or greater status, such as an elder, whereas the plain forms are reserved for another of lesser status. There are also humble verbs used to express deference to an elder or one of greater status.

Korean has an extensive set of address and reference terms that are sensitive to degrees of social stratification and distance between the speaker and addressee and between the speaker and referent. The most frequently used terms for a social superior or an adult distant equal are composed of an occupational title followed by the gender-neutral honorific suffix –님 (nim), such as 교수님 (gyo-su-nim) Professor.

This may be preceded by the full or family name. There are several titles. The most frequently used among younger co-workers or when speaking to a child or adolescent is the gender-neutral noun –씨 (ssi). This noun is affixed to one's full or given name. When speaking or referring to child, use either the given name alone or the full name without a title. When addressing a child by a given name, the name is followed by a particle. When the name ends with a consonant, the particle is 아 (a). When it ends with a vowel, the particle is 야 (ya).

In Korean, first person pronouns—the English "I" and "we"— have both plain and humble forms. The plain singular form is 나 (na) and the plain plural is 우리 (u-ri), while the humble singular is 저 (jeo) and the humble plural is 저희 (jeo-hui). The humble forms are used when speaking with an elder or an adult of higher social status. Second person pronouns, the equivalent of the English "you", are used only when speaking with children. The singular form is 너 (neo) and the plural is 너희 (neo-hui). When speaking with an adult, one must address them with their name and title. For example: 김선생님 (gim-seon-saeng-nim) / you, teacher Kim.

Korean is currently written using both Chinese characters and the Korean phonetic alphabet known as 한글 (hanguel/hangul). Chinese characters were used exclusively in written Korean until 1443, when King Sejong the Great, the fourth king of the 조선 (jo-seon)

Dynasty, created 한글 *(Hangul)* with his court scholars. 한글 has continued to enjoy increasing favor over Chinese characters. The latter's contemporary usage is largely restricted to newspapers and scholarly books, and even there it is limited. Chinese characters, however, are very useful in differentiating between words with identical pronunciation and 한글 spelling.

There are considerable differences between the Korean and English languages. Such differences range from pronunciation and grammar to vocabulary principles and writing systems to underlying traditions and culture. These differences make Korean one of the most challenging languages for a native English speaker to learn. We hope this book will help to make it one of the most rewarding.

Korean Alphabet &
Pronunciation Guide

핳 ㅏ ㄱㄹ

The Letters of the 한글 (Hangul/han-geul) Alphabet and Their Pronunciation

The current 한글 alphabet has 40 characters: 19 consonants, 8 vowels, and 13 diphthongs. A diphthong combines two separate vowel sounds. In English, examples include the "ou" sound in the word "out" and the "eo" sound in the word "people".

Korean allows a three-way voiceless contrast (plain, aspirate, and tense) in plosive consonants, and a two-way (plain and tense) or no contrast in fricative consonants. In addition to these consonants, Korean has the liquid consonant *l*, which is pronounced as *r* in initial position or between vowels, and three nasal consonants. The Korean consonant chart is illustrated below.

There are four kinds of consonants in Korean: plosive, fricative, liquid, and nasal. Plosive consonants have three kinds of contrasts: plain, aspirate, and tense. Twelve consonants are plosive, with four in each contrast. There are 3 fricative consonants, two using the plain contrast and the other using the tense contrast. The one liquid consonant is *l*, although it is pronounced as *r* when it begins a word or appears between two vowels. There are three nasal consonants, but they are not distinguished by contrasts. A pronunciation chart, which also indicates the proper tongue position when making the consonant sounds, appears below:

consonants

"plosive consonant: stop (stop airflow)"
"fricative consonant: consonant made by friction of breath in narrow openins producing turbulent air flow like f or th in enslish"

		Gum Ridge	Hard Palatal	Soft Palatal	Throat
	Lips				
PLOSIVE					
Plain	ㅂ [p/b] baby	ㄷ [t/d] day	ㅈ [ch/j] angel	ㄱ [k/g] begin	
Aspirate	ㅍ [p'] public	ㅌ [t'] atomic	ㅊ [ch'] achieve	ㅋ [k'] akin	
Tense	ㅃ [pp] spoon	ㄸ [tt] state	ㅉ [tch] pizza	ㄲ [kk] skate	
FRICATIVE					
Plain		ㅅ [s/sh] sheep			ㅎ [h] home
Tense		ㅆ [ss] assign			
LIQUID					
		ㄹ [l/r] leaf radio			
NASAL					
	ㅁ [m] me	ㄴ [n] now		ㅇ [ng] song	

Consonants change sounds depending on their position in a word. The 한글 spellings, however, do not change.

In standard Korean, there are 8 vowels and 13 diphthongs. The vowels are grouped into categories of front and back. Back vowels are further categorized as round and unround. (All front vowels are unround.) The Korean vowel chart, which indicates both these divisions and the tongue position during pronunciation, is below:

Handwritten top margin: 호ᅡ 구 ⟩ 호=h ᅡ=a ㄴ=n ㄱ=g ㅡ=u (eu) ㄹ=l

Tongue Position	Front		Back	
	Unround	Round	Unround	Round
High	ㅣ [i] beet		ㅡ [û] good	ㅜ [u] buoy
Mid	ㅔ [e] bet		ㅓ [ô] mother	ㅗ [o] awkward
Low	ㅐ [ae] at		ㅏ [a] father	

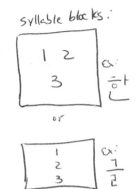

Handwritten (right margin): syllable blocks: 1 2 / 3 ex: 호ᅡ / or / 1 / 2 / 3 ex: 구ᄅ 1=consonant 2=vowel 3=consonant

There are two semi-vowels, *y* and *w*, and they combine with 8 vowels to make 13 diphthongs. The Korean diphthong chart is represented below.

	ㅏ	ㅓ	ㅗ	ㅜ	ㅡ	ㅣ	ㅔ	ㅐ
y	ㅑ [ya] yacht	ㅕ [yô] young	ㅛ [yo] yawn	ㅠ [yu] yukon	ㅢ [ûi]		ㅖ [ye] yet	ㅒ [yae] yak
w	ㅘ [wa] wander	ㅝ [wô] wonder			ㅟ [wi] win	ㅚ [we] west	ㅞ [we] west	ㅙ [wae] wangle

Syllable Blocks in Korean

한글 han-geul letters are combined into syllable blocks. The syllable blocks are constructed out of what is referred to as consonant, vowel, and diphthong positions. A square syllable block has the initial consonant position followed by a vowel or diphthong position. In the final consonant position, one or two consonants may occur. If a syllable does not begin with a consonant, the syllable block must have the letter ㅇ in the initial consonant position. The letter ㅇ is silent and functions as a zero consonant in the initial position of a syllable block.

If the vowel letter in the syllable block contains one or two long vertical strokes, it is written to the right of the initial consonant letter (e.g. 나 [na], 계 [gye]). If the vowel letter in the syllable block

Handwritten bottom margin: – vowel to the right if 1 or 2 vertical strokes – bellow if horizontal strokes

contains only a long horizontal stroke, the vowel letter is written below the initial consonant letter (e.g. 무 [mu], 교 [gyo]). If a diphthong letter contains a long horizontal stroke and a long vertical stroke, the initial consonant letter occurs in the upper left corner (e.g. 귀 [gwi], 놔 [nwa]). When a syllable ends with consonants, they occur beneath the vowel letter (e.g. 봤 [bwat], 김 [gim], 흙 [heuk, heulk]). Final consonants can be all single consonant letters and the following two-letter combinations: ㄲ (kk), ㅆ (ss), ㄳ (ks), ㄵ (nj), ㄶ (nh), ㄺ (lk), ㄻ (lm), ㄼ (lp), ㄽ (ls), ㄾ (lt'), ㄿ (lp'), ㅀ (lh), ㅄ (ps). When writing the letters in syllable blocks, they should be balanced to fill the space.

To demonstrate the construction of a word in written Korean, let us consider the word 한글 (han-geul). It has two syllable blocks, 한 (han) and 글 (geul). In the first syllable block, ㅎ (h), ㅏ (a), and ㄴ (n) combine like this:

한 (han)

In the second syllable block, the letters ㄱ (g), ㅡ (eu), and ㄹ (l) combine to form:

글 (gul)

Note how, in accordance with the rules outlined above, the initial consonant ㅎ (h) in 한 (han) appears with ㅏ (a) to its right and the final consonant ㄴ (n) below. With the syllable block 글 (geul), note how the initial consonant ㄱ (g) is placed first, with the vowel ㅡ (eu), which is written as a horizontal stroke, below it, and the final consonant ㄹ (l) appearing below the vowel.

The Romanization of Korean

(Korean Ministry of Culture and Tourism proclamation No. 2000-8)

1. Basic principles of romanization

(1) Romanization is based on standard Korean pronunciation.
(2) Symbols other than Roman letters are avoided to the greatest extent possible.

2. Summary of the romanization system

(1) Vowels are transcribed as follows:

Simple Vowels

ㅏ *a* / ㅓ *eo* / ㅗ *o* / ㅜ *u* / ㅡ *eu* / ㅣ *i* / ㅐ *ae* / ㅔ *e* / ㅚ *oe* / ㅟ *wi*

Diphthongs

ㅑ *ya* / ㅕ *yeo* / ㅛ *yo* / ㅠ *yu* / ㅒ *yae* / ㅖ *ye* / ㅘ *wa* / ㅙ *wae* / ㅝ *wo* / ㅞ *we* / ㅢ *ui*

Note 1: ㅢ is transcribed as *ui*, even when pronounced as ㅣ.

Note 2: Long vowels are not reflected in romanization.

(2) Consonants are transcribed as follows:

Plosives (Stops)

ㄱ *g, k* / ㄲ *kk* / ㅋ *k* / ㄷ *d, t* / ㄸ *tt* / ㅌ *t* / ㅂ *b, p* / ㅃ *pp* / ㅍ *p*

Affricates and Fricatives
ㅈ *j* / ㅉ *jj* / ㅊ *ch* / ㅅ *s* / ㅆ *ss* / ㅎ *h*

Nasals and Liquids
ㄴ *n* / ㅁ *m* / ㅇ *ng* / ㄹ *r, l*

Note 1: The sounds ㄱ, ㄷ, and ㅂ are transcribed respectively as *g*, *d*, and *b* when they appear before a vowel. They are transcribed as *k*, *t*, and *p* when followed by another consonant or forming the final sound of a word.

Note 2: ㄹ is transcribed as *r* when followed by a vowel, and *l* when followed by a consonant or when appearing at the end of a word. ㄹㄹ is transcribed as *ll*.

3. *Special provisions for romanization*

(1) When Korean sound values change as in the following cases, the results of those changes are romanized.

1) The case of assimilation of adjacent consonants
2) The case of the epenthetic [inserted within the body of a word] ㄴ and ㄹ
3) Cases of palatalization
4) Cases where ㄱ, ㄷ, ㅂ and ㅈ are adjacent to ㅎ

However, aspirated sounds are not reflected in case of nouns where ㅎ follows ㄱ, ㄷ, and ㅂ.

Note: Tense (or glottalized) sounds are not reflected in cases where morphemes [the smallest part of a word that has meaning] are compounded.

(2) When there is the possibility of confusion in pronunciation, a hyphen "-" may be used.

(3) The first letter is capitalized in proper names.

(4) Personal names are written by family name first, followed by a space and the given name. In principle, syllables in given names are not separated by hyphen, but the use of a hyphen between syllables is permitted.

  1) Assimilated sound changes between syllables in given names are not transcribed.
  2) Romanization of family names will be determined separately.

(5) Administrative units, such as 도 *do,* 시 *si,* 군 *gun,* 구 *gu,* 읍 *eup,* 면 *myeon,* 리 *ri,* 동 *dong,* and 가 *ga* are transcribed respectively as *do, si, gun, gu, eup, myeon, ri, dong,* and *ga,* and are preceded by a hyphen. Assimilated sound changes before and after the hyphen are not reflected in romanization.

Note: Terms for administrative units such as 시 *si,* 군 *gun,* 읍 *eup* may be omitted.

(6) Names of geographic features, cultural properties, and manmade structures may be written without hyphens.

(7) Proper names such as personal names and those of companies may continue to be written as they have been previously.

(8) When it is necessary to convert romanized Korean back to *hangul* in special cases such as in academic articles, romanization is done according to *hangul* spelling and not pronunciation. Each *hangul* letter is romanized as explained in section 2 except that ㄱ, ㄷ, ㅂ and ㄹ are always written as *g, d, b* and *l.* When ㅇ has no sound value, it is replaced by a hyphen. It may also be used when it is necessary to distinguish between syllables.

Pronunciation Rules

Rule 1. Resyllabification

When a syllable in a word ends with a consonant and the next syllable begins with a vowel, the consonant, when pronounced, is part of the latter syllable. For example, 한글은 (han-geul-eun) is pronounced han-geu-reun. In this case, the sound of ㄹ changes from *l* to *r* because ㄹ now appears between two vowels. Similarly, when a syllable block ends in a double consonant, the second consonant is pronounced before the vowel as part of the latter syllable, so the Korean word for 읽어요 (ilk-eo-yo) "read," is pronounced il-geo-yo.

Rule 2. Final closure in syllable pronunciation

At the end of a word or before a consonant, all Korean consonants are pronounced without releasing air. As a result, consonants at the end of words or preceding other consonants change sounds. For example, 꽃 (kkoch) is pronounced kkot and 꽃도 (kkoch-do) is pronounced kkot-do. The change of ㅊ to ㄷ happens here because the speech organs responsible for the articulation of the word-final and pre-consonantal ㅊ are not released. The sound of ㅊ (ch') becomes *t* because one does not release air when pronouncing it in these and similar words. The only consonant sounds that occur at the end of a word or before another consonant are the seven simple consonants: ㅂ (p/b), ㄷ (t/d), ㄱ (k/g), ㅁ (m), ㄴ (n), ㅇ (ng), and ㄹ (l/r). The sound changes are illustrated below.

ㅂ, ㅃ, ㅍ → ㅂ

ㄷ, ㄸ, ㄸ, ㅅ, ㅆ, ㅈ, ㅉ, ㅊ, ㅎ → ㄷ

ㄱ, ㄲ, ㅋ → ㄱ

ㅁ → ㅁ

ㄴ → ㄴ

ㅇ → ㅇ

ㄹ → ㄹ

Rule 3. Nasal assimilation

All plosive and fricative consonants become corresponding nasal consonants when preceding a nasal consonant. For example, 앞문 (ap-mun) "front gate" is pronounced am-mun and 일학년 (il-hak-nyeon) "first grade/first year" is pronounced il-hang-nyeon. The chart below fully illustrates the changes.

ㅂ, ㅃ, ㅍ → ㅁ

ㄷ, ㄸ, ㄸ, ㅅ, ㅆ, ㅈ, ㅉ, ㅊ, ㅎ → ㄴ

ㄱ, ㄲ, ㅋ → ㅇ

Rule 4. ㄴ *to* ㄹ *assimilation*

When ㄹ (l/r) and ㄴ (n) appear together in a word, the *n* sound is usually replaced by the *l/r* sound, as in the Korean word for "seven years," 칠년 (chil-lyeon). When *l/r* is followed by the vowel ㅣ (i) or the semivowel ㅑ (ya) in certain compound words, another *l/r* is inserted between them, as in the Korean word for "liquid medicine," 물약 (mul-lyak).

Rule 5. Tensification

When a plain plosive consonant (ㅂ (p/b), ㄷ (t/d), ㅈ (ch/j), ㄱ (k/g)) or the fricative consonant ㅅ (s/sh) is preceded by a plosive or fricative consonant (ㅂ, ㄷ, ㅈ, ㄱ, ㅍ[p'], ㅌ[t'], ㅊ[ch'], ㅋ[k'], ㅃ[pp], ㄸ[tt], ㅉ[tch], ㄲ[kk], ㅅ, ㅎ[h], ㅆ [ss]) it becomes a corresponding tense consonant, as in the words 학생 (hak-ssaeng) "students," 없다 (eop-tta) "not exist," and 학교 (hak-kkyo) "school."

Rule 6. Aspiration and the weakening of ㅎ

When the fricative consonant ㅎ (h) is preceded or followed by a plain plosive consonant (ㅂ [p/b], ㄷ [t/d], ㅈ [ch/j], ㄱ [k/g]), it merges with the consonant to produce a corresponding aspirate consonant (ㅍ [p'], ㅌ [t'], ㅊ [ch'], ㅋ [k']), as in the words for 좋다 (jo-ta) 'to be good', 입학 (i-pak) 'entering school', and 착하다 (cha-ka-da) 'to be kind'.

Rule 7. Double consonant reduction

As indicated in Rule 1, the second of the two consonants at the end of a syllable is, when pronounced, carried over to the following syllable if the latter syllable does not begin with a consonant. However, one of the two consonants becomes silent at the end of a word or before a consonant, as in the words for "price," 값 (gap) and 값도 (gap-tto). In English, up to three consonants may be combined in a syllable, but not even two may be combined in Korean. It is difficult to predict which of two consonants will become silent. The silent consonant is usually the second one, but there are exceptions.

Rule 8. Palatalization

When a word ending in ㄷ (t/d) or ㅌ (t') is followed by a suffix beginning with the vowel ㅣ (i) or the semivowel ㅕ (yeo), the ㄷ and ㅌ are pronounced, respectively, *ch/j and ch'*, as in the words for 닫혀요 (da-chyeo-yo) "to be closed," and 붙이다 (bu-chi-da) "to attach." This change is technically called "palatalization" because the original consonants, which are pronounced using the gum-ridge, are articulated with the hard palate.

한글
Reading Exercise

[연습문제]
Please read the words below. An answer key appears on the following page.

(1) 아이, 오이, 요요, 우유
(2) 나비, 나라, 사자, 가지, 고추, 개구리, 나무, 다리, 라디오, 모자, 무지개, 바지, 바구니, 사다리, 지도, 조개, 치마, 해바라기, 아기, 거미, 머리, 너구리, 소, 그네
(3) 눈사람, 당근, 독수리, 다람쥐, 리본, 물개, 말, 버섯, 선물, 사슴, 안경, 옥수수, 자동차, 잠자리, 바늘, 거북이, 오징어, 고래, 용, 눈, 물소, 드럼, 늑대, 기린, 진주
(4) 야구, 달걀, 야자수, 염소, 병아리, 주사위, 귤, 유람선
(5) 책상, 칠면조, 컵, 코끼리, 카메라, 코뿔소, 토끼, 타조, 태극기, 포도, 표범, 피아노, 풍차, 해, 호박, 편지, 도토리, 표지판, 우체통, 휴지통, 크레용, 피라밋
(6) 꼬리, 까마귀, 딸, 때, 빵, 싸움, 씨름, 짜장면, 꼴찌

[Answers]

(1) a-i, o-i, yo-yo, u-yu

(2) na-bi, na-ra, sa-ja, ga-ji, go-chu, gae-gu-ri, na-mu, da-ri, ra-di-o, mo-ja, mu-ji-gae, ba-ji, ba-gu-ni, sa-da-ri, ji-do, jo-gea, chi-ma, hae-ba-ra-gi, a-gi, geo-mi, meo-ri, neo-gu-ri, so, geu-ne

(3) nun-sa-ram, dang-geun, dok-su-ri, da-ram-jwi, ri-bon, mul-gae, mal, beo-seot, seon-mul, sa-seum, an-gyeong, ok-su-su, ja-dong-cha, jam-ja-ri, ba-neul, geo-bug-i, o-jing-eo, go-rae, yong, nun, mul-so, deu-reom, neuk-dae, gi-rin, jin-ju

(4) ya-gu, dal-gyal, ya-ja-su, byeong-a-ri, ju-sa-wi, gyul, yu-ram-seon

(5) chaek-sang, chil-myeon-jo, keop, ko-kki-ri, ka-me-ra, ko-ppul-so, to-kki, ta-jo, tae-guk-gi, po-do, pyo-beom, pi-a-no, pung-cha, hae, ho-bak, pyeon-ji, do-to-ri, pyo-ji-pan, u-che-tong, hyu-ji-tong, keu-re-yong, pi-ra-mit kko-ri, kka-ma-gwi, ttal, ttae, ppyam, ssa-um, ssi-reum, jja-jang-myeon, kkol-jji

Abbreviations

abbr.	abbreviation
adj.	adjective (including noun-modifier in Korean)
adv.	adverb
coll.	colloquial
conj.	conjunction
cop.	copula, i.e., linking verb
count.	counter
dat.	dative/indirect object particle
dir.	direction
e.g.	for example
fut.	future tense
hon.	honorific
loc.	location
n.	noun
num.	number
obj.	object/object particle
part.	particle
pl.	plural
pren.	pre-noun/noun modifier
pres.	present tense
pron.	pronoun
pst.	past tense
sing.	singular
subj.	subject/subject particle
top.	topic/topic particle
v.	verb (including both active verb and descriptive verb in Korean)

v. stem	verb stem
v. intr.	intransitive verb, i.e., cannot have an object
v. tr.	transitive verb, i.e., can have an object

제1과 인사

◇◇◇◇◇◇◇◇

Lesson 1: Greetings

표현 Patterns

안녕하십니까?
an-nyeong-ha-sim-ni-kka?
How are you? / Hello.

안녕히 가십시오.
an-nyeong-hi ga-sip-si-o.
Good-bye *(to the one leaving).*

안녕히 계십시오.
an-nyeong-hi gye-sip-si-o.
Good-bye *(to the one staying).*

처음 뵙겠습니다.
cheo-eum boep-get-seum-ni-da.
Nice to meet you. *(first time only)*

다음에 또 뵙겠습니다.
da-eum-e tto boep-get-seum-ni-da.
See you next time.

오래간만입니다.
o-rae-gan-man-im-ni-da.
Long time, no see.

그 동안 잘 지내셨습니까?
geu dong-an jal ji-nae-syeot-seum-ni-kka?
How have you been? *(lit.* Have you been doing well?*)*

요즘 어떻게 지내십니까?
yo-jeum eo-tteo-ke ji-nae-sim-ni-kka?
How are you these days?

덕분에 잘 지냈습니다.
deok-bun-e jal ji-naet-seum-ni-da.
I have been doing fine, thanks to you.

덕분에 잘 지냅니다.
deok-bun-e jal ji-naem-ni-da.
I am fine, thanks to you.

그저 그렇습니다.
geu-jeo geu-reot-seum-ni-da.
So-so.

만나 뵙게 돼서 반갑습니다.
man-na boep-ge dwae-seo ban-gap-seum-ni-da.
Nice to meet you.

만나 뵙게 돼서 정말 즐거웠습니다.
man-na boep-ge dwae-seo jeong-mal jeul-geo-wot-seum-ni-da.
I was glad to meet you.

다시 뵙게 돼서 정말 반갑습니다.
da-si boep-ge dwae-seo jeong-mal ban-gap-seum-ni-da.
Nice to see you again.

저도 반갑습니다.
jeo-do ban-gap-seum-ni-da.
I am glad, too.

저도 잘 지냅니다.
jeo-do jal ji-nam-ni-da.
I am doing fine, too.

저도 즐거웠습니다.
jeo-do jeul-geo-wot-seum-ni-da.
I was glad, too.

실례지만 성함이 어떻게 되십니까?
sil-lye-ji-man seong-ham-i eo-teo-ke doe-sim-ni-kka?
Excuse me, what is your name?

실례지만 어떤 일을 하십니까?
sil-lye-ji-man eo-tteon il-eul ha-sim-ni-kka?
Excuse me, but what do you do for living?

저는 김현준입니다.
jeo-neun gim-hyeon-jun-im-ni-da.
My name is Hyeon-Jun Kim. (*lit*. I am Hyeon-Jun Kim.)

저는 이정호라고 합니다.
jeo-neun i-jeong-ho-ra-go ham-ni-da.
My name is Jeong-Ho Lee. (*lit*. I am Jeong-Ho Lee)

저는 아직 학생입니다.
jeo-neun a-jik hak-saeng-im-ni-da.
I am still a student .

저는 컴퓨터 엔지니어입니다.
jeo-neun keop-pu-teo en-ji-ni-eo-im-ni-da.
I am a computer engineer.

저는 의과대학에 다닙니다.
jeo-neun ui-kkwa-dae-hag-e da-nim-ni-da.
I am attending medical school.

저는 IBM에서 근무합니다.
jeo-neun a-i-bi-em-e-seo geun-mu-ham-ni-da.
I am working at IBM.

대화 Model Conversations

(1)

이정호: 안녕하십니까? 처음 뵙겠습니다. 저는 이정호라고 합니다.

an-nyeong-ha-sim-ni-kka? cheo-eum boep-get-seum-ni-da.
jeo-neun i-jeong-ho-ra-go ham-ni-da.

실례지만 성함이 어떻게 되십니까?

sil-lye-ji-man seong-ham-i eo-tteo-ke doe-sim-ni-kka?

김현준: 안녕하십니까? 김현준입니다. 만나 뵙게 돼서 반갑습니다.

an-nyeong-ha-sim-ni-kka? gim-hyeon-jun-im-ni-da.
man-na-boep-ge dwae-seo ban-gap-seum-ni-da.

이정호: 저도 반갑습니다. 그런데 실례지만 김선생님은 어떤 일을 하십니까?

jeo-do ban-gap-seum-ni-da.
geu-reon-de sil-lye-ji-man gim-seon-saeng-nim-eun
eo-tteon il-eul ha-sim-ni-kka?

김현준: 저는 IBM에서 근무합니다. 컴퓨터 엔지니어입니다. 이선생님은 어떤 일을 하십니까?

jeo-neun a-i-bi-em-e-seo geun-mu-ham-ni-da.
keom-pu-teo en-ji-ni-eo-im-ni-da.
i-seon-saeng-nim-eun eo-tteon il-eul ha-sim-ni-kka?

이정호: 저는 아직 학생입니다. 의과대학에 다닙니다.

jeo-neun a-jik hak-seng-im-ni-da. ui-kkwa-dae-hag-e
da-nim-ni-da.

(2)

박성민: 안녕하십니까, 태민씨. 정말 오래간만입니다.

an-nyeong-ha-sim-ni-kka, tae-min-ssi. jeong-mal
o-rae-gan-man-im-ni-da.

최태민: 안녕하십니까, 성민씨. 요즘 어떻게 지내십니까?

an-nyeong-ha-sim-ni-kka, seong-min-ssi. yo-jeum
eo-tteo-ke ji-nae-sim-ni-kka?

박성민: 덕분에 잘 지냅니다. 태민씨는 요즘 어떻게
지내십니까?
deok-bun-e jal ji-naem-ni-da. tae-min-ssi-neun yo-jeum
eo-tteo-ke ji-nae-sim-ni-kka?

최태민: 저도 잘 지냅니다. 다시 뵙게 돼서 정말 반갑습니다.
jeo-do jal ji-naem-ni-da. da-si boep-ge dwae-seo
jeong-mal ban-gap-seum-ni-da.

박성민: 저도 정말 반갑습니다.
jeo-do jeong-mal ban-gap-seum-ni-da.

(3)
이정호: 김선생님, 만나 뵙게 돼서 정말 즐거웠습니다. 그럼
다음에 또 뵙겠습니다.
gim-seon-saeng-nim, man-na-boep-ge dwae-seo
jeong-mal jeul-geo-wot-seum-ni-da. geu-reom
da-eum-e tto boep-get-seum-ni-da.

김현준: 저도 즐거웠습니다. 안녕히 가십시오.
jeo-do jeul-geo-wot-seum-ni-da. an-nyeong-hi ga-sip-si-o.

이정호: 예, 안녕히 계십시오.
ye, an-nyeong-hi gye-sip-si-o.

영문번역 English Translation

(1)

Lee: How are you? Nice to meet you. My name is Jeong-Ho Lee. What is your name?

Kim: Hello. I am Hyeon-Jun Kim. Nice to meet you.

Lee: Nice to meet you, too. By the way, what do you do for living?

Kim: I am working at IBM. I am a computer engineer. What do you do for living, Mr. Lee?

Lee: I am still a student yet. I am attending medical school.

(2)

Park: Hello, Tae-min. Long time, no see. [*lit.* It has been a really long time, no see.]

Choi: Hi, Seong-min. How are you?

Park: I am fine. How are you doing these days?

Choi: I am doing fine, too. I am so glad to see you again.

Park: I am glad, too.

(3)

Lee: Mr. Kim, it was so nice [*lit.* happy] to meet you. See you next time.

Kim: It was nice to meet you, too. [*lit.* I was happy, too.] Good-bye.

Lee: OK. Good-bye.

어휘 Vocabulary

Nouns & Pronouns

김선생님 gim-seon-saeng-nim	Mr. Kim
김현준 gim-hyeon-jun	Kim, Hyeon-Jun
박성민 bak-seong-min	Park, Seong-Min
성민씨 seong-min-ssi	Seong-Min
성함 seong-ham	name *(hon.)*
엔지니어 en-ji-ni-eo	engineer
의과대학 ui-kkwa-dae-hak	medical school
이선생님 i-seon-saeng-nim	Mr. Lee
이정호 i-jeong-ho	Lee, Jeong-Ho
일 il	work, job
저 jeo	I *(pron., hum.)*
최태민 choe-tae-min	Choi, Tae-Min
컴퓨터 keom-pu-teo	computer
태민씨 tae-min-ssi	Tae-Min
학생 hak-saeng	student

Verbs

가다 ga-da	to go
계시다 gye-si-da	to stay *(hon.)*
근무하다 geun-mu-ha-da	to work at (company name)
다니다 da-ni-da	to attend
되다 doe-da	to become
만나뵙다 man-na-boep-da	to meet *(hon.)*
반갑다 ban-gap-da	to be glad
뵙다 boep-da	to meet, to see *(hon.)*
안녕하다 an-nyeong-ha-da	to be well
오래간만이다 o-rae-gan-man-i-da	long time no see
즐겁다 jeul-geop-da	to be happy

지내다 ji-nae-da   to spend time
하다 ha-da   to do

Adverbs & Conjunctions

그 동안 geu-dong-an   during the time
그런데 geu-reon-de   by the way (*when change topic*)
그럼 geu-reom   then
다시 da-si   again
다음에 da-eum-e   next time
덕분에 deok-bun-e   thanks to (you)
또 tto   again
실례지만 sil-lye-ji-man   Excuse me....
아직 a-jik   yet
안녕히 an-nyeong-hi   safely, peacefully
어떤 eo-tteon   which
어떻게 eo-tteo-ke   how
예 ye   yes, OK
요즘 yo-jeum   these days
잘 jal   well
정말 jeong-mal   really, so
처음 cheo-eum   for the first time

문법 Grammar

(1) More Useful Expressions

고맙습니다. go-map-seum-ni-da.	Thank you.
감사합니다. gam-sa-ham-ni-da.	Thank you.
천만에요. cheon-man-e-yo.	You are welcome.
별 말씀을요. byeol mal-sseum-eul-yo.	You are welcome.
무슨 말씀을요. mu-seun mal-sseum-eul-yo.	You are welcome.
죄송합니다. joe-song-ham-ni-da.	I am sorry.
괜찮습니다. gwaen-chan-seum-ni-da.	It's OK. / No problem.
어서 오세요. eo-seo o-se-yo.	Welcome.
실례합니다. sil-lye-ham-ni-da.	Excuse me.

Note:

In Korean, 안녕하십니까? (an-nyeong-ha-sim-ni-kka), which literally means, "Are you at peace?," is used as a greeting regardless of the time of day. It functions as the equivalent of "Good morning," "Good afternoon," and "Good evening." It can also mean, "How are you?," or "Nice to meet you." The appropriate response is 안녕하십니까? (an-nyeong-ha-sim-ni-kka). As for other greetings in the dialogues, 안녕히 가십시오 (an-nyeong-hi ga-sip-si-o) literally means "Please go in peace," and 안녕히 계십시오 (an-nyeong-hi gye-sip-si-o) means "Please stay in peace."

The expressions 처음 뵙겠습니다 (cheo-eum boep-get-sseum-ni-da), which literally means "It's the first time seeing you," and 만나 뵙게 돼서 반갑습니다 (man-na boep-ge dwae-seo ban-gap-seum-ni-da), the equivalent of "I am so glad to meet you," are used only when meeting someone for the first time. When parting, one says

다음에 또 뵙겠습니다 (da-eum-e tto boep-get-seum-ni-da), which means "See you again next time." Those who have previously met one another say 또 뵙게 돼서 반갑습니다 (tto boep-ge dwae-seo ban-gap-seum-ni-da) or 다시 뵙게 돼서 반갑습니다 (da-si boep-ge dwae-seo ban-gap-seum-ni-da). Both expressions mean "I am so glad to see you again."

When saying one's name, one uses the patterns 저는 [name] 입니다 (jeo-neun [name] im-ni-da) or 저는 [name] (이)라고 합니다 (jeo-neun [name] (i)-ra-go ham-ni-da). With 저는 [name] (이)라고 합니다, the 이 preceding 라고 합니다 only occurs when the name ends in a consonant. For example, 저는 김현준이라고 합니다 (jeo-neun gim-hyeon-jun-i-ra-go ham-ni-da)/"My name is Gim-Hyeon-Jun." The 저는 (jeo-neun) is optional with both patterns.

The Korean equivalent of "Thank you" is 고맙습니다 (go-map-seum-ni-da), or 감사합니다 (gam-sa-ham-ni-da). Appropriate replies include 천만에요 (cheon-man-e-yo), 별 말씀을요(byeol mal-sseum-eul-yo), and 무슨 말씀을요 (mu-seun mal-sseum-eul-yo). One may also smile silently or reply with네 (ne), the equivalent of "Yes." The expression 천만에요 means "Not at all," and both 별 말씀을요and 무슨 말씀을요 translate as "Don't mention it."

The proper response to 죄송합니다 (joe-song-ham-ni-da)/"I am sorry" is 괜찮습니다 (gwaen-chan-seum-ni-da)/"It's OK." If실례합니다 (sil-lye-ham-ni-da)/"Excuse me" is said, one should remember there is no appropriate reply in Korean. One responds through one's facial expression.

When visiting someone's home or entering a store, the host or sales-person will say the Korean equivalent of "Welcome," 어서 오세요 (eo-seo o-se-yo), which literally means "Please come hurry." The appropriate reply when visiting someone's home is 실례하겠습니

다 (sil-lye-ha-get-seum-ni-da), which means "Excuse me." One does not typically reply to a salesperson in this instance.

(2) Deferential Sentence Endings

The suffixes affixed to the verb at the close of a sentence indicate the relative social status and/or the personal relationship of the speaker and the addressee(s). There are four speech levels or categories for these relationships: deferential, polite, intimate, and plain.

	Statement	Question	Request	Suggestion
Deferential	~습/ㅂ니다. ~seum/m-ni-da. ~(으)십니다. (*hon.*) ~(eu)-sim-ni-da.	~습/ㅂ니까? ~seum/m-ni-kka? ~(으)십니까? (*hon.*) ~(eu)-sim-ni-kka?	~(으)십시오. (*hon.*) ~(eu)-sip-si-o.	~(으)시지요. (*hon.*) ~(eu)-si-ji-yo.
Polite	~아요/어요. ~a-yo. ~(으)세요. (*hon.*) ~(eu)-se-yo.	~아요/어요? ~a-yo? ~(으)세요? (*hon.*) ~(eu)-se-yo?	~아요/어요. ~a-yo. ~(으)세요. (*hon.*) ~(eu)-se-yo.	~아요/어요. ~a-yo. ~(으)세요. (*hon.*) ~(eu)-se-yo.
Intimate	~아/어. ~a/eo.	~아/어? ~a/eo?	~아/어. ~a/eo.	~아/어. ~a/eo.
Plain	~다 ~da.	~니/냐? ~ni/nya?	~아/어라 ~a/eo-ra.	~자 ~ja.

The deferential style of speech is generally spoken in formal settings, such as conferences, news broadcasts, business meetings, and formal speeches or interviews. By and large, males use this style more often than females, who generally use the polite style in these circumstances.

Additionally, the deferential style is frequently used when beginning a conversation. This occurs when people, usually males, meet for the first time. After introductions are made in the deferential style, further conversation uses the polite form , as a relationship is now established.

The table below illustrates the patterns used for speaking in the deferential in both the simple and honorific forms. The pattern is determined by whether the verb stem (e.g. 받 [bat] in 받다 [bat-da]/"to receive") ends in a vowel or a consonant. The consonant pattern is indicated with a C and is demonstrated with 받다. The vowel pattern is indicated with a V, with the forms demonstrated using the verb 가다 (ga-da)/"to go."

Statement	Question	Request	Suggestion
Simple			
C + ~습니다. ~seum-ni-da. → 받습니다. bat-seum-ni-da. V + ~ㅂ니다. ~m-ni-da. 갑니다. gam-ni-da.	C + ~습니까? ~seum-ni-kka? → 받습니까? bat-seum-ni-kka? V + ~ㅂ니까? ~m-ni-kka? 갑니까? gam-ni-kka?		
Honorific			
C + ~으십니다. ~eu-sim-ni-da. → 받으십니다. bad-eu-sim-ni-da. V + ~십니다. ~sim-ni-da. → 가십니다. ga-sim-ni-da.	C + ~으십니까? ~eu-sim-ni-kka? → 받으십니까? bad-eu-sim-ni-kka? V + ~십니까? ~ sim-ni-kka? → 가십니까? ga-sim-ni-kka?	C + ~으십시오. ~eu-sip-si-o. → 받으십시오. bad-eu-sip-si-o. V + ~십시오. ~ sip-si-o. → 가십시오. ga-sip-si-o.	C + ~으시지요. ~eu-si-ji-yo. → 받으시지요. bad-eu-si-ji-yo. V + ~시지요. ~ si-ji-yo. → 가시지요. ga-si-ji-yo.

(3) Case Particles

A. The Subject Particles ~이 (i) and 가 (ga)

The particles ~이 and 가 determine the subject of a sentence that depicts an action. The subject of a sentence is the noun denoting who or what is performing the action. The particle ~이 is attached to subject nouns that end in a consonant, such as 음식 (eum-sig)/ "food" in the sentence 음식이 맛있습니다 (eum-sig-i mas-it-seum-ni-da)/"The food is delicious." The particle ~가 is attached to subject nouns that end in a vowel, such as 한국어 (han-gug-eo)/ "the Korean language" in the sentence 한국어가 재미있습니다 (han-gug-eo-ga jae-mi-it-seum-ni-da)/ "Korean is fun."

B. The Object Particles ~을 (eul) and 를 (reul)

The particles ~을 and 를 indicate the object of a sentence that depicts an action. The object of a sentence is the noun denoting what or whom the action is being performed upon. The particle ~을 is attached to object nouns that end in a consonant, such as 아침 (a-chim)/ "breakfast" as in the sentence 정호가 아침을 먹습니다 (jeong-ho-ga a-chim-eul meok-seum-ni-da)/ "Jeong-Ho eats breakfast." The particle ~를 is attached to object nouns that end in a vowel, such as 커피 (keo-pi)/"coffee" in the sentence 마이클이 커피를 마십니다 (ma-i-keul-i keo-pi-reul ma-sim-ni-da)/ "Michael drinks a coffee."

C. The Topic Particles ~은 (eun) and ~는 (neun)

The particles ~은 and ~는 follow the topic noun of a descriptive sentence. The topic noun is the noun that the sentence describes. The particle ~은 is attached to nouns that end in a consonant, such as 마이클 (ma-i-keul)/"Michael" in the sentence 마이클은 키가 작습니다 (ma-i-keul-eun ki-ga jak-seum-ni-da)/ "Michael is small." The particle ~는is attached to nouns that end in a vowel, such as 정호 (jeong-ho)/"Jeong-Ho"in the sentence 정호는 키가 큽니다 (jeong-ho-neun ki-ga keum-ni-da)/ "Jeong-Ho is tall."

D. The Locative Particles ~에 (e) and ~에서 (e-seo)

The sentence pattern ~에 있다/없다 (e it-da/eop-da) is used to indicate where an object exists in space. Two things are presented: the noun's existence and its location, which, in the context of the sentence, is unchanging. For example:

신문이 테이블 위에 있습니다.
(sin-mun-i te-i-beul wi-*e* it-seum-ni-da)
The newspaper is ***on*** the table.

(**Note:** The verb 있다 (it-da) roughly translates as "to be." The verb 없다 (eop-da) is its negative, or "not to be." These verbs have conjugations, e.g. 있습니다 (it-seum-ni-da) in the above sentence. They are discussed further in Unit 4.)

When ~에 is used with directional verbs, such as 가다 (ga-da)/ "to go," 오다 (o-da)/ "to come," or 다니다 (da-ni-da) "to attend," it denotes the movement of the subject noun to the indicated location. Examples:

마이클은 내일LA에 갑니다.
(ma-i-keul-eun nae-il el-e-i-*e* gam-ni-da)
Michael goes ***to*** L.A. tomorrow.

정호씨는 의과대학에 다닙니다.
(jeong-ho-ssi-neun ui-kkwa-dae-hag-*e* da-nim-ni-da)
Jeong-Ho goes ***to*** (attends) a medical school.

The particle ~에서 to indicates the location or setting of an activity. Examples:

현준씨는 IBM에서 근무합니다.
(hyeon-jun-ssi-neun a-i-bi-em-***e-seo*** geun-mu-ham-ni-da)
Hyeon-Joon works ***at*** IBM.

정호씨는 병원에서 일합니다.
(jeong-ho-ssi-neun byeong-won-***e-seo*** il-ham-ni-da)
Jeong-Ho works ***at*** a hospital.

E. The Special Particles 은 (eun) / 는 (neun), 도 (do), and 만 (man)

The particles ~은/는, ~도, and ~만 are used when comparing things. Nouns ending in a consonant use 은, and nouns ending in a vowel use 는. The particles ~은/는 are always affixed to the first noun in the comparison.

The particles ~은/는, when affixed to all nouns being compared, denote difference. The nouns are being contrasted. For example:

정호는 의사입니다. 미셸은 선생님입니다.
(jeong-ho-***nuen*** ui-sa-im-ni-da. mi-syel-***eun***
    seon-saeng-nim-im-ni-da)
Jeong-Ho is a doctor. Michelle is a teacher.

The particle ~도 denotes similarity. It indicates that a noun is similar to the first one. For example:

정호는 의사입니다. 미셸도 의사입니다.
(jeong-ho-nuen ui-sa-im-ni-da. mi-syel-***do*** ui-sa-im-ni-da)
Jeong-Ho is a doctor. Michalle is a doctor, too.

The particle ~만 roughly translates as "only." It indicates that the final noun is unique among the other nouns in the comparison. For example:

미셸은 선생님입니다. 마이클도 선생님입니다. 정호<u>만</u> 의사입
니다.

(mi-syel-eun seon-saeng-nim-im-ni-da. ma-i-keul-do
seon-saeng-nim-im-ni-da. jeong-ho-***man*** ui-sa-im-ni-da)
Michelle is a teacher. Michael is a teacher, too. Only Jeong-Ho is
a doctor.

Note the use of ~도 to denote Michael's similarity to Michelle.

(4) Topic-Comment Structure

The topic-comment structure (Noun 1 is Noun 2) is one of the basic Korean sentence structures. It is a fundamental way of conveying ideas. The speaker picks a person, idea, or object and uses the structure to describe and comment on it.

The topic-comment sentence pattern in Korean is **[Noun 1]** 은/는 **[Noun 2]** 입니다([Noun 1]-eun/-neun [Noun 2]-im-ni-da.). The particle –이다 always comes after the second noun. Its presence changes the noun into a predicate. The pattern is commonly used when identifying oneself. Examples:

저<u>는</u> 김현준<u>입니다</u>.
(jeo-***neun*** gim-hyeon-jun-***im-ni-da***)
My name is Hyeon-Jun Kim. (*lit.* I Hyeon-Jun Kim am.)

저<u>는</u> 학생<u>입니다</u>.
(jeo-***neun*** hak-saeng-***im-ni-da***)
I am a student. (*lit.* I a student am.)

The negative of the topic-comment structure (Noun 1 isn't Noun 2) in Korean is **[Noun 1]** 은/는 **[Noun 2]** 이/가 아닙니다. ([Noun 1] -eun/-neun [Noun 2]-i/-ga a-nim-ni-da.). The particle 이/가 (-i/-ga) only occurs in negative constructions, and the word 아닙니다 (a-nim-ni-da) is the negative of 입니다 (im-ni-da). Examples:

저는 학생이 아닙니다.
(jeo-***neun*** hak-saeng-***i a-nim-ni-da***)
I am not a student.

미셸은 의사가 아닙니다.
(mi-syel-***eun*** ui-sa-***ga a-nim-ni-da***)
Michelle is not a doctor.

(5) The use of -(으)시- ((eu)-si) as an honorific.

When the characters ~(으)시~ are affixed to the verb stem, it indicates that the subject of the sentence is a person deserving of respect, such as an elderly person or someone of higher social status. For example:

할머니가 가십니다
(hal-meo-ni-ga ga-***si***m-ni-da)
Grandmother is going.

This may also be done as a sign of courtesy.

참고학습 **Further Study**

(1) Schools and Students

유치원 yu-chi-won	kindergarten
유치원생 yu-chi-won-saeng	kindergarten student
초등학교 cho-deung-hak-gyo	elementary school
초등학생 cho-deung-hak-saeng	elementary school student
중학교 jung-hak-gyo	middle school
중학생 jung-hak-saeng	middle school student
고등학교 go-deung-hak-go	high school
고등학생 go-deung-hak-saeng	high school student
대학교 dae-hak-gyo	college, university
대학생 dae-hak-saeng	college student
대학원 dae-hag-won	graduate school
대학원생 dae-hag-won-saeng	graduate student

In Korea, one attends elementary school for six years, middle school for three years, and high school for three years. Colleges and universities offer four-year undergraduate programs as well as graduate education. There are also two-year junior colleges (often called community colleges in the U.S.). The school year begins in March and ends in February.

Elementary school and middle school education are compulsory in Korea. Unlike the United States, kindergarten is not a part of Korean elementary school. Students between the ages of 4 and 7 have the option of attending private institutes called 유치원 (yu-chi-won) before they start their regular schooling. The 유치원 are the equivalent of U.S. preschools.

(2) Colleges in a University

법과대학 (법대) beop-gwa-dae-hak   law school
    (beop-dae)

의과대학 (의대) ui-kkwa-dae-hak   medical school
    (ui-dae)

치과대학 (치대) chi-kkwa-dae-hak   dental school
    (chi-dae)

약학대학 (약대) yak-hak-dae-hak   college of pharmacy
    (yak-dae)

사범대학 (사대) sa-beom-dae-hak   school of teacher education
    (sa-dae)

상경대학 (상대) sang-gyeong-dae-hak   school of business
    (sang-dae)

공과대학 (공대) gong-kkwa-dae-hak   engineering school
    (gong-dae)

음악대학 (음대) eum-ak-dae-hak   school of music
    (eum-dae)

미술대학 (미대) mi-sul-dae-hak   school of art
    (mi-dae)

체육대학 (체대) che-yuk-dae-hak   college of physical education
    (che-dae)

인문대학 (인문대) in-mun-dae-hak   school of humanities
    (in-mun-dae)

자연대학 (자연대) ja-yeon-dae-hak   school of sciences
    (ja-yeon-dae)

(3) Occupations

가수 ga-su   singer
간호원 gan-ho-won   nurse
공무원 gong-mu-won   civil servant
교수 gyo-su   professor
군인 gun-in   military personnel

기자 gi-ja   journalist
디자이너 di-ja-i-neo   designer
목사 mok-sa   pastor
변호사 byeon-ho-sa   lawyer
비서 bi-seo   secretary
사업가 sa-eop-ga   businessman
선생 seon-saeng   teacher
약사 yak-sa   pharmacist
엔지니어 en-ji-ni-eo   engineer
운동선수 un-dong-seon-su   sportsman
운전기사 un-jeon-gi-sa   driver
의사 ui-sa   doctor
작가 jak-ga   writer
학생 hak-saeng   student
회사원 hoe-sa-won   office employee

(4) Names of Majors

건축학 geon-chuk-hak   architecture
경영학 gyeong-yeong-hak   business management
경제학 gyeong-je-hak   economics
공학 gong-hak   engineering
교육학 gyo-yuk-hak   education
동양학 dong-yang-hak   Asian studies
문학 mun-hak   literature
물리학 mul-li-hak   physics
미술 mi-sul   fine arts
법학 beo-pak   law
사회학 sa-hoe-hak   sociology
생물학 saeng-mul-hak   biology
수학 su-hak   mathematics
심리학 sim-ni-hak   psychology
언어학 eon-eo-hak   linguistics
역사학 yeok-sa-hak   history

음악 eum-ak   music
의학 ui-hak   medicine
인류학 il-lyu-hak   anthropology
정치학 jeong-chi-hak   political science
화학 hwa-hak   chemistry

문화적 참고사항 Cultural Notes

(1) Korean Names

In Korean, the family name comes first, followed by the given name. Korean names generally have three syllables: one for the family name and two for the given name. For example, with the name 이정호 (i-jeong-ho), 이 (i) is the family name and 정호 (jeong-ho) is the given name. However, there are some two-syllable family names, such as 제갈 (je-gal) or 황보 (hwang-bo). Korea has approximately 300 family names. The five most common are 김 (gim)/Kim, 이 (i)/Lee, 박 (bak)/Park, 최 (choe)/Choi, and 정 (jeong)/Chung (or Jung).

(2) –선생님 (seon-saeng-nim) vs. –씨 (ssi)

The word 선생님 (seon-saeng-nim) literally means "teacher," but Koreans use the word as a standard form of address. It can be used as a simple honorific, the equivalent of "Mr.," "Mrs.," or "Ms.," or as a title when addressing one's elders, older people in general, or business colleagues with whom one does not have a personal relationship. The proper way of using the word 선생님 when addressing someone is to add it to the end of their full name or last name. Using it with the full name is more formal and polite.

The honorific suffix -씨 (-ssi), used in **Model Conversations** (2) above, is an expression of courtesy towards one's coworkers. It is not appropriate when speaking or referring to one's elders or older people. When using –씨, one should attach it to the addressee's first name or to the last name when preceded by the first name. Referring to someone by just his or her last name followed by –씨 is condescending.

(3) 실례지만 *(sil-lye-ji-man) Excuse me, but...*

The phrase 실례지만 (sil-lye-ji-man) always accompanies personal questions, such as those about one's age, job, or family life (including marriage). In Korean culture, such questions are always asked when meeting someone for the first time. The answers provide information that is necessary in determining the appropriate honorifics and sentence endings in further conversation.

(4) 덕분에 *(deok-bun-e) Thanks to you*

The expression 잘 지내셨습니까? (jal ji-nae-syeot-seum-ni-kka) is the equivalent of "How are you?" or "How have you been?" The usual Korean reply is 덕분에 잘 지냈습니다 (deok-bun-e jal ji-naet-seum-ni-da), which means "Thanks to you, I am fine," or "Thanks to you, I have been fine." The expression of gratitude reflects the traditional Korean belief that another's concern and blessing helps one to maintain a safe and happy life.

(5) *Greetings with a bow*

Bowing is the easiest and most common way to show courtesy when greeting someone. In general, the younger person initiates the bow and the older person reciprocates. Bowing is done by bending both head and waist about 15 degrees forward. Male adults often shake hands with one or both hands while bowing. During this greeting process, it is common courtesy to ask the addressee how they have been or whether they have eaten.

연습문제 Exercises

1. Please respond to the following:

(1) 안녕하십니까?
an-nyeong-ha-sim-ni-kka?
(2) 처음 뵙겠습니다. 만나서 반갑습니다.
cheo-eum boep-gess-eum-ni-da. man-na-seo ban-gap-seum-ni-da.
(3) 요즘 어떻게 지내십니까?
yo-jeum eo-tteo-ke ji-nae-sim-ni-kka?
(4) 실례지만 성함이 어떻게 되십니까?
sil-le-ji-man seong-ham-i eo-tteo-ke doe-sim-ni-kka?
(5) 실례지만 어떤 일을 하십니까?
sil-le-ji-man eo-tteon il-eul ha-sim-ni-kka?

2. Please translate the following into English:

(1) 감사합니다. gam-sa-ham-ni-da.
(2) 실례합니다. sil-le-ham-ni-da.
(3) 죄송합니다. joe-song-ham-ni-da.
(4) 어서 오세요. eo-seo o-se-yo.
(5) 별 말씀을요. byeol mal-sseum-eul-yo.

3. Please translate the following into Korean:

(1) How have you been?
(2) I have been doing fine, thanks to you.
(3) Long time, no see.
(4) See you next time.
(5) Nice to see you again.

4. Please write a paragraph introducing yourself (what your name is, where you work or study, etc.).

제2과 소개하기

Lesson 2: Asking about Something & Talking about Yourself

표현 Patterns

정호씨는 댁이 어디십니까?
jeong-ho-ssi-neun daeg-i eo-di-sim-ni-kka?
Where is your home, Jeong-Ho?

저희 집은 샌디에이고입니다.
jeo-hi jib-eun saen-di-e-i-go-im-ni-da.
My home is in San Diego.

저는 한국에서 왔습니다.
jeo-neun han-gug-e-seo wat-seum-ni-da.
I am from Korea.

저는 수원에서 삽니다.
jeo-neun su-won-e-seo sam-ni-da.
I live in Su-won.

현준씨는 한국 분이십니까?
hyeon-jun-ssi-neun han-guk bun-i-sim-ni-kka?
Are you Korean?

네, 그렇습니다. 저는 한국사람입니다.
ne, geu-reot-seum-ni-da. jeo-neun han-guk-sa-ram-im-ni-da.
Yes, I am. I am Korean.

아니오, 저는 한국사람이 아닙니다.
a-ni-o, jeo-neun han-guk-sa-ram-i a-nim-ni-da.
No, I am not Korean.

정호씨는요?
jeong-ho-ssi-neun-yo?
How about you, Jeong-Ho?

Barnes & Noble Booksellers #2115
800 Boylston Street Suite 179
Boston, MA 02199
617-247-6959

TR:2115 REG:001 TRN:8570 CSHR:Mariel R

BARNES & NOBLE MEMBER   EXP: 12/15/2019

Beginner's Korean with Online Audio
  9780781813778   T1
  (1 @ 24.95) Member Card 10% (2.50)
  (1 @ 22.45)   22.45

Subtotal   22.45
Sales Tax T1 (6.250%)   1.40
TOTAL   23.85
MASTERCARD DEBIT   23.85
  Card#:   XXXXXXXXXXXXX0818

  Application Label: Debit
  AID: a0000000042203
  PIN Verified
  TVR: 0000048000
  TSI: e800

MEMBER SAVINGS   2.50

Connect with us on Social

Facebook-   @BarnesandNobleBoston
Instagram- @bnbostonpru
Twitter-   @BNBostonPru

049.06B   04/16/2019 03:20PM

CUSTOMER COPY

at Barnes & Noble College bookstores that are listed for sale in the Barnes & Noble Booksellers inventory management system.

Opened music CDs, DVDs, vinyl records, audio books may not be returned, and can be exchanged only for the same title and only if defective. NOOKs purchased from other retailers or sellers are returnable only to the retailer or seller from which they are purchased, pursuant to such retailer's or seller's return policy. Magazines, newspapers, eBooks, digital downloads, and used books are not returnable or exchangeable. Defective NOOKs may be exchanged at the store in accordance with the applicable warranty.

Returns or exchanges will not be permitted (i) after 14 days or without receipt or (ii) for product not carried by Barnes & Noble or Barnes & Noble.com.

Policy on receipt may appear in two sections.

Return Policy

With a sales receipt or Barnes & Noble.com packing slip, a full refund in the original form of payment will be issued from any Barnes & Noble Booksellers store for returns of undamaged NOOKs, new and unread books, and unopened and undamaged music CDs, DVDs, vinyl records, toys/games and audio books made within 14 days of purchase from a Barnes & Noble Booksellers store or Barnes & Noble.com with the below exceptions:

A store credit for the purchase price will be issued (i) for purchases made by check less than 7 days prior to the date of return, (ii) when a gift receipt is presented within 60 days of purchase, (iii) for textbooks, (iv) when the original tender is PayPal, or (v) for products purchased at Barnes & Noble College bookstores that are listed for sale in the Barnes & Noble Booksellers inventory management system.

Opened music CDs, DVDs, vinyl records, audio books may not be returned, and can be exchanged only for the same title and only if defective. NOOKs purchased from other retailers or sellers are returnable only to the retailer or seller from which they are purchased, pursuant to such retailer's or seller's return policy. Magazines, newspapers, eBooks, digital downloads, and used books are not returnable or exchangeable. Defective NOOKs may be exchanged at the store in accordance with the applicable warranty.

Returns or exchanges will not be permitted (i) after 14 days or without receipt or (ii) for product not carried by Barnes & Noble or Barnes & Noble.com.

저는 한국계 미국인입니다.
jeo-neun han-guk-gye mi-gug-in-im-ni-da.
I am Korean-American.

저는 미시간에서 태어났습니다.
jeo-neun mi-si-gan-e-seo tae-eo-nat-seum-ni-da.
I was born in Michigan.

정호씨는 올해 연세가 어떻게 되십니까?
jeong-ho-ssi-neun ol-hae yeon-se-ga eo-tteo-ke doe-sim-ni-kka?
How old are you this year, Jeong-Ho?

서른 둘입니다.
seo-reun dul-im-ni-da.
I am thirty-two.

저도 서른 두살이에요.
jeo-do seo-reun du-sal-i-e-yo.
I am also thirty-two.

저하고 동갑이시군요.
jeo-ha-go dong-gab-i-si-gun-yo.
You are the same age as me.

저보다 좀 많으시군요.
jeo-bo-da jom man-eu-si-gun-yo.
You are a little older than me.

저보다 좀 적으시군요.
jeo-bo-da jom jeog-eu-si-gun-yo.
You are a little younger than me.

현준씨는 생일이 언제세요?
hyeon-jun-ssi-neun saeng-il-i eon-je-se-yo?
When is your birthday, Hyeon-Jun?

저는4월이에요.

jeo-neun sa-wol-i-e-yo.

It is in April.

저는 7월생이에요.

jeo-neun chil-wol-ssaeng-i-e-yo.

I was born in July.

정호씨는 결혼하셨어요?

jeong-ho-ssi-neun gyeol-hon-ha-syeoss-eo-yo?

Are you married, Jeong-Ho?

아니오, 저는 아직 혼자 살아요.

a-ni-o, jeo-neun a-jik hon-ja sal-a-yo.

No, I'm still single. (*lit.* No, I still live by myself.)

네, 저는 작년에 했어요.

ne, jeo-neun jang-nyeon-e haess-eo-yo.

Yes, I got married last year.

현준씨는 가족이 어떻게 되세요?

hyeon-jun-ssi-neun ga-jog-i eo-tteo-ke doe-se-yo?

How many people are in your family?

집사람하고 저하고 둘이에요.

jip-sa-ram-ha-go jeo-ha-go dul-i-e-yo.

Two people: my wife and I. (*lit.* My wife and I, all are two.)

아이는 아직 없으세요?

a-i-neun a-jik eops-eu-se-yo?

Do you have any children yet? (*lit.* Don't you have children yet?)

(Note: In Korean sometimes questions are asked in the negative because one wants to give the respondent the opportunity to answer no at all times without feeling uneasy. This is different than English, where negative questions are generally considered rude and confrontational.)

네, 아직 없어요.
ne, a-jik eops-eo-yo.
No, I still don't have any (*lit.* one).

아니오, 하나 있어요.
a-ni-o, ha-na iss-eo-yo.
Yes, I have one.

아이가 몇이세요?
a-i-ga myeoch-i-se-yo?
How many kids do you have?

딸 둘 아들 하나예요.
ttal dul a-deul ha-na-ye-yo.
I have two daughters and a son.

대화 Model Conversations

(1)

이정호: 실례지만 성함이 어떻게 되십니까?
sil-lye-ji-man seong-ham-i eo-tteo-ke doe-sim-ni-kka?

김현준: 저는 김현준입니다. 성함이 어떻게 되십니까?
jeo-neun gim-hyeon-jun-im-ni-da. seong-ham-i eo-tteo-ke doe-sim-ni-kka?

이정호: 저는 이정호라고 합니다. 그런데 실례지만 김선생님
은 어떤 일을 하십니까?
jeo-neun i-jeong-ho-ra-go ham-ni-da.
geu-reon-de sil-lye-ji-man gim-seon-saeng-nim-eun eo-tteon il-eul ha-sim-ni-kka?

김현준: 저는 IBM에서 근무합니다. 컴퓨터 엔지니어입니다.
이선생님은 어떤 일을 하십니까?
jeo-neun a-i-bi-em-e-seo geun-mu-ham-ni-da.
keom-pu-teo en-ji-ni-eo-im-ni-da.
i-seon-saeng-nim-eun eo-tteon il-eul ha-sim-ni-kka?

이정호: 저는 아직 학생입니다. 의과대학에 다닙니다.
jeo-neun a-jik hak-seng-im-ni-da. ui-kkwa-dae-hag-e da-nim-ni-da.

(2)

김현준: 정호씨는 댁이 어디십니까?
jeong-ho-ssi-neun daeg-i eo-di-sim-ni-kka?

이정호: 샌디에이고입니다. 현준씨는 댁이 어디십니까?
saen-di-e-i-go-im-ni-da. hyeon-jun-ssi-neun daeg-i eo-di-sim-ni-kka?

김현준: 저는 한국에서 왔습니다. 수원에서 삽니다.
Jeo-neun han-gug-e-seo wat-sum-ni-da. su-won-e-seo sam-ni-da.

이정호: 그럼 현준씨는 한국 분이십니까?
geu-reom hyeon-jun-ssi-neun han-guk bun-i-sim-ni-kka?

김현준: 네, 그렇습니다. 정호씨는요?
ne, geu-reot-seum-ni-da. jeong-ho-ssi-neun-yo?

이정호: 저는 한국계 미국인입니다. 미시간에서 태어났습니다.
jeo-neun han-guk-gye mi-gug-in-im-ni-da.
mi-si-gan-e-seo tae-eo-nat-seum-ni-da.

(3)
김현준: 실례지만 정호씨는 올해 연세가 어떻게 되십니까?
sil-lye-ji-man jeong-ho-ssi-neun ol-hae yeon-se-ga
eo-tteo-ke doe-sim-ni-kka?
이정호: 서른 둘입니다.
seo-reun-dul-im-ni-da.
김현준: 아, 그럼 저하고 동갑이시군요. 저도 서른 두살이에요.
a, geu-reom jeo-ha-go dong-gab-i-si-gun-yo. jeo-do
seo-reun du-sal-i-e-yo.
이정호: 그러세요? 그럼 생일이 언제세요?
geu-reo-se-yo? geu-reom saeng-il-i eon-je-se-yo?
김현준: 4월이에요.
sa-wol-i-e-yo.
이정호: 아, 그러세요? 그럼 저보다 좀 많으시군요. 저는 7월
생이에요.
a, geu-reo-se-yo? geu-reom jeo-bo-da jom
man-eu-si-gun-yo. jeo-neun chil-wol-ssaeng-i-e-yo.

(4)
김현준: 정호씨는 결혼하셨어요?
jeong-ho-ssi-neun gyeol-hon-ha-syeoss-eo-yo?
이정호: 아니오, 아직 혼자 살아요. 현준씨는요?
a-ni-o, a-jik hon-ja sal-a-yo. hyeon-jun-ssi-neun-yo?
김현준: 저는 작년에 했어요.
jeo-neun jang-nyeon-e haess-eo-yo.
이정호: 그럼 가족이 어떻게 되세요?
geu-reom ga-jog-i eo-tteo-ke doe-se-yo?
김현준: 집사람하고 저하고 둘이에요.
jip-sa-ram-ha-go jeo-ha-go dul-i-e-yo.
이정호: 아이는 아직 없으세요?
a-i-neun a-jik eops-eu-se-yo?
김현준: 네, 아직 없어요.
ne, a-jik eops-eo-yo.

영문번역 English Translation

(1)
Lee: Excuse me. May I have your name, please?
Kim: My name is Hyeon-Jun Kim. May I have your name, please?
Lee: My name is Jeong-Ho Lee. Excuse me, but do you mind if I ask what do you do for living?
Kim: I am working at IBM. I am a computer engineer. What do you do for living, Mr. Lee?
Lee: I am still a student. I am attending medical school.

(2)
Kim: Where is your home, Jeong-Ho?
Lee: It's in San Diego. Where is your home, Hyeong-Jun?
Kim: I am from Korea. I live in Su-won.
Lee: Are you Korean, then?
Kim: Yes, I am. How about you, Jeong-Ho?
Lee: I am Korean-American. I was born in Michigan.

(3)
Kim: Excuse me. How old are you this year, Jeong-Ho?
Lee: I am thirty-two.
Kim: Ah, then we are the same age. I am also thiry-two.
Lee: Is it? Then when is your birthday?
Kim: It's in April.
Lee: Ah, is that so? Then you are a little older than I am. I was born in July.

(4)
Kim: Are you married, Jeong-Ho?
Lee: No, I am still single. How about you, Hyeon-Jun?
Kim: I got married last year.
Lee: How many people are in your family, then?
Kim: My wife and I, there are only two.
Lee: Do you have children yet?
Kim: No, not yet.

어휘 Vocabulary

Nouns and Pronouns

4월 sa-wol	April
7월 생 chil-wol-saeng	born in July
가족 ga-jok	family
댁 daek	home, house *(hon.)*
동갑 dong-gap	same age
둘 dul	two
미국시민 mi-guk-si-min	American citizen
미시간 mi-si-gan	Michigan
샌디에이고 saen-di-e-i-go	San Diego, USA
생일 saeng-il	birthday
서른 둘 seo-reun-dul	thirty-two
수원 su-won	Su-won, Korea
아이 a-i	child, kid
연세 yeon-se	age *(hon.)*
올해 ol-hae	this year
작년 jang-nyeon	last year
집사람 jip-sa-ram	(my) wife
한국 분 han-guk-bun	Korean *(hon.)*
한국 han-guk	Korea
한국계 han-guk-gye	Korean-

Verbs

결혼하다 gyeol-hon-ha-da	to get married
그렇다 geu-reo-ta	it is, I am, s/he is
많다 man-ta	to be more
살다 sal-da	to live
없다 eop-da	not to exist, not to have
오다 o-da	to come
태어나다 tae-eo-na-da	to be born
하다 ha-da	to do

Adverbs and Conjunctions

네 ne	yes
아 a	ah
아니오 a-ni-o	no
아직 a-jik	yet, still
어디 eo-di	where
어떻게 eo-tteo-ke	how
언제 eon-je	when
좀 jom	a little
혼자 hon-ja	by oneself, alone

문법 Grammar

(1) The Possessive Particle ~의 (ui)

The possessive particle ~의 (generally pronounced like 에 [e]) indicates ownership and comes after the possessive noun, like "'s" in English. The noun that is possessed immediately follows. For example:

한국	+	의	+	대통령	→	한국의 대통령
han-guk		ui		dae-tong-nyeong		han-gug-e dae-tong-nyeong
Korea		(*part.*)		president		Korea's president / the President of Korea

However, ~의 is generally only used in written Korean. Most Korean speakers drop it in conversation. One only tends to hear it when the possessor and possessed both refer to abstract concepts. In other words, when someone says, for example, "Michael's wallet" in Korean, one will hear 마이클 지갑 (ma-i-keul ji-gap) instead of 마이클의 지갑 (ma-i-keul-e ji-gap).

(2) The Time Particle ~에 (e)

The particle ~에 is used when referring to the time of day, the days of the week, and the months of the year. It immediately follows the time word or phrase it follows, e.g.

일요일에 il-yo-il-e	on Sundays
주말에 ju-mal-e	on the weekend
12시에 yeol-ttu-si-e	at 12:00

Many time-related words and phrases do not use ~에. These include:

오늘	o-neul	today
어제	eo-je	yesterday
그제	geu-je	the day before yesterday
내일	nae-il	tomorrow
모레	mo-re	the day after tomorrow
매일	mae-il	every day
매주	mae-ju	every week
매달	mae-dal	every month
매년	mae-nyeon	every year

(3) The Dictionary Form of Verbs (verb stem + 다 da)

Verbs in Korean consist of both a stem and an ending. The ending changes based on the form of the verb used. The dictionary form of verbs ends in ~다 (da), creating the equivalent of the English infinitive, e.g.

이다 i-da	to be
아니다 a-ni-da	to not be
알다 al-da	to know
좋다 jo-ta	to be good
넓다 neolp-da	to be wide

The ~다 has no meaning other than its use in the dictionary form.

(4) The Polite Ending ~아/어요 (a/eo-yo)

The polite ending is the most commonly used ending in conversational
Korean. However, there are several variations depending on the
stem. In the examples below, which are taken from the verbs listed
in (3) immediately above, one begins with the dictionary form of the
verb. The ~다 ending is then dropped so that only the stem remains.
The polite form of the verb is then created by adding the appropriate
ending to the verb stem. The rules governing the appropriate ending
for a particular stem are as follows:

(1) Use ~아요 (a-yo) when the last vowel of the stem is either 아
   (a) or 오 (o), e.g.

알다	→	알	→	알아요
좋다	→	좋	→	좋아요

(2) Use ~어요 for all other stems, e.g.

먹다	→	먹	→	먹어요
넓다	→	넓	→	넓어요

(3) Some exceptions:

이다	→	이	→	이에요
아니다	→	아니	→	아니에요
하다	→	하	→	해요

An honorific form of the polite ending is ~(으)세요 ([eu]-se-yo),
which is a combination of the honorific marker ~(으)시 ([eu]-si) and
the polite ending ~어요 (eo-yo). The honorific form has two uses.
The first is to show respect for the person being talked about, e.g.

이선생님은 좋은 선생님이<u>세요</u>.
(i-seon-saeng-nim-eun jo-eun seon-saeng-nim-i-<u>se-yo</u>)
Mr. Lee is a good teacher.

The second is to show respect towards a person when asking he or
she to do something, including answering a question. For example:

안녕하세요? 여기 앉으세요. 요즘 어떻게 지내<u>세요</u>?
(an-nyeong-ha-se-yo? yeo-gi an-jeu-se-yo. yo-jeum eo-tteo-ke
    ji-nae-<u>se-yo</u>?)
Hello. Please sit here. How are you doing these days?

(5) The Past Tense of Verbs

Verbs in the past tense use the past tense markers 았/었 (at/eot), which
are placed between the verb stem and the sentence endings such as
the one used in the polite form. The marker 았 is used when the stem
ends in 아 (a) or 오 (o). The marker 었 is used with all other verbs.
Contractions are formed after the marker is added. The examples
below show how to create the past tense in the polite form:

to go   가다 ga-da → 가요 ga-yo
          → 가 +았+ 어요 → 갔어요 gass-eo-yo (*went*)

to be   이다 i-da → 이에요 i-e-yo
          → 이 +었+ 어요 → 이었어요 i-eoss-eo-yo (*was*)

The chart below shows several verbs in the present and past tenses in both the polite and honorific forms.

Dictionary Form	~아/어요 ~a/eo-yo (*polite present*)	~았/었어요 ~ass/eoss-eo-yo (*polite past*)	~(으)세요 ~(eu)-se-yo (*hon. present*)	~(으)셨어요 ~(eu)-syeoss-eo-yo (*hon. past*)
잡다 to catch jap-da	잡아요 jab-a-yo	잡았어요 jab-ass-eo-yo	잡으세요 jab-eu-se-yo	잡으셨어요 jab-eu-syeoss-eo-yo
섞다 to mix seok-da	섞어요 seokk-eo-yo	섞었어요 seokk-eoss-eo-yo	섞으세요 seokk-eu-se-yo	섞으셨어요 seokk-eu-syeoss-eo-yo
가다 to go ga-da	가요 ga-yo	갔어요 gass-eo-yo	가세요 ga-se-yo	가셨어요 ga-syeoss-eo-yo
서다 to stop seo-da	서요 seo-yo	섰어요 seoss-eo-yo	서세요 seo-se-yo	서셨어요 seo-syeoss-eo-yo
오다 to come o-da	와요 wa-yo	왔어요 wass-eo-yo	오세요 o-se-yo	오셨어요 o-syeoss-eo-yo
주다 to give ju-da	줘요 jwo-yo	줬어요 jwoss-eo-yo	주세요 ju-se-yo	주셨어요 ju-syeoss-eo-yo
바쁘다 to be busy ba-ppeu-da	바빠요 ba-ppa-yo	바빴어요 ba-ppass-eo-yo	바쁘세요 ba-ppeu-se-yo	바쁘셨어요 ba-ppeu-syeoss-eo-yo
예쁘다 to be pretty ye-ppeu-da	예뻐요 ye-ppeo-yo	예뻤어요 ye-ppeoss-eo-yo	예쁘세요 ye-ppeu-se-yo	예쁘셨어요 ye-ppeu-syeoss-eo-yo
지내다 to spend time ji-nae-da	지내요 ji-nae-yo	지냈어요 ji-naess-eo-yo	지내세요 ji-nae-se-yo	지내셨어요 ji-nae-syeoss-eo-yo
하다 to do ha-da	해요 hae-yo	했어요 haess-eo-yo	하세요 ha-se-yo	하셨어요 ha-syeoss-eo-yo
이다 to be i-da	이에요 i-e-yo	이었어요 i-eoss-eo-yo	이세요 i-se-yo	이셨어요 i-syeoss-eo-yo
아니다 not to be a-ni-da	아니에요 a-ni-e-yo	아니었어요 a-ni-eoss-eo-yo	아니세요 a-ni-se-yo	아니셨어요 a-ni-syeoss-eo-yo

(6) Answering Yes or No Questions

To answer yes to a yes-or-no question in the polite mode, one says
네 (ne), which is followed by the extended response. To answer yes
in the plain and intimate modes, one says 응 (eung) followed by the
extended response. An example in the polite mode:

한국사람이세요?   → 네, 한국사람이에요.
(han-guk-sa-ram-i-se-yo?)   (ne, han-guk-sa-ram-i-se-yo.)
Are you a Korean?   Yes, I am a Korean.

To answer no to a yes-or-no question in the polite mode, one says아
니오 (a-ni-o) or, followed by the extended reply. The word 아니
(a-ni) is used in the plain and intimate modes. An example in the
polite mode:

한국사람이세요?   → 아니오, 한국사람이 아니에요.
(han-guk-sa-ram-i-se-yo?)   (a-ni-o, han-guk-sa-ram-i
                                       a-ni-e-yo.)

Are you a Korean?   No, I am not a Korean.

One can precede a negative reply with 네 or a positive reply with
아니오 if the question is asked using the negative form. In these
instances, the English equivalents would be closer to "Yes, that's
correct," or "No, that's incorrect." For example:

한국사람이 아니세요?   → 네, 한국사람이 아니에요.
(han-guk-sa-ram-i a-ni-se-yo?)   (ne, han-guk-sa-ram-i a-ni-e-yo.)
Aren't you/You aren't a Korean?   Yes, that's correct, I am not a
                                       Korean.

                                   → 아니오, 한국사람이에요.
                                       (a-ni-o, han-guk-sa-ram-i-e-yo.)
                                       No, that's incorrect, I am a
                                       Korean.

(7) The Expression –군요 (gun-yo)

The expression ~군요 at the end of a statement is an equivalent of an English exclamation point. It used to indicate that the speaker has realized something for the first time. The ending ~네요 (ne-yo) can be used this way as well. Examples:

저하고 동갑이시군요.
(jeo-ha-go dong-gab-i-si-gun-yo.)
We are the same age!

저하고 동갑이시네요.
(jeo-ha-go dong-gab-i-si-ne-yo.)
We are the same age!

(8) The Sentence Ending –은요/는요? (eun-yo/neun-yo?)

The sentence endings ~은요/는요? (eun-yo/nenun-yo) are best translated as "How about...?" or "What about...?" The ending ~은요 is used when the noun ends in a vowel, e.g.

가족은요?
(ga-jog-eun-yo?)
How about your family?

The ending ~는요 is used when the noun ends in a consonant, e.g.

정호씨는요?
(jeong-ho-ssi-neun-yo?)
How about Jeong-Ho?

The ~는요 ending can also be used for such phrases as 주말에는요? (ju-mal-e-neun-yo?) / How about during the weekend?

참고학습 Further Study

(1) Naming a Language and Nationality/Ethnicity

The Korean name for a country's language is generally created by taking the name of the country and adding the suffix ~어(eo). The word for a country's nationality or ethnicity is created in the plain form by adding the suffix ~사람 (sa-ram). In the formal, one adds the suffix ~인 (in). The chart below illustrates these conversions. Note that, in some instances, the language and nationality listed are the proper ones, not derivations of the country's name.

| | | Nationality/Ethnicity | |
Country Name	Language Name	Plain Form	Formal Form
호주	영어	호주 사람	호주인
ho-ju	yeong-eo	ho-ju sa-ram	ho-ju-in
Australia	English	Australian	Australian
캐나다	영어	캐나다 사람	캐나다인
kae-na-da	yeong-eo	kae-na-da sa-ram	kae-na-da-in
Canada	English	Canadian	Canadian
중국	중국어	중국 사람	중국인
jung-guk	jung-gug-eo	gunk-guk sa-ram	gung-gug-in
China	Chinese	Chinese	Chinese
영국	영어	영국 사람	영국인
yeong-guk	yeong-eo	yeong-guk sa-ram	yeong-gug-in
England	English	British	British
프랑스	프랑스어	프랑스 사람	프랑스인
peu-rang-seu	peu-rang-seu-eo	peu-rang-seu sa-ram	peu-rang-seu-in
France	French	French	French

독일
dog-il
Germany

독일어
dog-il-eo
German

독일 사람
dog-il sa-ram
German

독일인
dog-il-in
German

일본
il-bon
Japan

일본어
il-bon-eo
Japanese

일본 사람
il-bon sa-ram
Japanese

일본인
il-bon-in
Japanese

한국
han-guk
Korea

한국어
gan-gug-eo
Korean

한국 사람
han-guk sa-ram
Korean

한국인
han-gug-in
Korean

멕시코
mek-si-ko
Mexico

스페인어
seu-pe-in-eo
Spanish

멕시코 사람
mek-si-ko sa-ram
Mexican

멕시코인
mek-si-ko-in
Mexican

뉴질랜드
nyu-jil-laen-deu
New Zealand

영어
yeong-eo
English

뉴질랜드 사람
nyu-jil-laen-deu sa-ram
New Zealander

뉴질랜드인
nyu-jil-laen-deu-in
New Zealander

러시아
reo-si-a
Russia

러시아어
reo-si-a-eo
Russian

러시아 사람
reo-si-a sa-ram
Russian

러시아인
reo-si-a-in
Russian

스페인
seu-pe-in
Spain

스페인어
seu-pe-in-eo
Spanish

스페인 사람
seu-pe-in sa-ram
Spanish

스페인인
seu-pe-in-in
Spanish

미국
mi-guk
United States
(U.S.)

영어
yeong-eo
English

미국 사람
mi-guk sa-ram
American

미국인
mi-gug-in
American

(2) *The Months of the Year*

1월 (일월) il-wol	January
2월 (이월) i-wol	February
3월 (삼월) sam-wol	March
4월 (사월) sa-wol	April
5월 (오월) o-wol	May
6월 (유월) yu-wol	June
7월 (칠월) chil-wol	July
8월 (팔월) pal-wol	August
9월 (구월) gu-wol	September
10월 (시월) si-wol	October
11월 (십일월) sib-il-wol	November
12월 (십이월) sib-i-wol	December

(3) *Years*

재작년 jae-jang-nyeon	the year before last year
작년 jang-nyeon	last year
올해 ol-hae	this year
금년 geum-nyeon	this year
내년 nae-nyeon	next year
내후년 nea-hu-nyeon	the year after next year

(4) *Family Terms*

가족 ga-jok	family, family members *(formal)*
식구 sik-gu	family, family members *(casual)*
집 jip	house
댁 daek	house *(hon.)*
할아버지 hal-a-beo-ji	grandfather
할머니 hal-meo-ni	grandmother
아버지 a-beo-ji	father
어머니 eo-meo-ni	mother

형 hyeong	man's older brother
오빠 o-ppa	woman's older brother
누나 nu-na	man's older sister
언니 eon-ni	woman's older sister
남동생 nam-dong-saeng	younger brother
여동생 yeo-dong-saeng	younger sister
남편 nam-pyeon	husband
아내 a-nae	wife
집사람 jip-sa-ram	wife
아들 a-deul	son
딸 ttal	daughter

문화적 참고사항 Cultural Notes

(1) Asking Personal Information

Koreans are almost certain to ask personal questions, such as one's age or marital status, when first meeting someone. The Korean language requires that information in order to determine the appropriate sentence endings when addressing another. Other questions that may arise include queries about one's job, hometown, or education. These are used to help build a rapport between speakers. As the relationship between the speakers develops, a shift will occur from the initial deferential mode of speech to a blend of the deferential and polite modes, and then, perhaps to the polite mode only.

(2) First-Person Possessive Pronouns and Korean Collectivism

The Korean equivalent of the English possessive pronoun "my" is 내 (nae) in the plain form and 제 (je) in the formal and deferential forms. However, one must keep in mind that Koreans consider things such as their country, school, family, and home as collective possessions. For these, the equivalent of the English "our" will always be used. In the plain form, this is 우리 (u-ri). In the formal and deferential forms, it is 저희 (jeo-hui).

The sense of a family member being a collective possession can extend even to one's wife or husband. The equivalent of "my wife" is 우리 집사람 (u-ri jip-sa-ram), while the equivalent of my husband is 우리 남편 (u-ri nam-pyeon).

(3) Husband and Wife

When referring to one's own spouse, one uses a different word than when referring to someone else's. The appropriate words are as follows:

남편 nam-pyeon	one's own husband
아내 a-nae	one's own wife
집사람 jip-sa-ram	one's own wife
바깥 어른 ba-kkat-eo-reun	another's husband
주인어른 ju-in-eo-reun	another's husband
부인 bu-in	another's wife
사모님 sa-mo-nim	another's wife

연습문제 Exercises

1.   Please respond to the following:

(1)   댁이 어디십니까? daeg-i eo-di-sim-ni-kka?
(2)   어느 나라 사람이십니까? eo-neu na-ra sa-ram-i-sim-ni-kka?
(3)   연세가 어떻게 되십니까? yeon-se-ga eo-tteo-ke
      doe-sim-ni-kka?
(4)   생일이 언제십니까? saeng-il-i eon-je-sim-ni-kka?
(5)   결혼하셨습니까? gyeol-hon-ha-syeot-seum-ni-kka?
(6)   가족이 어떻게 되십니까? ga-jog-i eo-tteo-ke doe-sim-ni-kka?

2.   Please translate the following into English:

(1)   저는 한국에서 왔습니다. 수원에서 삽니다.
      jeo-neun han-gug-e-seo wat-seum-ni-da. su-won-e-seo
      sam-ni-da.
(2)   저는 한국사람이 아닙니다. 중국사람입니다.
      jeo-neun han-guk-sa-ram-i a-nim-ni-da.
      jung-guk-sa-ram-im-ni-da.
(3)   저하고 동갑이시군요. 저도 서른 두살 입니다.
      jeo-ha-go dong-gab-i-si-gun-yo. jeo-do seo-reun-dul-im-ni-da.
(4)   아이는 아직 없어요. 집사람하고 저하고 둘이에요.
      a-i-neun a-jik eops-eo-yo. jip-sa-ram-ha-go jeo-ha-go
      dul-i-e-yo.

3.   Please translate the following into Korean:

(1)   I am a Korean-American.
(2)   I was born in Michigan.
(3)   I am from Canada.
(4)   I was born in July.
(5)   I have no brother and sister.

4.   Please write a paragraph introducing yourself (your name, hometown/nationality, age/birthday, family, etc.).

제3과 길 묻기

◇◇◇◇◇◇◇◇

Lesson 3: Asking Directions

표현 Patterns

이 근처에 대한은행이 어디 있습니까?
i geun-cheo-e dae-han-eun-haeng-i eo-di it-seum-ni-kka?
Where is Dae-Han Bank around here?

이 길로 똑바로 가세요.
i gil-lo ttok-ba-ro ga-se-yo.
Go straight down this street.

신호등을 건너서 오른쪽으로 쭉 가세요.
sin-ho-deung-eul geon-neo-seo o-reun-jjog-eu-ro jjuk ga-se-yo.
Cross (at) the traffic signal, turn right, and go straight .

길 건너편에 대한은행이 있어요.
gil geon-neo-pyeon-e dae-han-eun-haeng-i iss-eo-yo.
Dae-Han Bank is (on) across the street.

여기에서 대한은행까지 멉니까?
yeo-gi-e-seo dae-han-eun-haeng-kka-ji meom-ni-kka?
Is it far from here to Dae-Han Bank?

여기에서 대한은행까지 시간이 얼마나 걸립니까?
yeo-gi-e-seo dae-han-eun-haeng-kka-ji si-gan-i eol-ma-na
　　geol-lim-ni-kka?
How long does it take from here to Dae-Han Bank?

별로 안 멀어요.
byeol-lo an meol-eo-yo.
It's not very far.

걸어서 한 20분쯤 걸릴 거예요.
geol-eo-se han i-sip-bun-jjeum geol-lil geo-ye-yo.
It will take about 20 minutes by walking.

이 근처에서 제일 가까운 커피숍이 어디 있습니까?

i geun-cheo-e-seo je-il ga-kka-un keo-pi-syob-i eo-di it-seum-ni-kka?

Where is the nearest coffee shop around here (this area)?

회사 옆에 제일빌딩 아시지요?

hoe-sa yeop-e je-il-bil-ding a-si-ji-yo?

You know the Je-il building next to (our) company, right?

제일빌딩 바로 뒤에 한영서점 아시죠?

je-il-bil-ding ba-ro dwi-e han-yeong-seo-jeom a-si-jyo?

You know Han-Yeong Bookstore right behind the Je-il building,
    right?

그 빌딩 지하에 커피숍이 하나 있어요.

geu bil-ding ji-ha-e keo-pi-syob-i ha-na iss-eo-yo.

There is a coffee shop in the basement of the building.

한영서점 안에도 하나 있어요.

han-yeong-seo-jeom an-e-do ha-na iss-eo-yo.

There is also one inside Han-Yeong Bookstore.

그 빌딩은 요즘 공사중이라서 너무 복잡해서요.

geu bil-ding-eun yo-jeum gong-sa-jung-i-ra-seo neo-mu
    bok-ja-pae-seo-yo.

That building is under construction these days, so it's too crowded.

벽에 이상한 삼각형하고 사각형 타일이 붙은 가게 말이죠?

byeog-e i-sang-han sam-ga-kyeong-ha-go sa-ga-kyeong ta-il-i but-
    eun ga-ge mal-i-jyo?

You mean the store where strange-looking triangle and square tiles
    are attached to the wall, right?

이사 잘 하셨어요?

i-sa jal ha-syeoss-eo-yo?

Did your move go well? (*lit.* Did you move well?)

지난 주 금요일에 이사하고 주말 동안 대충 정리했어요.
ji-nal ju geum-yo-il-e i-sa-ha-go ju-mal ttong-an dae-chung
jeong-ri-haess-eo-yo.
I moved last Friday and almost finished putting things in order
during the weekend.

고생 많이 하셨군요.
go-saeng man-I ha-syeot-gun-yo.
You worked hard. (*lit.* You did a hard work.)

새로 이사하신 집은 어디세요?
sae-ro i-sa-ha-sin jib-eun eo-di-se-yo?
Where is the house you just (*lit.* newly) moved into?

병원에서 아주 가까워요.
byeong-won-e-seo a-ju ga-kka-wo-yo.
It is very close to the hospital (where I work).

한 **500**미터쯤 될 거예요.
han o-baeng-mi-teojjeum doel kkeo-ye-yo.
It is about 500 meters (from there).

저희 병원 근처에 서신 아파트 아세요?
jeo-hi byeong-won geun-cheo-e seo-sin a-pa-teu a-se-yo?
Do you know the Seo-Sin Apartment Complex near my hospital?

그 아파트 얼마 전에 새로 지었지요?
geu a-pa-teu eol-ma-jeon-e sae-ro ji-eot-ji-yo?
That apartment complex was recently built a (short) while ago,
right?

잘 됐네요.
jal dwaen-ne-yo.
That's good (for you).

아파트 단지 안에 상가가 있어서 아주 편리해요.

a-pa-teu dan-ji an-e sang-ga-ga iss-eo-seo a-ju pyeol-li-hae-yo.

There is a shopping center inside the apartment complex, so it is
very convenient.

대화 Model Conversations

(1)

김현준: 실례지만 이 근처에 대한은행이 어디 있습니까?

    sil-lye-ji-man i geun-cheo-e dae-han-eun-haeng-i eo-di it-seum-ni-kka?

행인: 이 길로 똑바로 가세요. 그리고 신호등을 건너서 오른쪽으로 쭉 가세요. 그럼 길 건너편에 대한은행이 있어요.

    i gil-lo ttok-ba-ro ga-se-yo. geu-ri-go sin-ho-deung-eul geon-neo-seo o-reun-jjog-eu-ro jjuk ga-se-yo. geu-reom gil geon-neo-pyeon-e dae-han-eun-haeng-i iss-eo-yo.

김현준: 감사합니다. 그런데 여기에서 대한은행까지 멉니까? 시간이 얼마나 걸립니까?

    gam-sa-ham-ni-da. geu-reon-de yeo-gi-e-seo dae-han-eun-haeng-kka-ji meom-ni-kka? si-gan-i eol-ma-na geol-lim-ni-kka?

행인: 별로 안 멀어요. 걸어서 한 20분쯤 걸릴 거예요.

    byeol-lo an meol-eo-yo. geol-eo-seo han i-sip-bun jjeum geol-lil kkeo-ye-yo.

김현준: 아, 알겠습니다. 감사합니다.

    a, al-get-seum-ni-da. gam-sa-ham-ni-da.

(2)

김현준: 성민씨, 이 근처에서 제일 가까운 커피숍이 어디 있습니까?

    seong-min-ssi, i geun-cheo-e-seo je-il ga-kka-un keo-pi-syob-i eo-di it-seum-ni-kka?

박성민: 회사 옆에 제일빌딩 아시지요? 파란색 건물이요. 그 빌딩 지하에 커피숍이 하나 있어요.

    hoe-sa yeop-e je-il-bil-ding a-si-ji-yo? pa-ran-saek geon-mul-i-yo. geu bil-ding ji-ha-e keo-pi-syob-i ha-na iss-eo-yo.

김현준: 그건 저도 알아요. 그런데 그 빌딩은 요즘 공사중이
라서 너무 복잡해서요.
geu-geon jeo-do al-a-yo. geu-reon-de geu bil-ding-eun
yo-jeum gong-sa-jung-i-ra-seo neo-mu bok-ja-pae-seo-yo.

박성민: 그렇군요. 그럼 제일빌딩 바로 뒤에 한영서점 아시
죠? 한영서점 안에도 하나 있어요.
geu-reo-kun-yo. geu-reom je-il-bil-ding dwi-e han-
yeong-seo-jeom a-si-jyo? han-yeong-seo-jeom an-e-do
ha-na iss-eo-yo.

김현준: 아, 벽에 이상한 삼각형하고 사각형 타일이 붙은 가
게 말이죠?
a, byeog-e i-sang-han sam-ga-kyeong-ha-go sa-ga-
kyeong ta-il-i but-eun ga-ge mal-i-jyo?

박성민: 네, 맞아요.
ne, maj-a-yo.

(3)
최태민: 정호씨, 이사 다 하셨어요?
jeong-ho-ssi, i-sa da ha-syeoss-eo-yo?

이정호: 네, 지난 주 금요일에 이사하고 주말 동안 대충 정리
했어요.
ne, ji-nan ju geum-yo-il-e i-sa-ha-go ju-mal ttong-an
dae-chung jeong-ri-haess-eo-yo.

최태민: 고생 많이 하셨군요. 그런데 새로 이사하신 집은 어
디세요?
go-saeng man-i ha-syeot-gun-yo. geu-reon-de sae-ro
i-sa-ha-sin jib-eun eo-di-se-yo?

이정호: 저희 병원에서 아주 가까워요. 한 500미터쯤 될 거예
요. 병원 근처에 서신 아파트 아세요?
jeo-hi byeong-won-e-seo a-ju ga-kka-wo-yo. han
o-baeng-mi-teo-jjeum doel geo-ye-yo.
byeong-won geun-cheo-e seo-sin a-pa-teu a-se-yo?

최태민: 네, 알아요. 그 아파트 얼마 전에 새로 지었지요? 잘
            됐네요.

            ne, al-a-yo. geu a-pa-teu eol-ma jeon-e sae-ro
            ji-eot-ji-yo? jal dwaen-ne-yo.

이정호: 네. 그리고 아파트 단지 안에 상가가 있어서 아주 편
            리해요.

            ne. geu-ri-go a-pa-teu dan-ji an-e sang-ga-ga iss-eo-seo
            a-ju pyeol-li-hae-yo.

영문번역 English Translation

(1)

Kim: Excuse me, where is the Dae-Han Bank around here?

Pedestrian: Go straight down this road. And cross at the signal light, turn right, and go straight. The Dae-Han Bank is right across the street.

Kim: Thank you. By the way, is the Dae-Han Bank far from here? How much time will it take to get there?

Pedestrian: It's not very far. It should take about 20 minutes by walking.

Kim: Ah, I see. Thank you.

(2)

Kim: Seong-Min, where is the closest coffee shop near here?

Park: You know the Je-Il building next to our office, right? I mean the blue colored building. There is a coffee shop in the basement of the building.

Kim: I know that one. But that building has had construction these past few days, so it is too crowded.

Park: That's right . . . Then you know the Han-Yeong Bookstore right behind the Je-Il building, right? There is one inside the Han-Yeong Bookstore, too.

Kim: Ah, you mean the store where the wall is covered with strange-looking triangle and square tiles, right?

Park: Yes, that's right.

(3)

Choi: Jeong-Ho, did your move go well?

Lee: Yes, I moved last Friday and almost finished putting things in order during the weekend.

Choi: You did a lot of hard work. By the way, where is the new house you moved to?

Lee: It is very close to the hospital where I work. It is
              about 500 meters from there. Do you know the
              Seo-Sin Apartment Complex near the hospital?
Choi: Yes, I know it. That apartment complex was recently
              built a short while ago, right? That's good for you.
Lee: Yes. And there is a shopping center inside the
              apartment complex, so it is very convenient.

어휘 Vocabulary

Nouns / Pronouns

20분쯤 i-sip-bun-jjeum	about 20 minutes
500미터쯤 o-bang-mi-teo-jjeum	about 500 meters
가게 ga-ge	store, shop
건너편 geon-neo-pyeon	the other side of a street
건물 geon-mul	building
고생 go-saeng	hard work
공사 중 gong-sa-jung	on the construction
근처 geun-cheo	near
금요일 geum-yo-il	Friday
길 gil	street, road
단지 dan-ji	(apartment) complex
대한은행 dae-han-eun-haeng	Dae-Han Bank
바로 뒤 ba-ro dwi	right behind
벽 byeok	wall
병원 byeong-won	hospital
사각형 sa-ga-kyeong	square
삼각형 sam-ga-kyeong	triangle
상가 sang-ga	mall, shopping center
서신아파트 seo-sin-a-pa-teu	Seo-Sin Apartment
시간 si-gan	time, hour
신호등 sin-ho-deung	traffic signal
아파트 a-pa-teu	apartment (complex)
안 an	inside
얼마 전 eol-ma jeon	a while ago
여기 yeo-gi	here
옆 yeop	beside
오른쪽 o-reun-jjok	right side
요즘 yo-jeum	these days
이사 i-sa	moving
제일빌딩 je-il-bil-ding	Je-Il Building

주말 ju-mal — weekend
지난 주 ji-nan ju — last week
지하 ji-ha — basement
커피숍 keo-pi-syop — coffee shop
타일 ta-il — tile
파란색 pa-ran-saek — blue color
하나 ha-na — one
한영서점 han-yeong-seo-jeom — Han-Yeong Bookstore
행인 haeng-in — passer-by
회사 hoe-sa — company, office

Verbs

가깝다 ga-kkap-da — to be close
감사하다 gam-sa-ha-da — to thank
건너다 geon-neo-da — to cross (a street)
걸리다 geol-li-da — to take time
맞다 mat-da — to be correct
멀다 meol-da — to be far
복잡하다 bok-ja-pa-da — to be crowded
붙다 but-da — to attach, to be attached
알다 al-da — to know
이사하다 i-sa-ha-da — to move
이상하다 i-sang-ha-da — to be strange, to be unusual
있다 it-da — to exist
잘 되다 jal doe-da — to be done well
정리하다 jeong-ri-ha-da — to organize
짓다 jit-da — to build
편리하다 pyeol-li-ha-da — to be convenient

Adverbs / Prepositions / Conjunctions

걸어서 geol-eo-seo	by walking
그 geu	that
그런데 geu-reon-de	but
그리고 geu-ri-go	and
너무 neo-mu	to much
대충 dae-chung	roughly
똑바로 ttok-ba-ro	straight
많이 man-i	a lot
별로 byeol-lo	not particularly
새로 sae-ro	newly
아주 a-ju	very, so
안 an	not
어디 eo-di	where
얼마나 eol-ma-na	how much/many/long
이 i	this
잘 jal	well
저희 jeo-hi	our *(hom.)*
제일 je-il	the most
쭉 jjuk	straight
한 han	approximately

문법 Grammar

(1) Demonstrative Expressions

The demonstrative pronouns 이 (i), 그 (geu), and 저 (jeo) are, respectively, the equivalents of the English "this," "that," and "that over there." When 이 appears before a word, the object denoted by that word is near the speaker. When 그 appears before a word, the object indicated is near the person being spoken to. When 저 appears before a word, the object indicated is something not near either person.

Once the object indicated has been mentioned once, one does not say the word for it again. One uses the word 것 (geot) instead. This is the Korean equivalent for the English word "thing." If one used 이 with the original noun, one says 이것 from that point on. Likewise, one would say 그것 for an item referred to with 그, and 저것 for something referred to with 저.

The shortened word 거 (geo) may be used instead of 것 in casual conversation. The word 거 may form a contraction with the following particle if that particle begins with a vowel. These contractions are shown below:

Full Form		Contracted Form
이것/그것/저것		이거/그거/저거
i-geot/geu-geot/jeo-geot		i-geo/geu-geo/jeo-geo
이것/그것/저것 + 은 → (*topic particle*)	이거/그거/저거 + 은 →	이건/그건/저건
i-geot/geu-geot/jeo-geot + eun	i-geo/geu-geo/jeo-geo + eun	i-geon/geu-geon/jeo-geon
이것/그것/저것 + 을 → (*object particle*)	이거/그거/저거 + 을 →	이걸/그걸/저걸
i-geot/geu-geot/jeo-geot + eul	i-geo/geu-geo/jeo-geo + eul	i-geol/geu-geol/jeo-geol

이것/그것/저것 + 이 →   이거/그거/저거 + 이 →   이게/그게/저게
  (*subject particle*)
i-geot/geu-geot/jeo-geot + i   i-geo/geu-geo/jeo-geo + i   i-ge/geu-ge/jeo-ge

(2) The Adverbial Pronouns 여기, 거기, and 저기

The Korean equivalents of "here," "there," and "over there," are, respectively, 여기 (yeo-gi), 거기 (geo-gi), and 저기 (jeo-gi). The word 여기 is used when indicating a location near oneself. The word 거기 is used when indicating a location near the person one is speaking to. The word 저기 is used when indicating a location that is not near either oneself or the person to whom one is speaking.

The use of the locative particle 에 (e), the equivalent of "at," with these words is optional. For example, one may say 여기서 (yeo-gi-seo) instead of 여기에서 (yeo-gi-e-seo).

(2) The Pattern ~부터 ~까지 vs. ~에서 ~까지

The pattern ~부터 ~까지 (bu-teo … kka-ji) is used when talking about a period of time with a distinct beginning and end. It is the equivalent of the English pattern "from [a beginning time] to [an ending time]." For example, consider the second part of this exchange:

매일 직장에 나가십니까?
(mae-il jik-jang-e na-ga-sim-ni-kka?)
Do you go to work everyday?

아니오, 월요일부터 금요일까지만 나가고 토요일과 일요일은
    쉽니다.
(a-ni-o, wol-yo-il-bu-teo geum-yo-il-kka-ji-man
    na-ga-go to-yo-il-gwa il-yo-il-eun swim-ni-da.)
No, I go to work from Monday to Friday, and take a rest on
    Saturday and Sunday.

The phrase 월요일부터 금요일까지만 나가고 (wol-yo-il-buteo geum-yo-il-kka-ji-man) means "from Monday to Friday." Note its use of this pattern.

Another "from...to..." pattern is ~에서~까지 (e-seo...kka-ji). This is used when the beginning and ending points are locations. Consider the first half of this exchange:

LA에서 서울까지 비행기로 시간이 얼마나 걸립니까?
(el-e-i-e-seo seo-ul-kka-ji bi-haeng-gi-ro si-gan-i eol-ma-na
    geol-lim-ni-kka?)
How long does it take from L.A. to Seoul by airplane?

한 열두시간쯤 걸려요.
(han yeo-ttu-si-gan-jjeum geol-lyeo-yo.)
It takes about 12 hours.

The phrase LA에서 서울까지 (el-e-i-e-seo seo-ul-kka-ji) means "from L.A. to Seoul." Again, note the use of the pattern.

(3) The future (prospective) tense of verbs

The pattern [Verb] + ~(으)ㄹ 거예요 is used to indicate that one is probably going to do something. An example is the second half of this exchange:

주말에 뭐 할 거예요?
(ju-mal-e mwo hal kkeo-ye-yo?)
What are you going to do the on weekend?

극장에 갈 거예요.
(geuk-jang-e gal kkeo-ye-yo.)
I will probably go to the movie theater.

When the verb ends in a consonant, use ~을 거예요. When it ends in a vowel, use ~ㄹ 거예요.

(4) Irregular Verbs

With irregular verbs, the final sound of the verb stem changes when affixed to certain suffixes. There are nine types.

ㄷ—Irregular Verbs

Verbs with stems that end in ㄷ are ㄷ-irregular verbs. Examples include 듣다 (deut-da) / "to listen," 걷다 (geot-da) / "to walk," and 묻다 (mut-da) / "to ask."

With ㄷ-irregular verbs, the ㄷ becomes ㄹ when followed by a vowel, as it does in the polite form:

듣다 (deut-da) → 듣 (deut) + 어요 (eo-yo) → 들어요 (deul-eo-yo)
걷다 (goet-da) → 걷 (geot) + 어요 (eo-yo) → 걸어요 (geol-eo-yo)
묻다 (mut-da) → 묻 (mut) + 어요 (eo-yo) → 물어요 (mul-eo-yo)

듣다 (deut-da) → 듣 (deut) + 으세요 (eu-se-yo) → 들으세요
   (deul- eu-se-yo)
걷다 (goet-da) → 걷 (geot) + 으세요 (eu-se-yo) → 걸으세요
   (geol- eu-se-yo)
묻다 (mut-da) → 묻 (mut) + 으세요 (eu-se-yo) → 물으세요
   (mul- eu-se-yo)

ㅂ—Irregular Verbs

Verbs with stems that end in ㅂ are ㅂ-irregular verbs. Examples include 가깝다 (ga-kkap-da) / "to be close," 어렵다 (eo-reop-da) / "to be difficult," and 무겁다 (mu-geop-da) / "to be heavy."

With ㅂ-irregular verbs, the ㅂ becomes 우 when followed by a vowel. Again, the examples demonstrate the conversion to the polite form:

가깝다 (ga-kkap-da) → 가깝 (ga-kkap) + 어요 (eo-yo) → 가까우 (ga-kka-u) + 어요 (eo-yo) → 가까워요 (ga-kka-wo-yo)
어렵다 (eo-reop-da) → 어렵 (eo-reop) + 어요 (eo-yo) → 어려우 (eo-ryeo-u) +어요 (eo-yo) → 어려워요 (eo-ryeo-wo-yo)
무겁다 (mu-geop-da) → 무겁 (mu-jeop) + 어요 (eo-yo) → 무거우 (mu-geo-u) + 어요 (eo-yo) → 무거워요 (mu-geo-wo-yo)

Note that in the polite form, the final 우 of the converted verb stem and the beginning 어 of the form-suffix form the contraction 워 (wo).

ㅅ—Irregular Verbs

Verbs with stems that end in ㅅ include짓다 (jit-da) / "to build," 붓다 (but-da) / "to pour," and 잇다 (it-da) / "to connect."

When the suffix begins with a vowel, as in the polite form, the ㅅ is dropped.

짓다 (jit-da) → 짓 (jit) + 어요 (eo-yo) → 지어요 (ji-eo-yo)
붓다 (but-da) → 붓 (but) + 어요 (eo-yo) → 부어요 (bu-eo-yo)
잇다 (it-da) → 잇 (it) + 어요 (eo-yo) → 이어요 (i-eo-yo)

으—Irregular Verbs

Verbs with stems that end in 으 include 쓰다 (sseu-da) / "to write," 크다 (keu-da) / "to be big," and 아프다 (a-peu-da) / "to be sick." If the form-suffix begins with a vowel, the 으 is dropped. Again, the conversions shown are in the polite form.

쓰다 (sseu-da) → 쓰 (sseu) + 어요 (eo-yo) → 써요 (sseo-yo)
크다 (keu-da) → 크 (keu) + 어요 (eo-yo) → 커요 (kkeo-yo)
아프다 (a-peu-da) → 아프 (a-peu) + 아요 (a-yo) → 아파요
 (a-pa-yo)
예쁘다 (ye-ppeu-da) → 예쁘 (ye-ppeu) + 어요 (eo-yo) → 예뻐요
 (ye-ppeo-yo)

Note that when the final syllable of the stem is 으, as in 아프-, 예
쁘-, the contraction syllable 파(pa) is formed with 아 Likewise, the
contraction syllable 뻐(ppeo) is formed when the final syllable of the
stem is 쁘 (ppeu) is formed with 어. When the second to the final
syllable vowel in a verb stem is 아, 오, or 애, the sentence ending
아요 is used, and 어요 is used when other vowels come in the same
position.

ㄹ—Irregular Verbs

Verbs with stems that end in ㄹ include 돌다 (dol-da) / "to turn," 늘
다 (neul-da) / "to play," and 알다 (al-da) / "to know." If the suffix
begins with the consonants ㄴ, ㅂ, or ㅅ, the ㄹ is dropped.

An example of this conversion in question form:

돌다 (dol-da) → 돌 (dol) + 니까 (ni-kka) → 도니까 (do-ni-kka)

An example in the deferential statement form:

늘다 (neul-da) → 늘 (neul) + ㅂ니다 (p-ni-da) → 늡니다 (neup-ni-da)

An example in the polite honorific form:

알다 (al-da) → 알 (al) + 세요 (se-yo) → 아세요 (a-se-yo)

르—Irregular Verbs

Verbs that end in 르 include 부르다 (bu-reu-da) / "to call," 모르다 (mo-reu-da) / "to not know," and 빠르다 (ppa-reu-da) / "to be fast."

With these verbs, the 르 that ends the stem becomes ㄹㄹ. The following examples show the conversion in the polite form:

부르다 (bu-reu-da) → 부르 (bu-reu) + 어요 (eo-yo) → 불러요 (bul-leo-yo)

모르다 (mo-reu-da) → 모르 (mo-reu) + 아요 (a-yo) → 몰라요 (mol-la-yo)

빠르다 (ppa-reu-da) →빠르 (ppa-reu) + 아요 (eo-yo) → 빨라요 (ppal-la-yo)

러—Irregular Verbs

This class of irregular verbs relates to verbs with stems that end in 르. These include 푸르다 (pu-reu-da) / "to be blue," 이르다 (i-reu-da) / "to be early," and 누르다 (nu-reu-da) / "to press." If a verb stem ends in 르 and is followed by the vowel 아 or 어, then there is a ㄹ insertion before the 아 or 어.

푸르다 (pu-reu-da) → 푸르 (pu-reu) + 어서 (eo-seo) → 푸르러서 (pu-reu-reo-seo)

이르다 (i-reu-da) → 이르 (i-reu) + 어서 (eo-seo) → 이르러서 (i-reu-reo-seo)

누르다 (nu-reu-da) → 누르 (nu-reu) + 어서 (eo-seo) → 누르러서 (nu-reu-reo-seo)

여—Irregular Verbs

This class of verbs relates to verbs with stems that end in 아. These include 하다 (ha-da) / "to do," 좋아하다 (jo-a-ha-da) / "to like," and 싫어하다 (sil-eo-ha-da) / "to dislike."

With these verbs, the ㅏ part of the syllable block 아 that ends the verb stem becomes ㅐ when the form-suffix begins with 어 or 아. The following examples show the conversion in the polite form.

하다 (ha-da) → 하 (ha) + 아요 (a-yo) → 해요 (hae-yo)
좋아하다 (jo-a-ha-da) → 좋아하 (jo-a-ha) + 아요 (a-yo) → 좋아
　해요 (jo-a-hae-yo)
싫어하다 (sil-eo-ha-da) → 싫어하 (sil-eo-ha) + 아요 (a-yo) → 싫
　어해요 (sil-eo-hae-yo)

ㅎ—Irregular Verbs

Verbs in this class have stems that end in ㅎ. They include 빨갛다 (ppal-ga-ta) / "to be red," 하얗다 (ha-ya-ta) / "to be blue," and 까맣다 (kka-ma-ta) / "to be black."

With these verbs, the ㅎ ending the stem is dropped if the suffix begins with ㄴ, ㄹ, or ㅁ. (These letters are the nasal consonants.)

The following example shows the sentence in the adjective-final form, in which descriptive verbs become adjectives. Here, the equivalent of the verb "to be red" becomes the equivalent of the adjective "red."

빨갛다 (ppal-ga-ta) → 빨갛 (ppal-ga) + ㄴ (n) → 빨간 (ppal-gan)

This example shows the sentence in the conditional form.

하얗다 (ha-ya-ta) → 하얗 (ha-ya) + 면 (myeon) →
　하야면 (ha-ya-myeon)

This example shows the sentence with the casual sentence ending (으)니까.

까맣다 (kka-ma-ta) → 까맣 (kka-ma) + 니까 (ni-kka) →
　까마니까 (kka-ma-ni-kka)

(5) The Causative Form of Verbs

When stating an action that is a cause or a reason, the verb is presented in the causative form. The suffixes ~아서 (a-seo) or ~어서 (eo-seo) are added to the verb stem, e.g.

가다 (ga-da) → 가 + 아서 (a-seo) → 가서 (ga-seo)
to go   Because I go, etc.

The suffix ~아서 is added if the verb stem ends in 아 (a)오 (o), or 애 (ae). The suffix ~어서 is used with all other verb stems.

Both causative and resulting actions are included in the same sentence. The cause is stated first, the result second. This sentence pattern is the equivalent of "Because..., I/he/they did..." It is often heard in response to a question asking 왜 (wae), the equivalent of the English "why." For example:

어제 왜 회사에 안 갔어요?
(eo-je wae hoe-sa-e an gass-eo-yo?)
Why you didn't go to work yesterday?

머리가 아파서 안 갔어요.
(meo-ri-ga a-pa-seo an gass-eo-to.)
I didn't go (to work) because I had a headache.

The clause 머리가 아파서 (meo-ri-ga a-pa-seo) / "because I had a headache" comes first, followed by the clause 안 갔어요 (an-gass-eo-to) / "I didn't go."

There is a rule regarding the use of the causative in casual conversation. When the causative verb is 이다 (i-da) / "to be" and follows a noun in the word order, 이다 becomes 이라서 (i-ra-seo) if the accompanying noun ends in a consonant, for example:

오늘은 일요일이라서 회사에 안 가요.
(o-neul-eun il-yo-il-i-ra-seo hoe-sa-e an ga-yo.)
Since today is Sunday, I am not going to work.

If the noun ends in a vowel, 이다 becomes라서 (ra-seo), e.g.

정호씨는 휴가라서 여행 갔어요.
(jeong-ho-ssi-neun hyu-ga-ra-seo yeo-haeng gass-eo-yo.)
Since it's a vacation, Jeong-Ho went traveling.

The English "because" and "since" are used interchangeably.

(6) The Adverb 별로

The adverb 별로 (byeol-lo) is the equivalent of the English "not particularly," "not really," and "not so much." The verb in the sentence,
if one appears, is usually negative. The following exchange high-
lights 별로 and its usage.

주말에 할 일이 많아요?
(ju-mal-e hal il-i man-a-yo?)
Do you have many things to do on the weekend?

아니오, 별로 없어요.
(a-ni-o, byeol-lo eops-eo-yo.)
No, not really.

(7) The Particles ~로 and ~으로

The particles ~로 (ro) and ~으로 (eu-ro) have multiple usages. The
particle ~로 is used with nouns ending in a vowel or the consonant ㄹ. The particle ~으로 is used with nouns ending in all other
consonants.

One meaning for ~로 and ~으로 is "by means of." Examples:

한국말로 이야기해 보세요.
(han-gung-mal-lo i-ya-gi-hae bo-se-yo.)
Please speak in Korean.

한국까지 비행기로 10시간 걸려요.
(han-guk-kka-ji bi-haeng-gi-ro yeol-ssi-gan geol-lyeo-yo.)
It takes 10 hours to come to Korea by airplane.

In these sentences, the Korean language and an airplane are the methods by which the action is carried out.

Another meaning for the particles is "to (a place)" or "towards (a place)," as in 서울로 (seo-ul-lo) / "to Seoul," or 은행으로 (eun-haeng-eu-ro) / "to the bank." It is also used when giving directions, e.g.

사거리에서 오른쪽으로 가세요.
(sa-geo-ri-e-seo o-reun-jjog-eu-ro ga-se-yo.)
Please turn right (*lit.* go to the right) at the intersection.

The particle ~에 (e) also indicates "to" or "towards." However, it is used when indicating a specific direction. The particles ~로 and ~으로 are used when the destination is more general.

참고학습 Further Study

Positional Words

가운데 ga-un-de	middle
뒤 dwi	back, behind
밑 mit	underneath
밖 bak / 바깥 ba-kkat	out, outside
속 sok	in, inside
아래 a-rae	under, below, down
안 an	in, inside
앞 ap	front
옆 yeop	side, nearby
위 wi	top, above, up

(1) Names of the Colors

Color	Noun	Adjective	Predicate
red	빨간색 ppal-gan-saek	빨간 ppal-gan	빨개요 ppal-gae-yo
black	까만색 kka-man-saek	까만 kka-man	까매요 kka-mae-yo
white	하얀색 ha-yan-saek	하얀 ha-yan	하얘요 ha-yae-yo
blue	파란색 pa-ran-saek	파란 pa-ran	파래요 pa-rae-yo
yellow	노란색 no-ran-saek	노란 no-ran	노래요 no-ra-yo
green	초록색 cho-rok-saek	초록색 cho-rok-saek	초록색이에요 cho-rok-saeg-i-e-yo
gray	회색 hoe-saek	회색 hoe-saek	회색이에요 hoe-saeg-i-e-yo
pink	분홍색 bun-hong-saek	분홍색 bun-hong-saek	분홍색이에요 bun-hong-saeg-i-e-yo

purple	보라색 bo-ra-saek	보라색 bo-ra-saek	보라색이에요 bo-ra-saeg-i-e-yo
orange	주황색 ju-hwang-saek	주황색 ju-hwang-saek	주황색이에요 ju-hwang-saeg-i-e-yo
pea	연두색 yeon-du-saek	연두색 yeon-du-saek	연두색이에요 yeon-du-saeg-i-e-yo

Example:

the color red	빨간색 ppal-gan-saek
a red apple	빨간 사과 ppal-gan sa-gwa
The apple is red.	사과가 빨개요. sa-gwa-ga ppal-gae-yo.

(2) The Names of Shapes

타원형 ta-won-hyeong	oval
원형 won-hyeong	round
동그라미 dong-geu-ra-mi	round
직사각형 jik-sa-ga-kyeong	rectangle
정사각형 jeong-sa-ga-kyeong	square
정삼각형 jeong-sam-ga-kyeong	triangle

(3) The Days of the Week

월요일 wol-yo-il	Monday (*day of the moon*)
화요일 hwa-yo-il	Tuesday (*day of fire*)
수요일 su-yo-il	Wednesday (*day of water*)
목요일 mog-yo-il	Thursday (*day of the trees*)
금요일 geum-yo-il	Friday (*day of metal*)
토요일 to-yo-il	Saturday (*day of soil*)
일요일 il-yo-il	Sunday (*day of the sun*)

The definitions in parentheses are the literal meanings of the Korean names for the days. They are named in honor of the sun, the moon, and the Five Elements according to Chinese philosophy. The seven-day week is a Western concept adopted by Korea and other East Asian countries.

주중 ju-jung	weekdays
주말 ju-mal	weekend
지난 주 ji-nan-ju	last week
이번 주 i-beon-jju	this week
다음 주 da-eum-jju	next week
지난 달 ji-nan-dal	last month
이번 달 i-beon-ttal	this month
다음 달 da-eum-ttal	next month
매일 mae-il	every day
매주 mae-ju	every week
매월 mae-wol	every month
매년 mae-nyeon	every year
월말 wol-mal	end of a month
연말 yeon-mal	end of a year

문화적 참고사항 Cultural Notes

(1) 아파트 (a-pa-teu)

The Korean 아파트, from the English "apartment," refers to the ubiquitous high-rise residential buildings in Korea. (The difference between the 아파트 and the U.S. "apartment" is that the Korean word refers to the building, not a rental unit inside.) The 아파트 are usually built in multi-building complexes that are named after the construction company, as in 현대아파트 (hyeon-dae a-pa-teu) and 삼익아파트 (sam-ik a-pa-teu). Nearly a quarter of the South Korean population lives in Seoul and the majority live in 아파트.

(2) 집들이 (jip-deul-i)

When people move into a new house, they are expected by their relatives, friends, and neighbors to have a 집들이, a housewarming party. This is especially true for newlyweds, and the party gives the bride an opportunity to demonstrate her cooking skills. Guests often bring modest gifts of soap or laundry detergent. These represent prosperity, i.e. a small amount produces a limitless amount of soap bubbles.

(3) 색깔 (saek-kkal)

The word for "color" in Korean is 색 (saek) or 색깔 (saek-kkal). The words for the different colors are used as nouns, as predicates, or as modifiers. The word 파란색 (pa-ran-saek) means "blue," but Koreans have traditionally used it to describe things that are either blue or green. An alternative word for green is 초록색 (cho-rok-saek), which literally means "grass green."

연습문제 Exercises

1. Please responsd to the following:

(1) 실례지만 이 근처에 지하철역이 어디 있습니까?
sil-le-ji-man i geun-cheo-e ji-ha-cheol yeog-i eo-di
it-seum-ni-kka?

(2) 여기에서 은행까지 멉니까?
yeo-gi-e-seo eun-haeng-kka-ji meom-ni-kka?

(3) 여기에서 은행까지 시간이 얼마나 걸립니까?
yeo-gi-e-seo eun-haeng-kka-ji si-gan-i eol-ma-na
geol-lim-ni-kka?

(4) 새로 이사하신 집은 어디세요?
sae-ro i-sa-ha-sin jib-eun eo-di-se-yo?

(5) 새로 이사하신 집이 어떠세요? 마음에 드세요?
sae-ro i-sa-ha-sin jib-i eo-tteo-se-yo? ma-eum-e deu-se-yo?

2. Please translate the following into English:

(1) 아파트 단지 안에 상가가 있어서 아주 편리해요.
(2) 지난주 금요일에 이사하고 주말동안 대충 정리했어요.
(3) 그 빌딩은 요즘 공사중이라 너무 복잡해서요.
(4) 제일빌딩 지하에 커피숍이 하나 있어요.
(5) 신호등을 건너서 오른쪽으로 쭉 가세요.

3. Please translate the following into Korean:

(1) There is a computer on the desk.
(2) My bag is under the coffee table.
(3) The telephone is beside my bed.
(4) The windows are behind a sofa.
(5) There is a door in front of the living room.

4. Please write a paragraph describing your room.

제4과 날짜와 시간 묻기

◇◇◇◇◇◇◇◇

Lesson 4: Asking the Date, Day and Time

표현 Patterns

오늘이 며칠이에요?
o-neul-i myeo-chil-i-e-yo?
What is the date today?

7월 15일이에요.
chil-wol sib-o-il-i-e-yo.
It's July 15th.

8월 7일이 무슨 요일이에요?
pal-wol chil-il-i mu-seun yo-il-i-e-yo?
What day is August 7th?

금요일이에요.
geum-yo-il-i-e-yo.
It's Friday.

지금 몇 시예요?
ji-geum myeot-si-ye-yo?
What time is it now?

5시 45분이에요.
da-seot-si sa-sib-o-bun-i-e-yo.
It's 5:45.

오빠가 몇 년생이세요?
o-ppa-ga myeon-nyeon-saeng-i-e-yo?
What year was (your) brother born in?

79년생이요.
chil-sip-gu-nyeon-saeng-i-yo.
(He was) born in 1979.

도영씨 언니는요?
do-yeong-ssi eon-ni-neun-yo?
How about your sister, Do-Yeong?

우리 언니도 79년생이에요.
u-ri eon-ni-do chil-sip-gu-nyeon-saeng-i-e-yo.
My sister was born in 1979 as well.

큰일 났네요.
keun-il nan-ne-yo.
I'm in a big trouble.

어제가 언니 생일이었는데 깜빡 잊어버렸어요.
eo-je-ga eon-ni saeng-il-i-eon-neun-de kkam-ppak ij-eo-beo-ryeoss-
   eo-yo.
Yesterday was my sister's birthday and I completely forgot.

우리 오빠 생일하고 똑같네요.
u-ri o-ppa saeng-il-ha-go ttok-gan-ne-yo.
It's the same as my brother's birthday.

우리 오빠 생일도 7월 14일인데요.
u-ri o-ppa saeng-il-do chil-wol sip-sa-il-in-de-yo.
My brother's birthday is July 14th, too.

정말 인연이네요.
jeong-mal in-yeon-i-ne-yo.
What a coincidence. (*lit.* There really are acts of Providence.)

왜요? 무슨 날이에요?
wae-yo? mu-seun nal-i-e-yo?
Why? Is it a special day?

대학 동창회가 있는 날이에요.
dae-hak dong-chang-hoe-ja in-neun nal-i-e-yo.
It's the day (my) college alumni reunion is on.

그래요? 좋겠어요.
geu-rae-yo? jo-ke-sseo-yo.
Really? Good for you.

새로 들어온 직원 환영회하고 시간이 겹치네요.
sae-ro deul-eo-on jig-won hwan-yeong-hoe-ha-ro si-gan-i
     gyeop-chi-ne-yo.
It falls on the same time as the new employee welcoming party.

그럼 어떻게 해요?
geu-reom eo-tteo-ke hae-yo?
Then what should you do?

할 수 없지요.
hal ssu eop-ji-yo.
There is nothing I can do.

회사 일이 먼저니까요.
hoe-sa il-i meon-jeo-ni-kka-yo.
Business is the first thing (to be done).

벌써 퇴근시간이 거의 다 됐네요.
beol-sseo toe-geun-si-gan-i geo-ui da dwaen-ne-yo.
It's already almost time to leave the office.

그럴 줄 알았어요.
geu-reol-jjul al-ass-eo-yo.
I knew it.

제 시계가 고장났나봐요.

je si-gye-ga go-jang-nan-na-bwa-yo.

It seems my watch is broken.

아직도 4시 10분밖에 안 됐어요.

a-jik-do ne-si sip-bun-bakk-e an dwaess-eo-yo.

It's still only 4:10.

혹시 배터리가 다 된 거 아니에요?

hok-si bae-teo-ri-ga da doen-geo a-ni-e-yo?

Do you think it might be because the battery is worn out?

그런가봐요.

geu-reon-ga-bwa-yo.

It might be.

집에 갈 때 시계방에 한번 들러 봐야겠어요.

jib-e gal-ttae si-gye-ppang-e han-beon deul-leo bwa-ya-gess-eo-yo.

I should stop by a watch repair shop when I go home.

대화 Model Conversations

(1)

이도영: 현주씨, 오늘이 며칠이에요?
　　　　heyon-ju-ssi, o-neul-i myeo-chil-i-e-yo?

정현주: 7월 15일이에요.
　　　　chil-wol sib-o-il-i-e-yo.

이도영: 아, 큰일났네요. 어제가 언니 생일이었는데 깜빡 잊
　　　　어버렸어요.
　　　　a, keun-il-nan-ne-yo. eo-je-ja eon-ni saeng-il-i-eon-
　　　　neun-de kkam-ppak ij-eo-beo-ryeoss-eo-yo.

정현주: 어머, 그러세요? 그럼 우리 오빠 생일하고 똑같네요.
　　　　우리 오빠 생일도 7월 14일인데요.
　　　　eo-meo, geu-reo-se-yo? geu-reom u-ri o-ppa saeng-il-ha-
　　　　go ttok-gan-ne-yo. u-ri o-ppa saeng-il-do chil-wol sip-sa-
　　　　il-in-de-yo.

이도영: 그러세요? 오빠가 몇년생이세요?
　　　　geu-reo-se-yo? o-ppa-ga myeon-nyeon-saeng-i-se-yo?

정현주: 79년생이요. 도영씨 언니는요?
　　　　chil-sip-gu-nyeon-saeng-i-yo. do-yeong-ssi
　　　　eon-ni-neun-yo?

이도영: 우리 언니도 79년생이에요. 정말 인연이네요.
　　　　u-ri eon-ni-do chil-sip-gu-nyeon-saeng-i-e-yo. jeong-mal
　　　　in-yeon-i-ne-yo.

(2)

정현주: 도영씨, 8월 7일이 무슨 요일이에요?
　　　　do-yeong-ssi, pal-wol chil-il-i mu-seun yo-il-i-e-yo?

이도영: 금요일이요. 왜요? 무슨 날이에요?
　　　　geum-yo-il-i-yo. wae-yo? mu-seun nal-i-e-yo?

정현주: 대학 동창회가 있는 날이에요.
　　　　dae-hak dong-chang-hoe-ga in-neun nal-i-e-yo.

이도영: 그래요? 좋겠어요.
　　　　geu-rae-yo? jo-kess-eo-yo.

정현주: 네. 그런데 그날 새로 들어온 직원 환영회하고 시간
이 겹치네요.

ne. geu-reon-de geu-nal sae-ro deul-eo-on jig-won
hwan-yeong-hoe-ha-go si-gan-i gyeop-chi-ne-yo.

이도영: 어머, 그래요? 그럼 어떻게 해요?

eo-meo, geu-rae-yo? geu-reom eo-tteo-ke hae-yo?

정현주: 할 수 없지요. 일이 먼저니까요.

hal-ssu eop-ji-yo. il-i meon-jeo-ni-kka-yo.

(3)

이도영: 현주씨, 지금 몇 시예요?

hyeon-ju-ssi, ji-geum myeot-si-ye-yo?

정현주: 5시 45분이요. 벌써 퇴근시간이 거의 다 됐네요.

da-seot-si sa-sib-o-bun-i-yo. beol-sseo toe-geun-si-gan-i
geo-ui da dwaen-ne-yo.

이도영: 그럴 줄 알았어요. 제 시계가 고장났나봐요. 아직도
4시 10분밖에 안 됐어요.

geu-reol jjul al-ass-eo-yo. je si-gye-ga go-jang-nan-na-
bwa-yo. a-jik-do ne-si sip-bun-bakk-e an-dwaess-eo-yo.

정현주: 혹시 배터리가 다 된 거 아니에요?

hok-si bae-teo-ri-ga da doen-geo a-ni-e-yo?

이도영: 그런가봐요. 집에 갈 때 시계방에 한번 들러 봐야겠
어요.

geu-reon-ga-bwa-yo. jib-e gal-ttae si-gye-ppang-e
han-beon deul-leo bwa-ya-gess-eo-yo.

영문번역 English Translation

(1)
Lee: Hyun-Ju, what is the date today?
Jung: It's July 15th.
Lee: Oh, I'm in big trouble. Yesterday was my sister's birthday and I completely forgot.
Jung: Wow, is that right? Then your sister's birthday is the same as my brother's. My brother's birthday is also July 14th.
Lee: Really? What year was he born in?
Jung: He was born in 1979. How about your sister, Do-Yeong?
Lee: My sister was born in 1979 as well. What a coincidence.

(2)
Jung: Do-Yeong, what day is August 7th?
Lee: It's Friday. Why? Is it a special day?
Jung: It's the day my college alumni reunion is on.
Lee: Really? Good for you.
Jung: Yes, but it conflicts with the reception for new employees.
Lee: Uh uh . . . really? Then what should you do?
Jung: Nothing I can do. My work is my first priority.

(3)
Lee: Hyeon-Ju, what time is it now?
Jung: It's 5:45. It's already almost time to go home.
Lee: I knew it. It seems my watch is broken. It's still only 4:10 on my watch.
Jung: Do you think it might be because the battery is worn out?
Lee: I think so. I should stop by a watch repair shop when I go home.

어휘 Vocabulary

Nouns & Pronouns

금요일 geum-yo-il	Friday
날 nal	day, date
대학 dae-hak	college
도영씨 do-yeong-ssi	Do-Yeong
동창회 dong-chang-hoe	alumni assembly
무슨 날 mu-seun nal	special day
배터리 bae-teo-ri	battery
생일 saeng-il	birthday
시간 si-gan	time, hour
시계 si-ge	watch, clock
시계 방 si-ge ppang	watch repair store
어제 eon-je	yesterday
언니 eon-ni	woman's older sister
오늘 o-neul	today
오빠 o-ppa	woman's older brother
이도영 i-do-yeong	Do-Yeong Lee
인연 in-yeon	act of Providence
일 il	work
정현주 jeong-hyeon-ju	Hyeon-Ju Jeong
지금 ji-geum	now
직원 jig-won	employee
집 jip	house
퇴근시간 toe-geun-si-gan	time to leave the office
현주씨 hyeon-ju-ssi	Hyeon-Ju
환영회 hwan-yeong-hoe	welcoming party
회사 hoe-sa	company
79년생 chil-sip-gu-nyeon-saeng	a person born in 1979
4시 10분 ne-si sip-bun	4:10
5시 45분 da-seot-si sa-sib-o-bun	5:45
7월 14일 chil-wol sip-sa-il	July 14th

7월 15일 chil-wol sib-o-il   July 15th
8월 7일 pal-wol chil-il   August 7th

Verbs

겹치다 gyeop-chi-da	to overlap
고장나다 go-jang-na-da	to be broken
다 되다 da doe-da	to be worn out, to be all done
들러 보다 deul-leo-bo-da	to stop by
들어오다 deul-eo-o-da	to enter
똑같다 ttok-gat-da	to be the same
있다 it-da	to exist, to have
잊어버리다 ij-eo-beo-ri-da	to forget
좋다 jo-ta	to be good
큰일나다 keun-il-na-da	to be in trouble
할 수 없다 hal sue op-da	cannot help, there is no other choice

Adverbs, Prepositions, and Conjunctions

거의 geo-ui	almost
그런데 geu-reon-de	but
깜빡 kkam-ppak	completely
다 da	all
먼저 meon-jeo	ahead, first
며칠 myeo-cil	what date?
몇 년생 myeon-nyeon-saeng	what year was one born?
몇 시 myeot-si	what time?
무슨 요일 mu-seun yo-il	what day?
벌써 beol-sseo	already
새로 sae-ro	newly
아직도 a-jik-do	yet, still
어떻게 eo-tteo-ke	how
왜 wae	why
우리 u-ri	our

정말 jeong-mal	really
제 je	my
한번 han-beon	once
혹시 hok-si	by any chance

문법 Grammar

(1) Numbers and Counters

A. Numbers

There are two sets of numbers used in Korean: the native Korean numbers and Sino-Korean numbers. Some counters take native Korean numbers, and others take Sino-Korean numbers. Some native Korean numbers have two forms, depending on whether they are followed by a counter or used in isolation. Since native Korean numbers count from 1 to 99, all factors of 100 use the Sino-Korean number system.

	Sino-Korean	Native Korean	Native Korean (with counter)
1	일 il	하나 ha-na	한 han
2	이 i	둘 dul	두 du
3	삼 sam	셋 set	세 se
4	사 sa	넷 net	네 ne
5	오 o	다섯 da-seot	다섯 da-seot
6	육 yuk	여섯 yeo-seot	여섯 yeo-seot
7	칠 chil	일곱 il-gop	일곱 il-gop
8	팔 pal	여덟 yeo-deol	여덟 yeo-deol
9	구 gu	아홉 a-hop	아홉 a-hop
10	십 sip	열 yeol	열 yeol
11	십일 sib-il	열하나 yeo-ha-na	열한 yeo-han
12	십이 sib-I	열둘 yeol-dul	열두 yeol-du
13	십삼 sip-sam	열셋 yeol-set	열세 yeol-se
14	십사 sip-sa	열넷 yeol-net	열네 yeol-ne
15	십오 sib-o	열다섯 yeol-da-seot	열다섯 yeol-da-seot
16	십육 sim-nyuk	열여섯 yeol-yeo-seot	열여섯 yeol-yeo-seot

17	십칠 sip-chil	열일곱 yeol-il-gop	열일곱 yeol-il-gop
18	십팔 sip-pal	열여덟 yeol-yeo-deol	열여덟 yeol-yeo-deol
19	십구 sip-gu	열아홉 yeol-a-hop	열아홉 yeol-a-hop
20	이십 i-sip	스물 seu-mul	스무 seu-mu
21	이십일 i-sib-il	스물하나 seu-mul-ha-na	스물한 seu-mul-han
22	이십이 i-sib-i	스물둘 seu-mul-dul	스물두 seu-mul-du
23	이십삼 i-sip-sam	스물셋 seu-mul-set	스물세 seu-mul-se
24	이십사 i-sip-sa	스물넷 seu-mul-net	스물네 seu-mul-ne
25	이십오 i-sib-o	스물다섯 seu-mul-da-seot	스물다섯 seu-mul-da-seot
26	이십육 i-sim-nyuk	스물여섯 seu-mul-yeo-seot	스물여섯 seu-mul-yeo-seot
27	이십칠 i-sip-chil	스물일곱 seu-mul-il-gop	스물일곱 seu-mul-il-gop
28	이십팔 i-sip-pal	스물여덟 seu-mul-yeo-deol	스물여덟 seu-mul-yeo-deol
29	이십구 i-sip-gu	스물아홉 seu-mul-a-hop	스물아홉 seu-mul-a-hop
30	삼십 sam-sip	서른 seo-reun	서른 seo-reun
40	사십 sa-sip	마흔 ma-heun	마흔 ma-heun
50	오십 o-sip	쉰 swin	쉰 swin
60	육십 yuk-sip	예순 ye-sun	예순 ye-sun
70	칠십 chil-sip	일흔 il-heun	일흔 il-heun
80	팔십 pal-sip	여든 yeo-deun	여든 yeo-deun
90	구십 gu-sip	아흔 a-heun	아흔 a-heun

100	백	baek
200	이백	i-baek
300	삼백	sam-baek
400	사백	sa-baek
500	오백	o-baek
600	육백	yuk-baek
700	칠백	chil-baek
800	팔백	pal-baek
900	구백	gu-baek
1,000	천	cheon
2,000	이천	i-cheon
3,000	삼천	sam-cheon
4,000	사천	sa-cheon
5,000	오천	o-cheon
6,000	육천	yuk-cheon
7,000	칠천	chil-cheon
8,000	팔천	pal-cheon
9,000	구천	gu-cheon
10,000	만	man
20,000	이만	i-man
30,000	삼만	sam-man
40,000	사만	sa-man
50,000	오만	o-man
60,000	육만	yung-man
70,000	칠만	chil-man

80,000	팔만 pal-man
90,000	구만 gu-man
100,000	십만 sim-man
1,000,000	백만 baeng-man
10,000,000	천만 cheon-man
100,000,000	억 eok
1,000,000,000	십억 sib-eok
10,000,000,000	백억 baeg-eok
100,000,000,000	천억 cheon-eok
1,000,000,000,000	조 jo

B. Noun Counters

Counters must be used when indicating a specific number of people, items, or other nouns, e.g. four men, two pens, or three months. Different counters are used for different entities or objects.

Whether native Korean or Sino-Korean numbers are used depends on the counter. Some counters use both, particularly when the number is 20 or greater. However, the native Korean numbers are generally used when the number indicates an amount. Sino-Korean numbers are used when the number is part of a numbered order, such as the chapters in a book, the stories in a building, or the months in a year.

Native-Korean numbers tend to be used with counters that have names rooted in the Korean language. Sino-Korean numbers tend to be used with counters that have names derived from other languages, such as Chinese. In other words, native-Korean numbers go with native-Korean counters, while Sino-Korean numbers are used with Sino-Korean counters.

The general word order when using counters is the noun first, the number second, the counter last. For example:

커피 (keo-pi) + 한 (han) + 잔 (jan) → 커피 한 잔 (keo-pi han jan)
coffee   one   (*counter for* cup)   one cup of coffee

책 (chaek) + 세 (se) + 권 (gwon) → 책 세 권 (chaek se gwon)
book   three   (*counter* for book)   three books

I. Counters with Native Korean Numbers

개 gae	items	세개 se-gae: 3 items
과 gwa	number of lessons	세과 se-gwa: 3 lessons
과목 gwa-mok	courses	세과목 se-gwa-mok: 3 courses
권 gwon	volumes	세권 se-gwon: 3 books
달 dal	months	세달 se-dal: 3 months
마리 ma-ri	animals	세마리 se-ma-ri: 3 animals
명 myeong / 사람 sa-ram	persons	세명 se-myeong, 세사람 se-sa-ram: 3 people
번 beon	times	세번 se-beon: 3 times
병 byeong	bottles	세병 se-byeong: 3 bottles
분 bun	persons (*honorific*)	세분 se-bun: 3 people (*honorific*)
시 si	o'clock	세시 se-si: 3 o'clock
시간 si-gan	hours	세시간 se-si-gan: 3 hours
상자 sang-ja	boxes	세상자 se-sang-ja: 3 boxes
잔 jan	cups, glasses	세잔 se-jan: 3 cups
장 jang	sheets	세장 se-jang: 3 sheets

II. Counters with Sino-Korean Numbers

과 gwa	numbered lessons	칠과 chil-gwa: lesson 7
년 nyeon	years	칠년 chil-lyeon: 7 years
달러 dal-leo / 불 bul	dollars	칠달러 chil-dal-la: 7 dollars
마일 ma-il	miles	칠마일 chil-ma-il: 7 miles
번 beon	number	칠번 chil-beon: number 7
분 bun	minutes	칠분 chil-bun: 7 minutes

센트 sen-teu	cents	칠센트 chil-sen-teu: 7 cents
원 won	Korean won	칠원 chil-won: 7 won
월 wol	months of the year	칠월 chil-wol: July
일 il	days of the month	칠일 chil-il: 7th
전화번호 jeon-hw-beon-ho	phone numbers	칠이사에 오팔삼구: 724-5839 chil-i-sa-e o-pal-sam-gu
층 cheung	layers, stories, floors	칠층 chil-cheung: 7th floor
파운드 pa-un-deu	pounds	칠파운드 chil-pa-un-deu: 7 pounds
학년 hang-nyeon	school year, grade	칠학년 chil-hang-nyeon: 7th grade

(2) The Noun-modifying Form (Relative Clauses)

An example of a relative clause in an English phrase is the "who is going" in "a person who is going." In Korean, such a phrase is translated by putting the particles ~는 (neun), ~은 (eun), or ~ㄴ (n) after the relative clause. There is no relative pronoun in Korean as exist in English. The Korean translation of the English phrase "a person who is going" is 가는 사람 (ga-neun sa-ram).

Korean relative clauses have the following characteristics:

a. The relative clause comes first, the clause particle second, and the modified noun last. This is true regardless of the tense. The phrase 가는 사람 begins with 가 / "to go," followed by the particle 는 / (the functional equivalent of "is … ~ing"), and ending with 사람/ "a person."

b. A relative clause in the present tense uses the particles ~는, ~은, and ㄴ. The particle ~는 follows a relative clause using an active verb (e.g. 먹다 [meok-da] / "to eat"). The particles ~은 and ~ㄴ follow a relative clause that uses a descriptive verb, such as 작다 (jak-da) / "to be small." The particle ~은 is used if the clause ends in a consonant. The particle ~ㄴ is used if it ends in a vowel, such as 예쁘다 (ye-ppeu-da) / "to be pretty."

c. Although the verbs 있다 (it-da) / " to be" and 없다 (eop-da) / "to not be" are classified as descriptive verbs, they follow the rules governing active verbs in relative clauses.

d. Relative clauses in the past tense are followed by the particles ~은 and ~ㄴ. For example, 마신 물 (ma-sin mul) / "the water that was drank," and 먹은 음식 (meog-eun eum-sik) / "the food that was eaten."

e. Relative clauses in the prospective or future tense are followed by the particles ~ㄹ(l) and ~을 (eul). For example, 마실 물 (ma-sil mul) / "water that will be drank," and 먹을 음식 (meog-eul eum-sik) / "food that will be eaten." The particle ~ㄹ follows clauses ending with a vowel, while ~을 follows clauses ending in a consonant.

The chart below shows the various kinds of verbs with the appropriate particles in the relative clause forms.

	Active Verb 먹다 / 자다 meok-da / ja-da	Descriptive Verb 작다 / 예쁘다 jak-da / ye-ppeu-da	있다 it-da/ 없다 eop-da 맛있다/맛없다 mas-it-da / mat-eop-da	이다 i-da 직원이다 jig-won-i-da
Past / Completed	먹은 meog-eun 잔 jan	작던 jak-deon 예쁘던 ye-ppeu-deon	맛있던 mas-it-deon 맛없던 mat-eop-deon	직원이던 jig-won-i-deon
Present / Ongoing	먹는 meong-neun 자는 ja-neun	작은 jag-eun 예쁜 ye-ppeun	맛있는 mas-in-neun 맛없는 mad-eom-neun	직원인 jig-won-in
Prospective / Unrealized	먹을 meog-eul 잘 jal	작을 jag-eul 예쁠 ye-ppeul	맛있을 mas-iss-eul 맛없을 mad-eops-eul	직원일 jig-won-il

(3) Question Words and IndefinitePronouns

Question Words

When asking a question, always stress the question word in the sentence. The Korean question words are listed below with sample sentences.

누가 nu-ga	who (*subject*)	누가 간호원이세요? nu-ga gan-ho-won-i-se-yo Who's the nurse?
누구 nu-gu	who	누구를 찾으세요? nu-gu-reul chaj-eu-se-yo Who are you looking for?
무슨 mu-seun	what kind of; what	무슨 일을 하세요? mu-seun il-eul ha-se-yo What kind of work do you do? / What do you do for a living?
무엇 mu-eot	what	무엇을 좋아하세요? mu-eos-eul jo-a-ha-se-yo What do you like?
뭐 mwo	what (*colloquial*)	뭐가 제일 어려우세요? mwo-ga je-il eo-ryeo-u-se-yo What is most difficult for you?
어느 eo-neu	which	어느 나라 사람이세요? eo-neu na-ra sa-ram-i-se-yo Which country are you from?

어디 eo-di	where	어디 사세요? eo-di sa-se-yo Where do you live?
어떻게 eo-tteo- ke	how	부산에 어떻게 가요? bu-san-e eo-tteo-ke ga-yo How can I get to Pusan?
어떤 eo-tteon	what kind of	어떤 사람을 좋아하세요? eo-tteon sa-ram-eul jo-a-ha-se-yo What kind of people do you like?
언제 eon-je	when	언제 한국에 가세요? eon-je han-gug-e ga-se-yo When are you leaving for Korea?

얼마나
eol-ma-
na
	how long/many/much	한국에 얼마나 계실 거예요?
		han-gug-e eol-ma-na gye-sil
		    geo-ye-yo
		How long are you staying in
		    Korea?

왜 wae	why	왜 한국에 가세요? wae han-gug-e ga-se-yo Why are you going to Korea?

Indefinite Pronouns

Question words, with the exception of 왜 (wae) / "why," can also be used as indefinite pronouns. Indefinite pronouns are not stressed in spoken Korean. The indefinite pronouns, their English equivalents, and sample sentences are listed below.

누가 nu-ga	someone/anyone	누가 왔어요. nu-ga wass-eo-yo Someone is coming. There is someone.
누구 nu-gu	someone/anyone	누구를 데리고 올 거예요. nu-gu-reul de-ri-go ol geo-ye-yo I am bringing someone.
무슨 mu-seun	some kind of	무슨 냄새가 나요. mu-seun naem-sae-ga na-yo I smell something.
뭐 mwo	something/anything	뭐 좀 샀어요. mwo jom sass-eo-yo I bought something.
무엇 mu-eot	something/anything	(*original form of* 뭐)

어느
 	
eo-neu
	some [*noun*]	어느 날 갑자기 귀가 잘 안 들렸
		      어요.
		eo-neu-nal gap-ja-gi gwi-ga jal an
		      deul-lyeoss-eo-yo
		One day I can't hear all of sudden.

어디	somewhere/anywhere	어디 좀 가고 싶어요.
eo-di		eo-di jom ga-go sip-eo-yo
		I want to go somewhere.

어떻게	somehow	어떻게 좀 해 보세요.
eo-tteo-ke		eo-tteo-ke jom hae bo-se-yo
		Please do something.

어떤	some	어떤 사람이 집에 왔어요.
eo-tteon		eo-tteon sa-ram-i jib-e wass-eo-yo
		Somebody came to our house.

언제	sometime/anytime	언제 한번 만날까요?
eon-je		eon-je han-beon man-nal-kka-yo
		Should we meet some time?

(4) Noun + ▮ (ttae) vs. Verb + ~(으)ㄹ ▮ ((eu)l-ttae)

When a noun is followed by the particle ~때 (ttae), it means "during [the noun]." For example:

| 시험 (si-heom) + ~때 (ttae) | → | 시험때 (si-heom-ttae) |
| test   during | | during the test |

However, if the noun is a time expression, the particle ~에 (e) is used. For example:

| 주말 (ju-mal) + ~에 (e) | → | 주말에 (ju-mal-e) |
| weekend   during | | during the weekend |

If a verb stem is followed by ~ㄹ 때 (l-ttae) or ~을때 (eul-ttae), it means "during [the action of the verb]" or "when [the action of the verb]." The ending ~ㄹ 때 is used with stems that end in a vowel, and ~을때 is used with stems that end in a consonant.

A sentence clause using the verb + ~ㄹ때 or ~을때 is always followed by another sentence clause. The second clause describes what happened during the first clause. For example:

한국에 갈 때 비행기를 타고 갔어요.
(han-gug-e gal-ttae bi-haeng-gi-reul ta-go gass-eo-yo)
When I went to Korea, I went by airplane.

These two actions occurred simultaneously. However, when the second action occurs in the midst of the first action (or after it), the verb stem changes to the stem in the past tense form. For example:

한국에 갔을 때 할머니를 처음 만났어요.
(han-gug-e gass-eul ttae hal-meo-ni-reul cheo-eum man-nass-eo-yo)
When I went to Korea, I met my grandmother for the first time.

Note that 가, the verb stem for the Korean equivalent of "to go," becomes the 갔 of 갔어요, the Korean equivalent of "went," in the first clause.

(5) The Particles ~하고, ~랑 & ~이랑, and ~와 & 과

The particle ~하고 (ha-go) is the equivalent of the English "and." It is the conjunction between two nouns. It is generally used in everyday speech and informal writing. Using ~하고, the Korean equivalent of "Jeong-Ho and Michael" is 정호하고 마이클 (jeong-ho-ha-go ma-i-keul).

The particles ~랑 (rang) and ~이랑(i-rang) are also used to say "and" in informal situations. The particle ~랑 is used after nouns that end in a vowel, while ~이랑 is used after nouns that end in a consonant. Using ~랑, the Korean equivalent of "Jeong-Ho and Michael" is 정호랑 마이클 (jeong-ho-rang ma-i-keul).

In formal situations, the particles ~와 (wa) and ~과 (gwa) are used. One uses ~와 when the noun ends in a vowel, and ~과 when the noun ends in a consonant. Using ~와, the Korean equivalent of Jeong-Ho and Michael is 정호와 마이클 (jeong-ho-wa ma-i-keul).

(6) The Particles ~나, ~이나, and ~밖에

The particles ~나 (na) and ~이나 (i-na) indicate surprise. They are used when a quantity is significantly greater than one's expectations. The particle ~나 is used when the preceding expression ends in a vowel. One uses ~이나 when the expression ends in a consonant.

The particle ~밖에 (bakk-e) is used when indicating that a quantity is smaller in comparison to another. One may also hear it when a quantity is less than expected. The second half of the following exchange demonstrates its use:

저는 형제가 다섯 명이나 있어요.
(jeo-neun hyeong-je-ga da-seot-myeong-i-na iss-eo-yo)
I have five siblings.

저는 두 명밖에 없어요.
(jeo-neun du-myeong-bakk-e eops-eo-yo)
I have only two.

Note that the noun construction 두 명 ("two siblings" in this context) comes first. The particle ~밖에 comes second, and the negative form of the verb follows. (The word 없어요 literally means "don't have.") All sentences featuring ~밖에 follow this pattern.

참고학습 Further Study

(1) How to tell time

Time

한시 han-si	1 o'clock
두시 du-si	2 o'clock
세시 se-si	3 o'clock
네시 ne-si	4 o'clock
다섯시 da-seot-si	5 o'clock
여섯시 yeo-seot-si	6 o'clock
일곱시 il-gop-si	7 o'clock
여덟시 yeo-deol-ssi	8 o'clock
아홉시 a-hop-si	9 o'clock
열시 yeol-ssi	10 o'clock
열한시 yeol-han-si	11 o'clock
열두시 yeol-ttu-si	12 o'clock

Minutes

오분 o-bun	5 minutes
십분 sip-bun	10 minutes
십오분 sib-o-bun	15 minutes
이십분 i-sip-bun	20 minutes
이십오분 i-sib-o-bun	25 minutes
삼십분 sam-sip-bun	30 minutes
반 ban	30 minutes
삼십오분 sam-sib-o-bun	35 minutes
사십분 sa-sip-bun	40 minutes
사십오분 sa-sib-o-bun	45 minutes
오십분 o-sip-bun	50 minutes
오십오분 o-sib-o-bun	55 minutes

Other Time Expressions

오전	o-jeon	A.M.
오후	o-hu	P.M.
새벽	sae-byeok	dawn
아침	a-chim	morning
점심	jeom-sim	afternoon
저녁	jeo-nyeok	evening
밤	bam night	

(2) The Days of the Month

1st	일일	il-il
2nd	이일	i-il
3rd	삼일	sam-il
4th	사일	sa-il
5th	오일	o-il
6th	육일	yug-il
7th	칠일	chil-il
8th	팔일	pal-il
9th	구일	gu-il
10th	십일	sib-il
11st	십일일	sib-il-il
12nd	십이일	sib-i-il
13rd	십삼일	sip-sam-il
14th	십사일	sip-sa-il
15th	십오일	sib-o-il
16th	십육일	sim-nyug-il
17th	십칠일	sip-chil-il
18th	십팔일	sip-pal-il
19th	십구일	sip-gu-il
20th	이십일	i-sib-il
21st	이십일일	i-sib-il-il
22nd	이십이일	i-sib-i-il

23rd	이십삼일	i-sip-sam-il
24th	이십사일	i-sip-sa-il
25th	이십오일	i-sib-o-il
26th	이십육일	i-sim-nyug-il
27th	이십칠일	i-sip-chil-il
28th	이십팔일	i-sip-pal-il
29th	이십구일	i-sip-gu-il
30th	삼십일	sam-sib-il
31st	삼십일일	sam-sib-il-il

(3) The Days of the Week

그제 geu-je / 그저께 geu-jeo-kke	the day before yesterday
어제 eo-je	yesterday
오늘 o-neul	today
내일 nae-il	tomorrow
모레 mo-re	the day after tomorrow

문화적 참고사항 Cultural Note

Birthday celebrations

Birthday celebrations are very important in Korean culture; they are seen as celebrations of a person's life. The first birthday is the day one is born. (Koreans, unlike Westerners, consider an infant a one-year-old at birth.)

An important birthday celebration is held on the day of 백일 (baek-il), the 100th day after the baby is born. There is a small family celebration with wine, fruit, rice cakes, and other delicacies. Rice cakes are traditionally given to one hundred neighbors, reflecting the belief that this will grant the child a long, healthy life. The rice cakes are presented in a bowl, which is returned to the family containing, yarn, rice, or money. The yarn signifies a wish that the child may enjoy a long life. The rice and money signify a wish for the prosperity of the child.

The most important birthdays are the first and the sixtieth. Family and friends are invited over, and the occasion is marked with the setting of a large table where food, wine, and gifts are set. Another large celebration commemorates a person's seventieth birthday.

연습문제 Exercises

1. Please respond to the following.

(1) 오늘이 며칠이에요? o-neul-i myeo-chil-i-e-yo?
(2) 내일이 무슨 요일이에요? nae-il-i mu-seun yo-il-i-e-yo?
(3) 지금 몇시예요? ji-geum myeot-si-ye-yo?
(4) 실례지만 몇 년생이세요? sil-le-ji-man myeon-nyeon-saeng-i-se-yo?
(5) 생일이 몇월 며칠이세요? saeng-il-i myeot-wol myeo-chil-i-se-yo?

2. Please translate the following into English.

(1) 어제가 언니 생일이었는데 깜빡 잊어버렸어요.
    eo-je-ga eon-ni saeng-il-i-eon-neun-de kkan-ppak ij-eo-beo-ryeoss-eo-yo.
(2) 새로 들어온 직원 환영회하고 시간이 겹치네요.
    sae-ro deul-eo-on jig-won hwan-yeong-hoe-ha-go si-gan-i gyeop-chi-ne-yo.
(3) 내일은 대학 동창회가 있는 날이에요.
    nae-il-eun dae-hak dong-chang-hoe-ga in-nun nal-i-e-yo.
(4) 벌써 퇴근시간이 거의 다 됐네요.
    beol-sseo toe-geun-si-gan-i geo-i da dwaen-ne-yo.
(5) 집에 갈 때 시계방에 한번 들러 봐야겠어요.
    jib-e gal-ttae si-gye-ppang-e han-beon deul-leo bwa-ya-gess-eo-yo.
(6) 혹시 배터리가 다 된 거 아니에요?
    hok-si bae-teo-ri-ga da doen geo a-ni-e-yo?

3. Please write the following in Korean:

(1) July 16th, 1997
(2) 12:30 P.M.

(3)   June 30th, 1965
(4)   3:45 P.M.
(5)   August 7th, 2004
(6)   7:15 A.M.
(7)   October 29th, 2000
(8)   9:20 A.M.
(9)   December 25th, 2006
(10) 10:40 A.M.

4.   Please write a paragraph describing your daily/weekly
     schedule.

제5과 전화 걸기

◇◇◇◇◇◇◇◇

Lesson 5: Making a Telephone Call

표현 Patterns

따르릉, 따르릉
tta-reu-reung, tta-reu-reung
ring-ring

여보세요? 거기 정현주씨 댁이지요?
yeo-bo-se-yo? geo-gi jeong-heon-ju-ssi daeg-i-ji-yo?
Hello. Is this Miss. Hyeon-Ju Jung's residence?

네, 그런데요.
ne, geu-reon-de-yo.
Yes, it is.

죄송하지만 혹시 현주씨 지금 계시면 좀 바꿔주시겠어요?
joe-song-ha-ji-man hok-si hyeon-ju-ssi ji-geum gye-si-myeon jom
    ba-kkwo ju-si-gess-eo-yo?
Excuse me, but may I talk to Hyeon-Ju if she is home now?

전데요. 실례지만 누구세요?
jeon-de-yo. sil-lye-ji-man nu-gu-se-yo?
This is she. Excuse me, but who is this?

현주씨, 저 이도영이에요.
hyeon-ju-ssi, jeo i-do-yeong-i-e-yo.
Hyeon-Ju, This is Do-Yeong Lee.

저는 정현주라고 하는데요.
jeo-neun jeong-hyeonju-ra-go ha-neun-de-yo.
I am Hyeon-Ju Jeong.

아침 일찍 전화 드려서 죄송해요.

a-chim il-jjik jeon-hwa deu-reo-seo joe-song-hae-yo.

I am sorry for calling you so early in the morning.

밤늦게 전화 드려서 죄송해요.

ban-neut-ge jeon-hwa deu-reo-seo joe-song-hae-yo.

I am sorry for calling you so late at night.

괜찮아요. 그런데 웬일이세요?

gwaen-chan-a-yo. geu-reon-de wen-il-i-se-yo?

It's OK. By the way, what is going on?

혹시 김현준 과장님 핸드폰 전화 번호 아세요?

hok-si gim-hyeon-jun gwa-jang-nim haen-deu-pon jeon-hwa-beon-
ho a-se-yo?

Do you happen to know the department manager Hyeon-Jun Kim's
cellular phone number?

급히 연락드릴 일이 있는데 전화번호를 몰라서요.

geu-pi yeol-lak deu-ril il-i in-neun-de jeon-hwa-beon-ho-reul mol-
la-seo-yo.

I have an urgent matter to contact him about, but I don't have his
phone number.

잠깐만 기다리세요.

jam-kkan-man gi-da-ri-se-yo.

Please wait for a moment.

여기 있어요. 011-399-3974예요.

yeo-gi iss-eo-yo. gong-il-il sam-gu-gu-e sam-gu-chil-sa-ye-yo.

Here it is. It's 011-399-3974.

내일 4시에 직원회의 있는 거 다들 알고 있지요?

nae-il ne-si-e jig-won-hoe-ui in-neun-geo da-deul al-go it-ji-yo?

Everyone knows there is a staff meeting tomorrow at 4:00, right?

어제 다 연락했는데 강재은씨만 아직 연락이 안 됐어요.

eo-je da yeol-la-kaen-neun-de gang-jae-eun-ssi-man a-jik yeol-lag-i
   an- dwaess-eo-yo.

I contacted everyone yesterday, but Ms. Jae-Eun Kang has not been
   contacted yet.

신호는 가는데 전화를 안 받아요.

sin-ho-neun ga-neun-de jeon-hwa-reul an bad-a-yo.

The telephone is ringing but no one answers.

그럼 지금 다시 한번 더 걸어 보실래요?

geu-reom ji-geum da-si han-beon deo geol-eo bo-sil-lae-yo?

Then would you please call her once again now?

네, 그러지요.

ne, geu-reo-ji-yo.

OK, I will do so.

자동 응답기가 받는데요.

ja-dong-eung-dap-gi-ga ban-neun-de-yo.

The answering machine is picking up.

그냥 메시지를 남길까요?

geu-nyang me-si-ji-reul nam-gil-kka-yo?

Should I just leave a message?

그러세요.

geu-reo-se-yo.

Please do.

전화 메시지 받으면 사무실로 바로 전화하라고 해 주세요.
jeon-hwa me-si-ji bad-eu-myeon sa-mu-sil-lo ba-ro jeon-hwa-ha-ra-
    go hae ju-se-yo.
Please say to call back to the office as soon as she gets the message.

알겠습니다.
al-get-seum-ni-da.
I understand.

오빠 지금 집에 없는데요.
o-ppa ji-geum jib-e eom-neun-de-yo.
My brother is not home now.

들어오면 뭐라고 전해 드릴까요?
deul-eo-o-myeon mwo-ra-go jeon-hae deu-ril-kka-yo?
What shall I tell him when he comes home?

아니오, 괜찮아요. 제가 나중에 다시 전화할게요.
a-ni-o, gwaen-chan-a-yo. jeo-ga na-jung-e da-si jeon-hwa-hal-kke-yo.
No, it's OK. I will just call him again later.

혹시 정호씨 몇 시쯤 집에 들어오는지 아세요?
hok-si jeong-ho-ssi myeot-si-jjeum jib-e deul-eo-o-neun-ji a-se-yo?
Do you know, by any chance, when he will be back home?

잘 모르겠는데요.
jal mo-reu-gen-neun-de-yo.
I don't well know. / I am not sure.

보통 저녁 6시쯤 오는데요.
bo-tong jeo-nyeok yeo-seot-si-jjeum o-neun-de-yo.
He usually comes home around 6:00 P.M.

오늘은 좀 늦을 거라고 했어요.

o-neul-eun jom neuj-eul kkeo-ra-go haess-eo-yo.

He said he would be a little late today.

그럼 제가 8시쯤 다시 전화해도 될까요?

geu-reom je-ga yeo-deol-ssi-jjeum da-si jeon-hwa-hae-do
    doel-kka-yo?

Then is it OK if I call back again around 8:00 P.M.?

대화 Model Conversations

(1)

정현주: (따르릉, 따르릉) 여보세요?

(tta-reu-reung, tta-reu-reung) yeo-bo-se-yo?

이도영: 여보세요? 거기 정현주씨 댁이지요?

yeo-bo-se-yo? geo-gi jeong-hyeon-ju-ssi daeg-i-ji-yo?

정현주: 네, 그런데요.

ne, geu-reon-de-yo.

이도영: 죄송하지만 혹시 현주씨 지금 계시면 좀 바꿔주시겠
어요?

joe-song-ha-ji-man hok-si hyeon-ju-ssi ji-geum
gye-si-myeon jom ba-kkwo-ju-si-gess-eo-yo?

정현주: 전데요. 실례지만 누구세요?

jeon-de-yo. sil-lye-ji-man nu-gu-se-yo?

이도영: 현주씨, 저 이도영이에요. 아침 일찍 전화 드려서 죄
송해요.

hyeon-ju-ssi, jeo i-do-yeong-i-e-yo. a-chim il-jjik
jeon-hwa deu-ryeo-seo joe-song-hae-yo.

정현주: 어머, 도영씨. 괜찮아요. 그런데 웬일이세요?

eo-meo, do-yeong-ssi. gwaen-chan-a-yo. geu-reon-de
wen-il-i-se-yo?

이도영: 혹시 김현준 과장님 핸드폰 전화 번호 아세요?

hok-si gim-hyeon-jun gwa-jang-nim haen-deu-pon
jeon-hwa-beon-ho a-se-yo?

급히 연락드릴 일이 있는데 전화번호를 몰라서요.

geu-pi yeol-lak-deu-ril il-i in-neun-de jeon-hwa-beon-ho-
reul mol-la-seo-yo.

정현주: 네, 알아요. 잠깐만 기다리세요. 아, 여기 있어요.

011-399-3974예요.

ne, al-a-yo. jam-kkan-man gi-da-ri-se-yo. a, yeo-gi
iss-eo-yo. gong-il-il sam-gu-gu-e sam-gu-chil-sa-ye-yo.

이도영: 감사합니다. 안녕히 계세요.

gam-sa-ham-ni-da. an-nyeon-hi gye-se-yo.

정현주: 네, 안녕히 계세요.

ne, an-nyeon-hi gye-se-yo.

(2)

정현주: 도영씨, 내일 4시에 직원회의 있는 거 다들 알고 있지요?

do-yeong-sii, nae-il ne-si-e jig-won-hoe-ui in-neun geo da-deul al-go it-ji-yo?

이도영: 어제 다 연락했는데 강재은씨만 아직 연락이 안 됐어요. 신호는 가는데 전화를 안 받아요.

eo-je da yeol-la-kaen-neun-de gang-jae-eun-ssi-man a-jik yeol-lag-i an-dwaess-eo-yo. sin-ho-neun ga-neu-de jeon-hwreul an bad-a-yo.

정현주: 그럼 지금 다시 한번 더 걸어 보실래요?

geu-reom ji-geum da-si han-beon deo geol-eo bo-sil-lae-yo?

이도영: 네, 그러지요.... (따르릉, 따르릉).... 자동 응답기가 받는데요. 그냥 메시지를 남길까요?

ne, geu-reo-ji-yo. (tta-reu-reung, tta-reu-reung) ja-dong eung-dap-gi-ga ban-neun-de-yo. geu-nyang me-si-ji-reul nam-gil-kka-yo?

정현주: 그러세요. 전화 메시지 받으면 사무실로 바로 전화하라고 해 주세요.

geu-reo-se-yo. jeon-hwa me-si-ji bad-eu-myeon sa-mu-sil-lo ba-ro jeon-hwa-ha-ra-go hae ju-se-yo.

이도영: 알겠습니다.

al-get-seum-ni-da.

(3)

정현주: 여보세요? 거기 이정호씨 댁이지요?

yeo-bo-se-yo? geo-gi i-jeong-ho-ssi daeg-i-ji-yo?

이정은: 네, 그런데요. 실례지만 누구세요?

ne, geu-reon-de-yo. sil-lye-ji-man nu-gu-se-yo?

정현주: 저는 정현주라고 하는데요. 혹시 이정호씨 지금 계시
면 좀 바꿔주시겠어요?

jeo-neun jeong-hyeon-ju-ra-go ha-neun-de-yo. hok-si i-
jeong-ho-ssi ji-geum gye-si-myeon jom ba-kkwo
ju-si-gess-eo-yo?

이정은: 어머, 현주언니. 저 정은이에요. 안녕하세요?

eo-meo, hyeon-ju-eon-ni. Jeo jeong-eun-i-e-yo. an-
nyeong-ha-se-yo?

오빠 지금 집에 없는데요. 들어오면 뭐라고 전해 드릴
까요?

o-ppa ji-geum jib-e eom-neun-de-yo. deul-eo-o-myeon
mwo-ra-go jeon-gae deu-lil-kka-yo?

정현주: 아니오, 괜찮아요. 제가 나중에 다시 전화할게요.

a-ni-o, gwaen-chan-a-yo. jeo-ga na-jung-e da-si
jeon-hwa-hal-kke-yo.

혹시 정호씨 몇 시쯤 집에 들어오는지 아세요?

Hok-si jeong-ho-ssi myeot-si-jjeum jib-e deul-eo-o-neun-
ji a-se-yo?

이정은: 잘 모르겠는데요. 보통 저녁 6시쯤 오는데, 오늘은 좀
늦을 거라고 했어요.

jal mo-reu-gen-neun-de-yo. bo-tong jeo-nyeok yeo-seot-
si-jjeum o-neun-de, o-neul-eun jom neuj-eul geo-ra-go
haess-eo-yo.

정현주: 그래요? 그럼 제가 8시쯤 다시 전화해도 될까요?

geu-rae-yo? geu-reom je-ga yeo-deol-ssi-jjeum da-si
jeon-hwa-hae-do doel-kka-yo?

이정은: 네, 그러세요. 안녕히 계세요.

ne, geu-reo-se-yo. an-nyeong-hi gye-se-yo.

영문번역 English Translation

(1)

Jung: (ring, ring) Hello.

Lee: Hello. Is this Miss. Hyeon-Ju Jung's residence?

Jung: Yes, it is.

Lee: I am sorry, but may I talk to Hyeon-Ju if she is available now?

Jung: This is she. Excuse me, but who am I talking with?

Lee: Hyeon-Ju, This is Do-Yeong Lee. I am sorry for calling you so early in the morning.

Jung: Ah, Do-Yeong. It's OK. By the way, what is going on?

Lee: Do you happen to know the department manager Hyeon-Jun Kim's cell phone number? I urgently need to contact him, but I don't have his phone number.

Jung: Yes, I know. Please wait for a moment. Oh, here it is. It's 011-399-3974.

Lee: Thank you. Good-bye.

Jung: OK, Good-bye.

(2)

Jung: Do-Yeong, everyone knows there is a staff meeting tomorrow at 4:00, right?

Lee: I contacted everyone yesterday, but I couldn't get a hold of Ms. Jae-Eun Kang. The phone is ringing but no one answers.

Jung: Then would you please call her once again now?

Lee: OK, I will. (ring, ring...) The answering machine is picking up. Should I just leave a message?

Jung: Yes. Please say to call back to the office as soon as she gets the message.

Lee: OK, alright.

(3)

Jung: Hello, is this Mr. Jeong-Ho Lee's residence?

Lee: Yes, it is. Excuse me, but who is this?

Jung: This is Hyeon-Ju Jung. May I please talk to Jeong-Ho Lee if he is home now?

Lee: Ah, Hyeon-Ju. This is Jeong-Eun. How are you? My brother is not home now. What shall I tell him when he comes home?

Jung: No, it's OK. I will just call him again later. Do you know, by any chance, when he will be back home?

Lee: I am not sure. He usually comes home around 6:00 P.M., but he said he would be a little late today.

Jung: Did he? Then is it OK if I call back again around 8:00 P.M.?

Lee: Yes, please. Good-bye.

어휘 Vocabulary

Nouns / Pronouns

강재은씨 gang-jae-eun-ssi	Ms. Jae-Eun Gang
과장님 gwa-jang-nim	department manager
누구 nu-gu	who
다들 da-deul	everyone, all
댁 daek	house (hon.)
메시지 me-se-ji	message
몇 시쯤 myeot-si-jjeum	approximately what time?
뭐 mwo	what?
사무실 sa-mu-sil	office
신호 sin-ho	signal
아침 a-chim	morning
연락 yeol-lak	contact
오늘 o-neul	today
웬일 wen-il	what thing?
일 il	something, work
자동 응답기 ja-dong eung-dap-gi	answering machine
저녁 jeo-nyeok	evening
전화 jeon-hwa	telephone
전화번호 jeon-hwa-beon-ho	telephone number
직원회의 jig-won-hoe-ui	staff meeting
핸드폰 haen-deu-pon	cellular phone
6시쯤 yeo-seot-si-jjeum	about 6:00
8시쯤 yeo-deol-si-jjum	about 8:00

Verbs

감사하다 gam-sa-ha-da	to thank
계시다 gye-si-da	to exist, to be (hon.)
괜찮다 gwen-chan-ta	to be OK
기다리다 gi-da-ri-da	to wait
남기다 nam-gi-da	to leave

늦다 neut-da	to be late
들어오다 deul-eo-o-da	to return home, to enter
모르다 mo-reu-da	not to know
바꿔주다 ba-kkwo-ju-da	to change, to switch (telephones)
받다 bat-da	to receive
알다 al-da	to know
연락 드리다 yeol-lak deu-ri-da	to contact (*hon.*)
연락하다 yeol-la-ka-da	to contact
오다 o-da	to come
전화 걸다 jeon-hwa geol-da	to make a phone call
전화 드리다 jeon-hwa deu-ri-da	to make a phone call (*hon.*)
전화하다 jeon-hwa-ha-da	to make a phone call
죄송하다 joe-song-ha-da	to be sorry

Adverbs / Conjunctions

거기 geo-gi	there
그냥 geu-nyang	just
급히 geu-pi	in a hurry
나중에 na-jung-e	later
다 da	all
다시 da-si	again
더 deo	more
따르릉 tta-reu-reung	ring ring….
바로 baro	a.s.a.p.
보통 bo-tong	in general
실례지만 sil-lye-ji-man	excuse me but…, I am sorry but…
아직 a-jik	yet
일찍 il-jjik	early
잘 jal	well
잠깐만 jam-kkan-man	for a moment
좀 jom	please
지금 ji-geum	now
한번 han-beon	once
혹시 hok-si	by any chance, just in case

문법 Grammar

(1) Indirect quotation

Directly or indirectly, a speaker often passes along what others have said. An indirect narrative occurs when someone else's words are passed along with modification. It takes the basic form of [Quoted Sentence + ~고 하다 (go ha-da)].

a.   to quote a general statement that is currently in circulation, use ~고 하다(go ha-da) with the appropriate sentence ending, such as ...고 해요/합니다 (... go hae-yo/ham-ni-da).

b.   to quote a specific statement in the past, use ~고 했다(go haet-da) with the appropriate sentence ending, such as...고 했어요/ 했습니다 (... go haess-eo-yo/haet-seum-ni-da)

c.   When the quoted statement is/was said by one who is respected, the honorific forms of 하다 (ha-da) are used. The sentence ending ...고 하세요/하십니다 (...go ha-se-yo/ha-sim-ni-da) is used for the present tense. The ending ...고 하셨어요/하셨습니 다 (...go ha-syeoss-eo-yo/ha-syeot-seum-ni-da) is used for the past tense.

The quoted statement also takes the different endings appropriate in the polite style, depending on the sentence type of the quote. Declarative sentences, questions, commands, and proposals take different forms, as do past and present.

Declarative sentences that are quoted use a variation of the sentence ending ~다고 해요 (da-go hae-yo). There are four types of declarative sentences used in quotations: those using an active verb stem, those using a descriptive verb stem, those using a copula, and those describing a past event. The sentence types and their endings:

active verb stems ending in a consonant
     ~는다고 해요 (neun-da-go hae-yo)

active verb stems ending in a vowel
   ~ㄴ다고 해요 (n-da-go hae-yo)

descriptive verb stems
   ~다고 해요 (da-go hae-yo)

copula (이)
   ~라고 해요 (ra-go hae-yo)

past events ending
   ~았다고 해요 (at-da-ga-hae-yo) or
   ~었다고 해요 (eot-da-go hae-yo)

In colloquial speech, ~다고 해요 may be shortened to ~대요 when quoting sentences that use active verbs or describe past events.

Questions that are quoted use a variation of the sentence ending ~느냐고 해요 (neu-nya-go hae-yo). As with declarative sentences, there are four types of questions used in quotations: those using active verb stems, those using descriptive verb stems, those using a copula, and those describing a past event. The question types and their endings:

active verb stems
   ~느냐고 해요 (neu-nya-go hae-yo)

descriptive verb stems
   ~(으)냐고 해요 ([eu-] nya-go hae-yo)

copula
   ~(으)냐고 해요 ([eu-] nya-go hae-yo)

past events
   ~았(느)냐고 해요 (at-neu-nya-go hae-yo) or
   ~었(느)냐고 해요 (eot-neu-nya-go hae-yo)

In colloquial speech, the ending can be shortened to ~느냬요 (neu-nyae-yo) with active verb stems, to ~(으)냬요 ([eu-] nyae-yo) with descriptive verb stems and copulas, and to ~었녜요 (eot-nyae-yo) with questions that describe past events.

Commands and requests that are quoted use a variation of the sentence ending ~라고 해요 (ra-go hae-yo).

Verbs stems ending in a vowel use ~라고 해요 (ra-go hae-yo), while those ending in a consonant use ~으라고 해요 (eu-ra-go hae-yo). In colloquial speech, the endings are shortened to ~래요 (rae-yo) with verb stems that end in a vowel, and to ~으래요 (eu-rae-yo) with stems that end in a consonant.

With a proposal, the ending ~자고 해요(ja-go hae-yo) is used with all verb stems. In colloquial speech, it can be shortened to ~재요 (jae-yo).

The act of speaking may be indicated by a different verb than 하다 (ha-da) if the specific kind of speech is specified. Examples include ~다/라고 전해주세요 (da/ra-go jeon-hae-ju-se-yo) "please convey/pass along the message that…," ~느냐/(으)냐고 물어봤어요 (neu-nya/[eu]-nya-go mul-eo-bwass-eo-yo) "asked if/whether…," and ~(으)라고 가르쳐 줬어요 ([eu]-ra-go ga-reu-cheo jwoss-eo-yo) "introduced someone to…."

(2) Honorific Expressions

Honorific expressions in Korean are systematized. Honorific forms appear in hierarchical address/reference terms and titles, some commonly used nouns and verbs, the pronoun system, particles, and verb suffixes. Sentences in Korean require knowledge of one's social relationships to the listener or the one about whom is speaking in terms of age, social status, and kinship. The following table is a summary of honorific forms.

	Plain	Honorific	Humble
Noun			
age	나이 na-i	연세 yeon-se	
name	이름 i-reum	성함 seong-ham	
birthday	생일 sang-il	생신 saeng-sin	
word	말 mal	말씀 mal-sseum	말씀 mal-sseum
house	집 jip	댁 daek	
meal	밥 bap	진지 jin-ji	
counter for people	사람 sa-ram/ 명 myeong	분 bun	
Pronoun			
he/she	이/그/저 사람 i/geu/jeo sa-ram	이/그/저 분 i/geu/jeo bun	
I	나는/내가 na-neun/je-ga		저는/제가 jeo-neun/je-ga
my	내 nae		제 je
we	우리 u-ri		저희 jeo-hi
Verb			
see/meet someone	만나다 man-na-da	만나시다 man-na-si-da	뵙다 boep-da
be at, exist, stay	있다 it-da	계시다 gye-si-da	
die	죽다 juk-da	돌아가시다 dol-a-ga-si-da	
be well, fine	잘 있다 jal it-da	안녕하시다 an-nyeong-ha-si-da	
sleep	자다 ja-da	주무시다 ju-mu-si-da	
eat	먹다 meok-da	잡수시다/드시다 jap-su-si-da / deu-si-da	
give	주다 ju-da	주시다 ju-si-da	드리다 deu-ri-da
speak	말하다 mal-ha-da	말씀하시다 mal-sseum-ha-si-da	말씀 드리다 mal-sseum deu-ri-da
ask	물어보다 mul-eo-bo-da	물어보시다 mul-eo-bo-sida	여쭈어 보다 yeo-jju-eo bo-da
Particle			
subject	이/가 i-ga	께서 kke-seo	
topic	은/는 eun-neun	께서는 kke-seo-neun	
goal	한테/에게 han-te/e-ge	께 kke	

Suffix 님 (Mr., Ms., Dr.)	부모 bu-mo 목사 mok-sa 사장 sa-jang 선생 seon-saeng 의사 ui-sa	부모님 bu-mo-nim 목사님 mok-sa-nim 사장님 sa-jang-nim 선생님 seon-saeng-nim 의사 선생님 ui-sa seon-saeng-nim	

Additionally, one uses the honorific suffixes ~(으)시 ([eu]-si) and ~(으)세 ([eu]-se) when discussing someone who is to be referred to with respect, such as a family elder, a business superior, a distant peer, or a stranger. The article ~께서 (kke-seo), at one's discretion, may be used instead of ~이 (i) or ~가 (ga) in order to show an additional level of respect to the subject of the sentence, regardless of whether the sentence subject is the person to whom one is speaking. The sentence endings ~아/어요 (a/eo-yo) and ~습니다 (seum-ni-da) show respect for the listener.

Examples of the different levels of honorific suffixes in use:

Plain

동생이 교회에 가.
dong-saeng-i gyo-hoe-e- ga.
My younger sibling goes to church.

Listener Honorific

동생이 교회에 가요.
dong-saen-i gyo-hoe-e ga-yo.
My younger sibling goes to church.

Subject Honorific

할머니께서 교회에 가셔.
hal-meo-ni-kke-seo gyo-hoe-e ga-syeo.
My grandmother goes to church.

Subject and Listener Honorific

할머니께서 교회에 가세요.
hal-meo-ni-kke-seo gyo-hoe-e ga-se-yo.
My grandmother goes to church.

(3) Name + 이 (i)

Korean names are composed of a family name followed by a given name. When a person is referred to in a friendly, intimate manner by given name, the suffix ~이 (i) is added to the name (without a title such as 씨 (ssi)) if it ends in a consonant, as in 현준이 (hyeon-jun-i) and 혜린이 (hye-rin-i). For given names ending in a vowel, no suffix is added, as in 정호 (jeong-ho) and 현주 (hyeon-ju). This rule does not apply to foreign names.

(4) ~는데요 (neun-de-yo)/~(으)ㄴ데요 ((eu)n-de-yo) Background information

The sentence endings ~는데요 and ~(으)ㄴ데요 are used when a speaker presents background information. The speaker is conveying information in an open-ended manner that will allow the listener to figure out what to do next. This is often a polite way of expressing things. For example:

A: 정호 있어요? (jeong-ho iss-eo-yo?) "Is Jeong-Ho there?"
B: 아니오, 지금 집에 없는데요. (a-ni-o, ji-geum jib-e eom-neun-de-yo.) "No, he is not at home now."

Speaker B uses 없는데요 (eom-neun-de-yo) to respond instead of 없어요 (eops-eo-yo). The response 없는데요 invites speaker A to follow up with another statement or action.

The endings also allow one to handle a potentially troublesome situation, such as disagreement, denial, or rejection, with diplomacy. They permit both parties to save face in a discussion. For example:

A: 오늘 씨월드에 같이 갈래요? (o-neul ssi-wol-deu-e ga-chi gal-lae-yo?) "Will you go to Sea World with me today?"

B: 미안하지만 오늘은 다른 약속이 있는데요. (mi-an-ha-ji-man o-neul-eun da-reun yak-sog-i in-neun-de-yo.) "I am sorry, but I have another appointment today."

Although speaker B is clearly declining the invitation (here, because of a schedule conflict), the use of 있는데요 helps avoid directly rejecting speaker A.

(5) ~지요? (ji-yo?) Tag question

The question ending ~지요? (ji-yo?) is used when one expects to hear confirmation of what one has said. The English equivalent is "is it right?" or "…, isn't it?" In spoken Korean, ~지요? (ji-yo?) is often shortened to ~죠? (jyo?). This is in contrast to the general ending of yes/no questions , ~아/어요? (a/eo-yo), in which the speaker has no apparent assumption about the answer.

(6) ~한테 (han-te) and ~한테서 (han-te-seo) 'to' and 'from'

The particle ~한테 (han-te) is used when the speaker wishes to indicate an arrival point for a movement, the range of the verb it is directed toward, or the cause of an action. When the recipient of an action is a respected elder, the particle ~께 should be used instead. The particle ~한테서 (han-te-seo) is used when the speaker wishes to indicate the source of an action or a point of departure. When not dealing with people, the particles ~한테 (han-te) and ~한테서 (han-te-seo) should be replaced with ~에 (e) and ~에서 (e-seo), respectively. The particle 도 (do) or 만 (man) is added after the particles ~한테 (han-te), ~한테서 (han-te-seo), ~에 (e), and ~에서 (e-seo).

정호한테 전화 왔어요.
jeong-ho-han-te jeon-hwa wass-eo-yo.
A phone call is to Jeong-Ho.

정호한테서 전화 왔어요.
jeong-ho-han-te-seo jeon-hwa wass-eo-yo.
A phone call is from Jeong-Ho.

회사에 전화 하세요.
hoe-sa-e jeon-hwa-ha-se-yo.
Please make a call to your office.

회사에서 전화 왔어요.
hoe-sa-e-seo jeon-hwa wass-eo-yo.
A phone call is from your office.

참고학습 Further Study

(1) Telephone Expressions

[person] 좀 바꿔주세요.
[person] jom ba-kkwo ju-se-yo.
May I speak to [person]?

[person] 한테 전화하세요.
[person] han-te jeon-hwa-ha-se-yo.
Please call [person].

[person] 한테서 전화 왔어요.
[person] han-te-seo jeon-hwa wass-eo-yo.
The phone call is from [person]

이따가 다시 전화할게요.
i-tta-ga da-si jeon-hwa-hal-kke-yo.
I will call later.

잠깐만 기다리세요.
jam-kkan-man gi-da-ri-se-yo.
Just a minute, please.

전화 받으세요.
jeon-hwa bad-eu-se-yo.
Please answer the phone.

전화해 주세요.
jeon-hwa-hae ju-se-yo.
Please give me a call.

통화 중이에요.
tong-hwa-jung-i-e-yo.
The line is busy.

신호는 가는데 전화를 안 받는데요.
sin-ho-neun ga-neun-de jeon-hwa-reul an ban-neun-de-yo.
It's ringing, but no one answers the phone.

자동 응답기가 받는데요.
ja-dong eung-dap-gi-ga ban-neun-de-yo.
The answering machine is on.

자동 응답기에 메모를 남겨 주세요.
ja-dong eung-dap-gi-e me-mo-reul nam-gyeo ju-se-yo.
Please leave a message in the answering machine.

전화가 계속 통화중이에요.
jeon-hwa-ga gye-sok tong-hwa-jung-i-e-yo.
The line is still busy.

전화가 고장난 것 같아요.
jeon-hwa-ga go-jang-nan geot gat-a-yo.
Maybe the phone is out of order.

전화가 끊어졌어요.
jeon-hwa-ga kkeun-eo-jeoss-eo-yo.
The line has been disconnected.

죄송합니다. 전화를 잘 못 건 것 같아요.
joe-song-ham-ni-da jeon-hwa-reul jal mot geon geot gat-a-yo.
I am sorry. I must have dialed the wrong number.

집에 아무도 없나봐요.
jib-e a-mu-do eom-na-bwa-yo.
It seems like no one is home.

혹시 이 번호로 팩스를 보내도 될까요?
hok-si i beon-ho-ro paek-seu-reul bo-nae-do doel-kka-yo?
Can I send a fax to this number?

혹시 집에 팩스가 있으세요?
hok-si jib-e paek-seu-ga iss-eu-se-yo?
Do you have a fax machine?

지역번호가 어떻게 되나요?
ji-yeok-beon-ho-ga eo-tteo-ke doe-na-yo?
What is the area code?

수신자 부담으로 전화를 좀 걸고 싶은데요.
su-sin-ja bu-dam-eu-ro jeon-hwa-reul jom geol-go sip-eun-de-yo.
I would like to make a collect call.

(2) Extended Family terms

시아버님 (or 시아버지) si-a-beo-nim   father-in-law
(female speaker)

시어머님 (or 시어머니) si-eo-meo-nim   mother-in-law
(female speaker)

장인어른 jang-in-eo-reun   father-in-law
(male speaker)

장모님 jang-mo-nim   mother-in-law
(male speaker)

며느리 myeo-neu-ri   daughter-in-law
사위 sa-wi   son-in-law
손녀 son-nyeo   granddaughter
손자 son-ja   grandson
손주 son-ju   grandchildren

큰아버지 keun-a-beo-ji   uncle (father's older
brother)

큰어머니 keun-eo-meo-ni   aunt (큰아버지's wife)

작은 아버지 jag-eun a-beo-ji	uncle (father's younger brother)
작은 어머니 jag-eun eo-meo-ni	aunt (작은 아버지's wife)
삼촌 sam-chon	uncle (general term for a father's brother)
외삼촌 oe-sam-chon	uncle (general term for a mother's brother)
외숙모 oe-sung-mo	aunt (외삼촌's wife)
고모 go-mo	aunt (father's sister)
고모부 go-mo-bu	uncle (고모's husband)
이모 i-mo	aunt (mother's sister)
이모부 i-mo-bu	uncle (이모's husband)
사촌 sa-chon	cousin (on the father's side)
외사촌 oe-sa-chon	cousin (on the mother's side)
(남자) 조카 (nam-ja) jo-ka	nephew
(여자) 조카 (yeo-ja) jo-ka	niece

문화적 참고사항 Cultural Note

Telephone cards are the most common means of paying with public telephones. They are available at most convenience stores. Some public telephones accept credit cards, but only a few accept coins. If one wishes to make an international call, one must enter the prefix 001, 002, 007, or 008, followed by the appropriate country prefix, and then the telephone number. When making a long-distance call, the number must be preceded the area code (see below). Apart from that, follow the same instructions as with regular telephones. Numbers can be looked up by using the telephone book or by dialing 114 for directory service. Telephone books can be usually be found under the telephone in the telephone booth.

In cases of emergency, the numbers 112 (the police department) or 119 (the fire department) can be dialed toll-free from any phone. These numbers are to an operator at an emergency service center. When speaking to the operator, one states one's name and location, what the problem is, and ask for appropriate assistance.

Internet cafes or computer access places are commonly found in most cities. Internet cafes are one of the most common hangouts for younger people. Some public libraries or post offices also offer Internet access. Most home have Internet access as well. ADSL and cable services are very common, and telephone line service is rare these days.

Terms of Address

Although people regularly use 저(jeo) and 나 (na) when referring to themselves, it is less common for people to address others using such personal pronouns. Instead, it is common to use kinship terms even when people are not actually related. A speaker will use the terms형 (hyeong)/오빠 (o-ppa) "older brother" and 누나 (nu-na)/언

ㄴㅣ (eon-ni) "older sister" to address someone who is somewhat older. The terms 아저씨 (a-jeo-ssi) "uncle" and 아줌마 (a-jum-ma) "aunt" are used to address someone who is a generation apart in age. When addressing an elderly person, one will use the terms 할아버지 (hal-a-beo-ji) "grandfather" and 할머니 (hal-meo-ni) "grandmother". When speaking to someone who is the same age or younger, one says the person's first name, followed by either ~아 (a) or ~야 (ya). The ending ~아 (a) is used if the name ends with a consonant, as with 현준아 (Hyeon-jun-a). The ending ~야 (ya) is used if the name ends in a vowel, as with 정호야 (Jeong-ho-ya).

연습문제 Exercises

1.   Please respond to the following:

(1)   여보세요. 거기 [your name] 씨 댁이지요?
      yeo-bo-se-yo. geo-gi _____ ssi daeg-i-ji-yo?

(2)   죄송하지만 혹시 [your name] 씨 지금 계시면 좀 바꿔 주시
      겠어요?
      joe-song-ha-ji-man hok-si _____ ssi ji-geum gye-si-
      myeon jom ba-kkwo ju-si-gess-eo-yo?

(3)   혹시 [your friend's name] 씨 핸드폰 전화 번호 아세요?
      hok-si _____ ssi haen-deu-pon jeon-hwa-beon-ho
      a-se-yo?

(4)   혹시[your friend's name] 씨 몇시쯤 집에 들어오는지 아세
      요?
      hok-si _____ ssi myeot-si-jjeum jib-e deul-eo-o-
      neun-ji a-se-yo?

(5)   [your friend's name] 씨 지금 집에 없는데요. 들어오면 뭐라
      고 전해 드릴까요?
      _____ ssi ji-geum jib-e eom-neun-de-yo. deul-eo-o-
      myeon mwo-ra-go jeon-hae deu-ril-kka-yo?

2.   Please translate the following into English:

(1)   전화 메시지 받으면 사무실로 바로 전화하라고 해 주세요.
      jeon-hwa me-si-ji bad-ei-myeon sa-mu-sil-lo ba-ro jeon-hwa-
      ha-ra-go hae ju-se-yo.

(2)   내일 4시에 직원회의 있는 거 다들 알고 있지요?
      nae-il ne-si-e jig-won-hoe-I in-neun geo da-deul al-go it-ji-yo?

(3)   어제 다 연락했는데 한사람만 아직 연락이 안 됐어요.
      eo-je da yeol-la-kaen-neun-de han sa-ram-man a-jik yeol-lag-i
      an dwaess-eo-yo.

(4) 과장님께 급히 연락드릴 일이 있는데 전화번호를
     몰라서요.

     gwa-jang-nim-kke geu-pi yeol-lak-deu-ril il-i in-neun-de jeon-
     hwa-beon-ho-reul mol-la-seo-yo.
(5) 밤 늦게 전화 드려서 죄송합니다.

     bam neut-ge jeon-hwa deu-ryeo-seo joe-song-ham-ni-da.

3.   Please translate the following into Korean:

(1) I would like to make a collect call.
(2) I am sorry. I must have dialed the wrong number.
(3) Please leave a message in the answering machine.
(4) It's ringing, but no one answers the phone.
(5) Maybe the phone is out of order.

4.   Please write a set of telephone dialogues.

제6과 날씨와 여가활동

◇◇◇◇◇◇◇◇

Lesson 6: Weather and Leisure Activities

표현 Patterns

요즘은 날씨가 정말 많이 덥네요.
yo-jeum-eun nal-ssi-ga jeong-mal man-i deop-ne-yo.
The weather is really hot these days.

매일 30도를 넘는데요.
mae-il sam-sip-do-reul neom-neun-de-yo.
The temperature goes over 30°C everyday.

요즘은 여름이 점점 더 더워지는 것 같아.
yo-jeum-eun yeo-reum-i jeom-jeom deo deo-wo-ji-neun geot gat-a.
It seems the weather is getting hotter and hotter in the summer
    nowadays.

내가 어렸을 때는 이렇게 안 더웠는데.
nae-ga eo-ryeoss-eul ttae-neun i-reo-ke an deo-won-neun-de.
It wasn't that hot when I was young.

한국뿐만 아니라 요즘은 전 세계적으로 이상기온 현상이 나타
    나잖아요.
han-guk ppun-man a-ni-ra yo-jeum-eun jeon se-gye-jeog-eu-ro
    i-sang-gi-on hyeon-sang-i na-ta-na-jan-a-yo.
It is showing unusually high temperatures not only in Korea but
    also all around the world these days.

한국은 여름에 습도가 높아서 더 지내기가 힘들지.
han-gug-eun yeo-reum-e seup-do-ga nop-a-seo deo ji-nae-gi-ga
    him-deul-ji.
It's harder to stay in Korea because the humidity is high in the
    summer.

요즘은 밤에도 낮처럼 덥잖아.
yo-jeum-eun bam-e-do nat-cheo-reom deop-jan-a.
It's as hot at night as it is in the day these days.

오래간만에 한국에 왔는데 날씨가 너무 덥고 끈끈해서 밖에 나
　가기가 싫네요.

o-rae-gan-man-e han-gug-e wan-neun-de nal-ssi-ga neo-mu
　　deop-go kkeunkkeun-hae-so bakk-e na-ga-gi-ga sil-le-yo.

It's been a while since I have been in Korea, but it's so hot and
　humid that I don't want to go out.

이렇게 더운 날에는 집에서 에어컨 틀어 놓고 시원한 수박이나
　먹는 게 최고지.

i-reo-ke deo-un nal-e-neun jib-e-seo e-eo-keon teul-eo no-ko si-
　　won-han su-bag-i-na meong-neun ge choe-go-ji.

During these hot days, it is best to stay home, turn on the air condi-
　tioner, and eat some watermelon.

내일 시간 있으면 나하고 같이 수영장에 갈래?

nae-il si-gan iss-eu-myeon na-ha-go ga-chi su-yeong-jang-e
　　gal-lae?

Would you go to the swimming pool with me if you have time
　tomorrow?

날씨가 너무 더워서 정말 죽겠다.

nal-ssi-ga neo-mu deo-wo-seo jeong-mal juk-get-da.

(I feel like) I am going to die because it's so hot.

아침에 일기예보 못 봤어요?

a-chim-e il-gi-ye-bo mot bwass-eo-yo?

Didn't you see the weather forecast in the morning?

내일 오후에 비 온대요.

nae-il o-hu-e bi on-dae-yo.

It's going to rain tomorrow afternoon.

그래도 상관없어.

geu-rae-do sang-gwan-eops-eo.

It doesn't matter.

할머니 댁 근처에 있는 실내 수영장에 가려고 하거든.
hal-meo-ni daek geun-cheo-e in-neun sil-lae su-yeong-jang-e
    ga-ryeo-go ha-geo-deun.
I am going to go to the indoor pool near grandma's place.

사실은 내일 제 동생 혜근이랑 같이 영화 보러 가기로 했거든요.
sa-sil-eun nae-il je dong-saeng hye-geun-i-rang ga-chi yeong-hwa
    bo-reo ga-gi-ro haet-geo-deun-yo.
Actually, I had planned to go to see a movie tomorrow with my
    little sister Hye-Geun.

그럼 우리 다 같이 일찍 수영장에 갔다가 점심 먹고 영화 보러
    가면 어때요?
geu-reom u-ri da ga-chi il-jjik su-yeong-jang-e gat-da-ga jeom-sim
    meok-go yeong-hwa bo-reo ga-myeon eo-ttae-yo?
Then how about us all going to the pool together early, and go to
    see the movie after lunch?

새로 나온 첩보영화인데 아주 재미있대요.
sae-ro na-on cheop-bo-yeong-hwa-in-de a-ju jae-mi-it-dae-yo.
It's a new spy movie and supposed to be really good.

그래, 그러자.
geu-rae, geu-reo-ja.
OK. Let's do that.

그럼 내일 아침 9시까지 할머니 댁으로 올래?
geu-reom nae-il a-hop-si-kka-ji hal-meo-ni daeg-eu-ro ol-lae?
Then will you come to grandma's place by 9:00 tomorrow morning?

늦어도 10시까지는 갈게요.
neuj-eo-do yeol-ssi-kka-ji-neun gal-kke-yo.
I will be there at 10:00 by the latest.

요즘 방학이라서 혜근이가 좀 늦게 일어나거든요.
yo-jeum bang-hag-i-ra-seo hye-geun-i-ga jom neut-ge
    il-eo-na-geo-deun-yo.
Since it's vacation, Hye-Geun gets up a little later these days.

샌디에이고는 보통 날씨가 어때요?
Saen-di-e-i-go-neun bo-tong nal-ssi-ga eo-ttae-yo?
How is the weather in San Diego in general?

샌디에이고 날씨는 항상 비슷해.
Saen-di-e-i-go nal-ssi-neun hang-sang bi-seu-tae.
San Diego weather is always the same.

여름에도 별로 안 덥고 겨울에도 별로 안 추워.
yeo-reum-e-do byeol-lo an deop-go gyeo-ul-e-do byeol-lo an
    chu-wo.
It's not too hot in the summer, and not too cold in the winter.

한국 봄 가을 날씨하고 비슷한 것 같아.
han-guk bom ga-eul nal-ssi-ha-go bi-seu-tan geot gat-a.
It seems to be similar to the spring and fall weather in Korea.

보통 겨울에 며칠 비가 좀 오지.
bo-tong gyeo-ul-e myeo-chil bi-ga jom o-ji.
Usually it rains for a few days in the winter.

겨울에 비가 와요? 눈이 아니고요?
gyeo-ul-e bi-ga wa-yo? nun-i a-ni-go-yo?
It rains in winter? It doesn't snow?

우리 동네는 바다 쪽이라서 눈이 안 와.
u-ri dong-ne-neun ba-da jjog-i-ra-seo nun-i an wa.
My town is by the ocean so it doesn't snow.

산 쪽으로 한 한시간 정도 운전해서 가면 눈이 오지.

san-jjog-eu-ro han han-si-gan jeong-do un-jeon-hae-seo ga-myeon
    nun-i o-ji.

If you drive for about an hour towards the mountains, it snows.

상상이 잘 안 되는데요.

sang-sang-i jal an doe-neun-de-yo.

I cannot imagine it.

같은 샌디에이고인데 한쪽에는 비가 오고 한쪽에는 눈이 와요?

gat-eun saen-di-e-i-go-in-de han-jjog-e-neun bi-ga o-go
    han-jjog-e-neun nun-i wa-yo?

It's the same in San Diego, but it rains on one side and snows on
    the other?

그게 이상하니?

geu-ge i-sang-ha-ni?

Is that weird?

산은 보통 다른 데보다 더 춥잖아.

san-eun bo-tong da-reun de-bo-da deo chup-jan-a.

The mountains are usually colder than other places, you know.

맞아, 그렇구나.

maj-a, geu-reo-ku-na.

Ah, that's right.

대화 Model Conversations

(1)

이정호: 할머니, 요즘은 날씨가 정말 많이 덥네요. 매일 30도
를 넘는데요.

hal-meo-ni, yo-jeum-eun nalssi-ga jeong-mal man-i
deom-ne-yo. mae-il sam-sip-do-reul neom-neun-de-yo.

할머니: 요즘은 여름이 점점 더 더워지는 것 같아. 내가 어렸
을 때는 이렇게 안 더웠는데.

yo-jeum-eun yeo-reum-i jeom-jeom deo deo-wo-ji-neun
get gat-a. nae-ga eo-ryeoss-eul ttae-neun i-reo-ke an
deo-won-neun-de.

이정호: 한국뿐만 아니라 요즘은 전 세계적으로 이상기온 현
상이 나타나잖아요.

han-guk-ppun a-ni-ra yo-jeum-eun jeon se-gye-jeog-eu-ro
i-sang-gi-on hyeon-sang-i na-ta-na-jan-a-yo.

할머니: 한국은 여름에 습도가 높아서 더 지내기가 힘들지. 요
즘은 밤에도 낮처럼 덥잖아.

han-gug-eun yeo-reum-e seup-do-ga nop-a-seo deo
ji-nae-gi-ga him-deul-ji.
yo-jeum-eun bam-e-do nat-cheo-reom deop-jan-a.

이정호: 어휴, 오래간만에 한국에 왔는데 날씨가 너무 덥고 끈
끈해서 밖에 나가기가 싫네요.

eo-hyu, o-rae-gan-man-e han-gug-e wan-neun-de
nal-ssiga neo-mu deop-go kkeun-kkeun-hae-seo bakk-e
na-ga-gi-ga sil-le-yo.

할머니: 이렇게 더운 날에는 집에서 에어컨 틀어 놓고 시원한
수박이나 먹는 게 최고지.

i-reo-ke deo-un nal-e-neun jib-e-seo e-eo-keon teul-eo
no-ko si-won-han su-bag-i-na meong-neun ge choe-go-ji.

(2)

이정호: 대근아, 너 내일 시간 있으면 나하고 같이 수영장
          에 갈래? 날씨가 너무 더워서 정말 죽겠다.
          dae-geun-a, neo nae-il si-gan iss-eu-myeon na-ha-go
          ga-chi su-yeong-jang-e gal-lae?
          nal-ssi-ga neo-mu deo-wo-seo jeong-mal
          juk-get-da.

이대근: 수영장이요? 형 아침에 일기예보 못 봤어
(사촌동생) 요? 내일 오후에 비 온대요.
          (sa-chon-dong-saeng) su-yeong-jang-i-yo? hyeong
          a-chim-e il-gi-ye-bo mot bwass-eo-yo? nae-il o-hu-e
          bi on-dae-yo.

이정호: 그래? 그래도 상관없어. 할머니 댁 근처에 있는 실
          내 수영장에 가려고 하거든.
          geu-rae? geu-rae-do sang-gwan-eops-eo.
          hal-meo-ni daek geun-cheo-e in-neun sil-lae su-
          yeong-jang-e ga-ryeo-go ha-geo-deun.

이대근: 그래요? 그런데 사실은 내일 제 동생 혜근이랑 같
          이 영화 보러 가기로 했거든요.
          geu-rae-yo? geu-reon-de sa-sil-eun nae-il je dong-
          saeng hye-geun-i-rang ga-chi yeong-hwa bo-reo
          ga-gi-ro haet-geo-deun-yo.
          그럼 우리 다 같이 일찍 수영장에 갔다가 점심 먹
          고 영화 보러 가면 어때요?
          geu-reom u-ri da ga-chi il-jjik su-yeong-jang-e gat-da-
          ga jeon-sim meok-go yeong-hwa
          bo-reo ga-myeon eo-ttae-yo?
          새로 나온 첩보영화인데 아주 재미있대요.
          Sae-ro na-on cheop-bo-yeong-hwa-in-de a-ju
          jae-mi-it-dae-yo.

이정호: 그래, 그러자. 그럼 내일 아침 9시까지 할머니 댁
          으로 올래?
          geu-rae, geu-reo-ja. geu-reom nae-il a-chim a-hop-si-
          kka-ji hal-meo-ni daeg-eu-ro ol-lae?

이대근: 늦어도 10시까지는 갈게요. 요즘 방학이라서 혜근
　　　　 이가 좀 늦게 일어나거든요.
　　　　 neuj-eo-do yeol-ssi-kka-ji-neun gal-kke-yo. yo-
　　　　 jeum bang-hag-i-ra-seo hye-geun-i-ga jom neuj-ge
　　　　 il-eo-na-geo-deun-yo.

(3)

이혜근: 오빠, 샌디에이고는 보통 날씨가 어때요?
　　　　 o-ppa, saen-di-e-i-go-neun bo-tong nal-ssi-ga eo-ttae-yo?

이정호: 샌디에이고 날씨는 항상 비슷해. 여름에도 별로 안 덥
　　　　 고 겨울에도 별로 안 추워.
　　　　 saen-di-e-i-go nal-ssi-neun hang-sang bi-seu-tae.
　　　　 yeo-reum-e-do byeol-lo an deop-go gyeo-ul-e-do
　　　　 byeol-lo an chu-wo.
　　　　 한국 봄 가을 날씨하고 비슷한 것 같아. 보통 겨울에
　　　　 며칠 비가 좀 오지.
　　　　 Han-guk bom ga-eul nal-ssi-ha-go bi-seu-tan geot gat-a.
　　　　 bo-tong gyeo-ul-e myeo-chil bi-ga jom o-ji.

이혜근: 겨울에 비가 와요? 눈이 아니고요?
　　　　 gyeo-ul-e bi-ga wa-yo? nun-i a-ni-go-yo?

이정호: 우리 동네는 바다 쪽이라서 눈이 안 와. 산 쪽으로 한
　　　　 한시간 정도 운전해서 가면 눈이 오지.
　　　　 u-ri dong-ne-neun ba-da jjog-i-ra-seo nun-i an wa.
　　　　 san-jjog-eu-ro han han-si-gan jeong-do un-jeonhae-seo
　　　　 ga-myeon nun-i o-ji.

이혜근: 와, 상상이 잘 안 되는데요. 같은 샌디에이고인데 한
　　　　 쪽에는 비가 오고 한쪽에는 눈이 와요?
　　　　 wa, sang-sang-i jal an doe-neun-de-yo. gat-eun
　　　　 saen-di-e-i-go-in-de han-jjog-e-neun bi-ga o-go
　　　　 han-jjog-e-neun nun-i wa-yo?

이정호: 그게 이상하니? 산은 보통 다른 데보다 더 춥잖아.
　　　　 geu-ge i-sang-ha-ni? San-eun bo-tong da-reun de-bo-da
　　　　 deo chup-jan-a.

이혜근: 맞아, 그렇구나.
　　　　 maj-a, geu-reo-ku-na.

영문번역 English Translation

(1)

Lee: Grandma, it's really hot these days. The temperature goes over 30°C every day.

Grandma: It's getting hotter every summer recently. When I was young it was not this hot.

Lee: It is showing unusually high temperatures not only in Korea but also in all around the world these days.

Grandma: It's worse in Korea because it's so humid in the summer. It's hot at night as much as it is in the day.

Lee: Hwew . . . it's been a while since I have been in Korea. But it's so hot and humid that I don't want to go out.

Grandma: During these hot days, it is the best to stay home, turn on the air conditioner, and eat some watermelon.

(2)

Jeong-Ho: Dae-Geun, do you want to go to the swimming pool with me if you have time tomorrow? I feel like I am going to die because it's so hot.

Dae-Geun: Swimming pool? Didn't you see the weather forecast in the morning? It's going to rain tomorrow afternoon.

Jeong-Ho: Really? But that's OK. I want to go to the indoor pool near grandma's place.

Dae-Geun: Is that so? But actually I had planned to go to see a movie tomorrow with my little sister Hye-Geun. Then how about we all go to the pool together early, and go to see the movie after lunch? It's a new spy movie and supposed to be really good.

Jeong-Ho: OK. Let's do that. Then will you come to grandma's place by 9:00 tomorrow morning?

Dae-Geun: I will be there at 10:00 by the latest. Since it's vacation Hye-Geun gets up a little later these days.

(3)

Hye-Geun: Jeong-Ho, how is the weather in San Diego?

Jeong-Ho: San Diego weather is always the same. It's not too
            hot in the summer and not too cold in the winter. The
            weather is similar to the spring and fall weather in
            Korea. Usually it rains for a few days in the winter.

Hye-Geun: It rains in the winter? It doesn't snow?

Jeong-Ho: My town is by the ocean so it doesn't snow. If you
            drive for about an hour towards the mountains, it
            snows.

Hye-Geun: Wow, I cannot imagine. It's the same city, but it rains
            on one side and snows on the other?

Jeong-Ho: Is that weird? The mountains are usually colder than
            other places, you know.

Hye-Geun: Ah, that's right.

어휘 Vocabulary

Nouns / Pronouns

가을 ga-eul	fall, autumn
겨울 gyeo-ul	winter
근처 geun-cheo	near, nearby
날씨 nal-ssi	weather, climate
낮 nat	day
내일 nae-il	tomorrow
눈 nun	snow
다른 데 da-reun de	other places
대근아 dae-geun-a	Hey, Dae-Geun
댁 daek	house (hon.)
더운 날 deo-un nal	hot day
동네 dong-ne	village, town
동생 dong-saeng	younger sibling
며칠 myeo-chil	several days
바다 쪽 ba-da jjok	sea side
밖 bak	outside
밤 bam	night
방학 bang-hak	(school) vacation
봄 bom	spring
비 bi	rain
사촌동생 sa-chon-dong-saeng	cousin
산 san	mountain
산 쪽 san jjok	mountain side
샌디에이고 saen-di-e-i-go	San Diego
수박 su-bak	watermelon
수영장 su-yeong-jang	swimming pool
습도 seup-do	humidity
실내 수영장 sil-lae su-yeong-jang	indoor swimming pool
아침 a-chim	morning

어렸을 때 eo-reoss-eul ttae — when (someone was) young

에어컨 e-eo-keon — air conditioner
여름 yeo-reum — summer
오후 o-hu — afternoon
요즘 yo-jeum — these days
우리 u-ri — we, us
이상기온 현상 i-sang-gi-on hyeon-sang — abnormal temperature effect
일기예보 il-gi-ye-yo — weather forecast
집 jip — house
첩보영화 cheop-bo-yeong-hwa — secret agent movie, spy movie

한 시간 han-si-gan — one hour
한 쪽 han jjok — one side
한국 han-guk — Korea
할머니 hal-meo-ni — grandmother
할머니 댁 hal-meo-ni daek — grandmother's house (hon.)

형 hyeong — (man's) older brother
혜근이 hye-geun-I — Hye-Geun
30도 sam-sip-do — 30 degrees Celsius/ Centigrade (30°C)

Verbs

가다 ga-da — to go
같다 gat-da — to be the same
끈끈하다 kkeun-kkeun-ha-da — to be humid, to be sticky
나가다 na-ga-da — to go out
나타나다 na-ta-na-da — to appear
넘다 neom-tta — to go over
높다 nop-da — to be high
눈이 오다 nun-i o-da — to snow

더워지다 deo-wo-ji-da	to become hot
덥다 deop-da	to be hot
맞다 mat-da	to be correct
먹다 meok-da	to eat
못 보다 mot bo-da	to not see
비가 오다 bi-ga o-da	to rain
비슷하다 bi-seu-ta-da	to be similar
상관없다 sang-gwan-eop-da	to be all right, to not matter
상상이 안 되다 sang-sang-i an-doe-da	to be beyond imagination, cannot imagine
새로 나오다 sae-ro na-o-da	to be newly released
시간(이) 있다 si-gan(-i) it-da	to have some time
시원하다 si-won-ha-da	to be cool
영화 보다 yeong-hwa bo-da	to watch a movie
오다 o-da	to come
운전하다 un-jeon-ha-da	to drive
이상하다 i-sang-ha-da	to be strange
일어나다 il-eo-na-da	to wake up
재미있다 jae-mi-it-da	to be fun
점심 먹다 jeom-sim meok-da	to eat lunch
지내다 ji-nae-da	to spend time, to live
춥다 chup-da	to be cold
틀어 놓다 teul-eo no-ta	to turn on

Adverbs / Conjunctions

그래도 geu-rae-do	even it is true
그러자 geu-reo-ja	let's do that
그럼 geu-reom	then
그렇구나 geu-reo-ku-na	that's right
너무 neo-mu	too, too much
늦게 nut-ge	late
늦어도 nuj-eo-do	at latest

다 같이 da ga-chi	all together
더 deo	more
많이 man-i	a lot
매일 mae-il	every day
별로 byeol-lo	not particularly
보통 bo-tong	in general
사실은 sa-sil-eun	in fact
아주 a-ju	very, very much
어휴 eo-hu	alas
오래간만에 o-rae-gan-man-e	after a long time
와 wa	wow
이렇게 i-reo-ke	like this
일찍 il-jjik	early
전 세계적으로 jeon se-gye-jeog-eu-ro	world-widely
점점 jeom-jeom	gradually
정말 jeong-mal	really
좀 jom	a little, a few
한 … 정도 han … jeong-do	approximately, about
항상 hang-sang	always
10시까지 yeol-si-kka-ji	by 10:00
9시까지 a-hop-si-kka-ji	by 9:00

문법 Grammar

(1) The Intimate Speech Style and the Plain Speech Style

The intimate speech style is used between people who share a close relationship, such as spouses, siblings, and childhood friends. Intimate speech uses the pattern Verb + ~아/어 (a/eo) where

~아 (a) is attached if the final vowel of the verb stem is either 아 (a) or 오 (o)

     많다 (man-ta) "to be many"
     → 많 (man) + ~아 (a)
     → 많아 (man-a)

~아 (a) is omitted if the verb stem ends with the vowel 아 (a) or 애 (ae) without a final consonant

     자다 (ja-da) "to sleep"
     → 자 (ja) + ~아 (a)
     → 자 (ja)

~어 is attached for all other verb stems

     먹다 (meok-da) "to eat"
     → 먹 (meok) + ~어 (eo)
     → 먹어 (meog-eo)

~어 (eo) is attached to the any past tense marker ~았/었 (at/eot)

~야 (ya) is attached after the copula 이 (i), as in 나야 (na-ya) "(it's) me," or 갈 거야 (gal kkeo-ya) "(I) will go"

There are also special cases when contraction and/or omission occurs:

- With the predicate ~하다 (ha-da), the stem 하 (ha) + ~아 (a) contracts to 해 (hae)

  전화하다 (jeon-hwa-ha-da) "to make a telephone call"
  전화하 (jeon-hwa-ha) + ~아 (a)
  →전화해 (jeon-hwa-hae)

- With verb stems that end in 오, there is a contraction to 와
  오다 (o-da) "to come"
  오 (o) + ~아 (a)
  와 (wa)

- With verb stems that end in 우, there is a contraction to 워
  주다 (ju-da) "to give"
  주 (ju) + ~어 (eo)
  줘 (jwo)

- With irregular verbs that end in ~ㅂ, the ㅂ is omitted and vowel contracts to ~워

  덥다 (deop-da) "to be hot"
  덥 (deop) + ~어 (eo)
  더 (deo) + 우 (u) + ~어 (eo)
  더워 (deo-wo)

The one exception is 돕다 (dop-da) "to help," which has a 와(wa) contraction.

With other endings, one speaks in the intimate style form by omitting the marker ~요 (yo) from the polite style form.

The plain speech style is used extensively in published writing, including newspapers, magazines, and academic journals. It can be used in conjunction with the intimate style, especially when speaking to a child, a younger sibling, or a childhood friend. Different sentence endings are used according to the type of sentence:

- With a statement, use ~다 (da).

- With a question, use ~니? (ni?) or ~나? (na?).

- With a request, use ~아/어라 (a/eo-ra).

- With a suggestion, use ~자 (ja) as in 가다 (ga-da), 가니? (ga-ni?), 가라 (ga-ra), and 가자 (ga-ja).

(2) ~아/어 지다 (a/eo ji-da) "become"

The descriptive verb pattern verb stem + ~아/어 지다expresses a change from one state (or condition) to another. Since it denotes a state of *becoming* or *happening*, it changes a descriptive verb into an active verb. Descriptive verbs using the construction ~아/어 지다 denote the resulting state or condition, as in 여름에는 날씨가 더워져요 (yeo-reum-e-neun nal-ssi-ga deo-wo-jyeo-yo) "In summer, the weather becomes hotter." If a present state is a result of a change in the past, the past tense form is used, as in 방이 더러워졌어요. (bang-i deo-reo-wo-jyeoss-eo-yo) "The room has become dirty."

(3) ~잖아요 (jan-a-yo) " . . . , you know"

When the speaker assumes that the listener will agree with him/her, or wants to reconfirm facts, the speaker will use the pattern ~잖아요 at the end of the verb stem. Although this pattern is derived from the negative question ~지 않아요?, there is no negative connotation. As it is not a question, there is no rising intonation.

이번 주가 휴가잖아요.
(i-beon ju-ga hyu-ga jan-a-yo.)
"This week is my vacation."

휴가동안 집에서 쉴 거잖아요.
(hyu-ga-dong-an jib-e-seo swil kkeo-jan-a-yo.)
"You are going to rest at home during the vacation."

(4) ~기로 하다 (gi-ro ha-da) "plan to, decide to"

One uses the pattern ~기로 하다 (gi-ro ha-da) to express or determination or a decision. This pattern expresses more resolve than other patterns that convey a decidedness to do something. One uses ~(으)ㄹ 까 하다 ([eu]l-kka ha-da), ~(으)ㄹ 거예요 ([eu]l kkeo-ye-yo), or ~기로 했어요 (gi-ro haess-eo-yo) to express the increased degree of resolve. With statements, one always uses the past tense marker ~기로 했어요(gi-ro haess-eo-yo). The present tense form, ~기로 해요 (gi-ro hae-yo), always indicates a suggestion or recommendation.

여름 휴가 동안에 한국에 가기로 했어요.
(yeo-reum hu-ga-dong-an han-gug-e ga-gi-ro haess-eo-yo.)
I decided to go to Korea during summer vacation.

여름 휴가 동안에 한국에 가기로 해요.
(yeo-reum hu-ga-dong-an han-gug-e ga-gi-ro hae-yo.)
Let's go to Korea during summer vacation.

(5) ~보다 (더/덜) (bo-da (deo/deol)) "more/less than~"

Use the pattern noun 1 + ~보다 + noun 2 with the optional adverb 더 (deo) "more," or덜 (deol) "less" when comparing two or more items. The first item of comparison is attached to ~보다. The following item comes directly after it. Although the order of items can be changed, it is important to note that the second item should be used to describe the comparison. When necessary, use the pattern ~중에서 to convey the expression *between* or *among*. To express a superlative construction (*the most*), use 제일 or 가장. In written Korean, 가장 is preferred.

미국이 한국보다 더 커요.
(mi-gug-i han-guk-bo-da deo keo-yo)
America is bigger than Korea.

유미가 유진이보다 덜 예뻐요.
(yu-mi-ga yu-jin-i-bo-da deol ye-ppeo-yo)
Yumi is less pretty than Yujin.

(6) ~(이)나 ((i)-na) "or something"

Use the pattern ~(이)나 to make a mild suggestion. When this pattern is used, there is no implication that the suggestion given is the best or only one, and the item suggested is not absolute or fixed.Rather, it is one of many possible alternatives. In this instance, ~(이)나 means "just" or "or something."

커피나 한잔 할까요?
keo-pi-na han-jan hal-kka-yo?
Shall we have a cup of coffee or something together?

(7) Adverb Formation

To express the way that something has occurred, attach ~게 (ge) to an descriptive verb stem to form an adverb. The adverbial form ~게 (ge) refers to the manner or way in which something happens.

재미있다 to be interesting   재미있게 interestingly
jae-mi-it-da   jae-mi-it-ge

늦다 to be late
neut-da

늦게 late
neut-ge

바쁘다 to be busy
ba-ppeu-da

바쁘게 busily
ba-ppeu-ge

시끄럽다 to be loud
si-kkeu-reop-da

시끄럽게 loudly
si-kkeu-reop-ge

(8) ~(으)러 *((eu)-reo) "to do ~, in order to~"*

Use the pattern ~(으)러, "in order to," to show the purpose of an action. It is used with directional verbs (examples include 가다, 오다, 다니다) to indicate the purpose of going or coming.

점심 먹고 영화 보러 가자.
jeom-sim-meok-go yeong-hwa-bo-reo ga-ja.
Let's go to see a movie after we eat lunch.

참고학습 Further Study

(1) 날씨와 계절에 관한 표현들

봄 bom	spring
여름 yeo-reum	summer
가을 ga-eul	fall
겨울 geo-wul	winter
일기예보 il-gi-ye-bo	weather forecast
온도 on-do	temperature
영상 yeong-sang	above zero
영하 yeong-ha	below zero
섭씨 seop-ssi	Celsius
화씨 hwa-ssi	Fahrenheit
기온이 낮다 gi-on-i nat-da	the temperature is low
기온이 높다 gi-on-i nop-da	the temperature is high
날씨가 나쁘다 nal-ssi-ga na-ppeu-da	the weather is bad
날씨가 좋다 nal-ssi-ga jo-ta	the weather is good
끈끈하다 kkeun-kkeun-ha-da	to be muggy
구름이 끼다 gu-reum-i kki-da	to get cloudy
눈이 오다 nun-i o-da	to snow
비가 오다 bi-ga o-da	to rain
바람이 불다 ba-ram-i bul-da	the wind blows
얼음이 얼다 eol-eum-i eol-da	the ice freezes
덥다 deop-da	to be hot
따뜻하다 tta-tteu-ta-da	to be warm
시원하다 si-won-ha-da	to be cool
쌀쌀하다 ssal-ssal-ha-da	to be chilly
춥다 chup-da	to be cold

더워지다 deo-wo-ji-da	to get hot
맑아지다 malg-a-ji-da	to become clean
추워지다 chu-wo-ji-da	to get cold
흐려지다 heu-ryeo-ji-da	to get cloudy

(2) 여가활동에 관한 표현들

Sports

권투를 하다 gwon-tu-reul ha-da	to box
레슬링을 하다 re-seul-ling-eul ha-da	to wrestle
산책을 하다 san-chaeg-eul ha-da	to go for a walk
수영을 하다 su-yeong-eul ha-da	to swim
조깅을 하다 jo-ging-eul ha-da	to jog

농구를 하다 nong-gu-reul ha-da	to play basketball
미식축구를 하다 mi-sik-chuk-gu-reul ha-da	to play football
배구를 하다 bae-gu-reul ha-da	to play volleyball
야구를 하다 ya-gu-reul ha-da	to play baseball
축구를 하다 chuk-gu-reul ha-da	to play soccer

등산을 하다/가다 deung-san-eul ha-da/ga-da	to climb a mountain
여행을 하다/가다 yeo-haeng-eul ha-da/ga-da	to travel

스케이트를 타다 seu-ke-i-teu-reul ta-da	to skate
스키를 타다 seu-ki-reul ta-da	to ski
자전거를 타다 ja-jeon-geo-reul ta-da	to ride a bicycle

골프를 치다 gol-peu-reul chi-da — to play golf
탁구를 치다 tak-gu-reul chi-da — to play ping-pong
테니스를 치다 te-ni-seu-reul chi-da — to play tennis

Musical instruments

플룻을 불다 peul-lus-eul bul-da — to play the flute
클라리넷을 불다 keul-la-ri-net-eul bul-da — to play the clarinet
트럼펫을 불다 teu-reom-pes-eul bul-da — to play the trumpet
피아노를 치다 pi-a-no-reul chi-da — to play the piano
드럼을 치다 deu-reom-eul chi-da — to play the drums
기타를 치다 gi-ta-reul chi-da — to play the guitar
바이올린을 켜다 va-i-ol-in-eul kyeo-da — to play the violin
첼로를 켜다 chel-lo-reul kyeo-da — to play the cello
비올라를 켜다 vi-ol-la-reul kyeo-da — to play the viola

Etc.

낚시를 가다/하다 nak-si-reul ga-da/ha-da — to go fishing
연극 구경을 가다/하다
    yeon-geuk gu-gyeong-eul ga-da/ha-da — to go to see a play
영화 구경을 가다/하다 — to go to see a movie
    yeong-hwa gu-gyeong-eul ga-da/ha-da
카드놀이를 하다 ka-deu nol-i-reul ha-da — to play a card game
컴퓨터 게임을 하다 — to play a computer
    keom-pyu-teo ge-im-eul ha-da — game

노래방에 가다 no-rae-bang-e ga-da — to go to a karaoke room
미술관에 가다 mi-sul-gwan-e ga-da — to go to an art gallery
박물관에 가다 bang-mul-gwan-e ga-da — to go to a museum
음악회에 가다 eum-a-koe-e ga-da — to go to a concert

비디오를 보다 vi-di-o-reul bo-da   to watch a videotape
영화를 보다 yeong-hwa-reul bo-da   to watch a movie
텔레비전을 보다 tel-le-bi-jeon-eul bo-da   to watch TV

그림을 그리다 geu-rim-eul geu-ri-da   to draw a picture
노래를 부르다 no-rae-reul bu-reu-da   to sing a song
사진을 찍다 sa-jin-eul jjik-da   to take a photograph
음악을 듣다 eum-ag-eul deut-da   to listen to music
잠을 자다 jam-eul ja-da   to sleep
책을 읽다 chaeg-eul ilk-da   to read a book
춤을 추다 chum-eul chu-da   to dance
트럼프를 치다 teu-reom-peu-reul chi-da   to play a card game

문화적 참고사항 Cultural Note

(1) 한국의 날씨

Korea is located in the East Asian monsoon belt and has four distinct seasons. Due to its location, Korea has monsoon season in the summer. A storm with abundant rainfall and strong, gusting winds, called a typhoon, is an unwelcome annual visitor. About 70% of rainfall comes between June and August. The hottest month is August, and the coldest month is January. The average temperature in August is above 25°C (about 77°F). In January, it is below –4°C (approximately 30°F).

연습문제 Exercises

1. Please respond to the following:

(1) 한국은 여름에 보통 날씨가 어때요?
  han-gug-eun yeo-reum-e bo-tong nal-ssi-ga eo-ttae-yo?
(2) 내일 같이 점심먹고 영화 보러 가실래요?
  nae-il ga-chi jeom-sim-meok-go yeong-hwa bo-reo
  ga-sil-lae-yo?
(3) 어떤 스포츠를 좋아하세요?
  eo-tteo seu-po-cheu-reul jo-a-ha-se-yo?
(4) 주말에는 보통 뭐 하세요?
  ju-mal-e-neun bo-tong mwo ha-se-yo?
(5) 이번 휴가동안 뭐 하셨어요?
  i-beon hyu-ga-ttong-an mwo ha-syeoss-eo-yo?

2. Please translate the following into English:

(1) 요즘은 전 세계적으로 이상기온 현상이 나타나잖아요.
  yo-jeum-eun jeon se-ge-jeog-eu-ro i-sang-gi-on hyeon-sang-i
  na-ta-najan-a-yo.
(2) 한국은 여름에 습도가 높아서 더 지내기가 힘들지.
  han-gug-eun yeo-reum-e seup-do-ga no-pa-seo deo ji-nae-gi-ga
  him-deul-ji.
(3) 날씨가 너무 덥고 끈끈해서 밖에 나가기가 싫네요.
  nal-ssi-ga neo-mu deop-go kkeun-kkeun-hae-seo bakk-e
  na-ga-gi-ga sil-ne-yo.
(4) 사실은 내일 친구하고 같이 영화보러 가기로 했거든요.
  sa-sil-eun nae-il chin-gu-ha-go ga-chi yeong-hwa bo-reo
  ga-gi-ro hat-geo-deun-yo.
(5) 새로 나온 첩보영화인데 아주 재미있대요.
  sae-ro na-on cheop-bo-yeong-hwa-in-de a-ju jae-mi-it-dae-yo.

3. Please translate into Korean:

(1) I like to watch TV during the weekend, but this weekend was too busy.
(2) My hobby is taking pictures, and my brother's is playing a piano.
(3) In Korea, the weather during winter is very cold and windy.
(4) When I have time, I love to visit a museum or an art gallery.
(5) We will have a lot of rain in San Diego tomorrow.

4. Please write a paragraph describing the weather in your town.

제7과 쇼핑

◇◇◇◇◇◇◇

Lesson 7: Shopping

표현 Patterns

어서 오세요. 뭐 찾으세요?
eo-seo- o-se-yo. mwo chaj-eu-se-yo?
Welcome. (*lit.* Come quickly). What are you looking for?

바지 한 벌 사려고 하는데 구경 좀 해도 돼요?
ba-ji han beol sa-ryeo-go ha-neun-de gu-gyeong jom hae-do
    dwae-yo?
I am trying to buy a pair of pants. Is it OK if I look around?

이리 들어오세요.
i-ri deul-eo-o-se-yo.
Come on in here, please.

어떤 색깔 바지를 찾으시는데요?
eo-tteon saek-kkal ba-ji-reul chaj-eu-si-neun-de-yo?
What color of pants are you looking for?

그냥 아무 옷에나 잘 어울리는 무난한 색깔이면 좋겠는데요.
geu-nyang a-mu os-e-na jal eo-ul-li-neun mu-nan-han
    saek-kkal-i-myeon jo-kken-neun-de-yo.
A plain color—one that fits well with any clothes—would be good.

그럼 짙은 청색이나 연한 갈색이 좋겠네요.
geu-reom jit-eun cheong-saeg-i-na yeon-han gal-ssaeg-i
    jo-kken-ne-yo.
Then either navy blue or light brown would be good.

잠깐만요. 제가 좀 찾아 볼게요.
jam-kkan-man-yo. je-ga jom chaj-a bo-kke-yo.
Just a moment, please. I will check and find some.

사이즈는 몇 입으세요?
ssa-i-jeu-neun myeot ib-eu-se-yo?
What's your waist size?

32나 33이요.
sam-sib-i-na sam-sip-sam-i-yo.
Either 32 or 33.

이건 어떠세요?
i-geon eo-tteo-se-yo?
How about this?

이게 요즘 제일 많이 팔리는 디자인인데요.
i-ge yo-jeum je-il man-i pal-li-neun di-ja-in-in-de-yo.
This is the design that sells the most these days.

손님한테도 잘 어울리겠는데요.
son-nim-han-te-do jal eo-ul-li-gen-neun-de-yo.
It seems to be go well with you, too.

괜찮아 보이네요.
gwaen-chan-a bo-i-ne-yo.
It looks good.

이거 한번 입어 봐도 돼요?
i-geo han-beon ib-eo bwa-do dwae-yo?
Is it OK if I try it on?

저쪽에 탈의실이 보이시죠?
jeo-jjog-e tal-ui-sil-I bo-i-si-jyo?
Can you see the dressing room over there?

저를 따라 오세요. 제가 모셔다 드릴게요.

jeo-reul tta-ra o-se-yo. je-ga mo-syeo-da deu-ril-kke-yo.

Please follow me. I will take you there.

어떠세요? 제가 보기엔 잘 맞는 것 같은데요.

eo-tteo-se-yo? je-ga bo-gi-en jal man-neun geot gat-eun-de-yo.

How is it? To me, it looks good on you.

잘 맞네요.

jal man-ne-yo.

It fits well.

그런데 이거 드라이 해야 되는 거 아닌가요?

geu-reon-de i-geo deu-ra-i hae-ya doe-neun geo a-nin-ga-yo?

But doesn't this need to be dry-cleaned?

요즘엔 정장 바지도 드라이 안 해도 되는 게 많이 나와요.

yo-jeum-en jeong-jang-ba-ji-do deu-ra-i an hae-do doe-neun ge
    man-i na-wa-yo.

A lot of dress pants that come out these days don't need to be
    dry-cleaned.

그냥 세탁기에 넣고 돌리셔도 돼요.

geu-nyang se-tak-gi-e neo-ko dol-li-syeo-do dwae-yo.

You can just put it in a washer and run.

잘 털어서 말리면 다림질도 안 하셔도 되고요.

jal teol-eo-seo mal-li-myeon da-rim-jil-do an ha-syeo-do doe-go-yo.

If you shake it well and line-dry, you don't have to iron it.

참 편리해서 마음에 드네요.

cham pyeol-li-hae-seo ma-eum-e deu-ne-yo.

I like it because it is convenient (to handle).

가격은 얼마나 하는데요?

ga-gyeog-eun eol-ma-na ha-neun-de-yo?

How much is the price?

정가는 10만원인데 요즘 세일기간이라서 25프로 세일해 드리
고 있어요.

jeong-kka-neun sim-man-won-in-de yo-jeum sse-il-gi-gan-i-ra-seo
i-sib-o-peu-ro sse-il-hae deu-ri-go iss-eo-yo.

The regular price is 100,000 won, but there's a sale, so we take
off 25%.

그럼 이거 두 벌 다 주세요.

geu-reom i-geo du-beol da ju-se-yo.

Then please give me both of them.

카드도 받으시죠?

Ka-deu-do bad-eu-si-jyo?

You accept credit cards, right?

그럼요. 이쪽으로 오세요.

geu-reom-yo. i-jjog-eu-ro o-se-yo.

Sure. Come this way.

넥타이하고 와이셔츠도 좀 봤으면 좋겠는데요.

nek-ta-i-ha-go wa-i-syeo-cheu-do jom bwass-eu-myeon
jo-ken-neun-de-yo.

I would like to see some ties and dress shirts, too.

손님이 입으실 거예요, 아니면 누구한테 선물하실 거예요?

son-nim-i ib-eu-sil kkeo-ye-yo, a-ni-myeon nu-gu-han-te seon-mul-
ha-sil kkeo-ye-yo?

Is it for yourself to wear or a gift for someone else?

할아버지 드릴 건데요.
hal-a-beo-ji deu-ril kkeon-de-yo.
It's for my grandpa.

점잖은 걸로 몇 가지 좀 보여 주세요.
jeom-jan-eun geol-lo myeot ga-ji jom bo-yeo ju-se-yo.
Please show me some of the ones in plain colors.

요즘엔 나이드신 분들이 점잖은 색깔을 더 싫어하세요.
yo-jeum-en na-i-deu-sin bun-deul-i jeom-jan-eun saek-kkal-eul deo
    sil-eo-ha-se-yo.
These days, elderly people like plain colors less than young
    people do.

요즘엔 노인용으로도 이렇게 산뜻하고 밝은 색상들이 많이 나
    와요.
yo-jeum-en no-in-yong-eu-ro-do i-reo-ke san-tteu-ta-go balg-eun
    saek-sang-deul-i man-i na-wa-yo.
Many vivid and brightly colored items, like this, for elderly people
    these days.

이것 보세요.
i-geot bo-se-yo.
Look at this.

이 겨자색 와이셔츠하고 줄무늬 넥타이가 잘 어울릴 것
    같은데요.
i gyeo-ja-saek wa-i-syeo-cheu-ha-go jul-mu-ni nek-ta-i-ga jal
    eo-ul-lil- kkeot gat-eun-de-yo.
I think this dark yellow dress shirt and striped tie would go well
    together.

제가 보기엔 괜찮은 것 같은데요.
Je-ga bo-gi-en gwaen-chan-eun geot gat-eun-de-yo.
To me, it looks good.

그래도 혹시 할아버지가 마음에 안 들어 하시면 바꾸러 와도
　되지요?

geu-rae-do hok-si hal-a-beo-ji-ga ma-eum-e an deul-eo ha-si-myeon
　ba-kku-reo wa-do doe-ji-yo?

But just in case if my grandpa doesn't like it, I can exchange it,
　right?

30일 안에 오시면 언제든지 교환해 드려요.

sam-sib-il an-e o-si-myeon eon-je-deun-ji gyo-hwan-hae
　deu-ryeo-yo.

If you come within 30 days, we will exchange it for you.

영수증 꼭 가지고 오시고요.

yeong-su-jeung kkok ga-ji-go o-si-go-yo.

Please be sure to bring your receipt.

대화 Model Conversations

(1)

점원: 어서 오세요, 손님. 뭐 찾으세요?

eo-seo o-se-yo, son-nim. mwo chaj-eu-se-yo?

이정호: 바지 한 벌 사려고 하는데 구경 좀 해도 돼요?

ba-ji han-beol sa-ryeo-go ha-neun-de gu-gyeong jom
hae-do dwae-yo?

점원: 그럼요. 이리 들어오세요. 어떤 색깔 바지를 찾으시는
데요?

geu-reom-yo. i-ri deul-eo-o-se-yo. eo-tteon saek-kkal
ba-ji-reul chaj-eu-si-neun-de-yo?

이정호: 그냥 아무 옷에나 잘 어울리는 무난한 색깔이면 좋겠
는데요.

geu-nyang a-nu os-e-na jal eo-ul-li-neun mu-nan-han
saek-kkal-i-myeon jo-ken-neun-de-yo.

점원: 그럼 짙은 청색이나 연한 갈색이 좋겠네요. 잠깐만요.

geu-reom jit-eun cheong-saeg-i-na yeon-han gal-ssaeg-i
jo-ken-ne-yo. jam-kkan-man-yo.

제가 좀 찾아 볼게요. 사이즈는 몇 입으세요?

je-ga jom chaj-a bol-kke-yo. ssa-i-jeu-neun myeot
ib-eu-se-yo?

이정호: 32나 33이요.

sam-sib-i-na sam-sip-sam-i-yo.

점원: 이건 어떠세요? 이게 요즘 제일 많이 팔리는 디자인
인데요. 손님한테도 잘 어울리겠는데요.

i-geon eo-tteo-se-yo? i-ge yo-jeum je-il man-I
pal-li-meun di-ja-in-in-de-yo. son-nim-han-te-do jal
eo-ul-li-gen-neun-de-yo.

이정호: 괜찮아 보이네요. 이거 한번 입어 봐도 돼요?

gwaen-chan-a bo-i-ne-yo. i-geo han-beon ib-eo bwa-do
dwae-yo?

점원: 그럼요. 저쪽에 탈의실이 보이시죠? 따라 오세요. 제가 모셔다 드릴게요.

geu-reom-yo. jeo-jjog-e tal-ui-sil-i bo-i-si-jyo? tta-ra-o-se-yo. je-ga mo-syeo-da deu-reil-kke-yo.

(2)

점원: 어떠세요? 제가 보기엔 잘 맞는 것 같은데요.

eo-tteo-se-yo? je-ga bo-gi-en jal man-neun-geot gat-eun-de-yo.

이정호: 네, 잘 맞네요. 그런데 이거 드라이 해야 되는 거 아닌가요?

ne, jal man-ne-yo. geu-reon-de i-geo deu-ra-i hae-ya doe-neun geo a-nin-ga-yo?

점원: 아니오, 요즘엔 정장 바지도 드라이 안 해도 되는 게 많이 나와요.

a-ni-o, yo-jeum-en jeong-jang ba-ji-do deu-ra-i an hae-do doe-neun ge man-i na-wa-yo.

그냥 세탁기에 넣고 돌리셔도 돼요. 잘 털어서 말리면 다림질도 안 하셔도 되고요.

geu-nyang se-tak-gi-e neo-ko dol-li-syeo-do dwae-yo. jal teol-eo-se mal-li-myeon da-rim-jil-do an ha-syeo-do doe-go-yo.

이정호: 그래요? 참 편리해서 마음에 드네요. 가격은 얼마나 하는데요?

geu-rae-yo? cham pyeol-li-hae-seo ma-eum-e deu-ne-yo. ga-gyeog-eun eol-ma-na ha-neun-de-yo?

점원: 정가는 10만원인데 요즘 세일기간이라서 25프로 세일해 드리고 있어요.

jeong-kka-neun sim-man-won-in-de yo-jeum sse-il-gi-gan-i-ra-seo i-sib-o-peu-ro sse-il-hae deu-ri-go iss-eo-yo.

이정호: 그럼 이거 두 벌 다 주세요. 카드도 받으시죠?

geu-reom i-geo du-beol da ju-se-yo. ka-deu-do bad-eu-si-jyo?

점원: 그럼요. 이쪽으로 오세요.
           geu-reom-yo. i-jjog-eu-ro o-se-yo.

(3)
이정호: 아참, 넥타이하고 와이셔츠도 좀 봤으면 좋겠는데요.
           a-cham, nek-ta-i-ha-go wa-i-syeo-cheu-do jom
           bwass-eu-myeon jo-kken-neun-de-yo.
점원: 그러세요? 손님이 입으실 거예요, 아니면 누구한테 선
           물하실 거예요?
           geu-reo-se-yo? son-nim-i ib-eu-sil kkeo-ye-yo,
           a-ni-myeon nu-gu-han-te seon-mul-ha-sil kkeo-ye-yo?
이정호: 할아버지 드릴 건데요. 좀 점잖은 걸로 몇 가지 좀 보
           여 주세요.
           hal-a-beo-ji deu-ril kkeon-de-yo. jom jeom-jan-eun
           geol-lo myeot ga-ji jom bo-yeo ju-se-yo.
점원: 어머, 요즘엔 나이드신 분들이 점잖은 색깔을 더 싫어
           하세요.
           eo-meo, yo-jeum-en na-i-deu-sin bun-deul-i jeom-jan-eun
           saek-kkal-eul deo sil-eo-ha-se-yo.
           요즘엔 노인용으로도 이렇게 산뜻하고 밝은 색상들
           이 많이 나와요.
           yo-jeum-en no-in-yong-eu-ro-do i-reo-ke san-tteu-ta-go
           balg-eun saek-sang-deul-i man-i na-wa-yo.
           이것 보세요. 이 겨자색 와이셔츠하고 줄무늬 넥타이
           가 잘 어울릴 것 같은데요.
           i-geot bo-se-yo. i gyeo-ja-saek wa-i-syeo-cheu-ha-go
           jul-mu-ni nek-ta-i-ga jal eo-ul-lil kkeot gat-eun-de-yo.
이정호: 흠 . . . 제가 보기엔 괜찮은 것 같은데요.
           heum . . . je-ga bo-gi-en gwaen-chan-eun geot
           gat-eun-de-yo.
           그래도 혹시 할아버지가 마음에 안 들어 하시면 바꾸
           러 와도 되지요?
           geu-rae-do hok-si hal-a-beo-ji-ga ma-eum-e an deul-eo
           ha-si-myeon ba-kku-reo wa-do doe-ji-yo?

점원: 그럼요. 30일 안에 오시면 언제든지 교환해 드려요.
          영수증 꼭 가지고 오시고요.
          geu-reom-yo. sam-sib-il an-e o-si-myeon eon-je-deun-ji
          gyo-hwan-hae deu-ryeo-yo. yeong-su-jeung kkok
          ga-ji-go o-si-go-yo.

영문번역 English Translation

(1)

Salesperson:	Hello. May I help you?
Lee:	I am trying to buy a pair of pants. Can I look around?
Salesperson:	Sure. Come on in, please. What color of pants are you looking for?
Lee:	A plain color one that goes well with any clothes would be great.
Salesperson:	Then either navy blue or light brown would be good. One moment, please. I will check and find some. What's your waist size?
Lee:	Either 32 or 33.
Salesperson:	How about this? This design sells the most these days. I think it will look good on you, too.
Lee:	It looks good. Can I try it on?
Salesperson:	Of course. Can you see the dressing room over there? Please follow me; I will take you there.

(2)

Salesperson:	How is it? I think it looks good on you.
Lee:	Yes, it fits well. But doesn't this need to be dry-cleaned?
Salesperson:	No, these days we get a lot of dress pants that don't need to be dry-cleaned. You can just put it in a washer. If you shake it well and line-dry, you don't have to iron it.
Lee:	Really? I like that it is convenient. How much is it?
Salesperson:	The regular price is 100,000 won, but there's a sale, so it will be 25% off.
Lee:	Then I will get two pairs altogether. You accept credit cards, right?
Salesperson:	Sure. Come on this way.

(3)

Lee:	Oh, I want to see some ties and dress shirts, too.
Salesperson:	Really? Is it for yourself or a gift for someone else?
Lee:	It's for my grandpa. Can you show me some of the plain color ones?
Salesperson:	Oh no, actually elderly people like plain colors less than young people do these days. There are many vivid and bright color items, like this, for elderly people. Check this out. I think this dark yellow dress shirt and striped tie would match well.
Lee:	Hmm . . . I think it will look alright. But if my grandpa doesn't like it, I can still exchange it, right?
Salesperson:	Of course. If you come within 30 days, you can exchange it. Please be sure to bring your receipt.

어휘 Vocabulary

Nouns / Pronouns

가격 ga-gyeok	price
갈색 gal-saek	light brown
겨자색 gyeo-ja-saek	dark yellow
나이드신 분들 na-i-deu-sin bun-deul	elderly people
넥타이 nek-ta-i	necktie
노인용 no-in-yong	things for elderly people
누구 nu-gu	who, someone
두 벌 du-beol	two pairs
드라이 deu-ra-i	dry cleaning
드릴 거 deu-ril geo	things to give (hon.)
디자인 di-ja-in	design
몇 myeot	what
몇 가지 myeot ga-ji	a couple of, several
뭐 mwo	what, something
바지 ba-ji	pants
사이즈 sa-i-jeu	size
색깔 saek-kkal	color
색상 saek-sang	color and shape
세일기간 se-il-gi-gan	sale period
세탁기 se-tak-gi	washing machine
손님 son-nim	customer
영수증 yeong-su-jeung	receipt
옷 ot	clothes
와이셔츠 wa-i-syeo-cheu	dress shirt
이쪽 i-jjok	this side
저쪽 jeo-jjok	that side
점원 jeom-won	salesperson
점잖은 것 jeom-jan-eun geot	plain-color item
정가 jeong-kka	original price
정장 바지 jeong-jang ba-ji	dress pants

청색 cheong-saek	navy blue
카드 ka-deu	credit card
탈의실 tal-ui-sil	fitting room
한 벌 han beol	one pair
할아버지 hal-a-beo-ji	grandfather
10만원 sip-man-won	10,000 won
25프로 i-sib-o peu-ro	25 percent
30일 sam-sib-il	30 days

Verbs

가지고 오다 ga-ji-go o-da	to bring something
괜찮다 gwaen-chan-ta	to be OK
괜찮아 보이다 gwaen-chan-a bo-i-da	to look good
교환해 드리다 gyo-hwan-hae deu-ri-da	to exchange (hon.)
구경하다 gu-gyeong-ha-da	to just look around
나오다 na-o-da	to come out
넣다 neo-ta	to put inside
다림질하다 da-rim-jil-ha-da	to iron
돌리다 dol-li-da	to turn
드라이하다 deu-ra-i ha-da	to dry clean
들어오다 deul-eo-o-da	to enter
따라오다 tta-ra-o-da	to follow
마음에 들다 ma-eum-e deul-da	to like, to fit someone's taste
마음에 안 들어 하다 ma-eum-e an deul-eo-ha-da	not to like
말리다 mal-li-da	to dry
모셔다 드리다 mo-syeo-da deu-ri-da	to take someone (hon.)
무난하다 mu-nan-ha-da	to be decent
바꾸러 오다 ba-kku-reo o-da	to come to exchange
받다 bat-da	to receive
밝다 balk-da	to be bright
보다 bo-da	to see

보여 주다 bo-yeo ju-da — to show
보이다 bo-i-da — to be seen
사다 sa-da — to buy
산뜻하다 san-tteu-ta-da — to be neat and fresh
선물하다 seon-mul-ha-da — to give a present
세일해 드리다 se-il-hae deu-ri-da — to discount (hon.)
싫어하다 sil-eo-ha-da — to dislike
어울리다 eo-ul-li-da — to match well
연하다 yeon-ha-da — to be light
오다 o-da — to come
입다 ip-da — to wear
입어 보다 ib-eo-bo-da — to try on (clothes), to wear
잘 맞다 jal mat-da — to fit well
점잖다 jeom-jan-ta — to be decent
좋다 jo-ta — to be good
주다 ju-da — to give
줄무늬 jul-mu-ni — stripe
짙다 jit-da — to be dark
찾다 chat-da — to look for, to find
찾아 보다 chaj-a-bo-da — to look for
털다 teol-da — to shake off
팔리다 pal-li-da — to be sold
편리하다 pyeol-li-ha-da — to be convenient

Adverbs / Pre-Nouns / Conjunctions

그냥 geu-nyang — just, only
그래도 geu-rae-do — even it is true
그러세요? geu-reo-se-yo — really?
그런데 geu-reon-de — but, by the way
그럼 geu-reom — then
그럼요 geu-reom-yo — of course
꼭 kkok — for sure
많이 man-i — a lot

아니면 a-ni-myeon	or, if not ~
아무 a-mu	any
아참 a-cham	oh,
어떠세요? eo-tteo-se-yo	How about ~
어떤 eo-tteon	which, a certain
어머 eo-meo	uh-uh (no)
어서 eo-seo	quickly, please
언제든지 eon-je-deun-ji	whenever
얼마나 eol-ma-na	how much
요즘 yo-jeum	these days
이렇게 i-reo-ke	like this
이리 i-ri	this way
잘 jal	well
잠깐만 jam-kkan-man	for a minute
제가 보기엔 je-ga bo-gi-en	in my point of view
제일 je-il	the most, the first
좀 jom	a little, please
참 cham	oh,
한번 han-beon	once
혹시 hok-si	just in case
흠 . . . heum	hmmm . . .

문법 Grammar

(1) Passive Verbs

In English, one often hears such sentence structures as "the window was broken." This is the passive form. In Korean, the passive construction is formed by attaching the suffix ~이(i), ~히 (hi), ~리 (li), or ~기 (gi) to a verb stem. Since all verbs cannot be made passive, the ones that can must be memorized along with the suffix used.

With passive verbs, the subject (which would be the object of a transitive sentence) is marked by the subject particles 이(i) or가(ga), or the topic markers 은(eun) or 는(neun).The agent (the subject of a transitive sentence) is marked with the dative particle 한테 (han-te) when the agent is a person or animal. If the agent is an inanimate object, the particle 에 (e) is used. Below are some verbs classified according to passive suffix.

Active	Passive	Sample Sentence
보다	보이다	저기 신호등이 보여요.
bo-da	bo-i-da	jeo-gi sin-ho-deung-i bo-yeo-yo
to see	to be seen	I see the traffic light over there.
쓰다	쓰이다	이 약이 감기에 잘 쓰여요.
sseu-da	sseu-i-da	i-yag-i gam-gi-e jal sseu-yeo-yo
to use	to be used	This medicine is often used for colds.
닫다	닫히다	바람에 문이 닫혔어요.
dat-da	da-chi-da	ba-ram-e mun-i da-chyeoss-eo-yo
to close	to be closed	The door became closed because of the wind.

막다
mak-da

to block

막히다
ma-ki-da

to be blocked

차가 많아서 길이 막혀요.
cha-ga man-a-seo gil-i
  ma-kyeo-yo
The street is blocked due to
  many cars.

잡다
jap-da

to catch

잡히다
ja-pi-da

to be caught

도둑이 경찰한테 잡혔어요.
do-dug-i gyeong-chal-han-te
  ja-pyess-eo-yo
The thief was caught by the
  policeman.

물다
mul-da

to bite

물리다
mul-li-da

to be bitten

우체부가 개한테 물렸어요.
u-che-bu-ga gae-han-te
  mul-lyeoss-eo-yo
The mailman was bitten by
  a dog.

열다
yeol-da
to open

열리다
yeol-li-da
to be open

가게문이 열렸어요.
ga-ge-mun-i yeol-lyeoss-eo-yo
The store door is open.

듣다
deut-da
to hear

들리다
deul-li-da
to be heard

음악 소리가 들려요.
eum-ak so-ri-ga deul-lyeo-yo
I heard music.

팔다
pal-da
to sell

팔리다
pal-li-da
to be sold

요즘 집이 잘 팔려요.
yo-jeum jib-i jal pal-lyeo-yo
Houses are sold quickly
  these days.

뺏다
ppaet-da

to take away

뺏기다
ppaet-gi-da

to be taken away

개한테 사과를 뺏겼어요.
gae-han-te sa-gwa-reul
  ppaet-gyeoss-eo-yo
My apple has been taken away
  by the dog.

안다	안기다	아이가 엄마한테 안겼어요.
an-tta	an-gi-da	a-i-ga eom-ma-ha-te an-gyeoss-eo-yo
to hold	to be held	The baby was being held by the mom.
쫓다	쫓기다	쥐가 고양이한테 쫓겨요.
jjot-da	jjot-gi-da	jwi-ga go-yang-i han-te jjot-gyeo-yo
to chase	to be chased	A mouse is being chased by a cat.

(2) ~고 있다 (go it-da) vs. ~고 계시다 (go gye-si-da) progressive "be ...ing"

When indicating the progression or repetition of an action, add the suffix ~고 있다 (go it-da) to the verb. The honorific form uses the suffix ~고 계시다 (go gye-si-da). The past tense plain uses the suffix ~고 있었어요 (go iss-eoss-eo-yo), and the past tense honorific uses ~고 계셨어요 (go gye-syeoss-eo-yo).

The future tense uses ~고 있을 거예요 (go iss-eul kkeo-ye-yo) and ~고 계실 거예요 (go gye-sil kkeo-ye-yo), respectively.

(3) ~(으)면 ((eu)-myeon) "if, when~"

Use the suffix ~(으)면 to create either a conditional statement (in English, one that uses "if"), or to express when. When the verb stem ends in a consonant other than ㄹ, use ~으면 (eu-myeon). When it ends in a vowel or ㄹ, use ~면 (myeon).

(4) ~(으)ㄹ게요 ((eu)l-kke-yo) vs. ~(으)ㄹ래요 ((eu)l-lae-yo) and expressing intention

The ending ~(으)ㄹ게요 (-[eu]l-kke-yo) expresses the determination of or a promise by the speaker to do something. It denotes willingness, assurance, and promise. The English equivalent is "I am going to do." It may be used only in the first person and only in the form of statement. It cannot be used in a question. When expressing intention in a statement, use the sentence ending ~(으)ㄹ래요 –(eu)l-lae-yo. Also use it when asking the intention of the listener. It denotes intention and assertion. The English equivalent is "planning to do." These patterns occur only in casual language. In a formal setting, one uses ~(으)시겠습니까? ([eu]-si-get-seum-ni-kka?) instead of ~(으)ㄹ게요, and ~겠습니다 (get-seum-ni-da) instead of ~(으)ㄹ래요.

Examples:

저는 비빔밥을 먹을래요.
jeo-neun bi-bim-ppab-eul meog-eul-kke-yo.
I am going to eat bi-bim-ppap. (*casual*)

저는 비빔밥을 먹을게요.
jeo-neun bi-bim-ppab-eul meog-eul-lae-yo.
I am planning to eat bi-bim-ppap. (*casual*)

저는 비빔밥을 먹겠습니다.
jeo-neun bi-bim-ppab-eul meok-get-seum-ni-da.
I am planning to eat bi-bim-ppap. (*formal*)

비빔밥을 먹을래요?
bi-bim-ppab-eul meog-eul-lae-yo?
Are you planning to eat bi-bim-ppap? (*casual*)

비빔밥을 드시겠습니까?
bi-bim-ppab-eul deu-si-get-seum-ni-kka?
Are you planning to eat bi-bim-ppap? (*formal*)

(5) Noun Formation: ~는 것 (neun geot) vs. ~기(gi)

To express a verb as a noun, add the suffix ~는 것 to the verb. This is the equivalent of adding the suffix *-ing* to a verb in English. Depending on the sentence, a particle may be added, causing contraction. In writing, the forms ~는 것이, ~는 것을, and ~는 것은 are not shortened into contractions. Contractions are used colloquially. The contractions occur like so:

~는 것이 (neun geot-i)	→	~는 게 (neun ge)
~는 것을 (neun geot-eul)	→	~는 걸 (neun geol)
~는 것은 (neun geot-eun)	→	~는 건 (neun geon)

The ending ~기(-gi) is also used to form a noun from a verb. Sometimes ~는 것 and ~기 are used interchangeably, but not always. To make a list of things to do, ~기 is used.

걷다
geot-da
walk

걷기 / 걷는 것
geot-gi / geon-neun geot
walking

노래하다
no-rae-ha-da
sing

노래하기 / 노래하는 것
no-rae-ha-gi / no-rae-ha-neun geot
singing

쇼핑가다
syo-ping-ga-da
go shopping

쇼핑가기 / 쇼핑가는 것
syo-ping-ga-gi / syo-ping-ga-neun geot
shopping

자다
ja-da
sleep

자기 / 자는 것
ja-gi / ja-neun geot
sleeping

(6) Permission ~아/어도 되다 (a/eo-do doe-da) vs. Prohibition ~(으)면 안되다 ((eu)-myeon an-doe-da)

To ask for or grant permission to do something in a general sense, use the pattern ~아/어도 돼요 (a/eo-do dae-yo). The negative forms are 안 ~아/어도 돼요 (an ~a/eo-do dae-yo) and ~지 않아도 돼요 (ji an-a-do dae-yo). To askfor or grant permission to do something in particular, do not use ~되다 (doe-da). Use ~좋다 (jo-ta) or ~괜찮다 (gwaen-chan-ta) instead.

To refuse permission, forbid an action, or issue a warning, use the ending ~(으)면 안돼요 ([eu]-myeon an-dae-yo), which directly translates as "it is not all right if . . ."

(7) Expressing "old"

Although *old* in English signifies "aged" in most instances, the Korean equivalents have distinct connotations and are quite specific in terms of what is being described.

For items, use 오래되다 (o-rae-doe-da) to express a positive meaning, e.g.

> 이 그림은 오래된 것이다.
> (i geu-rim-eun o-rae-doen geos-i-da.)
> This picture is old and venerable.

The word 낡다 (nalk-da) is used to emphasize a negative meaning, e.g.
> 이 책상은 낡았다.
> (i chaek-sang-eun nalg-at-da.)
> This desk is old and run-down.

When referring to oneself, younger people or animals, one uses the word 늙다 (neulk-da). For example:

> 나도 이제 늙었다.
> (na-do i-je neulg-eot-da.)
> Now I am old.

The word 나이가 많다 (na-i-ga man-ta) is used to describe oneself or other people regardless of age. However, the honorific marker ~시 (-si) should be attached if necessary, e.g.

> 부모님이 나이가 많으시다.
> (bu-mo-nim-i na-i-ga man-eu-si-da.)
> My parents are old.

When speaking of someone in a humble or deferential manner, one uses the word 연세가 많으시다 (yeon-se-ga man-eu-si-da), e.g.

> 부모님이 연세가 많으시다.
> (bu-mo-nim-i yeon-se-ga man-eu-si-da.)
> My parents are old.

참고학습 Further Study

(1) Kinds of Stores

꽃집 kkot-jip, 화원 hwa-won   florist/flower shop
다방 da-bang, 카페 ka-pe   café, coffee shop
백화점 bae-kwa-jeom   department store
빵집 ppang-jjip, 제과점 je-gwa-jeom   bakery
사진관 sa-jin-gwan   photo shop
서점 seo-jeom, 책방 chaek-bang   bookstore
슈퍼마켓 syu-peo-ma-ket   supermarket
신발가게 sin-bal-kka-ge   shoe store
약국 yak-guk, 약방 yak-bang   drugstore
옷가게 ot-ga-ge   clothing store
우체국 u-che-guk   post office
은행 eun-haeng   bank
장난감 가게 jang-nan-kkam ga-ge   toy store
편의점 pyeon-ui-jeom, 가게 ga-ge   convenience store

(2) Clothing

남방 nam-bang   T-shirts, tennis/golf shirts
넥타이 nek-ta-i   necktie
모자 mo-ja   hat
목도리 mok-do-ri   muffler/scarf
바지 ba-ji   pants
블라우스 beul-la-u-seu   blouse
셔츠 syeo-cheu   shirt
속옷 sog-ot   underwear
스웨터 seu-we-teo   sweater
스카프 seu-ka-peu   scarf
스타킹 seu-ta-king   panty hose
양말 yang-mal   socks

와이셔츠 wa-i-syeo-cheu	dress shirt
원피스 won-pi-seu	dress
자켓 ja-ket	jacket
장갑 jang-gap	glove
정장 jeong-jang	suit
치마 chi-ma	skirt
캐주얼 kae-ju-eol	casual
코트 co-teu	coat

Putting On and Taking Off Clothes

Korean has different verbs for "to put on" or "to wear," and "to take off," depending on how the item is worn. For example, 입다 (ip-da) is for apparel other than headgear, footwear, or gloves. The verb 신다 (sin-tta) is for footwear, and the verb 끼다 (kki-da) is for things that fit tightly, such as gloves.

Items	Putting On Verb	Taking Off Verb
옷 ot clothes	입다 ip-da	벗다 beot-da
양말 yang-mal socks	신다 sin-tta	벗다 beot-da
신발 sin-bal, shoes	신다 sin-tta	벗다 beot-da
모자 mo-ja hat, cap	쓰다 sseu-da	벗다 beot-da
안경 an-gyeong glasses	끼다 kki-da	벗다 beot-da, 빼다 ppae-da

장갑 jang-gap   끼다 kki-da   벗다 beot-da,
gloves, mittens   빼다 ppae-da

반지 ban-ji   끼다 kki-da   빼다 ppae-da
ring

머리핀 meo-ri-pin   꽂다 kkot-da   빼다 ppae-da
hairpin

목도리 mok-do-ri,   매다 mae-da,   풀다 pul-da,
scarf   두르다 du-reu-da   끄르다 kkeu-reu-da

넥타이 nek-ta-i   매다 mae-da   풀다 pul-da,
necktie   끄르다 kkeu-reu-da

벨트 bel-teu   차다 cha-da,   풀다 pul-da,
belt   하다 ha-da   끄르다 kkeu-reu-da

The verb 하다 (ha-da) is used with necklaces, earrings, and other accessories.

Darkness and Patterns

light	연(한) yeon(-han)
e.g. light yellow	연한 노란색 yeon-han no-ran-saek
	연노란색 yeon-no-ran-saek
	연노랑색 yeon-no-rang-saek
dark	진(한) jin(-han)
e.g. dark yellow	진한 노란색 jin-han no-ran-saek
	진노란색 jin-no-ran-saek
	진노랑색 jin-no-rang-saek
checkered	체크무늬 che-keu-mu-nui, che-keu-mu-ni
striped	줄무늬 jul-mu-nui, jul-mu-ni
flower-patterned	꽃무늬 kkon-mu-nui, kkon-mu-ni

문화적 참고사항 Cultural Note

In Korea, negotiating prices is common except in department stores and supermarkets, where all items have price tags. Although growing numbers of merchants accept credit cards, they still prefer cash to plastic. Tax is included in the price. Most shops are open until 10 PM and some are open until midnight or 24 hours. It is advisable to carry sufficient cash as ATM machines are not easily found apart from banks. One needs to know one's clothing size as many clothing stores are reluctant to allow the trying-on of clothes prior to purchase. A full refund for cash is rare, but exchanges for other products are possible.

연습문제 Exercises

1. Please respond to the following:

(1) 어서 오세요, 손님. 뭐 찾으세요?
　　eo-seo o-se-yo, son-nim. mwo chaj-eu-se-yo?
(2) 어떤 바지하고 셔츠를 찾으시는데요?
　　eo-tteon ba-ji-ha-go cyeo-cheu-reul chaj-eu-si-neun-de-yo?
(3) 사이즈는 몇 입으세요?
　　ssa-i-jeu-neun myeot ib-eu-se-yo?
(4) 손님이 입으실 건가요, 다른 분한테 선물하실 건가요?
　　son-nim-i ib-eu-sil kkeon-ga-yo, da-reun bun-han-te
　　seon-mul-ha-sil kkeon-ga-yo?
(5) 제가 보기엔 잘 어울리는 것 같은데 손님은 어떠세요?
　　je-ga bo-gi-e-neun jal eo-ul-li-neun geot gat-eun-de
　　son-nim-eun eo-tteo-se-yo?

2. Please translate the following into English:

(1) 이게 요즘 제일 많이 팔리는 디자인인데요.
　　i-ge yo-jeum je-il man-i pal-li-neun di-ja-in-in-de-yo.
(2) 그런데 이거 드라이 해야 되는 거 아닌가요?
　　geu-reon-de i-geo deu-ra-i hae-ya doe-neun geo a-nin-ga-yo?
(3) 요즘엔 정장바지도 드라이 안 해도 되는 게 많이 나와요.
　　yo-jeum-en jeong-jang-ba-ji-do deu-ra-i an hae-do doe-neun ge
　　man-i na-wa-yo.
(4) 정가는 10만원인데 요즘 세일기간이라서 25프로 세일해 드
　　리고 있어요.
　　jeong-kka-neun sim-man-won-in-de yo-jeum sse-il-g-gan-i-ra-
　　seo i-sib-o-peu-ro sse-il-hae deu-ri-go iss-eo-yo.
(5) 요즘엔 나이드신 분들이 점잖은 색깔을 더 싫어하세요.
　　yo-jeum-en na-i-deu-sin bun-deul-i jeom-jan-eun saek-kkal-eul
　　deo sil-eo-ha-se-yo.

(6) 이 겨자색 와이셔츠하고 줄무늬 넥타이가 잘 어울릴 것 같
은데요.

i gyeo-ja-saek wa-i-syeo-cheu-ha-go jul-mu-ni nek-ta-i-ga jal
eo-ul-li-gen-neun-de-yo.

(7) 그냥 아무 옷에나 잘 어울리는 무난한 색깔이면 좋겠는데요.

geu-nyang a-mu os-e-na jal eo-ul-li-neun mu-nan-han
saek-kkal-i-myeon jo-ken-neun-de-yo.

3. Please fill in the blanks with appropriate passive verbs:

(1) 아이가 엄마한테 (안다:_____). a-i-ga eom-ma-ha-te
(an-tta)

(2) 저기 신호등이 (보다:_____). jeo-gi sin-ho-deung-i
(bo-da)

(3) 차가 많아서 길이 (막다:_____). cha-ga man-a-seo gil-i
(mak-da)

(4) 우체부가 개한테 (물다:_____). u-che-bu-ga gae-han-te
(mul-da)

(5) 개한테 사과를 (뺏다:_____). gae-han-te sa-gwa-reul
(ppaet-da)

4. Please fill in the blanks with appropriate words:

현준씨는 아침에 양복을 (1.   ), 넥타이
를 (2.   ), 구두를 (3.   ), 안경을
(4.   ), 모자를 (5.   ) 회사에
갑니다. 저녁에 집에 돌아오면 양복을 (6.   ),
넥타이를 (7.   ), 구두를 (8.   ),
안경을 (9.   ), 모자를 (10.   )
쉽니다.

5. Please write a paragraph describing your favorite fashion.

제8과 음식과 음식점

◇◇◇◇◇◇◇

Lesson 8: Food & Restaurants

표현 Patterns

좋은 아침입니다.
jo-eun a-chim-im-ni-da.
Good morning.

일찍 나오셨네요.
il-jjik na-o-syeon-ne-yo.
You came out early.

오늘은 이것 저것 일이 좀 많아서요.
o-neul-eun i-geot jeo-geot il-i jom man-a-seo-yo.
That's because I have quite a lot of work to do today.

왜 벌써 나오셨어요?
wae beol-sseo na-o-syeoss-eo-yo?
Why did you come so early?

오늘은 길이 별로 복잡하지 않아서 좀 일찍 도착했습니다.
o-neul-eun gil-i byeol-lo bok-ja-pa-ji an-a-seo jom il-jjik
    do-cha-kaet-seum-ni-da.
There wasn't too much traffic today, so I arrived a little early.

일 시작하기 전에 같이 커피나 한잔 할까요?
il si-ja-ka-gi jeon-e ga-chi keo-pi-na han-jan hal-kka-yo?
Shall we have some coffee together before we start work?

마침 저쪽에 음료수 자판기가 있네요.
ma-chim jeo-jjog-e eum-nyo-su ja-pan-gi-ga in-ne-yo.
Coincidentally, a drink vending machine is over there.

나는 냉커피나 한잔 할까 하는데 성민씨는 뭘로 하시겠어요?
na-neun naeng-keo-pi-na han-jan hal-kka ha-neun-de
    seong-min-ssi-neun mwol-lo ha-si-gess-eo-yo?
I would like to have a can of iced coffee, and what would you like
    to have, Seong-Min?

저도 냉커피로 하지요.
jeo-do naeng-keo-pi-ro ha-ji-yo.
I would like to have an iced coffee also.

벌써 점심시간이 다 됐군요.
beol-sseo jeom-sim-si-gan-i da dwaet-gun-yo.
It is already about time for lunch.

오늘은 정말 시간이 빨리 가네요.
o-neul-eun jeong-mal si-gan-i ppal-li ga-ne-yo.
The time (seems to) be going by so fast today.

회사 앞에 한식집이 새로 생겼는데 가 보셨습니까?
hoe-sa ap-e han-sik-jib-i sae-ro saeng-gyeon-neun-de gab
    o-syeot-seum-ni-kka?
A Korean restaurant has just opened in front of the office, and have
    you been there?

아니오, 아직 안 가 봤어요.
a-ni-o, a-jik an ga bwass-eo-yo.
No, I have not been there yet.

그 집은 뭘 잘 합니까?
geu jib-eun mwol jal ham-ni-kka?
What kind of dishes are good there (*lit.* in the house)?

냉면도 잘 하고, 비빔밥도 맛있습니다.
naeng-myeon-do jal ha-go, bi-bim-ppap-do mas-it-seum-ni-da.
Naeng-myeon is good, and bi-bim-bap is also good.

비교적 다 괜찮습니다.
bi-gyo-jeok da gwaen-chan-seum-ni-da.
All (the foods) are relatively good (there).

가게도 깨끗하고요.
ga-ge-do kkae-kkeu-ta-go-yo.
The restaurant is clean also.

그럼 날씨도 더운데 오늘은 냉면이나 한 그릇 먹어 볼까요?
geu-reom nal-ssi-do deo-un-de o-neul-eun naeng-myeon-i-na han
    geu-reut meog-eo bol-kka-yo?
Then shall we (go to) have some naeng-myeon today since the
    weather is hot?

그럼 같이 나가시죠.
geu-reom ga-chi na-ga-si-jyo.
Then let's go together.

오늘은 제가 모시겠습니다.
o-neul-eun je-ga mo-si-get-seum-ni-da.
This is my treat today. (*lit.* I will treat you today.)

어서 오세요.
eo-seo o-se-yo.
Welcome. (*lit.* Come quickly.)

장사 잘 되시지요?
jang-sa jal doe-si-ji-yo?
Your business is doing well, right?

또 오셨네요.

tto o-syeon-ne-yo.

You are here again. (*lit.* You came again.)

어서 이리 들어오세요.

eo-seo i-ri deul-eo-o-se-yo.

Please come this way.

여기 선풍기 앞이 제일 시원해요.

yeo-gi seon-pung-gi ap-i je-il si-won-hae-yo.

This, in front of the fan, is the coolest spot.

오늘은 제가 우리 과장님도 모시고 왔으니까 특별히 더 잘 해
주셔야 됩니다.

o-neul-eun je-ga u-ri gwa-jang-nim-do mo-sigo wass-eu-ni-kka
teuk-byeol-hi deo jal hae ju-syeo-ya doem-ni-da.

Since I brought my manager with me today, please be
especially nice.

그런 건 걱정 마세요.

geu-reon geon geok-jeong-ha-ji ma-se-yo.

Don't worry about that.

오늘은 뭘로 해 드릴까요?

o-neul-eun mwol-lo hae deu-ril-kka-yo?

What would you like today? (*lit.* What do you want me to cook
for you?)

물냉면으로 하시겠습니까, 비빔냉면으로 하시겠습니까?

mul-lang-myeon-eu-ro ha-si-get-seum-ni-kka,
bi-bim-naeng-myeon-eu-ro ha-si-get-seum-ni-kka?

Would you like to have naeng-myeon soup or hot-paste
naeng-myeon?

나는 물냉면이 좋겠네요.
na-neun mul-lang-myeon-i jo-ken-ne-yo.
Naeng-myeon soup sounds good to me. (*lit.* Naeng-myeon soup
　would be good for me.)

여기 물냉면 하나하고 비빔냉면 하나 빨리 좀 갖다 주세요.
yeo-gi mul-lang-myeon ha-na-ha-go bi-bim-naeng-myeon ha-na
　ppal-li jom gat-da ju-se-yo.
Please bring a naeng-myeon soup and a hot-paste naeng-myeon
　here quickly.

비빔냉면은 너무 맵지 않게 해 주세요.
bi-bim-naeng-myeon-eun neo-mu maep-ji an-ke hae ju-se-yo.
Please do not make the hot-paste naeng-myeon too spicy.

냉수하고 물수건도 좀 갖다 주세요.
naeng-su-ha-go mul-ssu-geon-do jom gat-da ju-se-yo.
Please give us some cold water and wet towels too.

금방 갖다 드릴게요.
geum-bang gat-da deu-ril-kke-yo.
I will bring it right away.

여기 냉면 나왔습니다.
yeo-gi naeng-myeon na-wat-seum-ni-da.
Here comes your naeng-myeon.

이 파전은 서비스로 드리는 거니까 맛있게 드세요.
i pa-jeon-eun sseo-bi-sseu-ro deu-ri-neun geo-ni-kka mas-it-ge
　deu-se-yo.
This scallion pancake is on the house, so please enjoy it.

잘 먹겠습니다.
jal meok-get-seum-ni-da.
We will enjoy it.

음식이 입에 맞으십니까?
eum-sig-i ib-e maj-eu-sim-ni-kka?
Did you like the food? (*lit.* The food fits your taste?)

정말 국물도 시원하고 참 맛있네요.
jeong-mal gung-mul-do si-won-ha-go cham mas-in-ne-yo.
The soup is very cool and nice, and quite delicious.

앞으로 자주 와야겠어요.
ap-eu-ro ja-ju wa-ya-gess-eo-yo.
I should come more often from now on.

그래서 저도 요즘 이 집 단골이 됐지 않습니까?
geu-rae-seo jeo-do yo-jeum i jip dan-gol-i dwaet-ji an-seum-ni-kka?
That's why I am a regular customer at this place, you know?

덕분에 잘 먹었습니다.
deok-bun-e jal meog-eot-seum-ni-da.
Thanks to you, I had a great meal.

다음 번엔 내가 사지요.
da-eum beon-en nae-ga sa-ji-yo.
I will treat you next time.

그럼 이제 일어날까요?
geu-reom i-je il-eo-nal-kka-yo?
Should we leave now?

여기 모두 얼마입니까?
yeo-gi mo-du eol-ma-im-ni-kka?
How much was that altogether here?

여기 있습니다.
yeo-gi it-seum-ni-da.
Here it is.

많이 파세요.

man-i pa-se-yo.

Do a lot of business. (*lit.* Sell a lot.)

또 오세요.

tto o-se-yo.

Come again please.

대화 Model Conversations

(1)

김현준: 안녕하세요, 박성민씨. 좋은 아침입니다.

an-nyeong-ha-se-yo, bak-seong-min-ssi. jo-eun
a-chim-im-ni-da.

박성민: 안녕하십니까, 김과장님. 일찍 나오셨네요.

an-nyeong-ha-sim-ni-kka, gim-gwa-jang-nim. il-jjik
na-o-syeon-ne-yo.

김현준: 네, 오늘은 이것 저것 일이 좀 많아서요. 그런데 성민
씨는 왜 벌써 나오셨어요?

ne, o-neul-eun i-geot jeo-geot il-i jom man-a-seo-
yo. geu-reon-de seong-min-ssi-neun wae beol-sseo
na-o-syeoss-eo-yo?

박성민: 오늘은 길이 별로 복잡하지 않아서 좀 일찍 도착했습
니다.

o-neul-eun gil-i byeol-lo bok-ja-pa-ji an-a-seo jom il-jjik
do-cha-kaet-seum-ni-da.

김현준: 그렇군요. 그럼 우리 일 시작하기 전에 같이 커피나
한잔 할까요?

geu-reo-kun-yo. geu-reom u-ri il si-ja-ka-gi jeon-e ga-chi
keo-pi-na han-jan hal-kka-yo?

박성민: 네, 좋습니다. 마침 저쪽에 음료수 자판기가 있네요.

ne, jot-seum-ni-da. ma-chim jeo-jjog-e eum-nyo-su ja-
pan-gi-ga in-ne-yo.

김현준: 나는 냉커피나 한잔 할까 하는데 성민씨는 뭘로 하시
겠어요?

na-neun naeng-keo-pi-na han-jan hal-kka ha-neun-de
seong-min-ssi-neun mwol-lo ha-si-gess-eo-yo?

박성민: 저도 냉커피로 하지요.

jeo-do naeng-keo-pi-ro ha-ji-yo.

(2)

김현준: 아이구, 벌써 점심시간이 다 됐군요. 오늘은 정말 시간이 빨리 가네요.

a-i-gu, beol-sseo jeom-sim-si-gan-i da dwaet-gun-yo.
o-neul-eun jeong-mal si-gan-i ppal-li ga-ne-yo.

박성민: 과장님, 회사 앞에 한식집이 새로 생겼는데 가 보셨습니까?

gwa-jang-nim, hoe-sa ap-e han-sik-jib-i sae-ro saeng-gyeon-neun-de gab o-syeot-seum-ni-kka?

김현준: 아니오, 아직 안 가 봤어요. 그 집은 뭘 잘 합니까?

a-ni-o, a-jik an ga bwass-eo-yo. gu jib-eun mwol jal ham-ni-kka?

박성민: 냉면도 잘 하고, 비빔밥도 맛있고, 비교적 다 괜찮습니다. 가게도 깨끗하고요.

naeng-myeon-do jal ha-go, bi-bim-ppap-do mas-it-go,
bi-gyo-jeok da gwaen-chan-sseum-ni-da.
ga-ge-do kkae-kkeu-ka-go-yo.

김현준: 그래요? 그럼 날씨도 더운데 오늘은 냉면이나 한 그릇 먹어 볼까요?

geu-rae-yo? geu-reom nal-ssi-do deo-un-de o-neul-eun
naeng-myeon-i-na han geu-reut meog-eo bol-kka-yo?

박성민: 그럼 같이 나가시죠. 오늘은 제가 모시겠습니다.

geu-reom ga-chi na-ga-si-jyo. o-neul-eun je-ga
mo-si-get-seum-ni-da.

(3)

주인: 어서 오세요.

eo-seo o-se-yo.

박성민: 아주머니, 안녕하세요? 장사 잘 되시지요?

a-ju-meo-ni, an-nyeong-ha-se-yo? jang-sa jal
doe-si-ji-yo?

주인: 아이구, 또 오셨네요. 어서 이리 들어오세요. 여기 선풍기 앞이 제일 시원해요.

a-i-gu, tto o-syeon-ne-yo. eo-seo i-ri deul-eo o-se-yo.
yeo-gi seon-pung-gi ap-i je-il si-won-hae-yo.

박성민: 오늘은 제가 우리 과장님도 모시고 왔으니까 특별히 더 잘 해 주셔야 됩니다.

o-neul-eun je-ga u-ri gwa-jang-nim-do mo-si-go wass-eu-ni-kka teuk-byeol-hi deo jal hae ju-syeo-ya doem-ni-da.

주인: 그럼요, 그런 건 걱정 마세요. 그런데 오늘은 뭘로 해 드릴까요?

geu-reom-yo, geu-reon geon geok-jeong ma-se-yo. geu-reon-de o-neul-eun mwol-lo hae deu-ril-kka-yo?

박성민: 과장님, 물냉면으로 하시겠습니까, 비빔냉면으로 하시겠습니까?

gwa-jang-nim, mul-laeng-myeon-eu-ro ha-si-gess-eum-ni-kka, bi-bim-naeng-myeon-eu-ro ha-si-gess-eum-ni-kka?

김현준: 글쎄요 ... 나는 물냉면이 좋겠네요.

geul-sse-yo... na-neun mul-laeng-myeon-i jo-ken-ne-yo.

박성민: 아주머니, 그럼 여기 물냉면 하나하고 비빔냉면 하나 빨리 좀 갖다 주세요.

a-ju-meo-ni, geu-reom yeo-gi mul-laeng-myeon ha-na-ha-go bi-bim-naeng-myeon ha-na ppal-li jom gat-da ju-se-yo.

비빔냉면은 너무 맵지 않게 해 주시고요, 냉수하고 물수건도 좀 갖다 주세요.

bi-bim-naeng-myeon-eun meo-mu maep-ji an-ke hae ju-si-go-yo, naeng-su-ha-go mul-ssu-geon-do jom gat-da ju-se-yo.

주인: 네, 알겠습니다. 금방 갖다 드릴게요.

ne, al-get-seum-ni-da. geum-bang gat-da deu-ril-kke-yo.

(4)
(잠시 후 jam-si hu)

주인: 여기 냉면 나왔습니다. 그리고 이 파전은 서비스로 드리는 거니까 맛있게 드세요.

yeo-gi naeng-myeon na-wass-eum-ni-da. geu-ri-go i pa-jeon-eun sseo-bi-sseu-ro deu-ri-neun geo-ni-kka mas-it-ge deu-se-yo.

박성민: 고맙습니다, 아주머니. 잘 먹겠습니다.
          go-map-seum-ni-da, a-ju-meo-ni. jal
          meok-get-seum-ni-da.

(식사 후 sik-sa hu)

박성민: 과장님, 음식이 입에 맞으십니까?
          gwa-jang-nim eum-sig-i ib-e maj-eu-sim-ni-kka?

김현준: 정말 국물도 시원하고 참 맛있네요. 앞으로 자주 와야
          겠어요.
          jeong-mal gung-mul-do si-won-ha-go cham mas-in-ne-
          yo. ap-eu-ro ja-ju wa-ya-gess-eo-yo.

박성민: 그래서 저도 요즘 이 집 단골이 됐지 않습니까?
          geu-rae-seo jeo-do yo-jeum i jip dan-gol-i dwaet-ji
          an-sseum-ni-kka?

김현준: 그렇군요. 덕분에 잘 먹었습니다. 다음 번엔 내가 사
          지요. 그럼 이제 일어날까요?
          geu-reo-kun-yo. deok-bun-e jal meog-eot-seum-ni-
          da. da-eum-ppeon-en ne-ga sa-ji-yo. geu-reom i-je
          il-eo-nal-kka-yo?

박성민: 그러시죠. 아주머니, 여기 모두 얼마입니까?
          geu-reo-si-jyo. a-ju-meo-ni, yeo-gi mo-du
          eol-ma-im-ni-kka?

주인: 잠깐만요 ... 만이천원이네요.
          jam-kkan-man-yo. man-i-cheon-won-i-ne-yo.

박성민: 여기 있습니다. 많이 파세요.
          Yeo-gi it-seum-ni-da. man-i pa-se-yo.

주인: 네, 안녕히 가세요. 또 오세요.
          ne, an-nyeong-hi ga-se-yo. tto o-se-yo.

영문번역 English Translation

(1)

Kim: Hello, Mr. Seong-Min Park. Good morning.

Park: Hello, manager Mr. Kim. You came out early.

Kim: Yes, I have quite a lot of work to do today. By the way, why did you come to work so early?

Park: There wasn't too much traffic today, so I arrived a little early.

Kim: I see. Then would you like to have a coffee with me before we start work?

Park: Yes, that sounds good. Luckily a drink vending machine is over there.

Kim: I would like to have a can of iced coffee, and what would you like to have?

Park: I would like to have iced coffee also.

(2)

Kim: Wow, it is already time for lunch. The time seems to be going by so fast today.

Park: Manager, a Korean restaurant has just opened in front of the office, and have you been there?

Kim: No, I have not been there yet. What kinds of dishes are good there?

Park: Naeng-myeon is good, bi-bim-bap is good, and all the foods are relatively good there. The restaurant is clean also.

Kim: Really? Then, since the weather is hot, shall we go to try some naeng-myeon today?

Park: Then let's go together. This is my treat today.

(3)

Owner: Welcome.

Park: Hello, ma'am. How are you? Your business is doing well, right?

Owner: Oh, you are here again. Please come this way. This, in front of the fan, is the coolest spot.

Park: Since I brought my manager with me today, please be especially nice.

Owner: Of course, don't worry about that. By the way, what would you like today?

Park: Sir, would you like naeng-myeon soup or hot-paste naeng-myeon?

Kim: Well . . . naeng-myeon soup sounds good to me.

Park: Ma'am, please bring us a naeng-myeon soup and a hot-paste naeng-myeon quickly. Please do not make the hot-paste naeng-myeon too spicy, and give us some cold water and wet towels too.

Owner: Sure. I will bring it right away.

(4)

(A bit later)

Owner: Here is your naeng-myeon. And this scallion pancake is on the house, so please enjoy it.

Park: Thank you, maam. We will enjoy it.

(After the meal)

Park: Manager, did you like the food?

Kim: The soup was really cool and nice, and very delicious. I should come more often.

Park: That's why I am a regular customer at this place, you know?

Kim: I see. Thanks to you, I had a great meal. I will treat you next time. Should we leave now?

Park: OK. Ma'am, how much was that altogether?

Owner: One moment . . . That will be twelve thousand won.

Park: Here it is. Do a lot of business.

Owner: Thank you. Good-bye. Come again.

어휘 Vocabulary

Nouns / Pronouns

가게 ga-ge	store, shop
과장님 gwa-jang-nim	department manager
국물 gung-mul	soup
길 gil	street, road
냉면 naeng-myeon	cold noodle
냉수 naeng-su	ice water
냉커피 naeng-keo-pi	iced coffee
다음 번 da-eum-beon	next time
단골 dan-gol	regular customer
만이천원 man-i-cheon-won	1200 won
많다 man-ta	to be many
물냉면 mul-laeng-myeon	cold noodle soup
물수건 mul-ssu-geon	wet towel
비빔냉면 bi-bim-naeng-myeon	cold noodle with hot paste
비빔밥 bi-bim-ppap	rice with mixed vegetable
서비스 sseo-bi-sseu	service
선풍기 seon-pung-gi	fan
시간 si-gan	time
식사 후 sik-sa hu	after a/the meal
아주머니 a-ju-meo-ni	middle-aged woman
앞 ap	front
여기 yeo-gi	here
오늘 o-neul	today
우리 u-ri	we, us
음료수 eum-nyo-su	drink
음식 eum-sik	food
이것 저것 i-geot jeo-geot	this and that
일 il	things, work
자판기 ja-pan-gi	banding machine
잠시 후 jam-si hu	after a while

장사 jang-sa	business
점심시간 jeom-sim-si-gan	lunch time
좋은 아침 jo-eun a-chim	good morning
주인 ju-in	owner
집 jip	house
커피 keo-pi	coffee
파전 pa-jeon	scallion pancake
하나 ha-na	one
한식집 han-sik-jip	Korean restaurant
회사 hoe-sa	company

Verbs

가 보다 ga bo-da	to have been
갖다 드리다 gat-da deu-ri-da	to bring or take something (*hon.*)
갖다 주다 gat-da ju-da	to bring or take something
괜찮다 gwaen-chan-ta	to be OK
깨끗하다 kkae-kkeu-ta-da	to be clean
나가다 na-ga-da	to go out
나오다 na-o-da	to come out
다 되다 da doe-da	to be all done
단골이 되다 dan-gol-i doe-da	to become a regular customer
덥다 deop-da	to be hot
도착하다 do-cha-ka-da	to arrive
드리다 deu-ri-da	to give (*hon.*)
들다 deul-da	to eat (*hon.*)
들어오다 deul-eo-o-da	to enter
맛있다 mass-it-da	to be tasty
먹다 meok-da	to eat
먹어 보다 meog-eo bo-da	to try to eat
모시고 오다 mo-si-go o-da	to bring someone (*hon.*)
모시다 mo-si-da	to take care (*hon.*)
복잡하다 bok-ja-pa-da	to be busy
사다 sa-da	to buy

생기다 saeng-gi-da	to open
시원하다 si-won-ha-da	to be cool
시작하다 si-ja-ka-da	to start
일어나다 il-eo-na-da	to get up
입에 맞다 ib-e mat-da	to fit someone's taste
있다 it-da	to exist
잘 되다 jal doe-da	to be going well
잘 먹다 jal meok-da	to eat well
잘 해 주다 jal hae ju-da	to give special care
팔다 pal-da	to sell

Adverbs / Conjunctions

같이 ga-chi	together
금방 geum-bang	soon
너무 neo-mu	too
덕분에 deok-bun-e	thanks to
또 tto	again
마침 ma-chim	just in time
맛있게 mas-it-ge	to be tasty
맵지 않게 maep-ji an-ke	to not be hot
모두 mo-du	all
벌써 beol-sseo	already
별로 byeol-lo	not particularly
비교적 bi-gyo-jeok	relatively
빨리 ppal-li	fast
새로 sae-ro	newly
아이구 a-i-gu	oh
아직 a-jik	yet
앞으로 ap-eu-ro	from now on
어서 eo-seo	quickly
얼마 eol-ma	how much?
왜 wae	why?
요즘 yo-jeum	these days

이리 i-ri	this way
이제 i-je	now
일찍 il-jjik	early
자주 ja-ju	often
잠깐만 jam-kkan-man	for a minute
정말 jeong-mal	really
제일 je-il	the most, the first
참 cham	really
특별히 teuk-byeol-hi	especially

문법 Grammar

(1) Coming and Going: 오다 *vs.* 가다

In Korean, a movement may be described differently depending on whether the motionis away from or towards the speaker. The direction determines whether to use a form of 오다 (*come*) or 가다 (*go*) to describe the motion.

Away from the speaker: 가다 (ga-da) to go
나가다 (na-ga-da) to go out
들어가다 (deul-eo-ga-da) to enter
올라가다 (ol-la-ga-da) to go up
내려가다 (nae-ryeo-ga-da) to go down

Towards the speaker: 오다 (o-da) to come
나오다 (na-o-da) to come out
들어오다 (deul-eo-o-da) to enter
올라오다 (ol-la-o-da) to come up
내려오다 (nae-ryeo-o-da) to come down

However, this rule does not apply when a speaker talks about his or her own action. Notice Jeong-Ho says지금 가요 (ji-geum ga-yo), not 지금 와요 (ji-geum wa-yo) in the following exchange:

Example:

A: 정호씨 왜 안 오세요?
(jeong-ho-ssi wae an o-se-yo?)
Jeong-Ho, why you do not come?

B: 지금 가요.
(ji-geum ga-yo.)
I am coming.

(2) Before and After: ~기 전에 (gi jeon-e) vs. ~고 나서 (go na-seo) and ~(으)ㄴ 다음에/후에 ((eu)n da-eum-e/hu-e)

The pattern [verb + ~기 전에 (gi jeon-e) indicates that the second action occurs before the first one is completed. As such, the first clause never uses the past tense. When a noun is used in place of a verb, add 전에 to the noun. For example:

휴가가 시작하기 전에... (hyu-ga-ga si-ja-ka-gi jeon-e)
Before the vacation starts...

휴가 시작 전에... (hyu-ga si-jak jeon-e)
Before the start of the vacation...

The pattern [verb + ~고 나서 (go na-seo) indicates that the first action has been completed and the second is forthcoming. It is never used with a descriptive verb stem and does not use a past tense marker. Expressions that can be used interchangeably are ~(은) 다음에, and, in written Korean,

휴가가 시작하고 나서... (hyu-ga-ga si-ja-ka-go na-seo)
After the vacation starts...

휴가가 시작한 다음에... (hyu-ga-ga si-ja-kan da-eum-e)
After the start of the vacation...

(3) Negation (the negative form of predicates)

To negate a predicate using short-form negative markers, place the negative adverb 안 (do not) or 못 (cannot) immediately before the predicate. The negative of the predicate 가요 (ga-yo) is 안 가요 (an ga-yo) and 못 가요 (mot ga-yo), the negative of 먹어요 (meog-eo-yo) is 안 먹어요 (an meog-eo-yo) and 못 먹어요 (mot meog-eo-yo), and the negative of 와요 (wa-yo) is 안 와요 (an wa-yo) and 못 와요 (mot wa-yo).

The word 못 (*cannot*) is used instead of 안 (*do not*) when one's circumstances do not permit the action of the verb.

To negate an action verb following the pattern of [noun] +하다, place 안 or 못 between the noun and the verb, as in:

전화 안 해요. (jeon-hwa an hae-yo.)
I do not call.

일 안 해요. (il an hae-yo.)
I do not work.

전화 못 해요. (jeon-hwa not hae-yo.)
I cannot call.

일 못 해요. (il mot hae-yo.)
I cannot work.

To negate a descriptive verb using the pattern of [noun] +하다, place 안 before the noun. Examples:

안 피곤해요. (an pi-gon-hae-yo.)
I am not tired.

안 착해요. (an cha-kae-yo.)
I am not kind/nice.

To use the more formal long-form negative marker often found in writing, add the endings ~지 않다 (ji an-ta) or ~지 못하다 (ji mo-ta-da) to the verb, e.g.

저는 가지 못해요. (jeo-neun ga-ji mo-tae-yo.)
I can't go.

저는 먹지 못해요. (jeo-neun meok-ji mo-tae-yo.)
I can't eat.

저는 가지 않아요. (jeo-neun ga-ji an-a-yo.)
I don't go.

저는 먹지 않아요. (jeo-neun meok-ji an-an-yo.)
I don't eat.

To indicate not to do something, use the ending ~지 마세요 (ji ma-se-yo), e.g.

커피 마시지 마세요. (keo-pi ma-si-ji ma-se-yo.)
Please don't drink coffee.

To express the idea of *Please don't do A; do B instead*, use the pattern ~지 말고 ... ~(으)세요 (ji aml-go ... (eu)-se-yo). For example:

커피 마시지 말고 물을 마시세요.
(keo-pi ma-si-ji mal-go mul-eul ma-si-se-yo.)
Please don't drink coffee; drink water instead.

There are verbs that have unique negative forms. Examples:

있다 vs. 없다	있어요 there is ...	없어요 there is not ...
it-da / eop-ta	iss-eo-yo	eops-eo-yo
이다 vs. 아니다	이에요 it is ...	아니에요 it is not ...
i-da / a-ni-da	i-e-yo	a-ni-e-yo
알다 vs. 모르다	알아요 I know ...	몰라요 I don't know ...
al-da / mo-reu-da	al-a-yo	mol-la-yo
좋다 vs. 싫다	좋아요 I like ...	싫어요 I don't like ...
jo-ta / sil-ta	jo-a-yo	sil-eo-yo

좋아하다 vs. 싫어하다   좋아해요 she/he likes ...   싫어해요 she/he doesn't like ...
jo-a-ha-da / sil-eo-ha-da   jo-a-hae-yo   sil-eo-hae-yo

(4) *"Doing something for someone"*: ~**아/어 주다** *(a/eo ju-da)* vs. ~**아/어 드리다** *(a/eo deu-ri-da)*

When the pattern ~아/어 주다 is used, it means that one is performing the action of the verb for the benefit of another person. The past tense is ~아/어 줬어요 (a/eo jwoss-eo-yo), and the future tense is ~아/어 줄 거예요 (a/eo jul kkeo-ye-yo).

읽어주다 (ilg-eo-ju-da)   to read for someone's benefit
놀아주다 (nol-a-ju-da)   to play for someone's benefit
빌려주다 (bil-lyeo-ju-da)   to lend for someone's benefit
도와주다 (do-wa-ju-da)   to help for someone's benefit

When requesting something for the benefit of the speaker, use ~아/어 주세요. This means, "Please do . . . for me." Examples:

좀 도와주세요. (jom do-wa ju-seyo.)
Please help me.

다시 한번 말씀해 주세요. (da-si han-beon mal-sseum-hae ju-se-yo.)
Please say that again for me

The pattern ~아/어 주셔서 감사합니다/고맙습니다 expresses gratitude for performing an action. The adverb 대단히, the equivalent of "very much," can be added before the equivalent of "thank you" for added emphasis.

The ending ~아/어 주셔서 감사합니다/고맙습니다 is used to express gratitude. The adverb 대단히 may be added. Examples:

도와 주셔서 (대단히) 감사합니다.
(do-wa ju-syeo-seo (dae-dan-hi) gam-sa-ham-ni-da.)
Thank you (very much) for helping me.

와 주셔서 고맙습니다. (wa ju-syeo-seo go-map-seum-ni-da.)
Thank you for coming.

The plain form of ~아/어 주다 is used with a person of lower social status or age. The humble form ~아/어 드리다 is used with someone of a higher social status or age.

~아/어 주다 *(plain)*:

친구가 점심을 사 주었습니다.
(chin-gu-ga jeom-sim-eul sa ju-eot-seum-ni-da.)
My friend bought me a lunch.

~아/어 주시다 *(subject honorific)*:

아버지께서 점심을 사 주셨습니다.
(a-beo-ji-kke-seo jeom-sim-eul sa ju-syeot-seum-ni-da.)
My father bought me a lunch.

~아/어 드리다 *(humble)*:

제가 아버지께 점심을 사 드렸습니다.
(je-ga a-beo-ji-kke jeom-sim-eul sa deu-ryeot-seum-ni-da.)
I bought a lunch for my father.

~아/어 드리시다 *(subject honorific & humble)*:

아버지께서 할머니께 점심을 사 드리셨습니다.
(a-beo-ji-kke-seo hal-meo-ni-kke jeom-sim-eul sa
    deu-ryeot-seum-ni-da.)
My father bought a lunch for my grandmother.

(5) "Have to, must": ~아/어야 되다 (a/eo-ya doe-da)

When indicating that one has to or must do something, the ending ~아/어야 되다 is used. Examples:

지금 가야 돼요. (ji-geum ga-ya dwae-yo.)
I have to go now.

조용히 해야 돼요. (jo-yong-hi hae-ya dwae-yo.)
We must be quiet.

(6) "Be thinking of ~ing" ~(으)ㄹ까 하다 ((eu)l-kka ha-da)

The construction of the verb stem + ~(으)ㄹ까 하다 is used to express a tentative thought about what one might do. The pattern means "I am/we are thinking of ~ing." Examples:

오늘은 피곤해서 일찍 잘까 해요.
(o-neul-eun pi-gon-hae-seo il-jjik jal-kka hae-yo.)
Since I am tired today, I am thinking of going to bed early.

저녁에 피자나 먹을까 해요.
(jeo-nyeog-e pi-ja-na meog-eul-kka hae-yo.)
I am thinking of having a pizza at dinner.

(7) Expressing experience: ~아/어 보다 (a/e obo-da)

The pattern ~아/어 보다 conveys that the action of the main verb indicates an experience, an attempt, or a suggestion that someone try something.

서울에 가 보셨어요? (seo-ul-e gab o-syeoss-eo-yo?)
Have you been in Korea?

아니오, 아직 안 가 봤어요. (a-ni-o, a-jik an ga bwass-eo-yo.)
No, I haven't yet.

그래요? 그러면 한번 가 보세요.
(geu-rae-yo? geu-reo-myeon han-beon gab o-se-yo.)
Really? Then please do/try it once.

(8) Bringing (someone or something) / Taking (someone or something)

It is important to know two things when deciding on the correct equivalent for *bring* and *take*. The first is whether what is being brought or taken is a person. The second, if it is a person, is to determine whether age and/or standing necessitates the more deferential term. First it should be determined. One uses 가지고 오다 (ga-ji-go o-da) or 가지고 가다 (ga-ji-da ga-da) for items, e.g.

공을 가지고 왔다. (gong-eul ga-ji-go wat-da.)
I brought the ball.

With younger people or those of lower status, one uses 데리고 오다 (de-ri-go o-da) or 데리고 가다 (de-ri-go ga-da), e.g.

동생을 데리고 왔다. (dong-saeng-eul de-ri-go wat-da.)
I brought my younger sibling.

With older people or those of higher status, one uses the honorific 모시고 오다 (mo-si-go o-da) or 모시고 가다 (mo-si-go ga-da), e.g.

부모님을 모시고 왔다. (bu-mo-nim-eul mo-si-go wat-da.)
I brought my parents.

참고학습 Further Study

Meals

아침 a-chim	breakfast
점심 jeom-sim	lunch
저녁 jeo-nyeok	dinner

아침을 먹다 a-chim-eul meok-da	to have breakfast
점심을 먹다 jeom-sim-eul meok-da	to have lunch
저녁을 먹다 jeo-nyeog-eul meok-da	to have dinner

Restaurants

양식 yang-sik	Western food
양식당 yang-sik-dang	Western restaurant
일식 il-ssik	Japanese food
일식당 il-ssik-dang	Japanese restaurant
중식 jung-sik	Chinese food
중식당 jung-sik-dang	Chinese restaurant
한식 han-sik	Korean food
한식당 han-sik-dang	Korean restaurant

손님 son-nim	customer
종업원 jong-eob-won	waiter, waitress
계산서 gye-san-seo	check, bill
거스름돈 geo-seu-reum-tton	change
음식 eum-sik	food
음료수 eum-nyo-su	beverage
메뉴 me-nyu	menu
자리 ja-ri	seat
주문하다 ju-mun-ha-da	to order
시키다 si-ki-da	to order

Tastes

싱겁다 sing-geop-da	to be blended
짜다 jja-da	to be salty
시다 si-da	to be sour
맵다 maep-da	to be spicy/hot
달다 dal-da	to be sweet
쓰다 tteu-da	to be tart

배가 부르다 bae-ga bu-reu-da	to be full
배가 고프다 bae-ga go-peu-da	to be hungry
목이 마르다 mog-i ma-reu-da	to be thirsty
맛이 있다 mas-i it-da	to be delicious
맛이 없다 mas-i eop-da	to not be delicious

Basics for Korean-style Dishes

밥 bap	cooked rice (usually steamed rice)
국 guk	soup
김치 gim-chi	kimchi
반찬 ban-chan	side dishes

Meat 고기 go-gi

소고기 so-go-gi	beef
닭고기 dak-go-gi	chicken
생선 saeng-seon	fish
돼지고기 dwae-ji-go-gi	pork

Drinks 마실 것/음료수 ma-sil-kkeot/eum-nyo-su

물 mul	water
커피 keo-pi	coffee

콜라 kol-la	cola
사이다 sa-i-da	7-Up
주스 ju-seu	juice
맥주 maek-ju	beer
소주 so-ju	soju
양주 yang-ju	Western liquor
포도주 po-do-ju	wine

문화적 참고사항 Cultural Note

A restaurant is sometimes called a 집 (jip), or *house*, especially when referring to the type of food in which it specializes. In most Korean restaurants, it is not necessary to wait to be seated. Feel free to seat oneself at any open table. Many restaurants post their menus on the wall. As such, one should wave or call the waitress over when one is ready to order. Middle-aged waitresses are referred to as 아줌마 (a-jum-ma). Along with the order, one receives several side dishes and a bowl of rice The rice is refilled at a nominal or no charge. When multiple people are eating together at one table, there will only be one bill unless individual bills are requested. This is because friends usually take turns paying for the whole meal. Although fine restaurants produce a bill stating the amount owed, most regular restaurants do not provide one.The customer is expected to pay at the counter on the way out. There is no sales tax and tipping is not customary. If you sit at a table with chairs, shoes are not removed. However, if one is seated on the floor, usually in a separate room, shoes must be removed.

Hotel restaurants are similar to American-style ones in that they do not follow many of these rules. Regular customers may even receive a delicacy as a side dish for free.

연습문제 Exercises

1. Please respond to the following:

(1) 우리 일 시작하기 전에 같이 커피나 한잔 할까요?
u-ri il si-ja-ka-gi jeon-e ga-chi keo-pi-na han-jan hal-kka-yo?

(2) 저는 커피 마실건데 your name씨는 뭘로 하시겠어요?
jeo-neun keo-pi ma-sil-kkeon-de _____ssi-neun mwol-lo
ha-si-gess-eo-yo?

(3) 회사 앞에 음식점이 새로 생겼는데 가 보셨어요?
hoe-sa ap-e eum-sik-jeom-i se-ro saeng-gyeon-neun-de ga
bo-syeoss-eo-yo?

(4) 오늘은 왜 이렇게 일찍 나오셨어요?
o-neul-eun wae i-reo-ke il-jjik na-o-syeoss-eo-yo?

(5) 오늘은 뭘 드시겠습니까?
o-neul-eun mwol deu-si-get-seum-ni-kka?

(6) 음식이 입에 맞으십니까?
eum-sig-i ib-e maj-eu-sim-ni-kka?

2. Please translate the following into English:

(1) 오늘은 정말 시간이 빨리 가네요.
o-neul-eun jeong-mal si-gan-i ppal-li ga-ne-yo.

(2) 비교적 음식이 다 괜찮습니다. 가게도 깨끗하고요.
bi-gyo-jeok eum-sig-i da gwaen-chan-seum-ni-da. ga-ge-do
kkae-kkeu-ta-go-yo.

(3) 오늘은 제가 모시겠습니다.
o-neul-eun je-ga mo-si-get-seum-ni-da.

(4) 오늘은 제가 손님도 모시고 왔으니까 특별히 더 잘 해 주셔
야 합니다.
o-neul-eun je-ga son-nim-do mo-si-go was-eu-ni-kka teuk-
byeol-hi deo jal hae ju-syeo-ya ham-ni-da.

(5) 여기 냉수하고 물수건도 좀 갖다 주세요.
yeo-gi naeng-su-ha-go mul-ssu-geon jom gat-da ju-se-yo.

(6) 그래서 저도 요즘 이 집 단골이 됐지 않습니까?
geu-rae-seo jeo-do yo-jeum i jip dan-gol-I dwaet-ji
an-seum-ni-kka?

3. Please translate the following into Korean:

(1) How much was that altogether?
(2) Do a lot of business.
(3) Thanks to you, I enjoyed the food.
(4) I will treat you next time.
(5) Your business is doing well, right?
(6) You came out early.

4. Please change the following sentences to the negative:

(1) 책상 위에 컴퓨터가 있어요. chaek-sang wi-e keop-pu-teo-ga
iss-eo-yo.
(2) 우리 아버지는 선생님이세요. u-ri a-beo-ji-neun
seon-saeng-nim-i-se-yo.
(3) 저는 한국어를 잘 알아요. jeo-neun han-gug-eo-reul jal
al-a-yo.
(4) 저는 한국음식을 좋아해요. jeo-neun han-gug-eum-sig-eul
jo-a-hae-yo.
(5) 제 여자친구는 아주 예뻐요. je yeo-ja-chin-gu-neun a-ju
ye-ppeo-yo.

5. Please write a paragraph describing your favorite food and how
to make it.

제9과 이발소와 미장원

◇◇◇◇◇◇◇◇

Lesson 9: Barbershops & Beauty Salons

표현 Patterns

어느 분 찾아 오셨어요?
eo-neu bun chaj-a o-syeoss-eo-yo?
Are you looking for anybody? (*lit.* How are you looking for?)

아무 분이나 괜찮아요.
a-mu bun-i-na gwaen-chan-a-yo.
Any one is fine.

파마 하실 건가요?
pa-ma ha-sil kken-ga-yo?
Are you going to get a perm for your hair?

저는 파마 할 거고요, 오빠는 커트만 할 건데요.
jeo-neun pa-ma hal kkeo-go-yo, o-ppa-neun keo-teu-man hal
　　kkeon-de-yo.
I am going to get a perm, and my brother is just getting a haircut.

얼마나 기다려야 돼요?
eol-ma-na gi-da-ryeo-ya dwae-yo?
How long do we have to wait?

한 15분만 기다리시면 될 것 같은데요.
han sib-o-bun-man gi-da-ri-si-myeon doel kkeot gat-eun-de-yo.
About 15 minutes. (*lit.* It seems to be done if you wait only about
　　15 minutes.)

저쪽에 앉아서 잠깐만 기다리세요.
jeo-jjog-e anj-a-seo jam-kkan-man gi-da-ri-se-yo.
Please sit over there and wait a little.

기다리시는 동안 뭐 마실 것 좀 갖다 드릴까요?
gi-da-ri-si-neun dong-an mwo ma-sil kkeot jom gat-da
   deu-ril-kka-yo?
Would you like something to drink while you are waiting?

저는 커피 한잔 주시겠어요?
jeo-neun keo-pi han-jan ju-si-gess-eo-yo?
Would you please give me a cup of coffee?

저는 괜찮아요.
jeo-neun gwaen-chan-a-yo.
I am fine.

그냥 찬물이나 한잔 주세요.
geu-nyang chan-mul-i-na han-jan ju-se-yo.
Just give me a cup of cold water, please.

여기 커피하고 물 있습니다.
yeo-gi keo-pi-ha-go mul it-seum-ni-da.
Here is your coffee and your water.

기다리시는 동안 이 잡지 좀 보시겠어요?
gi-da-ri-si-neun dong-an i jap-ji jom bo-si-gess-eo-yo?
Would you like to look at these magazines while you are waiting?

손님, 이쪽으로 앉으세요.
son-nim, i-jjog-eu-ro anj-eu-se-yo.
Please sit here, ma'am (*lit.* customer).

머리 어떻게 해 드릴까요?
meo-ri eo-tteo-ke hae deu-ril-kka-yo?
How would you like your hair done? (*lit.* How would you like for
  me to do your hair?)

스트레이트 파마 하려고 하는데요.
seu-teu-re-i-teu pa-ma ha-ryeo-go ha-neun-de-yo.
I would like (*lit.* am trying) to get my hair straightened
(*lit.* straight perm).

머리 길이는 자르지 마시고요.
meo-ri gil-i-neun ja-reu-ji ma-si-go-yo.
Don't cut the hair (*lit.* hair length), please.

제가 보기에는 앞머리 길이에 맞춰서 옆머리도 레이어를 좀 주
는 게 더 나을 것 같은데요.
je-ga bo-gi-e-neun ap-meo-ri gil-i-e- mat-chwo-seo yeop-meo-ri-do
le-i-eo-reul jom ju-neun ge deo na-eul kkeot gat-eun-de-yo.
The way I look at it, layering (*lit.* giving some layer on) your side
hair by matching it with the length of your bangs would be
much better.

머리 숱이 많아서 레이어가 없으면 너무 답답해 보일 것 같아요.
meo-ri su-chi man-a-seo le-i-eo-ga eops-eu-myeon neo-mu dap-da-
pae bo-il kkeot gat-a-yo.
Your hair is pretty thick, so it will look stuffy without the layering.

그럼 그렇게 해 주세요.
geu-reom geu-reo-ke hae ju-se-yo.
Then please do it that way.

머리색깔이 너무 까마니까 염색 한번 해 보세요.
meo-ri saek-kkal-i neo-mu kka-ma-ni-kka yeom-saek han-beon hae
bo-se-yo.
Your hair color is quite (*lit.* too) dark, so try tinting your hair.

그럼 인상이 훨씬 부드러워 보여요.
geu-reom in-sang-i hwol-ssin bu-deu-reo-wo bo-yeo-yo.
Then your face (will) look softer.

머리를 염색하면 어떻게 손질해야 돼요?

meo-ri-reul yeom-sae-ka-myeon eo-tteo-ke son-jil-hae-ya dwae-yo?

After tinting my hair, how should I take care of it?

머리 감고 나서 수건으로 잘 말린 다음에 헤어 크림만 조금 발
　라 주시면 돼요.

meo-ri gam-kko na-seo su-geon-eu-ro jal mal-lin da-eum-e he-eo-
　keu-rim-man jo-geum bal-la ju-si-myeon dwae-yo.

After washing your hair, dry it well with a towel, and put a little
　hair cream on it.

머리 결이 많이 상하니까 드라이는 안 하시는 게 낫고요.

meo-ri kkyeol-i man-i sang-ha-ni-kka deu-ra-i-neun an ha-si-neun
　ge nat-go-yo.

Because your hair will be damaged, it is better not to blow-dry
　the hair.

그럼 알아서 해 주세요.

geu-reom al-a-seo hae ju-se-yo.

Then please do what you think would look good (on me).

저한테 잘 어울리게 예쁘게 해 주세요.

jeo-han-te jal eo-il-li-ge ye-ppeu-ge hae ju-se-yo.

Please do it so it would look good on me. (*lit.* Please do it pretty
　and match well with me.)

어떻게 잘라 드릴까요?

eo-tteo-ke jal-la deu-ril-kka-yo?

How would you like your hair cut?

머리 모양은 바꾸지 마시고 그냥 좀 짧게 다듬어 주세요.

meo-ri mo-yang-eun ba-kku-ji ma-si-go geu-nyang jom jjalp-ge
　da-deum-eo ju-se-yo.

Don't change the shape of the hair and just trim it so it's a little
　shorter.

뒷머리하고 옆머리는 좀 짧게 깎고 앞머리는 너무 짧지 않게 해
　주세요.
dwin-meo-ri-ha-go yeom-meo-ri-neun jom jjalp-ge kkak-go
　　am-meo-ri-neun neo-mu jjalp-ji an-ke hae ju-se-yo.
Please cut the hair on the back and on the sides a little shorter, but
　do not cut the front hair too short.

머리가 많이 기네요.
meo-ri-ga man-i gi-ne-yo.
Your hair is pretty long.

언제 머리 자르셨어요?
eon-je meo-ri ja-reu-syeoss-eo-yo?
When was the last time you had your hair cut? (*lit.* When did you
　have a haircut?)

두 달 밖에 안 됐는데 그래요.
du-dal bakk-e an dwaen-neun-de geu-rae-yo.
It has been only two months.

머리가 남들보다 빨리 자라나봐요.
meo-ri-ga nam-deul-bo-da ppal-li ja-ra-na-bwa-yo.
I guess my hair grows faster than other people's.

어떠세요? 마음에 드세요?
eo-tteo-se-yo? ma-eum-e deu-se-yo?
How is it? Do you like it?

괜찮은 것 같은데요.
gwaen-chan-eun geot gat-eun-de-yo.
It looks fine.

그럼 이쪽으로 오세요. 머리 감아 드릴게요.
geu-reom i-jjog-eu-ro o-se-yo. meo-ri gam-a deu-ril-kke-yo.
Then come over here, please. I will wash your hair.

다 됐습니다. 두분 다 수고 많이 하셨습니다.

da dwaet-seum-ni-da. du-bun da su-go man-i ha-syeot-seum-ni-da.

It's all done. You both had a lot of work done (*lit.* went through a
   lot of work).

대화 Model Conversations

(1)

종업원: 어서 오세요, 손님. 어느 분 찾아 오셨어요?

eo-seo o-se-yo, son-nim.eo-neu bun chaj-a
o-syeoss-eo-yo?

이혜근: 아무 분이나 괜찮아요.

a-mu bun-i-na gwaen-chan-a-yo.

종업원: 파마 하실 건가요?

pa-ma ha-sil kkeon-ga-yo?

이혜근: 네, 저는 파마 할 거고요, 오빠는 커트만 할 건데요. 얼
마나 기다려야 돼요?

ne, jeo-neun pa-ma hal kkeo-go-yo, o-ppa-neun keo-teu-
man hal kkeon-de-yo. eol-ma-na gi-da-ryeo-ya dwae-yo?

종업원: 한 15분만 기다리시면 될 것 같은데요. 저쪽에 앉아서
잠깐만 기다리세요.

han sib-o-bun-man gi-da-ri-si-myeon doel kket gat-eun-
de-yo. jeo-jjog-e anj-a-seo jam-kkan-man gi-da-ri-se-yo.
기다리시는 동안 뭐 마실 것 좀 갖다 드릴까요?

gi-da-ri-si-neun dong-an mwo ma-sil kkeot jom gat-da
deu-ril-kka-yo?

이혜근: 네, 그럼 저는 커피 한잔 주시겠어요?

ne, geu-reom jeo-neun keo-pi han-jan ju-si-gess-eo-yo?

이정호: 저는 괜찮아요. 그냥 찬물이나 한잔 주세요.

jeo-neun gwaen-chan-a-yo. geu-nyang chan-mul-i-na
han-jan ju-se-yo.

종업원: (잠시 후) 여기 커피하고 물 있습니다. 기다리시는 동
안 이 잡지 좀 보시겠어요?

(jam-si- hu) yeo-gi keo-pi-ha-go mul it-seum-ni-da.
gi-da-ri-si-neun dong-an i jap-ji jom bo-si-gess-eo-yo?
이혜근: 네, 고맙습니다.

ne, go-map-seum-ni-da.

(2)

미용사: 손님, 이쪽으로 앉으세요. 머리 어떻게 해 드릴까요?
son-nim, i-jjog-eu-ro anj-eu-seoyo. meo-ri eo-tteo-ke hae
deu-ril-kka-yo?

이혜근: 스트레이트 파마 하려고 하는데요. 머리 길이는 자르
지 마시고요.
seu-teu-re-i-teu pa-ma ha-ryeo-go ha-neun-de-yo. meo-ri
gil-i-neun jja-reu-ji ma-si-go-yo.

미용사: 제가 보기에는 앞머리 길이에 맞춰서 옆머리도 레이
어를 좀 주는 게 더 나을 것 같은데요.
jeo-ga bo-gi-e-neun ap-meo-ri gil-i-e mat-chwo-seo
yeop-meo-ri-do le-i-eo-reul jom ju-neun ge deo na-eul
kkeot gat-eun-de-yo.
머리 숱이 많아서 레이어가 없으면 너무 답답해 보일
것 같아요.
meo-ri su-chi man-a-seo le-i-eo-ga eops-eu-myeon
neo-mu dap-da-pae bo-il kket gat-a-yo.

이혜근: 그럼 그렇게 해 주세요.
geu-reom geu-reo-ke hae ju-se-yo.

미용사: 그리고 머리색깔이 너무 까마니까 염색 한번 해 보세
요. 그럼 인상이 훨씬 부드러워 보여요.
geu-ri-go meo-ri-saek-kkal-I neo-mu kka-ma-ni-kka
yeom-saek han-beonhae bo-se-yo. geu-reom in-sang-i
hwol-ssin bu-deu-reo-wo bo-yeo-yo.

이혜근: 그래요? 그런데 머리를 염색하면 어떻게 손질해야
돼요?
geu-rae-yo? geu-reon-de meo-ri-reul yeom-sae-ka-myeon
eo-tteo-ke son-jil-hae-ya dwae-yo?

미용사: 똑 같아요. 머리 감고 나서 수건으로 잘 말린 다음에
헤어크림만 조금 발라 주시면 돼요.
ttok gat-a-yo. meo-ri gam-go na-seo su-geon-eu-ro jal
mal-lin da-eum-e he-eo-keu-rim-man jo-geum bal-la
ju-si-myeon dwae-yo.

머리 결이 많이 상하니까 드라이는 안 하시는 게
낫고요.
meo-ri kkyeol-i man-i sang-ha-ni-kka deu-ra-i-neun an
ha-si-neun ge nat-go-yo.

이혜근: 그럼 알아서 저한테 잘 어울리게 예쁘게 해 주세요.
geu-reom al-a-seo jeo-han-te jal eo-ul-li-ge ye-ppeu-ge
hae ju-se-yo.

(3)

미용사: 오빠도 이쪽으로 앉으세요. 어떻게 잘라 드릴까요?
o-ppa-do i-jjog-eu-ro anj-eu-se-yo. eo-tteo-ke jal-la
deu-ril-kka-yo?

이정호: 머리 모양은 바꾸지 마시고 그냥 좀 짧게 다듬어
주세요.
meo-ri mo-yang-eun ba-kku-ji ma-si-go geu-nyang jom
jjalp-ge da-deum-eo ju-se-yo.
뒷머리하고 옆머리는 좀 짧게 깎고 앞머리는 너무 짧
지 않게 해 주세요.
dwin-meo-ri-ha-go yeom-meo-ri-neun jom jjalp-ge kkak-
go am-meo-ri-neun neo-mu jjalp-gi an-ke hae ju-se-yo.

미용사: 알겠습니다. 어휴... 머리가 많이 기네요. 언제 머리
자르셨어요?
al-get-seum-ni-da. eo-hyu. Meo-ri-ga man-i gi-ne-yo.
eon-je meo-ri jja-reu-syeoss-eo-yo?

이정호: 두 달밖에 안 됐는데 그래요. 머리가 남들보다 빨리
자라나봐요.
du dal-bakk-e an dwaen-neun-de geu-rae-yo. meo-ri-ga
nam-deul-bo-da ppal-li ja-ra-na-bwa-yo.

미용사: (잠시 후) 어떠세요? 마음에 드세요?
(jam-si hu) eo-tteo-se-yo? ma-eum-e deu-se-yo?

이정호: 네, 괜찮은 것 같은데요.
ne, gwaen-chan-eun geot gat-eun-de-yo.

미용사: 그럼 이쪽으로 오세요. 머리 감아 드릴게요.
geu-reom i-jjog-eu-ro o-se-yo. meo-ri gam-a
deu-ril-kke-yo.
(잠시 후) 다 됐습니다. 두분 다 수고 많이 하셨습니다.
안녕히 가세요.
(jam-si hu) da dwaet-seum-ni-da. du-bun da su-go man-i
ha-syeoss-eum-ni-da. an-nyeong-hi ga-se-yo.

영문번역 English Translation

(1)

Employee: Please come in , ma'am (*lit.* customer). Are you looking for anybody?

Hye-Geun: Anyone is fine.

Employee: Are you going to have your hair permed?

Hye-Geun: Yes, I am going to get a perm, and my brother is just getting a haircut. How long do we have to wait?

Employee: About 15 minutes will do. Please sit over there and wait a little. Would you like something to drink while you are waiting?

Hye-Geun: Yes, then would you give me a cup of coffee?

Jeong-Ho: I am fine. Just give me a cup of water, please.

(after a while)

Employee: Here is your coffee and your water. Would you like to look at some magazines while you are waiting?

Hye-Geun: Yes, thank you.

(2)

Hairdresser: Come sit here please, ma'am. How would you like your hair done?

Hye-Geun: I would like to get my hair straightened. Don't cut the hair, please.

Hairdresser: The way I look at it, layering the side hair by matching it with the length of your bangs will be much better. Your hair is pretty thick, so without the layering, it will look stuffy.

Hye-Geun: Then do it that way.

Hairdresser: Also your hair is quite dark, so let's try tinting your hair. Then your face will look softer.

Hye-Geun: Really? But after the tinting, how do I take care of it?

Hairdresser:	The same. After washing your hair, dry it well with a towel, and rub a little hair cream on it. Because your hair will be damaged, it is better not to blow-dry the hair.
Hye-Geun:	Then do what you think would look good on me.

(3)

Hairdresser:	Sir (*lit.* Brother), come sit here, please. How would you like your hair cut?
Jeong-Ho:	Don't change the shape of the hair and just trim it a little. Please cut the hair on the back and on the sides a little shorter, but do not cut the front hair too much.
Hairdresser:	I understand. Whew... Your hair is pretty long. When was the last time you had your hair cut?
Jeong-Ho:	It has been only two months. I guess my hair grows faster than other people's.

(after a while)

Hairdresser:	How is it? Do you like it?
Jeong-Ho:	Yes, it looks fine.
Hairdresser:	Then come over here, please. I will wash your hair.

(after a while)

Hairdresser:	It's all done. You both had a lot of work done. Good-bye.

어휘 Vocabulary

Nouns / Pronouns

길이 gil-i	length
남들 nam-deul	other people
두 달 du-dal	two months
두 분 du-bun	two people (*hon.*)
뒷머리 dwin-meo-ri	back hair
드라이 deu-ra-i	blow dry
레이어 le-i-eo	layer
마실 것 ma-sil kkeot	something to drink
머리 meo-ri	head, hair
머리 결 meo-ri kkyeol	hair quality
머리 숱 meo-ri sut	hair volume, hair density
머리색깔 meo-ri-saek-kkal	hair color
모양 mo-yang	shape
물 mul	water
뭐 mwo	what, something
손님 son-nim	customer
수건 su-geon	towel
스트레이트 파마 seu-teu-re-i-teu pa-ma	hair straightening (*lit.* straight perm)
아무 분 a-mu bun	anyone
앞머리 am-meo-ri	front hair
어느 분 eo-neu-bun	which person
여기 yeo-gi	here
염색 yeom-saek	dying
옆머리 yeom-meo-ri	side hair
인상 in-sang	facial impression
잡지 jap-ji	magazine
종업원 jong-eop-won	employee
찬물 chan-mul	cold water
커피 keo-pi	coffee

한 15분 han sib-o-bun	about 15 minutes
한번 han-beon	once
한잔 han jan	one cup
헤어 크림 he-eo keu-rim	hair cream

Verbs

갖다 드리다 gat-da deu-ri-da	to bring something (*hon.*)
고맙다 go-map-da	to thank
괜찮다 gwaen-chan-ta	to be OK, to be good
기다리다 gi-da-ri-da	to wait
길다 gil-da	to be long
까맣다 kka-ma-ta	to be black
깎다 kkak-da	to have a haircut
다 되다 da doe-da	to be all done
다듬어 주다 da-deum-eo ju-da	to trim
답답해 보이다 dap-dap-hae bo-i-da	to look heavy
똑 같다 ttok gat-da	to be same
레이어를 주다 le-i-eo-reul ju-da	to layer
마음에 들다 ma-eum-e deul-da	to like
많다 man-ta	to be many
말리다 mal-li-da	to dry
맞추다 mat-chu-da	to fit, to set, to adjust
머리 감다 meo-ri gam-tta	to wash hair
바꾸다 ba-kku-da	to change, to switch
발라 주다 bal-la ju-da	to put on
부드럽다 bu-deu-reop-da	to be soft
부드러워 보이다 bu-deu-reo-wo bo-i-da	to look soft
상하다 sang-ha-da	to be damaged
손질하다 son-jil-ha-da	to take care
수고하다 su-go-ha-da	to work hard
앉다 an-tta	to sit
알다 al-da	to know

알아서 하다 al-a-seo ha-da	to do (what someone thinks is) right
없다 op-da	to not exist
염색하다 yeom-sae-ka-da	to dye
자라다 ja-ra-da	to grow
자르다 ja-reu-da	to have cut, to cut
잘라 드리다 jal-la deu-ri-da	to cut something for someone (*hon.*)
짧다 jjalp-da	to be short
찾아 오다 chaj-a o-da	to come to see
커트 하다 keo-teu-ha-da	to have a haircut
파마 하다 pa-ma-ha-da	to have a perm

Adverbs / Conjunctions

그냥 geu-nyang	just
그런데 geu-reon-de	by the way
그렇게 geu-reo-ke	like that
그리고 geu-ri-go	and
너무 neo-mu	too
다음에 da-eum-e	next time
빨리 ppal-li	fast
알아서 al-a-seo	as (someone thinks is) right/good
어떠세요? eo-tteo-se-yo	How is it?
어떻게 eo-tteo-ke	how/somehow
어서 eo-seo	quickly, please
어울리게 eo-ul-li-ge	match well
어휴.... eo-hyu	wow....
언제 eon-je	when/sometime
얼마나 eol-ma-na	how long/much/many
예쁘게 ye-ppeu-ge	pretty, beautifully
잘 jal	well
잠깐만 jam-kkan-man	for a minute

잠시 후 jam-si hu	after a while
제가 보기에는 je-ga bo-gi-e-neun	in my point of view
조금 jo-geum	a little
짧게 jjalp-ge	short, shortly
훨씬 hwol-ssin	much more

문법 Grammar

(1) Causative Verbs

A causative verb is used when one thing or person *causes* another person or thing to do something. They are derived from more general verbs, using one of seven suffixes. Theseare ~이 (i), ~히 (hi), ~리 (li), ~기 (gi), ~우 (u), ~구 (gu), and 추 (chu). One must memorize the verbs that can become causatives and the corresponding suffixes.

Verb	Causative Derivation	Sample Sentence
먹다	먹이다	엄마가 아기한테 우유를 먹여요.
meok-da	meog-i-da	eom-ma-ga a-gi-han-te u-yu-reul meog-yeo-yo
to eat	to feed someone	Mom is feeding the baby.
죽다	죽이다	제가 파리를 죽였어요.
juk-da	jug-i-da	je-ga pa-ri-reul jug-yeoss-eo-yo
to die	to kill	I killed the fly.
끓다	끓이다	라면을 먹으려고 물을 끓여요.
kkeul-ta	kkeul-i-da	ra-myeon-eul meog-eu-ryeo-go mul-eul kkeul-yeo-yo
to boil	to boil something	I'm boiling water to cook ramen.
입다	입히다	엄마가 아기한테 옷을 입혀요.
ip-da	i-pi-da	eom-ma-ga a-gi-han-te os-eul i-pyeo-yo
to wear	to dress someone	Mom is dressing the baby.

눕다	눕히다	엄마가 아기를 침대에 눕혀요.
nup-da	nu-pi-da	eom-ma-ga a-gi-reul chim-dae-e nu-pyeo-yo
to lie down	to lay someone down	Mom is laying the baby down on the bed.

앉다	앉히다	엄마가 아기를 의자에 앉혀요.
an-tta	an-chi-da	eom-ma-ga a-gi-reul ui-ja-e an-chyeo-yo
to sit	to seat someone	Mom is seating the baby on the chair.

울다	울리다	형이 동생을 울려요.
ul-da	ul-li-da	hyeong-i dong-saeng-eul ul-lyeo-yo
to cry	to make someone cry	The older brother makes his younger sibling cry.

얼다	얼리다	물을 얼려서 얼음을 만들어요.
eol-da	eol-li-da	mul-eul eol-lyeo-seo eol-eum-eul man-deul-eo-yo
to freeze	to freeze something	You can freeze water to make ice.

벗다	벗기다	엄마가 아기 옷을 벗겨요.
beot-da	beot-gi-da	eom-ma-ga a-gi os-eul beot-geo-yo
to take off	to undress someone	Mom is undressing the baby.

웃다 웃기다 형이 동생을 웃겨요.

ut-da ut-gi-da hyeong-i dong-saeng-eul
ut-gyeo-yo

to laugh to make someone laugh The older brother makes his
younger sibling laugh.

신다 신기다 엄마가 아기한테 신발을 신
겨요.

sin-tta sin-gi-da eom-ma-ga a-gi-han-te sin-
bal-eul sin-gyeo-yo

to wear to put shoes on someone Mom is putting shoes on the
baby.

자다 재우다 엄마가 아기를 침대에
재워요.

ja-da jae-u-da eom-ma-ga a-gi-reul chim-
dae-e jae-wo-yo

to sleep to make someone sleep Mom is putting the baby to
sleep on the bed.

타다 태우다 실수로 생선을 태웠어요.

ta-da tae-u-da sil-su-ro saeng-seon-eul
tae-woss-eo-yo

to burn to burn something I burned the fish by mistake.

깨다 깨우다 엄마가 아침에 아이를
깨워요.

kkae-da kkae-u-da eom-ma-ga a-chim-e a-i-reul
kkae-wo-yo

to wake to wake someone up Mom is waking up the baby in
the morning.

낮다	낮추다	의자가 너무 높으니까 조금 낮춰 주세요.
nat-da	nat-chu-da	ui-ja-ga neo-mu nop-eu-ni-kka jo-geum nat-chwo ju-se-yo
to be low	to make something low	This chair is too high, so please make it a little lower.

맞다	맞추다	길이가 잘 안 맞으니까 좀 맞춰 주세요.
mat-da	mat-chu-da	gil-i-ga jal an maj-eu-ni-kka jom mat-chwo ju-se-yo
to fit	to make something fit	The length does not fit, so please make it fit.

(2) "It seems, it looks like...": ~(으)ㄴ/~는/~(으)ㄹ 것 같다 ((eu)n/neun/(eu)l geot gat-da)

The pattern ~(으)ㄴ/는/(으)ㄹ 것 같다 conveys that something seems or looks like something else. It is common to use this pattern as an indirect, polite expression even when the similarity is obvious.

	Active Verb	**Descriptive Verb**
Past:	~(으)ㄴ 것 같다 (eu)n geot gat-da	~았/었던 것 같다 at/eot-deon geot gat-da
	잔 것 같아요 jan geot ga-ta-yo	예뻤던 것 같아요 ye-ppeot-deon geot ga-ta-yo
	it seems he slept	it seems she was pretty

Present: ~는 것 같다   ~(으)ㄴ 것 같다
       neun geot gat-da   (eu)n geot gat-da

       자는 것 같아요   예쁜 것 같아요
       ja-neun geot ga-ta-yo   ye-ppeun geot ga-ta-yo
       it seems he is sleeping   it seems she is pretty

Future: ~(으)ㄹ 것 같다   ~(으)ㄹ 것 같다
       (eu)l geot gat-da   (eu)l geot gat-da

       잘 것 같아요   예쁠 것 같아요
       jal geot ga-ta-yo   ye-ppeul geot ga-ta-yo
       it seems he is going to sleep it seems she will be pretty

One only uses ~같다 after a noun, e.g.

저기가 영화관 같아요.
(jeo-gi-ga yeong-hwa-gwan gat-a-yo)
It looks that one over there is a movie theater.

저분이 김선생님 같아요.
(jeo-bun-i gim-seon-saeng-nim gat-a-yo)
That person looks like Mr. Kim.

(3) Sentence Conjunctions and Clause Connectives

Sentence conjunctions and clause connectives share a close relationship, as detailed below.

그리고	and	아파트가 조용해요. 그리고 깨끗해요.
geu-ri-go		a-pa-teu-ga jo-yong-hae-yo geu-ri-go kkae-kkeu-tae-yo

아파트가 조용하고 깨끗해요.

a-pa-teu-ga jo-yong-hae-yo
  kkae-kkeu-tae-yo

The apartment is quiet and clean.

그래서	so	아파트가 멀어요. 그래서 버스 타고 와요.
geu-rae-seo		a-pa-teu-ga meol-eo-yo geu-rae-seo beo-seu ta-go wa-yo

아파트가 멀어서 버스(를) 타고 와요.

a-pa-teu-ga meol-eo-yo beo-seu ta-go
  wa-yo

The apartment is far so I took the bus.

그런데	but	아파트가 조용해요. 그런데 안 깨끗 해요.
geu-reon-de		a-pa-teu-ga jo-yong-hae-yo geu-reon-de an kkae-kkeu-tae-yo

아파트가 조용한데 안 깨끗해요.

a-pa-teu-ga jo-yong-hae-yo an
  kkae-kkeu-tae-yo

The apartment is quiet but not clean.

그렇지만	but	아파트가 조용해요. 그렇지만 안 깨 끗해요.
geu-reo-chi-man		a-pa-teu-ga jo-yong-hae-yo geu-reo-chi-man an kkae-kkeu-tae-yo

아파트가 조용하지만 안 깨끗해요.

a-pa-teu-ga jo-yong-hae-yo geu-reo-
  chi-man an kkae-kkeu-tae-yo

The apartment is quiet. However, it is
  not clean.

그러면	if then	아파트가 좋아요. 그러면 비싸요.
geu-reo-myeon		a-pa-teu-ga jo-a-yo. geu-reo-myeon bi-ssa-yo
		아파트가 좋으면 비싸요.
		a-pa-teu-ga jo-a-yo bi-ssa-yo
		If the apartment is good, the price is high.

(4) "To make or have someone or something…": ~게 하다 (ge ha-da)

The pattern ~게 하다 indicates that a person is deliberately putting someone or something in a new situation or making someone do something, e.g.

선생님이 학생들을 공부하게 했어요.
seon-saeng-nim-i hak-saeng-deul-eul gong-bu-ha-ge haess-eo-yo.
The teacher made the students study.

The pattern ~게 해 주세요 (ge hae ju-se-yo) frames this sort of statement as a polite request. Examples:

머리를 예쁘게 해 주세요.
meo-ri-reul ye-ppeu-ge hae ju-se-yo.
Please make my hair pretty.

아이들이 못 들어오게 해 주세요.
a-i-deul-i mot deul-eo-o-ge hae ju-se-yo.
Please do not let the children come in.

(5) "Someone or something appears or looks…": ~**아/어 보 이다** *(a/e obo-i-da)*

The pattern of adescriptive verb followed by the ending ~아/어 보 이다 is used to state an opinion about the appearance of somebody or something. It literally means a person or object appears or looks like something. The speaker does not claim that the statement is objectively true.

머리가 너무 무거워 보여요.
(meo-ri-ga neo-mu mu-geo-wo bo-yeo-yo.)
The hair looks too heavy.

아파 보여요.
(a-pa bo-yeo-yo.)
You look sick.

(6) 아무 *Noun* (이) 나 *(a-mu …(i)-na)* "any Noun"

The word 아무, followed by a noun (이)나 means "any [noun]." It indicates that no matter what the noun is, it makes no difference. When the noun refers to a person, it is usually omitted, as in 아무 나 (a-mu-na) "anyone." Some useful expressions: 아무 거나 (a-mu geo-na) "whatever it may be" or "anything," 아무 데나 (a-mu de-na) "wherever" or "anywhere," and 아무 때나 (a-mu ttae-na) "whenever" or "anytime."

참고학습 Further Study

Style

짧은 머리 jjalb-eun meo-ri	short hair
긴 머리 gin meo-ri	long hair
가는 머리 ga-neun meo-ri	thin hair
굵은 머리 gulg-eun meo-ri	thick hair
곱슬머리 gop-seul meo-ri	curly hair
뻣뻣한 머리 ppeot-ppeo-tan meo-ri	thick hair
부드러운 머리 bu-deu-reo-un meo-ri	soft hair
대머리 dae-meo-ri	bald
파마머리 pa-ma meo-ri	permanent-wave hair
단발머리 dan-bal meo-ri	shoulder-length hair
스트레이트 파마 seu-teu-re-i-teu pa-ma	hair straightening
굵은 파마 gulg-eun pa-ma	perm with large rolls
미용사 mi-yong-sa, 헤어 디자이너 he-eo di-ja-i-neo	woman's hairdresser
이발사 i-bal-ssa	man's hairdresser
머리를 감다 meo-ri-reul gam-tta	to shampoo
머리를 깎다 meo-ri-reul kkak-da	to have a haircut (*for men*)
머리를 다듬다 meo-ri-reul da-deum-tta	to trim hair
머리를 말리다 meo-ri-reul mal-li-da	to have a towel-dry
머리를 빗다 meo-ri-reul bit-da	to brush hair
머리를 자르다 meo-ri-reul ja-reu-da	to have a haircut (*for women*)

머리를 헹구다 meo-ri-reul heng-gu-da — to rinse, to wash out

드라이하다 deu-ra-i-ha-da — to have a blow-dry

린스 하다 rin-seu ha-da — to rinse out, to wash out

무스/젤
→ 젤을 바르다 mu-sseu/jel-li-reul ba-reu-da — to put on hair mousse/gel

샴푸하다 syam-pu-ha-da — to shampoo

스프레이를 하다
→ 스프레이를 뿌리다 seu-peu-re-i-reul ha-da — to put on hair spray

염색하다 yeom-sae-ka-da — to dye/tint

파마하다 pa-ma-ha-da — to have a permanent

문화적 참고사항 Cultural Note

Reservations are not required for a barbershop or beauty salon. Even without a reservation one will be quickly served. While waiting, some shops provide one with tea or a soft drink free of charge. Only men go to barbershops, with more expensive places providing shaves and a massage in addition to haircuts. There are both male and female barbers. Hair salons have traditionally been used only by women, but now younger men also go there for haircuts, permanents, and other services. An older man will usually go to a barbershop. Younger men prefer hair salons to barbershops since haircuts at salons are more stylish. Tipping in either place is not required. Permanents are very popular with women of all ages, and having some or all of one's hair tinted is not uncommon. Hair fashions change rapidly in Korea, and these changes are quite noticeable as fashion is important to a large portion of the population.

연습문제 Exercises

1. Please respond to the following:

(1) 어서 오세요. 어느 분 찾아 오셨어요?

  eo-seo o-se-yo. eo-neu bun chaj-a o-syeoss-eo-yo?

(2) 기다리시는 동안 뭐 마실 것 좀 갖다 드릴까요?

  gi-da-ri-si-neun dong-an mwo ma-sil kkeot jom gat-da
  deu-ril-kka-yo?

(3) 머리 어떻게 해 드릴까요?

  meo-ri eo-tteo-ke hae deu-ril-kka-yo?

(4) 머리가 많이 기네요. 언제 머리 자르셨어요?

  meo-ri-ga man-i gi-ne-yo. eon-je meo-ri ja-reu-syeoss-eo-yo?

(5) 다 됐습니다. 어떠세요? 마음에 드세요?

  da dwaet-seum-ni-da eo-tteo-se-yo? ma-eum-e deu-se-yo?

2. Please translate the following into English:

(1) 기다리시는 동안 이 잡지 좀 보시겠어요?

  gi-da-ri-si-neun dong-an i jap-ji jom bo-si-gess-eo-yo?

(2) 머리 숱이 많아서 레이어가 없으면 좀 답답해 보일 것
  같아요.

  meo-ri su-chi man-a-seo le-i-eo-ga eops-eu-myeon jom sap-da-
  hae bo-il kkeot gat-a-yo.

(3) 머리 색깔이 너무 까마니까 염색 한번 해 보세요.

  meo-ri saek-kkal-i neo-nu kka-ma-ni-kka yeom-saek han-beon
  hae bo-se-yo.

(4) 머리 모양은 바꾸지 마시고 그냥 짧게 좀 다듬어 주세요.

  meo-ri mo-yang-eun ba-kku-ji ma-si-go geu-nyang jjalp-ge jom
  da-deum-eo ju-se-yo.

(5) 머리가 남들보다 빨리 자라나봐요.

  meo-ri nam-deul-bo-da ppal-li ja-ra-na-bwa-yo.

3. Please fill in the blanks with appropriate causative verbs:

(1) 실수로 생선을 (타다:). sil-su-ro saeng-seon-eul
tae-woss-eo-yo

(2) 라면을 먹으려고 물을 (끓다:). ra-myeon-eul meog-
eu-ryeo-go mul-eul kkeul-yeo-yo

(3) 형이 동생을 (울다:). hyeong-i dong-saeng-eul
ul-lyeo-yo

(4) 엄마가 아기 옷을 (벗다:). eom-ma-ga a-gi os-eul
beot-geo-yo

(5) 엄마가 아기한테 옷을 (입다:). eom-ma-ga a-gi-han-
te os-eul i-pyeo-yo

(6) 의자가 너무 높으니까 조금 (낮다:).
ui-ja-ga neo-mu nop-eu-ni-kka jo-geum nat-chwo ju-se-yo

(7) 엄마가 아기를 침대에 (자다:). eom-ma-ga a-gi-reul
chim-dae-e jae-wo-yo

4. Please fill in the blanks with the appropriate conjunction.

(그렇지만, 그런데, 그러면 (그럼), 그리고, 그래서)

A: 어디 가세요?
B: 내일이 여자친구 생일이에요. (1)_____ 선물 사러 백화
점에 가요.
A: 그러세요? (2)_____ 지난 주말에는 어떻게 지내셨어요?
B: 토요일에는 친구하고 영화를 봤어요. (3)_____ 일요
일에는 교회에 갔어요.
A: 아, 그러셨군요. (4)_____ 요즘 어떻게 지내세요?
B: 요즘은 일이 좀 적어요. (5)_____ 좀 한가해요.
A: 그러세요? (6)_____ 시간 있으실 때 저하고 같이 테니
스 치실래요?
B: 좋지요. (7)_____ 요즘은 제가 몸이 별로 안 좋으니까 다
음 주가 좋겠는데요.

5. Please write a paragraph describing your experience in a barber-shop or a beauty salon.

제10과 교통

◇◇◇◇◇◇◇

Lesson 10: Transportation

표현 Patterns

어디까지 가십니까?
eo-di-kka-ji ga-sim-ni-kka?
Where would you like to go?

대학로까지 좀 부탁합니다.
dae-hang-no-kka-ji jom bu-ta-kam-ni-da.
To the college's street, please.

죄송하지만 합승 좀 해도 되겠습니까?
joe-song-ha-ji-man hap-seung jom hae-do doe-get-seum-ni-kka?
I'm sorry, but would it be OK if I take another passenger?

길이 많이 막히네요.
gil-i man-i ma-ki-ne-yo.
All the roads are congested.

서울 시내는 언제나 이래요.
seo-ul si-nae-neun eon-je-na i-rae-yo.
This is quite typical on the streets in Seoul. (*lit.* In downtown Seoul, the traffic is always just like this.)

그래도 주중이 주말보다 좀 낫지 않아요?
geu-rae-do ju-jung-i ju-mal-bo-da jom nat-ji an-a-yo?
But don't you think traffic is a lot smoother during weekdays than on the weekends?

큰일 났네요. 약속시간에 늦었는데...
keun-il nan-ne-yo. yak-sok-si-gan-e neuj-eon-neun-de...
I have a problem (*lit.* I am in trouble.) I am late for a meeting...

거의 다 왔는데 어디 세워 드릴까요?
geo-i da wan-neun-de eo-di se-wo deu-ril-kka-yo?
(We are) almost there, and where can I drop you off?

저기 육교 밑에 세워 주세요.

jeo-gi yuk-gyo mit-e se-wo ju-se-yo.

Please drop me off under the overpass over there.

요금은 9,600원 나왔습니다.

yo-geum-eun gu-cheon-yuk-baeg-won na-wat-seum-ni-da.

The fare comes out to 9600 won.

여기 10,000원이요. 잔돈은 그냥 가지세요.

yeo-gi man-won-i-yo. jan-don-eun geu-nyang ga-ji-se-yo.

Here is 10,000 won. Please keep the change.

여권하고 비행기표 좀 주시겠습니까?

yeo-kkwon-ha-go bi-haeng-gi-pyo jom ju-si-get-seum-ni-kka?

May I have your passport and plane ticket?

여기 있습니다.

yeo-gi it-seum-ni-da.

Here they are.

짐은 몇 개나 부치실 겁니까?

jim-eun myeot gae-na bu-chi-sil kkeom-ni-kka?

How many pieces of luggage will you being taking (*lit.* shipping)?

두 개요. 그리고 이건 가지고 타도 되죠?

du-gae-yo. geu-ri-go i-geon ga-ji-go ta-do doe-jyo?

Just two. And I can take this one on board with me, right?

두 개까지 괜찮습니다.

du-gae-kka-ji gwaen-chan-seum-ni-da.

You may take up to two pieces of luggage with you. (*lit.* Up to two, it's OK.)

좌석은 어느 쪽으로 드릴까요?
jwa-seog-eun eo-neu jjog-eu-ro deu-ril-kka-yo?
With the seat, which side do you prefer? (*lit.* Which side of seat
    should I give you?)

창측으로 주세요.
chang-cheug-eu-ro ju-se-yo.
A window seat, please.

혹시 더 필요한 게 있으십니까?
hok-si deo pil-yo-ha-sin ge iss-eu-sim-ni-kka?
Is there anything more I can do for you? (*lit.* Are there any more
    things you need?)

이 카드에 마일리지 좀 넣어 주시겠어요?
i ka-deu-e ma-il-li-ji jom neo-eo ju-si-gess-eo-yo?
Can you please add my mileage (for this flight) onto this card?

이리 주십시오.
i-ri ju-sip-si-o.
May I have your card, please? (*lit.* Please give it to me.)

여기 손님 여권하고 보딩패스 있습니다.
yeo-gi son-nim yeo-kkwon-ha-go bo-ding-pae-sseu it-seum-ni-da.
Here are your passport and boarding pass.

게이트는 38번이고 좌석번호는 27A입니다.
ge-i-teu-neun sam-sip-pal-beon-i-go jwa-seok-beon-ho-neun
    i-sep-chil-e-i-im-ni-da.
The gate number is 38 and your seat number is 27A.

즐거운 여행 되십시오.
jeul-geo-un yeo-haeng doe-sim-si-o.
Have a pleasant flight.

부산행12시 30분 표 두 장만 주세요.
bu-san-haeng yeol-ttu-si sam-sip-bun pyo du-jang-man ju-se-yo.
Please give me two tickets for the train that departs at 12:30
    to Pusan.

두 장이요. 20,000원입니다.
du-jang-i-yo. i-man-won-im-ni-da.
Two tickets. That comes to 20,000 won.

12시 30분에 출발하면 몇 시에 부산에 도착하나요?
yeol-ttu-si sam-sip-bun-e chul-bal-ha-myeon myeot-si-e
    bu-san-e do-cha-ka-na-yo?
If the train leaves at 12:30, what time will it arrive in Pusan?

보통 5시간 정도 걸려요.
bo-tong da-seot-si-gan jeong-do geol-lyeo-yo.
It usually takes about 5 hours.

기차 타는 데가 어디죠?
gi-cha ta-neun de-ga eo-di-jyo?
Where can I go to board the train? (*lit.* Where is the place to board
    the train?)

저기 건너편 첫 번째 플랫폼에 '부산행'이라고 써 있지요?
jeo-gi geon-neo-pyeon cheot-beon-jjae peul-laet-pom-e
    bu-san-haeng-i-ra-go sseo it-ji-yo?
You see the first platform across the track where a sign says
    "To Pusan," right?

그 쪽에 가서 기다리세요.
geu-jjog-e ga-seo gi-da-ri-se-yo.
Please go there and wait.

중간에 기차를 갈아타야 되나요, 아니면 바로 가나요?

jung-gan-e gi-cha-reul gal-a-ta-ya doe-na-yo, a-ni-myeon ba-ro
  ga-na-yo?

Do I have to change trains, or would this train take me directly
  there? (*lit.* Would I have to transfer trains or would this train go
  there directly?)

직행이니까 갈아타지 않으셔도 돼요.

ji-kaeng-i-ni-kka gal-a-ta-ji an-eu-syeo-do dwae-yo.

This train will take you directly there, so you will not need to
  change trains. (*lit.* Since this train goes there directly, you don't
  need to transfer.)

대화 Model Conversations

(1) 택시 타기 taek-si-ta-gi

기사: 어디까지 가십니까?
eo-di-kka-ji ga-sim-ni-kka?

이정호: 대학로까지 좀 부탁합니다.
dae-hang-no-kka-ji jom bu-ta-kam-ni-da.

기사: 알겠습니다. 그런데 죄송하지만 합승 좀 해도 되겠습
니까?
al-get-seum-ni-da. geu-reon-de joe-song-ha-ji-man
hap-seung jom hae-do doe-get-seum-ni-kka?

이정호: 네, 괜찮아요. 그러세요. 그런데 길이 많이 막히네요.
ne, gwaen-chan-a-yo. geu-reo-se-yo. geu-reon-de gil-i
man-i ma-ki-ne-yo.

기사: 서울 시내는 언제나 이래요. 그래도 주중이 주말보다
좀 낫지 않아요?
seo-ul si-nae-neun eon-je-na i-rae-yo. geu-rae-do
ju-jung-i ju-mal-bo-da jom nat-ji an-a-yo?

이정호: 큰일 났네요. 약속시간에 늦었는데...
keun-il nan-ne-yo. yak-sok-si-gan-e neuj-eon-neun-de.

기사: (잠시 후) 거의 다 왔는데 어디 세워 드릴까요?
(jam-si hu) geo-ui da wan-neun-de eo-di se-wo
deu-ril-kka-yo?

이정호: 저기 육교 밑에 세워 주세요.
jeo-gi yuk-gyo mit-e se-wo ju-se-yo.

기사: 요금은 9,600원 나왔습니다.
yo-geum-eun gu-cheon-yuk-baeg-won
na-wat-seum-ni-da.

이정호: 여기 10,000원이요. 잔돈은 그냥 가지세요.
yeo-gi man-won-i-yo. jan-don-eun geu-nyang ga-ji-se-yo.

기사: 고맙습니다. 안녕히 가세요.
      go-map-seum-ni-da. an-nyeong-hi ga-se-yo.

(2) 비행기 타기 bi-haeng-gi ta-gi

직원: 어서 오십시오. 여권하고 비행기표 좀 주시겠습니까?
      eo-seo o-sip-si-o. yeo-kkwon-ha-go bi-haeng-gi-pyo jom
      ju-si-get-seum-ni-kka?

이정호: 여기 있습니다.
       yeo-gi iss-eum-ni-da.

직원: 짐은 몇 개나 부치실 겁니까?
      jim-eun myeot gae-na bu-chi-sil kkeom-ni-kka?

이정호: 두 개요. 그리고 이건 가지고 타도 되죠?
       du-gae-yo. geu-ri-go i-geon ga-ji-go ta-do doe-jyo?

직원: 네. 두 개까지 괜찮습니다. 좌석은 어느 쪽으로 드릴
      까요?
      ne. du-gae-kka-ji gwaen-chan-seum-ni-da. jwa-seog-eun
      eo-neu jjog-eu-ro deu-ril-kka-yo?

이정호: 창측으로 주세요.
       chang-cheug-eu-ro ju-se-yo.

직원: 혹시 더 필요한 게 있으십니까?
      hok-si deo pil-yo-han ge iss-eu-sim-ni-kka?

이정호: 이 카드에 마일리지 좀 넣어 주시겠어요?
       i ka-deu-e ma-il-li-ji jom neo-eo ju-si-gess-eo-yo?

직원: 네, 이리 주십시오. (잠시 후) 여기 손님 여권하고 보딩
      패스 있습니다
      ne, i-ri ju-sip-si-o. (jam-si hu) yeo-gi son-nim yeo-
      kkwon-ha-go bo-ding-pae-sseu it-seum-ni-da.

      게이트는 38번이고 좌석번호는 27A입니다. 즐거운
      여행 되십시오.
      ge-i-teu-neun sam-sip-pal-beon-i-go jwa-seok-beon-
      ho-neun i-sip-chil-e-i-im-ni-da. jeul-geo-un yeo-haeng
      doe-sip-si-o.

이정호: 감사합니다.
      gam-sa-ham-ni-da.

(3) 기차/고속버스 타기gi-cha/go-sok-ppeo-sseu ta-gi

이정호: 부산행12시 30분 표 두 장만 주세요.
      bu-san-haeng yeol-ttu-si sam-sip-bun pyo du-jang-man
      ju-se-yo.

직원: 두 장이요. 20,000원입니다.
      du-jang-i-yo. i-man-won-im-ni-da.

이정호: 12시 30분에 출발하면 몇 시에 부산에 도착하나요?
      yeol-ttu-si sam-sip-bun-e chul-bal-ha-myeon myeot si-e
      bu-san-e do-cha-ka-na-yo?

직원: 보통 5시간 정도 걸려요.
      bo-tong da-seot-si-gan jeong-do geol-lyeo-yo.

이정호: 그런데 기차 타는 데가 어디죠?
      geu-reon-de gi-cha ta-neun de-ga eo-di-jyo?

직원: 저기 건너편 첫 번째 플랫폼에 '부산행'이라고 써 있
      지요? 그 쪽에 가서 기다리세요.
      jeo-gi geon-neo-pyeon cheot-beon-jjae peul-laet-pom-
      e bu-san-haeng-i-ra-go sseo it-ji-yo? geu-jjog-e ga-seo
      gi-da-ri-se-yo.

이정호: 중간에 기차를 갈아타야 되나요, 아니면 바로 가나요?
      jung-gan-e gi-cha-reul gal-a-ta-ya doe-na-yo, a-ni-myeon
      ba-ro ga-na-yo?

직원: 직행이니까 갈아타지 않으셔도 돼요.
      ji-kaeng-i-ni-kka gal-a-ta-ji an-eu-syeo-do dwae-yo.

영문번역 English Translation

(1) Riding a taxi

Driver:	Where would you like to go, sir?
Lee:	To the college's street, please.
Driver:	OK. I'm sorry, but would it be OK if I take another passenger?
Lee:	Sure, it's OK. Please do. It seems like all the roads are congested.
Driver:	This is quite typical on the streets in Seoul. But don't you think traffic is a lot smoother during the weekdays than on the weekends?
Lee:	I have a problem. I am late for a meeting…

(after a while)

Driver:	We are almost there, and where can I drop you off?
Lee:	Please drop me off under the overpass over there.
Driver:	The cab fare comes to 9600 won.
Lee:	Here is 10,000 won. Please keep the change.
Driver:	Thank you. Good-bye.

(2) Riding an airplane

Employee:	Welcome. May I have your passport and plane ticket?
Lee:	Here they are.
Employee:	How many pieces of luggage will you being taking?
Lee:	Just two. And I can take this one on board with me, right?
Employee:	Sure. You may take up to two pieces of luggage with you. With the seat, which side do you prefer?
Lee:	A window seat, please.
Employee:	Is there anything more I can do for you?
Lee:	Can you please add my mileage for this flight onto my card?

Employee: Sure. May I have your card please? *(after a while)*
Here are your passport and boarding pass. The gate
number is 38 and your seat number is 27A. Hope you
have a pleasant flight.

Lee: Thank you.

(3) Riding a train/express bus

Lee: May I get two tickets for the train that departs at 12:30
to Pusan?

Employee: Two tickets. That comes to 20,000 won.

Lee: If the train leaves at 12:30, what time should I expect
to arrive in Pusan?

Employee: It usually takes about 5 hours.

Lee: By the way, where do I go to board the train?

Employee: Do you see the first platform across the track where a
sign says "To Pusan"? Please go there and wait.

Lee: Do I have to make a change trains, or does this train
take me directly to Pusan?

Employee: This train will take you directly to Pusan, so you will
not need to change trains.

어휘 **Vocabulary**

Nouns / Pronouns

건너편 geon-neo-pyeon	across the street
게이트 ge-i-teu	gate
고속버스 go-sok-beo-seu	express bus
그 쪽 geu jjok	that side
기사 gi-sa	driver
기차 gi-cha	train
길 gil	street, road
대학로 dae-hang-no	university street
두 개 du-gae	two items
두 장 du-jang	two sheets of paper
마일리지 ma-il-li-ji	mileage
몇 개 myeot-gae	how many items?
몇 시 myeot-si	what time?
밑 mit	under, beneath
보딩패스 bo-ding-pae-sseu	boarding pass
부산 bu-san	Pusan
부산행 bu-san-haeng	going to Pusan
비행기 bi-haeng-gi	airplane
비행기표 bi-haeng-gi-pyo	airplane ticket
서울 seo-ul	Seoul
손님 son-nim	guest, visitor, customer
시내 si-nae	downtown
약속시간 yak-sok-si-gan	appointment time
어느 쪽 eo-neu jjok	which way?
어디 eo-di	where?
여권 yeo-kkwon	passport
여기 yeo-gi	here
여행 yeo-haeng	travel
요금 yo-geum	fare
육교 yuk-gyo	over pass

잔돈 jan-don	change
저기 jeo-gi	there
좌석 jwa-seok	seat
좌석번호 jwa-seok-beon-ho	seat number
주중 ju-jung	weekdays
주말 ju-mal	weekend
직원 jig-won	employee
직행 jik-haeng	non-stop, direct
짐 jim	baggage
창측 chang-cheuk	window side
첫번째 cheot-beon-jjae	first
카드 ka-deu	card
타기 ta-gi	riding
타는 데 ta-neun de	place to ride
택시 taek-si	taxi
표 pyo	ticket
플랫폼 peul-laet-pom	platform
필요한 것 pil-yo-han geot	things to be needed
10,000원 sim-man-won	10,000 won
12시 30분 yeol-ttu-si sam-sip-bun	12:30 pm
20,000원 i- sim-man-won	20,000 won
38번 sam-sip-pal-beon	the number 38
5시간 da-seot-si-gan	5 hours
9,600원 gu-cheon-yuk-baeg-won	9,600 won

Verbs

가다 ga-da	to go
가지고 타다 ga-ji-go ta-da	to ride having something
가지다 ga-ji-da	to have
갈아타다 gal-a-ta-da	to transfer
걸리다 geol-li-da	to take time
괜찮다 gwaen-chan-ta	to be OK
그러다 geu-reo-da	to do so

기다리다 gi-da-ri-da | to wait
나오다 na-o-da | to come out
낫다 nat-da | to be better
넣어 주다 neo-eo ju-da | to put on something (*for someone*)

늦다 neut-da | to be late
도착하다 do-cha-ka-da | to arrive
되다 doe-da | to become
드리다 deu-ri-da | to give (*hon.*)
막히다 ma-ki-da | to be blocked, to be jammed

바로 가다 ba-ro ga-da | to go directly
부치다 bu-chi-da | to send
부탁하다 bu-ta-ka-da | to request
세워 드리다 se-wo deu-ri-da | to stop (*hon.*)
세워 주다 se-wo ju-da | to stop
써 있다 sseo it-da | to be written
알다 al-da | to know
오다 o-da | to come
죄송하다 joe-song-ha-da | to be sorry
주다 ju-da | to give
즐겁다 jeul-geop-da | to be happy
출발하다 chul-bal-ha-da | to depart
큰일 나다 keun-il na-da | to have a problem, to have trouble

타다 ta-da | to ride
합승 하다 hap-seung-ha-da | to share a ride

Adverbs / Conjunctions

거의 geo-ui | almost
그냥 geu-nyang | just
그래도 geu-rae-do | although, even though
보통 bo-tong | in general

아니면 a-ni-myeon	if not
어서 eo-seo	quickly
언제나 eon-je-na	always
잠시 후 jam-si hu	after a while
좀 jom	a little, please
중간에 jung-gan-e	in the middle, on the way
혹시 hok-si	just in case

문법 Grammar

(1) Ordinal Numbers

	Native ordinal numbers	Sino-Korean ordinal numbers
1st	첫째 cheot-jjae, 첫 번째 cheot-beon-jjae	제 일 회 je-il-hoe
2nd	둘째 dul-jjae, 두 번째 du-beon-jjae	제 이 회 je-i-hoe
3rd	셋째 set-jjae, 세 번째 se-beon-jjae	제 삼 회 je-sam-hoe
4th	넷째 net-jjae, 네 번째 ne-beon-jjae	제 사 회 je-sa-hoe
5th	다섯째 da-seot-jjae, 다섯 번째vda-seot-beon-jjae	제 오 회 je-o-hoe
6th	여섯째 yeo-seot-jjae, 여섯 번째 yeo-seot-beon-jjae	제 육 회 je-yu-koe
7th	일곱째 il-gop-jjae, 일곱 번째 il-gop-beon-jjae	제 칠 회 je-chil-hoe
8th	여덟째 yeo-deol-jjae, 여덟 번째 yeo-deol-ppeon-jjae	제 팔 회 je-pal-hoe
9th	아홉째 a-hop-jjae, 아홉 번째 a-hop-beon-jjae	제 구 회 je-gu-hoe
10th	열째 yeol-jjae, 열 번째 yeol-ppeon-jjae	제 십 회 je-si-poe
11th	열한 번째 yeol-han-beon-jjae	제 십일 회 je-sib-il-hoe
12th	열두 번째 yeol-ttu-beon-jjae	제 십이 회 je-sib-il-hoe
13th	열네 번째 yeol-sse-beon-jjae	제 십삼 회 je-sip-sam-hoe
14th	열네 번째 yeol-le-beon-jjae	제 십사 회 je-sip-sa-hoe
15th	열다섯 번째 yeol-tta-seot-beon-jjae	제 십오 회 je-sib-o-hoe
16th	열여섯 번째 yeol-lyeo-seot-beon-jjae	제 십육 회 je-sim-nyu-koe
17th	열일곱 번째 yeol-lil-gop-beon-jjae	제 십칠 회 je-sip-chil-hoe
18th	열여덟 번째 yeol-lyeo-deol-ppeon-jjae	제 십팔 회 je-sip-pal-hoe
19th	열아홉 번째 yeol-a-hop-beon-jjae	제 십구 회 je-sip-gu-hoe
20th	스무 번째 seu-mu-beon-jjae	제 이십 회 je-i-si-poe
21st	스물 한 번째 seu-mul-han-beon-jjae	제 이십일 회 je-i-sib-il-hoe
22nd	스물 두 번째 seu-mul-ttu-beon-jjae	제 이십이 회 je-i-sib-i-hoe
29th	스물 아홉 번째 seu-mul-a-hop-beon-jjae	제 이십구 회 je-i-sip-gu-hoe
30th	서른 번째 seo-reun-beon-jjae	제 삼십 회 je-sam-si-poe
40th	마흔 번째 ma-heun-beon-jjae	제 사십 회 je-sa-si-poe
50th	쉰 번째 swin-beon-jjae	제 오십 회 je-o-si-poe
60th	예순 번째 ye-sun-beon-jjae	제 육십 회 je-yuk-si-poe
70th	일흔 번째 il-heun-beon-jjae	제 칠십 회 je-chil-si-poe
80th	여든 번째 yeo-deun-beon-jjae	제 팔십 회 je-pal-si-poe
90th	아흔 번째 a-heun-beon-jjae	제 구십 회 je-gu-si-poe
100th	백 번째 baek-beon-jjae	제 백 회 je-bae-koe
which	몇 째 myeot-jjae, 몇 번째 myeot-beon-jjae	몇 회 myeo-toe

(2) Compound Sentences: ~아/어서 (a/eo-seo) vs. ~고 (go)

The ending ~아/어서 is used to connect two action or event clauses describing an action or event. The clauses are in chronological order, with the first always a precondition or cause of the second. The verb in the first clause cannot use the past tense, and the subject of the two clauses must be the same.

친구를 만나서 영화를 봤어요.
chin-gu-reul man-na-seo yeong-hwa-reul bwass-eo-yo.
I met my friend and then we went to see a movie.

When listing unrelated events, the ending ~고 is used. For example:

친구를 만나고 영화를 봤어요.
chin-gu-reul man-na-go yeong-hwa-reul bwass-eo-yo.
I met my friend, and I went to see a movie.

(3) State of Being: ~아/어 있다 (a/eo it-da)

The pattern ~아/어 있다 means "in the state of being." It describes the continuation of a state after a result has been had. The focus is on the current state and not on the action that led to the result. Examples:

상자 안에 사과가 들어 있다.
sang-ja an-e sa-gwa-ga deul-eo it-da.
Apples are in the box.

정호는 한국에 가 있어요.
jeong-ho-neun han-gug-e ga iss-eo-yo.
Jung-Ho is in Korea.

The use of this ending contrasts with the use of ~고 있다, which indicates that a person or thing is in the midst of a process, e.g. 정호는 지금 한국에 가고 있어요. (jeong-ho-neun ji-geum han-gug-e ga-go iss-eo-yo) "Jeong-Ho is now going to Korea."

(4) Background Information: ~(았/었)는데 ((at/eot)-neun-de)

To supply background information about the situation in the main clause, the ending ~는데 is used. It occurs in the following circumstances: whenthe speaker and listener are sharing information; when two clauses are contrasted; and when a request or proposal is justified. There are alternative forms. The ending ~는데 is used with an active verb stem ending in 있/없, or ~았/었~. The ending ~(으)ㄴ데 is used with a descriptive verb stem. With a copula stem, the ending ~ㄴ데 is used. In the past tense, ~았/었 is placed before ~는데.

(5) Expressing Surprise, Admiration, or Sympathy: ~네요 (ne-yo)

The ending ~네요indicates an exclamation. It is heard when the speaker hears something that contradicts their knowledge of a matter. The ending may be used in any tense, but it must always occur in a declarative sentence. It differs from the ending ~아/어요, which indicates a neutral reaction.

(6) Rhetorical Questions: ~지 않아요? (ji an-a-yo?)

The long form of the negative, or ~지 않아요?, can be used as a rhetorical question. Using a negative question is a more polite way of stating a belief or an opinion. If the listener agrees, the response begins with네 (ne), as in this exchange:

요즘 날씨가 정말 춥지 않아요?
yo-jeum nal-ssi-ga jeong-mal chup-ji an-a-yo?
Isn't the weather these days really cold?

네, 정말 그렇네요.

ne, jeong-mal geu-reon-ne-yo.

Yes, it really is.

The words 맞아요 (maj-a-yo) and 그래요 (geu-rae-yo) may also be used to begin the sentence.

If the listener disagrees with the speaker, the appropriate response is 아니오 (a-ni-o). If the listener is uncertain, he or she responds with 글쎄요 (geul-sse-yo).

참고학습 Further Study

(1) Means of Transportation

고속버스 go-sok-ppeo-seu	express bus
기차 gi-cha	train
렌트카 ren-teu-ka	rental car
배 bae	boat, ship
버스 beo-seu	bus
비행기 bi-haeng-gi	airplane
오토바이 o-to-ba-i	motorcycle
자동차 ja-dong-cha/자가용 ja-ga-yong	car (*personal*)
자전거 ja-jeon-geo	bike
지하철 ji-ha-cheol	subway
택시 taek-si	taxi
걸어서 geol-eo-seo	on foot, by walking
뛰어서 ttwi-eo-seo	by running
운전해서 un-jeon-hae-seo	by driving
N(을/를) 타고 (eul/reul) ta-go	by riding (something)
출발하는 곳 chul-bal-ha-neun got	departure
차 타는 곳 cha ta-neun got	ground transportation
보딩패스 bo-ding-pae-sseu	boarding pass
여권 yeo-kkwon	passport
비자 bi-ja	visa
비행기표 bi-haeng-gi-pyo	airline ticket
비행장 bi-haeng-jang / 공항 gong-hang	airport
국내선 gung-nae-seon	domestic airlines
국제선 guk-je-seon	international airlines
나가는 곳 na-ga-neun got	exit
갈아타는 곳 gal-a-ta-neun got	subway platform
왼쪽 oen-jjok	left
오른쪽 o-reun-jjok	right

신호등 sin-ho-deung	traffic signal
횡단보도 hoeng-dan-bo-do	crosswalk
육교 yuk-gyo	overpass
지하도 ji-ha-do	underpass
사거리 sa-geo-ri	four-way intersection

직진하다 jik-jin-ha-da	to go straight
똑바로 가다 ttok-ba-ro ga-da	to go straight
되돌아 가다 doe-dol-a ga-da	to go back
좌회전하다 jwa-hoe-jeon-ha-da	to turn left
왼쪽으로 가다 oen-jjog-eu-ro ga-da	to turn left
우회전하다 u-hoe-jeon-ha-da	to turn right
오른쪽으로 가다 o-reun-jjog-eu-ro ga-da	to turn right
무단횡단을 하다 mu-dan hoeng-dan-eul ha-da	to jaywalk

앰뷸런스 aem-byul-leon-seu	ambulance
구급차 gu-geup-cha	ambulance
소방서 so-bang-seo	fire department
소방차 so-bang-cha	fire truck
경찰 gyeong-chal	police
경찰서 gyeong-chal-sseo	police department

문화적 참고사항 Cultural Note

Traveling in Korea

When traveling in Korea, public transportation has many advantages. Street signs are inadequate in most places and Seoul has heavy traffic almost all day long. Using the subway is the most time-efficient wy of traveling. Tickets can be purchased at either vending machines or ticket windows. The city bus routes are difficult to understand if one is not familiar with them. One may call in advance for taxi service, but most people simply hail them when they pass by.

Though officially discouraged, ride-sharing in taxis (합승 hap-seung) is very common during peak hours. Taxi drivers stop several times to pick up additional passengers, and each party pays a separate fare. Tipping is not required, but, since many passengers dislike waiting for small change, they will often tell the driver to keep the balance of the payment.

Trains and express buses are the most common way of traveling between regions. One may use a car, but under normal traffic conditions, it takes about five hours to get from Seoul to Pusan, which is longer than most people care to drive. On the trains and buses, one is generally issued a one-way ticket, with a return ticket being purchased after arriving at one's destination.

When driving, beware of people jaywalking. It is very common in the cities. When stopping at a gas station, remember that most stations will pump your gas for you; self-service is very rare. Tipping is not required at the station, and the posted price for gas is by the liter.

연습문제 Exercises

1. Please respond to the following:

(1) 어디까지 가십니까?
    eo-di-kka-ji ga-sim-ni-kka?
(2) 죄송하지만 합승 좀 해도 되겠습니까?
    joe-song-ha-ji-man hap-seung jom hae-do doe-get-seum-ni-kka?
(3) 거의 다 왔는데 어디 세워 드릴까요?
    geo-i da wan-neun-de eo-di se-wo deu-ril-kka-yo?
(4) 짐은 몇 개나 부치실 겁니까?
    jim-eun myeot gae-na bu-chi-sil kkeom-ni-kka?
(5) 좌석은 어느 쪽으로 드릴까요?
    jwa-seog-eun eo-neu jjog-eu-ro deu-ril-kka-yo?
(6) 혹시 더 필요한 게 있으십니까?
    hok-si deo pil-yo-han ge iss-eu-sim-ni-kka?

2. Please translate the following into English:

(1) 그래도 주중이 주말보다 좀 낫지 않아요?
    geu-rae-do ju-jung-i ju-mal-bo-da jom nat-ji an-a-yo?
(2) 여권하고 비행기표 좀 주시겠습니까?
    yeo-kkwon-ha-go bi-haeng-gi-pyo jom ju-si-get-seum-ni-kka?
(3) 12시에 출발하면 몇시에 부산에 도착하나요?
    yeol-ttu-si-e chul-bal-ha-myeon myeot-si-e bu-san-e
    do-cha-ka-na-yo?
(4) 직행이니까 기차를 갈아타지 않으셔도 돼요.
    ji-kaeng-i-ni-kka gi-cha-reul gal-a-ta-ji an-eu-syeo-do dwae-yo.
(5) 게이트는 38번이고 좌석번호는 27A입니다.
    ge-i-teu-neun sam-sip-pal-beon-i-go jwa-seok-beon-ho-neun
    i-sip-chil-e-i-im-ni-da.

3. Please translate the following into Korean:

(1) It seems like all the roads are congested.
(2) Where can I go to board the train?
(3) Two tickets for the train departing at 1:00 for Pusan, please.
(4) Please drop me off under the overpass over there.
(5) Please keep the change.

4. Please write five things that you have to do during this week. Make sure to use ordinal numbers.

5. Please write a paragraph describing your experiences with public transportation.

제 11과 은행과 우체국

◇◇◇◇◇◇◇◇

Lesson 11: Banks & Post Offices

표현 Patterns

통장 만들기.
tong-jang man-deul-gi.
Opening a bank account.

어떻게 도와 드릴까요?
eo-tteo-ke do-wa deu-ril-kka-yo?
How may I help you?

통장을 하나 만들려고 하는데요.
tong-jang-eul ha-na man-deul-lyeo-go ha-neun-de-yo.
I would like to open an account. (*lit.* I would like to make an
    account keeping book.)

그러세요? 그럼 신분증하고 도장 좀 주시겠습니까?
geu-reo-se-yo? geu-reom sin-bun-jjeung-ha-go do-jang jom
    ju-si-get-seum-ni-kka?
Is that so? Then would you give me your ID and signature stamp?

신분증은 여권이면 되죠?
sin-bun-jjeung-eun yeo-kkwon-i-myeon doe-jyo?
My passport can be an ID, right?

그리고 도장은 없는데요.
geu-ri-go do-jang-eun eom-neun-de-yo.
And I don't have a signature stamp.

괜찮아요. 그냥 사인만 하셔도 돼요.
gwaen-chan-a-yo. geu-nyang ssa-in-man ha-syeo-do dwae-yo.
It's OK. You can just sign.

얼마나 예금하시겠습니까?
eol-ma-na ye-geum-ha-si-get-seum-ni-kka?
How much do you want to deposit?

이 신청서에 손님 성함하고 주소하고 비밀번호 좀 써 주십시오.
i sin-cheong-seo-e son-nim seong-ham-ha-go ju-so-ha-go bi-mil-
   beon-ho jom sseo ju-sip-si-o.
On this application, please write your name, address, and pin
   number.

이렇게 쓰면 되나요?
i-reo-ke sseu-myeon doe-na-yo?
Is it OK if I write like this?

네, 됐습니다. 현금카드도 필요하시죠?
ne, dwaet-seum-ni-da. hyeon-geum ka-deu-do pil-yo-ha-si-ji-yo?
Yes, it's done. You need an ATM card too, right?

네, 해 주세요.
ne, hae ju-se-yo.
Yes, please do it for me.

잠깐만 기다리세요.
jam-kkan-man gi-da-ri-se-yo.
Wait a minute, please.

여기 손님 통장하고 현금카드 있습니다.
yeo-gi son-nim tong-jang-ha-go hyeon-geum-ka-deu it-seum-ni-da.
Here is your balance (*lit.* account keeping) book and an ATM card.

환전하기
hwan-jeon-ha-gi
exchanging currency

환전을 좀 하고 싶은데요.
hwan-jeon-eul jom ha-go sip-eun-de-yo.
I would like to exchange some money.

오늘 환율이 어떻게 되나요?
o-neul hwan-nyul-i eo-tteo-ke doe-na-yo?
What is today's exchange rate?

달러당 1300원이에요.
dal-leo-dang cheon-sam-baeg-won-i-e-yo.
1300 won per dollar.

얼마나 바꾸시게요?
eol-ma-na ba-kku-si-ge-yo?
How much do you want to exchange?

500불만 바꿔 주세요.
o-baek-bul-man ba-kkwo ju-se-yo.
Just 500 dollars, please.

여기 신청서 좀 써 주시겠어요?
yeo-gi sin-cheong-seo jom sseo ju-si-gess-eo-yo?
Would you please fill out the application form here?

여권이나 신분증 좀 보여주세요.
yeo-kkwon-i-na sin-bun-jjeung jom bo-yeo-ju-se-yo.
Please show me your passport or ID.

돈은 현금으로 드릴까요, 아니면 수표로 드릴까요?
don-eun hyeon-geum-eu-ro deu-ril-kka-yo, a-ni-myeon su-pyo-ro
　　deu-ril-kka-yo?
Do you want your money in cash or checks?

전부 수표로 주시고 잔돈만 현금으로 주세요.
jeon-bu su-pyo-ro ju-si-go jan-don-man hyeon-geum-eu-ro
　　ju-se-yo.
Please give me everything in checks and only the change in cash.

수수료 5,000원 공제하고 드렸습니다.
su-su-ryo o-cheon-won gong-je-ha-go deu-ryeot-seun-ni-da.
I've taken out the 5,000 won processing fee and given you the rest.
   (lit. I gave you the rest after deducting the processing
   5,000-won fee.)

편지 부치기
pyeon-ji bu-chi-gi
sending mail

이거 샌디에이고까지 얼마나 걸릴까요?
i-geo saen-di-e-i-go-kka-ji eol-ma-na geol-lil-kka-yo?
How long will this take to get to San Diego?

어떻게 보내실 건데요?
eo-tteo-ke bo-nae-sil kkeon-de-yo?
How would you want to send it?

제일 빨리 가는 것으로 해 주세요.
je-il ppal-li ga-neun geos-eu-ro hae ju-se-yo.
The fastest way, please.

속달우편은 3일이면 되는데 좀 비싸요. 급하세요?
sok-dal-u-pyeon-eun sam-il-i-myeon doe-neun-de jom bi-ssa-yo.
   geu-pa-se-yo?
Express mail will take three days, but it's a little expensive. Are you
   in a hurry?

별로요. 그럼 어떤 게 좋을까요?
byeol-lo-yo. geu-reom eo-tteon ge jo-eul-kka-yo?
Not really. Then what do you think is better?

항공편으로 보내시면 한 일주일 정도 걸려요.
hang-gong-pyeon-eu-ro bo-nae-si-myeon han sil-jju-il jeong-do
    geol-lyeo-yo.
If you send it airmail, it will take about a week.

그럼 그걸로 할게요.
geu-reom geu-geol-lo hal-kke-yo.
Then I will take that.

등기우편으로 해 드릴까요?
deung-gi-u-pyeon-eu-ro hae deu-ril-kka-yo?
Do you want it to be registered mail?

아니오, 괜찮아요.
a-ni-o, gwaen-chan-a-yo.
No, that's OK.

여기에 받으실 분 주소하고 성함 좀 써 주시겠어요?
yeo-gi-e bad-eu-sil ppun ju-so-ha-go seong-ham jom sseo
    ju-si-gess-eo-yo?
Would you please write the receiver's name and address here?

이렇게 쓰면 되나요?
i-reo-ke sseu-myeon doe-na-yo?
Is it OK if I write like this?

됐습니다. 뭐 더 필요하신 게 있으십니까?
dwaet-seum-ni-da. mwo deo pil-yo-ha-sin ge iss-eu-sim-ni-kka?
Yes, it's done. Is there anything else I can do for you? (*lit.* Is there
    anything more you need?)

200원짜리 우표 10장만 주세요.
i-baeg-won-jja-ri u-pyo yeol-jjang-man ju-se-yo.
Please give me ten 200-won stamps.

지난 주부터 우편요금이 인상됐기 때문에 이젠 230원짜리를 사
　용하셔야 되는데요.

ji-nan ju-bu-teo u-pyeon-nyo-geum-i in-sang-dwaet-gi ttae-mun-
　e i-jen i-baek-sam-sib-won-jja-ri-reul sa-yong-ha-syeo-ya
　doe-neun-de-yo.

Because of the price increase last week, you will probably need to
　use 230-won stamps now.

그럼 230원짜리로 10장 주세요.

geu-reom i-baek-sam-sib-won-jja-ri-ro yeol-jjang ju-se-yo.

Then ten 230-won stamps, please.

대화 Model Conversations

(1) 통장 만들기 tong-jang man-deul-gi

직원: 어서 오세요, 손님. 어떻게 도와드릴까요?
eo-seo o-se-yo, son-nim. eo-tteo-ke
do-wa-deu-ril-kka-yo?

이정호: 통장을 하나 만들려고 하는데요.
tong-jang-eul ha-na man-deul-lyeo-go ha-neun-de-yo.

직원: 그러세요? 그럼 신분증하고 도장 좀 주시겠습니까?
geu-reo-se-yo? geu-reom sin-bun-jjeung-ha-go do-jang
jom ju-si-get-seum-ni-kka?

이정호: 신분증은 여권이면 되죠? 그리고 도장은 없는데요.
sin-bun-jjeung-eun yeo-kkwon-i-myeon doe-jyo? geu-ri-
go do-jang-eun eom-neun-de-yo.

직원: 괜찮아요. 그냥 사인만 하셔도 돼요. 얼마나 예금하시
겠습니까?
gwaen-chan-a-yo. geu-nyang sa-in-man ha-syeo-do
dwae-yo. eol-ma-na ye-geum-ha-si-get-seum-ni-kka?

이정호: 30만원이요.
sam-sim-man-won-i-yo.

직원: 이 신청서에 손님 성함하고 주소하고 비밀번호 좀 써
주십시오.
i sin-cheong-seo-e son-nim seong-ham-ha-go ju-so-ha-go
bi-mil-beon-ho jom sseo ju-sip-si-o.

이정호: (잠시 후) 이렇게 쓰면 되나요?
(jam-si hu) i-reo-ke sseu-myeon doe-na-yo?

직원: 네, 됐습니다. 현금카드도 필요하시죠?
ne dwaet-seum-ni-da. hyeon-geum ka-deu-do
pil-yo-ha-si-jyo?

이정호: 네, 해 주세요.
ne, hae ju-se-yo.

직원: 잠깐만 기다리세요.... (잠시 후) 여기 손님 통장하고
현금카드 있습니다. 안녕히 가십시오.

jam-kkan-man gi-da-ri-se-yo. (jam-si hu) yeo-gi son-nim
tong-jang-ha-go hyeon-geum-ka-deu it-seum-ni-da.
an-nyeong-hi ga-sip-si-o.

(2) 환전하기 hwan-jeon-ha-gi

이정호: 환전을 좀 하고 싶은데요. 오늘 환율이 어떻게 되나요?
hwan-heon-eul jom ha-go sip-eun-de-yo. o-neul
hwan-nyul-i eo-tteo-ke doe-na-yo?

직원: 달러당 1300원이에요. 얼마나 바꾸시게요?
dal-leo-dang cheon-sam-baeg-won-i-e-yo. eol-ma-na
ba-kku-si-ge-yo?

이정호: 500불만 바꿔 주세요.
o-baek-bul-man ba-kkwo ju-se-yo.

직원: 그럼 여기 신청서 좀 써 주시겠어요? 그리고 여권이
나 신분증 좀 보여주세요.

geu-reom yeo-gi sin-cheong-seo jom sseo ju-si-gess-
eo-yo? geu-ri-go yeo-kkwon-i-na sin-bun-jjeung jom
bo-yeo-ju-se-yo.

이정호: 여기 있습니다.
yeo-gi it-seum-ni-da.

직원: 돈은 현금으로 드릴까요, 아니면 수표로 드릴까요?
don-eun hyeon-geum-eu-ro deu-ril-kka-yo, a-ni-myeon
su-pyo-ro deu-ril-kka-yo?

이정호: 전부 수표로 주시고 잔돈만 현금으로 주세요.
jeon-bu su-pyo-ro ju-si-go jan-don-man hyeon-geum-eu-
ro ju-se-yo.

직원: (잠시 후) 여기 있습니다. 수수료 5,000원 공제하고 드
렸습니다. 안녕히 가십시오.

(jam-si hu) yeo-gi it-seum-ni-da. su-su-ryo o-cheon-
won gong-je-ha-go deu-ryeot-seum-ni-da. an-nyeong-hi
ga-sip-si-o.

이정호: 감사합니다.
gam-sa-ham-ni-da.

(3) 편지 부치기 pyeon-ji bu-chi-gi

이정호: 이거 샌디에이고까지 얼마나 걸릴까요?
i-geo saen-di-e-i-go-kka-ji eol-ma-na geol-lil-kka-yo?

직원: 어떻게 보내실 건데요?
eo-tteo-ke bo-nae-sil kkeon-de-yo?

이정호: 제일 빨리 가는 것으로 해 주세요.
je-il ppal-li ga-neun geos-eu-ro hae ju-se-yo.

직원: 속달우편은 3일이면 되는데 좀 비싸요. 급하세요?
sok-dal-u-pyeon-eun san-il-i-myeon doe-neun-de jom
bi-ssa-yo. geu-pa-se-yo?

이정호: 별로요. 그럼 어떤 게 좋을까요?
byeol-lo-yo. geu-reom eo-tteon ge jo-eul-kka-yo?

직원: 항공편으로 보내시면 한 일주일 정도 걸려요.
hang-gong-pyeon-eu-ro bo-nae-si-myeon han il-jju-il
jeong-do geol-lyeo-yo.

이정호: 그럼 그걸로 할게요.
geu-reom geu-geol-lo hal-kke-yo.

직원: 등기우편으로 해 드릴까요?
deung-gi-u-pyeon-eu-ro hae deu-ril-kka-yo?

이정호: 아니오, 괜찮아요.
a-ni-o, gwaen-chan-a-yo.

직원: 여기에 받으실 분 주소하고 성함 좀 써 주시겠어요?
yeo-gi-e bad-eu-sil bun ju-so-ha-go seong-ham jom sseo
ju-si-gess-eo-yo?

이정호: (잠시 후) 이렇게 쓰면 되나요?
(jam-si hu) i-reo-ke sseu-myeon doe-na-yo?

직원: 네, 됐습니다. 뭐 더 필요하신 게 있으십니까?
ne, dwaet-seum-ni-da. mwo deo pil-yo-ha-sin-ge
iss-eu-sim-ni-kka?

이정호: 200원짜리 우표 10장만 주세요.
i-baeg-won-jja-ri u-pyo yeol-jjang-man ju-se-yo.

직원:　　지난 주부터 우편요금이 인상됐기 때문에 이젠 230원
　　　　짜리를 사용하셔야 되는데요.

　　　　ji-nan ju-bu-teo u-pyeon-yo-geum-i in-sang-dwaet-gi
　　　　ttae-mun-e i-jen i-baek-sam-sib-won-jja-ri-reul sa-yong-
　　　　ha-syeo-ya doe-neun-de-yo.

이정호: 그래요? 그럼 230원짜리로 10장 주세요.

　　　　geu-rae-yo? geu-reom i-baek-sam-sib-won-jja-ri-ro yeol-
　　　　jjang ju-se-yo.

영문번역 English Translation

(1) Opening a bank account

Employee: Welcome, customer. How may I help you?

Lee: I would like to open an account.

Employee: Is that so? Then would you give me your ID and signature stamp?

Lee: My passort can be an ID, right? And I don't have a signature stamp.

Employee: It's OK. You can just sign. How much do you want to deposit?

Lee: 300,000 won, please.

Employee: On this application, please write your name, address, and pin number.

Lee: *(after a while)* Is it OK if I write like this?

Employee: Yes, it's done. You need an ATM card too, right?

Lee: Yes, please do it for me.

Employee: Wait a minute, please. *(after a while)* Here are your balance book and ATM card. Good-bye.

(2) Exchanging currency

Lee: I would like to exchange some money. What is today's exchange rate?

Employee: 1300 won per dollar. How much do you want to exchange?

Lee: Just 500 dollars, please.

Employee: Then would you please fill out this application form? And please show me your passport or ID.

Lee: Here it is.

Employee: Do you want your money in cash or checks?

Lee: Please give me everything in checks and only the change in cash.

Employee: *(after a while)* Here it is. I took out the 5,000-won processing fee and gave it to you the rest. Good-bye.

Lee: Thank you.

(3) Sending mail

Lee:	How long will this take to go to San Diego?
Employee:	How would you want to send it?
Lee:	The fastest way, please.
Employee:	Express mail will take three days but it's a little expensive. Are you in a hurry?
Lee:	Not really. Then what do you think is better?
Employee:	If you send it as airmail, it will take about a week.
Lee:	Then I will take that.
Employee:	Do you want it sent registered mail?
Lee:	No, that's OK.
Employee:	Would you please write the receiver's name and address here?
Lee:	*(after a while)* Is this OK?
Employee:	Yes, that's good. Is there anything else I can do for you?
Lee:	Please give me ten 200-won stamps.
Employee:	Because of the price increase last week, you will probably need to use 230-won stamps now.
Lee:	Really? Then ten 230-won stamps, please.

어휘 Vocabulary

Nouns / Pronouns

도장 do-jang	stamp, seal
돈 don	money
등기우편 deung-gi-u-pyeon	registered mail
뭐 mwo	what?
받으실 분 bad-eu-sil bun	receiver
비밀번호 bi-mil-beon-ho	pin (personal identification) number
사인 sa-in	signature
성함 seong-ham	name (*hon.*)
속달우편 sok-dal-u-pyeon	express mail
손님 son-nim	customer
수수료 su-su-ryo	fee, charge
수표 supyo	check
신분증 sin-bun-jjeung	ID card
신청서 sin-cheong-seo	application
어떤 거 eo-tteon geo	which one?
여권 yeo-kkwon	passport
오늘 o-neul	today
우편요금 u-pyeon-yo-geum	postage, postal charge
우표 u-pyo	stamp
이거 i-geo	this one
잔돈 jan-don	change
주소 ju-so	address
지난 주 ji-nan ju	last week
직원 jig-won	employee
통장 만들기 tong-jang man-deul-gi	opening a bank account
통장 tong-jang	bank account
편지 부치기 pyeon-ji bu-chi-gi	sending a piece of mail
필요하신 것 pil-yo-ha-sin geot	something needed (*hon.*)
하나 ha-na	one

현금 hyeon-geum	cash
현금카드 hyeon-geum-ka-deu	ATM card
환율 hwan-nyul	exchange rate
환전하기 hwan-jeon-ha-gi	exchanging currency
10장 yeol-jjang	ten sheets of paper
1300원 cheon-sam-baeg-won	1300 won
200원짜리 i-baeg-won-jja-ri	200-won value
230원짜리 i-baek-sam-sib-won-jja-ri	230-won value
30만원 sam-sim-man-won	300,000 won
3일 sam-il	three days
5,000원 o-cheon-won	5,000 won
500불 o-baek-bul	500 dollars

Verbs

가다 ga-da	to go
감사하다 gam-sa-ha-da	to thank
걸리다 geol-li-da	to take time
공제하다 gong-je-ha-da	to deduct
그렇다 geu-reo-ta	to be so
급하다 geu-pa-da	to be hurrying
기다리다 gi-da-ri-da	to wait
도와드리다 do-wa-deu-ri-da	to help (*hon.*)
되다 doe-da	to become
드리다 deu-ri-da	to give (*hon.*)
만들다 man-deul-da	to make
바꾸다 ba-kku-da	to change
바꿔 주다 ba-kkwo ju-da	to change
보내다 bo-nae-da	to send
보여주다 bo-yeo-ju-da	to show
비싸다 bi-ssa-da	to be expensive
사용하다 sa-yong-ha-da	to use
써 주다 sseo ju-da	to write
쓰다 sseu-da	to write

없다 eop-da	to not exist
예금하다 ye-geum-ha-da	to save money
오다 o-da	to come
인상되다 in-sang-doe-da	to be increased
좋다 jo-ta	to be good
필요하다 pil-yo-ha-da	to need
하다 ha-da	to do
해 드리다 hae deu-ri-da	to do (*hon.*)
해 주다 hae ju-da	to do
환전하다 hwan-jeon-ha-da	to exchange money

Adverbs / Conjunctions

그걸로 geu-geol-lo	that one
그냥 geu-nyang	just
그럼 geu-reom	then
그리고 geu-ri-go	and
달러당 dal-leo-dang	per dollar
별로 byeol-lo	not particularly
빨리 ppal-li	fast
아니면 a-ni-myeon	or, if not
안녕히 an-nyeong-hi	peacefully
어떻게 eo-tteo-ke	how?
어서 eo-seo	quickly
얼마나 eol-ma-na	how much?
여기 yeo-gi	here
이렇게 i-reo-ke	like this
잠깐만 jam-kkan-man	for a minute
잠시 후 jam-si-hu	after a while
전부 jeon-bu	all
제일 je-il	the most, the first
좀 jom	a little, please
한 일주일 정도 han il-jju-il jeong-do	about a week
항공편으로 hang-gong-pyeon-eu-ro	via airmail

문법 Grammar

(1) The Ending ~(으)ㄹ까요? ((eu)l-kka-yo?): "Shall I/ we...?," "Do you think ...?"

The basic function of the ending ~(으)ㄹ까요? is to ask for the listener's opinion. When the sentence's subject noun is "I" or "we" (when the speaker is the subject or a part of the subject), the ending ~(으)ㄹ까요? is used. In addition to asking the listener's opinion, it allows one to suggest or offer to do something. Examples:

뭐 먹을까요?
mwo meog-eul-kka-yo?
What are we going to eat?

커피 마실까요?
keo-pi ma-sil-kka-yo?
Shall we drink some coffee?

When used in the third person, the speaker is asking for the listener's opinion (i.e. "do you think ...?"). Examples:

길이 복잡할까요?
gil-i bok-ja-pal-kka-yo?
Do you think the traffic will be busy?

일이 어려울까요?
il-i eo-ryeo-ul-kka-yo?
Do you think the task is difficult?

When used in the form ~(으)ㄹ까요,... ~(으)ㄹ까요? the listener is given alternatives from which to choose. For example:

커피를 마실까요, 주스를 마실까요?
keo-pi-reul ma-sil-kka-yo, ju-seu-reul ma-sil-kka-yo?
Shall we drink coffee or juice?

Use ~을까요 when the verb stem ends in any consonant except ㄹ. When the consonant is ㄹ, use ~까요. When the stem ends in a vowel, ~ㄹ까요 is used.

(2) The Volitional: ~고 싶다 (go sip-da) vs. ~고 싶어하다 (go sip-eo-ha-da) "want to," " would like to"

The pattern ~고 싶다 is used to state either what the speaker wishes to do or to ask what the listener would want. When indicating what a third person would want, one uses the ending ~고 싶어하다.

The past tense of ~고 싶어요 (go sip-eo-yo) /~고 싶어해요 (go sip-eo-hae-yo) is ~고 싶었어요 (go sip-eoss-eo-yo) /~고 싶어했어요 (go sip-eo-haess-eo-yo), respectively; and the future prospective tense is ~고 싶을 거예요 (go sip-eul kkeo-ye-yo) /~고 싶어할 거예요 (go sip-eo-hal kkeo-ye-yo).

Examples:

저는 한국에 가고 싶어요.
jeo-neun han-gug-e ga-go sip-eo-yo.
I want to go to Korea.

정호는 한국에 가고 싶어해요.
jeong-ho-neun han-gug-e ga-go sip-eo-hae-yo.
Jeong-ho wants to go to Korea.

저는 한국에 가고 싶었어요.

jeo-neun han-gug-e ga-go sip-eoss-eo-yo.

I wanted to go to Korea.

정호는 한국에 가고 싶어했어요.

jeong-ho-neun han-gug-e ga-go sip-eo-haess-eo-yo.

Jeong-ho wanted to go to Korea.

저는 한국에 가고 싶을 거예요.

jeo-neun han-gug-e ga-go sip-eul kkeo-yeo-yo.

I will want to go to Korea.

정호는 한국에 가고 싶어할 거예요.

jeong-ho-neun han-gug-e ga-go sip-eo-hal kkeo-ye-yo.

Jeong-ho will want to go to Korea.

(3) *Stating Cause*: 때문에 *(ttae-mun-e)*, ~기 때문에 *(gi ttae-mun-e)*, *and* ~아/어서 *(a/eo-seo)* "because, because of"

The pattern ~기 때문에 is used when the speaker wishes to give a reason for something. It is the equivalent of the English prepositions "because" or "because of." It is affixed to the verb stem, and can be used with a tense marker. It tends to be formal and often occurs in formal settings and in writing. The word 때문에 is used when the cause referred to is a noun.

When the sentence relates that something progresses from something else, rather than being its cause, the ending ~아/어서 is used. It cannot take any tense marker, and is most appropriate in the context of an apology, excuse, or when expressing gratitude. For example:

늦어서 죄송합니다.

neuj-eo-seo joe-song-ham-ni-da.

I am sorry [because] I am late.

Neither ~기 때문에 or ~아/어서 may be used with a command (the imperative), or when making a proposition or suggestion.

(4) Expressing Intention: ~(으) 려고 하다 ((eu)-ryeo-go ha-da) vs. ~(으)러 ((eu)-reo)

To express an intention to perform a future action or to convey that something is about to happen, one uses the pattern ~(으)려고 하다. It can be used with any verb. This is in contrast to the pattern ~(으)러, with which only verbs of coming or going can be used. Examples:

오늘을 일찍 자려고 해요.
o-neul-eun il-jjik ja-ryeo-go hae-yo.
I plan to go to sleep early today.

버스가 지금 떠나려고 해요.
beo-sseu-ga ji-geum tteo-na-ryeo-go hae-yo.
The bus is about to depart.

텔레비전을 보려고 해요.
tel-le-bi-jeon-eul bo-ryeo-go hae-yo.
I am going to watch TV.

일하러 회사에 가요.
il-ha-reo hoe-sa-e ga-yo.
I go to the office to work.

의사 선생님을 만나러 병원에 왔어요.
ui-sa seon-saeng-nim-eul man-na-reo byeong-won-e
    wass-eo-yo.
I came to the hospital to meet a doctor.

(5) The Pattern ~(으)면 되다 ((eu)-myeon doe-da) "it would do if...," "it would be good/all right if ..."

The pattern ~(으)면 되다, which means "it would do if...," or " it would be good/all right if...," is used when indicating what is needed to perform an action or resolve a situation. When emphasizing that only one thing is needed, follow the noun with 만 (man) and affix ~(으)면 돼요 to the verb stem. This pattern is best translated as "all one has to do is..."

(6) Money-related Expressions

돈을 찾다 don-eul chat-da	to withdraw money
돈을 벌다 don-eul beol-da	to earn money
돈을 쓰다 don-eul sseu-da	to spend money
돈을 부치다 don-eul bu-chi-da	to send money
돈을 받다 don-eul bat-da	to receive money
돈을 주다 don-eul ju-da	to give money
돈을 따다 don-eul tta-da	to win money
돈을 잃다 don-eul il-ta	to lose money
돈을 잃어버리다 don-eul il-eo-beo-ri-da	to misplace money
돈을 줍다 don-eul jup-da	to find money
돈을 맞기다 don-eul mat-gi-da	to save money
돈이 들다 don-i deul-da	to need money

참고학습 Further Study

Korean Currency

The unit of Korean currency is the won (원), which comes from the Chinese character for "circle." There are five different coins in use:

> 1원 (일원 il-won)
> 10원 (십원 sib-won)
> 50원 (오십원 o-sib-won)
> 100원 (백원 baeg-won)
> 500원 (오백원 o-baeg-won)

There are three denominations of paper currency:

> 1000원 (천원 cheon-won)
> 5000원 (오천원 o-cheon-won)
> 10,000원 (만원 man-won)

Official checks are similar to traveler's checks, and are issued at a bank.

> Checks:　　수표 su-pyo (자기앞수표 ja-gi-ap su-pyo)

One U.S. dollar is equal to approximately 1000 won.

Additional Vocabulary:

환율 hwan-nyul	exchange rate
수수료 su-su-ryo	fee, charge
은행거래신청서 eun-haeng-geo-rae-sin-cheong-seo	bank account application
입금표 ip-geum-pyo	deposit slip

출금표 chul-geum-pyo	withdrawal slip
비밀번호 bi-mil-beon-ho	pin number
통장 tong-jang	deposit and withdrawal record
도장 do-jang	seal, stamp
현금카드 hyeon-geum-ka-deu	ATM card
현금지급기 hyeon-geum-gi-geup-gi	ATM machine
환율이 내리다 hwan-nyul-i nae-ri-da	the exchange rate goes down
환율이 오르다 hwan-nyul-i o-reu-da	the exchange rate goes up
환전을 하다 hwan-jeon-eul-ha-da	to exchange money
돈을 찾다 don-eul chat-da	to withdraw
저금하다 jeo-geum-ha-da	to deposit
예금하다 ye-geum-ha-da	to deposit
우표를 사다 u-pyo-reul sa-da	to buy a stamp
우표를 붙이다 u-pyo-reul bu-chi-da	to put on a stamp
편지/소포를 받다 pyeon-ji/so-po-reul bat-da	to receive a letter/ package
편지/소포를 부치다 pyeon-ji/so-po-reul bu-chi-da	to send a letter/ package
편지를 쓰다 pyeon-ji-reul sseu-da	to write a letter
답장을 쓰다 dap-jang-eul sseu-da	to write a reply
주소를 쓰다 ju-so-reul sseu-da	to write an address
받는 사람 ban-neun sa-ram	recipient
보내는 사람 bo-nae-neun sa-ram	sender
주소 ju-so	address
성함 seong-ham	name
성명 seong-myeong	name
이름 i-reum	name
중앙우체국 jung-ang-u-che-guk	central post office

우체통 u-che-tong	mailbox
우체국 직원 u-che-guk jig-won	post office employee
우편요금 u-pyeon-nyo-geum	postage
우체부 u-che-bu	postman
우편번호 u-pyeon-beon-ho	zip code
항공 우편 hang-gong u-pyeon	air mail, first-class mail
빠른 우편 ppa-reun u-pyeon (속달우편 sok-dal-u-pyeon)	express mail
등기 우편 deung-gi u-pyeon	registered mail
보통 우편 bo-tong u-pyeon (일반우편 il-ban u-pyeon)	regular mail, ground mail
상자 sang-ja	box
편지봉투 pyeon-ji-bong-tu	envelope
편지 pyeon-ji	letter
편지지 pyeon-ji-ji	letter paper
소포 so-po	package
엽서 yeop-seo	postcard

문화적 참고사항 Cultural Note

Banks in Korea are usually open from 9:00 A.M. to 4:30 P.M. during the weekdays and closed on weekends. All banks provide currency exchange services. Customers pay utility bills at the bank, and any number of services, including balance transfers, can be done at an ATM.

Korea is cash oriented society. Many small shops do not accept credit cards, and personal checks do not exist. Only banks can issue checks.

Post offices are usually open on weekdays from 9:00 A.M. to 5:00 P.M., and Saturdays from 9:00 A.M. to 1:00 P.M. They offer a great deal more than the U.S. postal service. One can do one's banking, mail-order local specialties, make train reservations, or buy express bus tickets. In the majority of offices, one can buy stamps from vending machines. When sending mail, one must address the envelope in macro-to-micro style, beginning with the country and ending with the person's name.

연습문제 Exercises

1. Please respond to the following:

(1) 어서 오세요, 손님. 어떻게 도와드릴까요?
    eo-seo o-se-yo, son-nim. eo-tteo-ke do-wa-deu-ril-kka-yo?
(2) 얼마나 예금하시겠습니까?
    eol-ma-na ye-geum-ha-si-get-seum-ni-kka?
(3) 얼마나 바꿔 드릴까요?
    eol-ma-na ba-kkwo deu-ril-kka-yo?
(4) 돈은 현금으로 드릴까요, 수표로 드릴까요?
    don-eun hyeon-geum-eu-ro deu-ril-kka-yo, su-pyo-ro
    deu-ril-kka-yo?
(5) 이 소포 어떻게 보내실 겁니까?
    i so-po eo-tteo-ke bo-nae-sil kkeom-ni-kka?

2. Please translate the following into English:

(1) 신분증은 여권이면 되죠? 그리고 도장은 없는데요.
    sin-bun-jjeung-eun yeo-kkwon-i-myeon doe-jyo? geu-ri-go
    do-jang-eun eom-neun-de-yo.
(2) 이 신청서에 손님 성함하고 주소하고 비밀번호 좀 써 주십
    시오.
    i sin-cheong-seo-e son-nim seong-ham-ha-go ju-so-ha-go
    bi-mil-beon-ho jom sseo ju-sip-si-o.
(3) 돈은 전부 수표로 주시고 잔돈만 현금으로 주세요.
    don-eun jeon-bu su-pyo-ro ju-si-go jan-don-man
    hyeon-geum-eu-ro ju-se-yo.
(4) 속달우편은 3일이면 되는데 좀 비싸요. 급하세요?
    sok-dal u-pyeon-eun sam-il-i-myeon doe-neun-de jom
    bi-ssa-yo. geu-pa-se-yo?
(5) 항공편으로 보내시면 한 일주일 정도 걸려요.
    hang-gong-pyeon-eu-ro bo-nae-si-myeon han il-jju-il jeong-do
    geol-lyeo-yo.

(6) 지난 주부터 우편요금이 인상됐기 때문에 이젠 230원짜리
를 사용하셔야 되는데요.
ji-nan ju-bu-teo u-pyeon-nyo-geum-i in-sang-dwaet-gi ttae-
mun-e i-jen i-baek-sam-sib-won-jja-ri-reul sa-yong-ha-syeo-ya
doe-neun-de-yo.

3. Please translate the following into Korean:

(1) I would like to have a bank account.
(2) Would you please give me your ID and signature stamp?
(3) You need an ATM card, right?
(4) What is today's exchange rate?
(5) I took out the 5,000-won processing fee is taken out and gave
you the rest.

4. Please write the meaning of the phrases below and write
sentences using them:

(1) 돈을 찾다 don-eul chat-da
(2) 돈을 벌다 don-eul beol-da
(3) 돈을 부치다 don-eul bu-chi-da
(4) 돈을 따다 don-eul tta-da
(5) 돈이 들다 don-i deul-da

5. Please read the following numbers in Korean:

(1) 250원
(2) 78,350원
(3) 469,700원
(4) 1,257,800원
(5) 34,500,000원

6. Please write a paragraph about an experience in either a bank or a post office.

제12과 병원과 약국

◇◇◇◇◇◇◇◇

Lesson 12: Hospitals & Drugstores

표현 Patterns

어서 오세요. 어떻게 오셨어요?
eo-seo o-se-yo. eo-tteo-ke o-syeoss-eo-yo?
Welcome. What brings you here? (*lit.* What did you come here for?)

감기에 걸린 것 같아서요.
gam-gi-e geol-lin geot gat-a-seo-yo.
It's because I think I caught a cold.

요즘 감기가 정말 독하지요?
yo-jeum gam-gi-ga jeong-mal do-ka-ji-yo?
The colds these days are really severe, right?

잠깐만 저기 앉아서 기다리세요.
jam-kkan-man jeo-gi anj-a-seo gi-da-ri-se-yo.
Please sit there and wait a moment.

보험카드 좀 주시겠어요?
bo-heom-ka-deu jom ju-si-gess-eo-yo?
Would you please give me your health insurance card?

여기 있어요.
yeo-gi iss-eo-yo.
Here it is.

어디가 어떻게 아프세요?
eo-di-ga eo-tteo-ke a-peu-se-yo?
Where and how do you feel sick?

감기에 걸린 것 같은데 어지럽고 기운이 없어요.
gam-gi-e geol-lin geot gat-eun-de eo-ji-reop-go gi-un-i eops-eo-yo.
I think I have a cold; I feel dizzy and have no energy.

춥고 땀이 나면서 기침을 자꾸 해요.
chup-go ttam-i na-myeon-seo gi-chim-eul ja-kku hae-yo.
I feel cold and I am sweating, and I'm coughing constantly.

목도 아프고요. 숨도 잘 못 쉬겠어요.
mok-do a-peu-go-yo. sum-do jal mot swi-gess-eo-yo.
My throat also hurts. And I cannot breathe easily.

어제 밤새도록 설사하고 토했어요.
eo-je bam-sae-do-rok seol-ssa-ha-go to-haess-eo-yo.
I had diarrhea and threw up all night yesterday.

너무 어지러워서 앉아 있을 수가 없어요.
neo-mu eo-ji-reo-wo-seo anj-a iss-eul ssu-ga eops-eo-yo.
I feel so dizzy that I cannot stay seated.

지금도 자꾸 눕고 싶어요.
ji-geum-do ja-kku nup-go sip-eo-yo.
Even now I want to lie down.

언제부터 설사하기 시작했어요?
eon-je-bu-teo seol-ssa-ha-gi si-ja-kaess-eo-yo?
When did your diarrhea start?

한 이틀 전부터요.
han i-teul jeon-bu-teo-yo.
About two days ago.

이쪽으로 앉아 보세요.
i-jjog-eu-ro anj-a bo-se-yo.
Please sit here.

숨을 크게 쉬어 보세요.
sum-eul keu-ge swi-eo bo-se-yo.
Take a deep breath, please.

'아' 해 보세요.
a hae bo-se-yo.
Please say "Ah!"

검사를 좀 해야 되겠는데요.
geom-sa-reul jom hae-ya doe-gen-neun-de-yo.
We need to do some tests.

마지막으로 생리하신 게 언제지요?
ma-ji-mag-eu-ro saeng-ri-ha-sin ge eon-je-ji-yo?
How long has it been since your last period? (*lit.* When was the last
　　time you had a period?)

지난 달 15일이요.
ji-nan dal sib-o-il-i-yo.
I had it on the15th of last month.

상태가 어떤가요?
sang-tae-ga eo-tteon-ga-yo?
How is my condition?

검사를 해 봐야 알겠지만 장염에 걸린 것 같아요.
geom-sa-reul hae-bwa-ya al-get-ji-man jang-yeom-e geol-lin geot
　　gat-a-yo.
We need more examinations/tests to know details, but I think you
　　have enteritis.

그럼 어떻게 하지요?
geu-reom eo-tteo-ke ha-ji-yo?
Then what am I supposed to do?

요즘은 좋은 약이 많으니까 걱정 많이 안 하셔도 괜찮아요.
yo-jeum-eun jo-eun yag-i man-eu-ni-kka geok-jeong man-i an
　　ha-syeo-do gwaen-chan-a-yo.
Because there are lots of good medicines these days, you don't need
　　to worry too much.

그럼 다행이네요.

geu-reom da-haeng-i-ne-yo.

That's good. (*lit.* That would be fortunate.)

어떻게 오셨습니까?

eo-tteo-ke o-syeot-seum-ni-kka?

What brings you here?

잇몸이 자주 붓고 양치질할 때 잇몸에서 자꾸 피가 나요.

in-mom-i ja-ju but-go yang-chi-jil hal ttae in-mom-e-seo ja-kku
    pi-ga na-yo.

My gums are frequently swollen, and I often bleed when I brush
    my teeth.

그래요? 좀 볼까요?

geu-rae-yo? jom bol-kka-yo?

Really? Can I see it for a moment?

증상이 별로 심하지는 않군요.

jeung-sang-i byeol-lo sim-ha-ji-neun an-kun-yo.

It is not that serious. (*lit.* The symptom is not that serious.)

그래도 치료를 좀 해야겠습니다.

geu-rae-do chi-ryo-reul jom hae-ya-get-seum-ni-da.

But you have to get some treatment. (lit. But we still have to
    treat it.)

좀 아프실 겁니다. 조금만 참으세요.

jom a-peu-sil kkeom-ni-da. jo-geum-man cham-eu-se-yo.

It will hurt a little bit. Just endure it for a bit, please.

다 됐습니다. 이제 양치질 하십시오.

da dwaet-seum-ni-da. i-je yang-chi-jil ha-sip-si-o.

It's all done. Now rinse your mouth, please.

잇몸이 왜 자꾸 그러지요?

in-mom-i wae ja-kku geu-reo-ji-yo?

Why is this happening with my gums constantly? (*lit.* Why my gum is often doing like this?)

잇몸이 좀 약한 사람들이 있어요.

in-mom-i jom ya-kan sa-ram-deul-i iss-eo-yo.

Some people have soft gums. (*lit.* There are some people who have weak gums.)

양치질할 때 꼭 치주염 예방용 치약을 사용하세요.

yang-chi-jil-hal ttae kkok chi-ju-yeom ye-bang-nyong chi-yag-eul sa-yong-ha-se-yo.

Please use an anti-peridentitis toothpaste whenever you brush your teeth.

플로스 사용하실 줄은 알지요?

peul-lo-sseu sa-yong-ha-sil jjul-eun al-ji-yo?

You know how to floss, right?

어서 오세요. 뭘 도와 드릴까요?

eo-seo o-se-yo. mwol do-wa deu-ril-kka-yo?

Welcome. What can I do for you? (lit. What should I help you?)

의사 선생님이 처방전을 주셨는데요.

ui-sa seon-saeng-nim-i cheo-bang-jeon-eul ju-syeon-neun-de-yo.

My doctor gave me a prescription.

그러세요? 이리 주세요.... 잠깐만 기다리세요.

geu-reo-se-yo? i-ri ju-se-yo... jam-kkan-man gi-da-ri-se-yo.

Is that so? Please give it to me. Please wait for a minute.

이 알약은 하루에 3번씩 식후에 2알씩 드세요.

i al-lyag-eun ha-ru-e se-beon-ssik si-ku-e du-al-ssik deu-se-yo.

With these pills, please take two after every meal, three times a day.

이 물약은 아침저녁 공복에 한컵씩 드세요.

i mul-lyag-eun a-chim-jeo-nyeok gong-bog-e han-keop-ssik
    deu-se-yo.

With this liquid, please take one cup in the morning and in the after-
    noon on an empty stomach.

치주염 예방용 치약하고 플로스랑 마우스워시도 하나 주세요.

chi-ju-yeom ye-bang-nyong chi-ya-ka-go peul-lo-sseu-rang ma-u-
    sseu-wo-ssi-do ha-na ju-se-yo.

Please give me an anti-peridentitis toothpaste, a box of floss, and a
    bottle of mouthwash, too.

어떤 회사 제품으로 드릴까요?

eo-tteon hoe-sa je-pum-eu-ro deu-ril-kka-yo?

What brand do you prefer?

아무 회사 거나 다 괜찮아요.

a-mu hoe-sa kkeo-na da gwaen-chan-a-yo.

Any one would be OK.

대화 Model Conversations

(1) 병원에서 byeong-won-e-seo

간호원: 어서 오세요. 어떻게 오셨어요?
　　　　eo-seo o-se-yo. eo-tteo-ke o-syeoss-eo-yo?

이혜근: 감기에 걸린 것 같아서요.
　　　　gam-gi-e geol-lin-geot gat-a-seo-yo.

간호원: 요즘 감기가 정말 독하지요? 잠깐만 저기 앉아서 기
　　　　다리세요. 참, 보험카드 좀 주시겠어요?
　　　　yo-jeum gamogi-ga jeong-mal do-ka-ji-yo?
　　　　jam-kkan-man jeo-gi anj-a-seo gi-da-ri-se-yo.
　　　　cham, bo-heom-ka-deu jom ju-si-gess-eo-yo?

이혜근: 여기 있어요.
　　　　yeo-gi iss-eo-yo.

*(*잠시 후 *jam-si hu)*

의사: 어디가 어떻게 아프세요?
　　　eo-di-ga eo-tteo-ke a-peu-se-yo?

이혜근: 감기에 걸린 것 같은데 어지럽고 기운이 없어요.
　　　　gam-gi-e geol-lin geot gat-eun-de eo-ji-reop-go
　　　　gi-un-i eops-eo-yo.
　　　　춥고 땀이 나면서 기침을 자꾸 해요. 목도 아프고요.
　　　　chup-go ttam-i na-myeon-seo gi-chim-eul ja-kku hae-yo.
　　　　mok-do a-peu-go-yo.
　　　　그리고 숨도 잘 못 쉬겠고요, 어제 밤새도록 설사하고
　　　　토했어요.
　　　　geu-ri-go sum-do jal mot swi-get-go-yo, eo-je
　　　　bam-sae-do-rok seol-ssa-ha-go to-haess-eo-yo.
　　　　너무 어지러워서 앉아 있을 수가 없어요. 지금도 자꾸
　　　　눕고 싶어요.
　　　　neo-mu eo-ji-reo-wo-seo anj-a iss-eul su-ga eops-eo-yo.
　　　　ji-geum-do ja-kku nup-go sip-eo-yo.

의사: 언제부터 설사하기 시작했어요?

eon-je-bu-teo seol-ssa-ha-gi si-ja-kaess-eo-yo?

이혜근: 한 이틀 전부터요.

han i-teul jeon-bu-teo-yo.

의사: 이쪽으로 앉아 보세요... 숨을 크게 쉬어 보세요...
'아' 해 보세요...

i-jjok-eu-ro anj-a b-se-yo. sum-eul keu-ge swi-eo bo-se-yo. a hae bo-se-yo.

검사를 좀 해야 되겠는데요. 마지막으로 생리하신 게
언제지요?

geom-sa-reul jom hae-ya doe-gen-neun-de-yo.
ma-ji-mag-eu-ro saeng-ni-ha-sin ge eon-je-ji-yo?

이혜근: 지난 달 15일이요. 상태가 어떤가요?

ji-nan-dal sib-o-il-i-yo. sang-tae-ga eo-tteon-ga-yo?

의사: 검사를 해 봐야 알겠지만 장염에 걸린 것 같아요.

geom-sa-reul hae bwa-ya al-get-ji-man jang-yeom-e geol-lin geot gat-a-yo.

이혜근: 그래요? 그럼 어떻게 하지요?

geu-rae-yo? geu-reom eo-tteo-ke ha-ji-yo?

의사: 요즘은 좋은 약이 많으니까 걱정 많이 안 하셔도 괜찮
아요.

yo-jeum-eun jo-eun yag-i man-eu-ni-kka geok-jeong
man-i an ha-syeo-do gwaen-chan-a-yo.

이혜근: 그럼 다행이네요.

geu-reom da-haeng-i-ne-yo.

(2) 치과에서

의사: 어떻게 오셨습니까?

eo-tteo-ke o-syeot-seum-ni-kka?

이혜근: 잇몸이 자주 붓고 양치질할 때 잇몸에서 자꾸 피가
나요.

in-mom-i ja-ju but-go yang-chi-jil-hal ttae in-mom-e-seo
ja-kku pi-ga-na-yo.

의사: 그래요? 좀 볼까요? …. 증상이 별로 심하지는 않군요.
          geu-rae-yo? jom bol-kka-yo? jeung-sang-i byeol-lo
          sim-han-ji-neun an-kun-yo.
          그래도 치료를 좀 해야겠습니다.
          geu-rae-do chi-ryo-reul jom hae-ya-gess-eum-ni-da.
          좀 아프실 겁니다. 조금만 참으세요.
          jom a-peu-sil kkeom-ni-da. jo-geum-man cham-eu-se-yo.
          (잠시 후) 다 됐습니다. 이제 양치질 하십시오.
          (jam-si hu) da dwaet-seum-ni-da. i-je yang-chi-jil
          ha-sip-si-o.

이혜근: 잇몸이 왜 자꾸 그러지요?
          in-mom-i wae ja-kku geu-reo-ji-yo?

의사: 잇몸이 좀 약한 사람들이 있어요. 양치질할 때 꼭 치
          주염 예방용 치약을 사용하세요.
          in-mom-i jom ya-kan sa-ram-deul-I iss-eo-yo.
          yang-chil-jil-hal ttae kkok chi-ju-yeom ye-bang-nyong
          chi-yag-eul sa-yong-ha-se-yo.
          그리고 양치질 한 다음에 플로스하고 마우스워시 꼭
          하시고요.
          geu-ri-go yang-chil-jil-han da-eum-e peul-lo-ssu-ha-go
          ma-u-ssu-wo-ssi kkok ha-si-go-yo.
          플로스 사용하실 줄은 알지요?
          peul-lo-ssu sa-yong-ha-sil jul-eun al-ji-yo?

이혜근: 네, 알아요.
          ne, al-a-yo.

(3) 약국에서 yak-gug-e-seo
약사: 어서 오세요. 뭘 도와 드릴까요?
          eo-seo o-se-yo. mwol do-wa deu-ril-kka-yo?

이혜근: 의사 선생님이 처방전을 주셨는데요.
          ui-sa seon-saeng-nim-i cheo-bang-jeon-eul
          ju-syeon-neun-de-yo.

약사: 그러세요? 이리 주세요… 잠깐만 기다리세요.
          geu-reo-se-yo? i-ri ju-se-yo. jam-kkan-man

gi-da-ri-se-yo.

(잠시 후) 이 알약은 하루에 3번(세번)씩 식후에
2(두)알씩 드세요.

(jam-si hu) i al-lyag-eun ha-ru-e se-beon-ssik si-ku-e du-al-ssik deu-se-yo.

그리고 이 물약은 아침저녁 공복에 한컵씩 드세요.

geu-ri-go i mul-lyag-eun a-chim-jeo-nyeok gong-bog-e han-keop-ssik du-se-yo.

이혜근: 네, 알겠습니다. 참, 그리고 치주염 예방용 치약하고
플로스랑 마우스워시도 하나 주세요.

ne, al-get-seum-ni-da. cham, geu-ri-go chi-ju-yeom ye-bang-nyong chi-ya-ka-go peul-lo-sseu-rang ma-u-sseu-wo-ssi-do ha-na ju-se-yo.

약사: 어떤 회사 제품으로 드릴까요?

eo-tteo hoe-sa je-pum-eu-ro deu-ril-kka-yo?

이혜근: 아무 회사 거나 다 괜찮아요.

a-mu hoe-sa kkeo-na da gwaen-chan-a-yo.

영문번역 English Translation

(1) At a hospital

Nurse: Welcome. How may I help you?

Lee: I think I have a cold.

Nurse: The colds these days are really severe, right? Please
            have sit there and just wait a moment. Oh, would you
            please give me your health insurance card?

Lee: Here it is.

(after a while)

Doctor: Where and how does it hurt?

Lee: I think I have a cold; I feel dizzy and have no energy.
            I am cold and sweating, and I am coughing constantly.
            My throat hurts, too. And I cannot breathe easily, and
            I had diarrhea and threw up all night yesterday. I feel
            so dizzy that I cannot sit down properly. Even now I
            would like to lie down.

Doctor: When did you start having diarrhea?

Lee: About two days ago.

Doctor: Please sit here... Take a deep breath. Say "Ah!" We
            need to do some tests. How long has it been since your
            last period?

Lee: I had it on the 15th of last month. How is my
            condition?

Doctor: I'll see the details after the tests, but I think you have
            enteritis.

Lee: Really? Then what should I do?

Doctor: Because there are lots of good medicines these days,
            you don't need to worry too much.

Lee: That would be good.

(2) At a dentistry

Dentist: What brings you here?

Lee: My gums get frequently swollen, and I often bleed when I brush my teeth.

Dentist: Really? Let me see… It is not that serious. But you still need some treatment. This will hurt a bit. Please be patient. (*after a while*) It's all done. Now rinse your mouth, please.

Lee: What's happening on my gum?

Dentist: There are some people who have weaker gums. For sure, please use an anti-peridentitis toothpaste whenever you brush your teeth. And don't forget to floss and use mouthwash every time you brush your teeth. You know how to use floss, right?

Lee: Yes, I know.

(3) At a pharmacy

Pharmacist: Welcome. How may I help you?

Lee: My doctor gave me a prescription.

Pharmacist: Is that so? Please give it to me. Please wait for a minute. (*after a while*) With these pills, please take two after every meal, three times a day. And with this liquid, please take one cup in the morning and in the afternoon on an empty stomach.

Lee: OK, I understand. Oh, and give me an anti-peridentitis toothpaste, a box of floss, and a bottle of mouthwash, please.

Pharmacist: Do you have any preference?

Lee: Any one would be OK.

어휘 Vocabulary

Nouns / Pronouns

간호원 gan-ho-won	nurse
감기 gam-gi	cold
마우스워시 ma-u-seu-wo-si	mouthwash
목 mok	throat, neck
물약 mul-lyak	liquid medicine
병원 byeong-won	hospital
보험카드 bo-heom-ka-deu	insurance card
사람들 sa-ram-deul	people
상태 sang-tae	condition
아침 a-chim	morning
알약 al-lyak	pill, tablet
약국 yak-guk	drugstore
약사 yak-sa	pharmacist
어제 eo-je	yesterday
예방용 ye-bang-nyong	prevention
의사 ui-sa	doctor
의사 선생님 ui-sa seon-saeng-nim	doctor
이쪽 i-jjok	this way
잇몸 in-mom	gum
장염 jang-yeom	enteritis (infection in the small intestine)
저녁 jeo-nyeok	evening
제품 je-pum	product
좋은 약 jo-eun yak	good medicine
증상 jeung-sang	symptom
지난 달 ji-nan dal	last month
처방전 cheo-bang-jeon	prescription
치과 chi-kkwa	dentistry
치실 chi-sil	floss
치약 chi-yak	toothpaste

치주염 chi-ju-yeom — gum disease
플로스 peul-lo-seu — floss
회사 hoe-sa — company
15일 sib-o-il — 15 days
2 (두) 알씩 du-al-ssik — 2 pills (each time)
3(세)번씩 se-beon-ssik — 3 times (a day)

Verbs

감기에 걸리다 gam-gi-e geol-li-da	to catch a cold
걱정하다 geok-jeong-ha-da	to worry
검사를 하다 geom-sa-reul ha-da	to get examined
그렇다 geu-reo-ta	to be so
기다리다 gi-da-ri-da	to wait
기운이 없다 gi-un-i eop-da	to have no energy
기침을 하다 gi-chim-eul ha-da	to cough
눕다 nup-da	to lay down
다 되다 da doe-da	to be finished
다행이다 da-haeng-i-da	to be lucky
도와 드리다 do-wa deu-ri-da	to help (*hon.*)
독하다 do-ka-da	to be strong, to be severe
드리다 deu-ri-da	to give (*hon.*)
들다 deul-da	to take
땀이 나다 ttam-i na-da	to sweat
많다 man-ta	to be many
보다 bo-da	to see
붓다 but-da	to be swollen
사용하다 sa-yong-ha-da	to use
생리하다 saeng-ri-ha-da	to be having one's period, to be menstruating
설사하다 seol-ssa-ha-da	to have diarrhea
숨을 쉬다 sum-eul swi-da	to breathe
심하다 sim-ha-da	to be serious
'아' 하다 a-ha-da	to say "ah"

아프다 a-peu-da	to be hurt, to be sick
아프다 a-peu-da	to be sick
앉다 an-tta	to sit
앉아 있다 anj-a it-da	to be sitting
알다 al-da	to know
약하다 ya-ka-da	to be weak
양치질하다 yang-chi-jil-ha-da	to brush one's teeth
어떻다 eo-tteo-ta	to be how?
어지럽다 eo-ji-reop-da	to be dizzy
장염에 걸리다 jang-yeom-e geol-li-da	to have intestinal trouble
참다 cham-tta	to be patient
춥다 chup-da	to feel cold, to be cold
치료를 하다 chi-ryo-reul ha-da	to treat
토하다 to-ha-da	to vomit
피가 나다 pi-ga na-da	to bleed

Adverbs / Prepositions / Conjunctions

공복에 gong-bog-e	on an empty stomach
그래도 geu-rae-do	even it is true
그리고 geu-ri-go	and
꼭 kkok	for sure
너무 neo-mu	too
마지막으로 ma-ji-mag-eu-ro	at last
밤새도록 bam-sae-do-rok	for all night
별로 byeol-lo	not particularly
식후에 sik-hu-e	after a meal
아무 a-mu	any
어디 eo-di	where
어떤 eo-tteon	which, a certain
어떻게 eo-tteo-ke	how
어서 eo-seo	quickly
언제 eon-je	when
왜 wae	why

요즘 yo-jeum	these days
이제 i-je	now
자꾸 ja-kku	again and again
자주 ja-ju	often
잠깐만 jam-kkan-man	for a minute
저기 jeo-gi	there
정말 jeong-mal	really
조금만 jo-geum-man	a little
지금도 ji-geum-do	even now
참 cham	oh
크게 keu-ge	widely, big, loudly
하루에 ha-ru-e	per day
한 이틀 전 han i-teul jeon	about two days ago
한 컵씩 han-keop-ssik	one cup (at a time)

문법 Grammar

(1) Number of Days (using cardinal numbers)

	Sino-Korean	Native Korean
one day	일일 il-il	하루 ha-ru
two days	이일 i-il	이틀 i-teul
three days	삼일 sam-il	사흘 sa-heul
four days	사일 sa-il	나흘 na-heul
five days	오일 o-il	닷새 tat-sae
six days	육일 yug-il	엿새 yeot-sae
seven days	칠일 chil-il	이레 i-re
eight days	팔일 pal-il	여드레 yeo-deu-re
nine days	구일 gu-il	아흐레 a-heu-re
ten days	십일 sib-il	열흘 yeol-heul
fifteen days	십오일 sib-o-il	열닷새 yeol-dat-sae / 보름 bo-reum
twenty days	이십일 i-sib-il	스무날 seu-mu-nal

(2) The Pattern ~기 시작하다 (gi si-ja-ka-da) "begin to...," "start to..."

One uses the pattern ~기 시작하다 to indicate that one is beginning or starting to perform an action. In the past tense (*began to, begun to*), one uses ~기 시작했어요 (gi si-ja-kaess-eo-yo). With the future tense (*will begin to*), the ending ~기 시작할 거예요 (gi si-ja-kal kkeo-ye-yo) is used.

(3) The Pattern ~(으)ㄹ 수 있다/없다 ((eu)l ssu it-da/eop-da) "can / cannot..." vs. ~(으)ㄹ 줄 알다/모른다 ((eu)l jjul al-da/mo-reu-da) "know / don't know how to..."

When the pattern ~(으)ㄹ 수있다/없다 is affixed to a verb, it indicates that one can or cannot perform the action in question. It is equivalent to the verb못 followed by the verb stem with the suffix ~지 못 하다. One's capability or lack thereof can be due to any number of reasons. Examples:

테니스를 칠 줄 알지만 비가 와서 오늘은 칠 수 없어요.
te-ni-seu-reul chil jul al-ji-man bi-ga wa-seo o-neul-eun chil sue ops-eo-yo.
I know how to play tennis, but I cannot play today because it is raining.

불고기를 만들 줄 알지만 고기가 없어서 지금은 만들 수 없어요.
bul-go-gi-reul man-deul jul al-ji-man go-gi-ga eops-eo-seo ji-geum-eun man-deul sue ops-eo-yo.
I know how to cook bul-go-gi, but I cannot make it now because I don't have beef.

The pattern ~(으)ㄹ 줄 알다/모르다 is restricted to indicating one's knowledge or lack of it regarding performing the action.

(4) Expressing Concurrent Actions: ~(으)면서 ((eu)-myeon-seo) "while..."

To indicate that two actions are concurrent, one uses the pattern ~(으)면서, the equivalent of the English "while." The tense of the actions should only be indicated in the final clause. Examples:

밥을 먹으면서 텔레비전을 봐요.
bab-eul meog-eu-myeon-seo tel-le-bi-jeon-eul bwa-yo.
I am watching TV while I am eating.

운전하면서 음악을 들어요.
un-jeon-ha-myeon-seo eum-ag-eul deul-eo-yo.
I am listening to music while I am driving.

(5) Washing

Although the word *wash* in English is used to describe most acts of hygiene and cleaning, Korean uses different verbs according to what is being washed.

손/발을 씻다 son/bal-eul ssit-da	to wash one's hands/feet
양치질을 하다 yang-chi-jil-eul ha-da	to brush one's teeth
이를 닦다 i-reul dak-da	to brush one's teeth
세수를 하다 se-su-reul ha-da	to wash one's face
머리를 감다 meo-ri-reul gam-tta	to wash one's hair
샤워를 하다 sya-wo-reul ha-da	to take a shower
목욕을 하다 mog-yog-eul ha-da	to take a bath
빨래를 하다 ppal-lae-reul ha-da	to do laundry
설거지를 하다 seol-geo-ji-reul ha-da	to wash dishes

(6) Emotions and Feelings

기쁘다 gi-ppeu-da	to be happy
슬프다 seul-peu-da	to be sad
스트레스가 많다/쌓이다	to be stressed
seu-teu-re-sseu-ga man-ta/ssa-i-da	
스트레스가 풀리다	to relieve stress
seu-teu-re-sseu-ga pul-li-da	
좋다 jo-ta	to be good
싫다 sil-ta	to not be likable
신나다 sin-na-da	to be excited
심심하다 sim-sim-ha-da	to feel bored
지루하다 ji-ru-ha-da	to be bored to death
피곤하다 pi-gon-ha-da	to be tired

무섭다 mu-seop-da	to be scared/afraid
행복하다 haeng-bo-ka-da	to be happy
화가 나다 hwa-ga na-da	to be angry
화가 풀리다 hwa-ga pul-li-da	to have anger subside

참고학습 Further Study

Hospitals and Calling for Medical Help

병원 byeong-won	hospital, clinic
내과 nae-kkwa	department of internal medicine
소아과 so-a-kkwa	pediatrics
안과 an-kkwa	ophthalmology (eye)
외과 oe-kkwa	department of external medicine
치과 chi-kkwa	dentistry
간호사 gan-ho-sa	nurse
간호원 gan-ho-won	nurse
약사 yak-sa	pharmacist
의사 ui-sa	doctor
의료보험카드 ui-ryo-bo-heom-ka-deu	health insurance card
처방전 cheo-bang-jeon	prescription
먹는 약 meong-neun nyak	pills
바르는 약 ba-reu-neun nyak	ointment
가루약 ga-ru-yak	powdered medicine
물약 mul-lyak	liquid medicine
알약 al-lyak	tablet/pill
식전(에) sik-jeon-(e)	before a meal
식후(에) si-ku-(e)	after a meal
공복에 gong-bog-e	on an empty stomach

Medical Services

약을 먹다 yag-eul meok-da	to take a medication
종합검사를 하다/받다 jong-hap-geom-sa-reul ha-da/bat-da	to get a general examination (testing)
주사를 맞다 ju-sa-reul mat-da	to get injected
진찰을 하다/받다 jin-chal-eul ha-da/bat-da	to be examined (in a hospital)
입원하다 ib-won-ha-da	to hospitalize
퇴원하다 toe-won-ha-da	to release

Body Parts

가슴 ga-seum	chest/breast
귀 gwi	ear
눈 nun	eye
다리 da-ri	leg
등 deung	back
머리 meo-ri	head
목 mok	neck
무릎 mu-reup	knee
발 bal	foot
발가락 bal-kka-rak	toe
배 bae	belly
손 son	hand
손가락 son-kka-rak	finger
어깨 eo-kkae	shoulder
얼굴 eol-gul	face
엉덩이 eong-deong-i	butt, hip
이 i	tooth
입 ip	mouth
코 ko	nose
턱 teok	chin
팔 pal	arm
허리 heo-ri	waist

Symptoms

감기에 걸리다 gam-gi-e geol-li-da	to have a cold
기운이 없다 gi-un-i eop-da	to be lacking in energy
기침을 하다 gi-chim-eul ha-da	to cough
다치다 da-chi-da	to get injured
머리가 아프다 meo-ri-ga a-peu-da	to have a headache
목감기에 걸리다 mok-gam-gi-e geol-li-da	to have a sore throat
목이 붓다 mog-i but-da	to have a sore throat
배가 아프다 bae-ga a-peu-da	to have stomach pain
상처가 나다 sang-cheo-ga na-da	to get hurt
설사를 하다 seol-ssa-reul ha-da	to have diarrhea
소화가 안 되다 so-hwa-ga an-doe-da	to have indigestion
숨쉬기가 힘들다 sum-swi-gi-ga him-deul-da	to have difficulty breathing
어지럽다 eo-ji-reop-da	to be dizzy
열이 나다 yeol-i na-da	to have a fever
이가 아프다 i-ga a-peu-da	to have a toothache
코가 막히다 ko-ga ma-ki-da	to have nasal congestion
콧물이 나다 kon-mul-i na-da	to have a runny nose
토하다 to-ha-da	to have been vomiting
피가 나다 pi-ga na-da	to bleed
피곤하다 pi-gon-ha-da	to be tired

문화적 참고사항 Cultural Note

Hospitals in Korea

In the United States, the terms "hospital," "medical clinic," and "doctor's office" indicate the size of the facility and the level of service provided. In Korea, all facilities are called 병원. Reservations are not required, but waits at general hospitals can be several hours. At other hospitals, the wait can be less than thirty minutes. One dials 119 for emergencies.

Most Korean citizens have medical insurance. In 1976, legislation was passed that required large companies to provide insurance for their employees. More recently, insurance benefits have been made mandatory for public employees and the employees of private schools. For those who do not qualify for these and other types of private insurance, the option is available to join a community health insurance plan. These are accepted at almost all 병원, whether they are general hospitals, dental clinics, midwife clinics, pharmacies, or facilities specializing in traditional Asian medicine.

연습문제 Exercises

1. Please respond to the following:

(1) 어서 오세요. 어떻게 오셨어요? eo-seo o-se-yo. eo-tteo-ke
  o-syeoss-eo-yo?
(2) 어디가 어떻게 아프세요? eo-di-ga eo-tteo-ke a-peu-se-yo?
(3) 언제부터 아프기 시작하셨어요? eon-je-bu-teo a-peu-gi
  si-ja-ka-syeoss-eo-yo?
(4) 어떤 회사 제품으로 드릴까요? eo-tteon hoe-sa je-pum-eu-ro
  deu-ril-kka-yo?
(5) 마지막으로 식사를 하신 게 언제지요? ma-ji-mag-eu-ro sik-
  sa-reul ha-sin ge eon-je-ji-yo?

2. Please translate the following into English:

(1) 감기에 걸린 것 같은데 어지럽고 기운이 없어요.
  gam-gi-e geol-lin geot gat-eun-de eo-ji-reop-go gi-un-i
  eops-eo-yo.
(2) 춥고 땀이 나면서 기침을 자꾸 해요.
  chup-go ttam-i na-myeon-seo gi-chim-eul ja-kku hae-yo.
(3) 어제 밤새도록 설사하고 토했어요.
  eo-je bam-sae-do-rok seol-ssa-ha-go to-haess-eo-yo.
(4) 너무 어지러워서 앉아 있을 수가 없어요.
  neo-mu eo-ji-reo-wo-seo anj-a iss-eul su-ga eops-eo-yo.
(5) 검사를 해 봐야 알겠지만 장염에 걸린 것 같아요.
  geom-sa-reul hae bwa-ya al-get-ji-man jang-yeom-e geol-lin
  geot gat-a-yo.
(6) 요즘엔 좋은 약이 많으니까 걱정 많이 안 하셔도 괜찮아요.
  yo-jeum-en jo-eun yag-i man-eu-ni-kka geok-jeong man-i an
  ha-syeo-do gwaen-chan-a-yo.

3. Please translate the following into Korean:

(1) My gums are frequently swollen, and I often bleed when I brush
    my teeth.
(2) For sure, please use an anti-peridentitis toothpaste when you
    brush your teeth
(3) With these pills, please take two after every meal, three times
    a day.
(4) Please give me an anti-peridentitis toothpaste, a box of floss,
    and a bottle of mouthwash.
(5) Please use floss and mouthwash for sure after you brush
    your teeth.

4. Please write the meaning of the words below and compose
    sentences using them:

(1) 심심하다 sim-sim-ha-da
(2) 지루하다 ji-ru-ha-da
(3) 피곤하다 pi-gon-ha-da
(4) 신나다 sin-na-da
(5) 무섭다 mu-seop-da

5. Please fill in the blanks with the appropriate words:

[내과, 외과, 소아과, 안과, 치과]

(1) 배가 아프거나 감기에 걸리면 _____에 가야 합니다.
(2) 눈이 아프면_____에 가야 합니다.
(3) 이가 아플 때는_____에 가야 합니다.
(4) 아기나 어린이가 아플 때는_____에 가야 합니다.
(5) 넘어졌을 때 피가 많이 나면_____에 가야 합니다.

6. Please write a paragraph about your experience in a hospital.

◇◇◇◇◇◇◇◇

Key to Exercises

Lesson 1

2.
(1) Thank you.
(2) Excuse me.
(3) I am sorry.
(4) Welcome.
(5) Don't mention it.

3.
(1) 그 동안 어떻게 지내셨습니까? geu-dong-an eo-tteo-ke ji-nae-syeot-seum-ni-kka?
(2) 덕분에 잘 지냈습니다. deok-bun-e jal ji-naet-seum-ni-da.
(3) 오래간만입니다. o-rae-gan-man-im-ni-da.
(4) 다음에 또 뵙겠습니다. da-eum-e tto boep-get-seum-ni-da.
(5) 다시 뵙게 돼서 반갑습니다. da-si boep-ge dwae-seo ban-gap-seum-ni-da.

Lesson 2

2.
(1) I come from Korea. I live in Su-won.
(2) I am not Korean. I am Chinese.
(3) You and I are the same age. I am 32 years old, too.
(4) We don't have a kid yet. There are only two of us, my wife and I.

3.
(1) 저는 한국계 미국인입니다. jeo-neun han-guk-gye mi-gug-in-im-ni-da.
(2) 저는 미시간에서 태어났습니다. jeo-neun mi-si-gan-e-seo tae-eo-nat-seum-ni-da.
(3) 저는 캐나다에서 왔습니다. jeo-neun kae-na-da-e-seo wat-seum-ni-da.

(4) 저는 칠월 생입니다. jeo-neun chil-wol-saeng-im-ni-da.

(5) 저는 형제가 없습니다. jeo-neun hyeong-je-ga eop-seum-ni-da.

Lesson 3

2.

(1) There is a shopping center inside the apartment complex, so it is very convenient.

(2) I moved last Friday and almost finished putting things in order during the weekend.

(3) That building has had construction these past few days, so it is too crowded.

(4) There is a coffee shop in the basement of the Je-il building.

(5) Please cross the signal light and go straight on your right-hand side.

3.

(1) 책상 위에 컴퓨터가 있어요. chaek-sang wi-e keom-pyu-teo-ga iss-eo-yo.

(2) 제 가방은 탁자 밑에 있어요. je ga-bang-eun tak-ja mit-e iss-eo-yo.

(3) 침대 옆에 전화기가 있어요. chim-dae yeop-e jeon-hwa-gi-ga iss-eo-yo.

(4) 창문은 소파 뒤에 있어요. chang-mun-eun sso-pa dwi-e iss-eo-yo.

(5) 거실 앞에 문이 있어요. geo-sil ap-e mun-i iss-eo-yo.

Lesson 4

2.

(1) Yesterday was my sister's birthday and I completely forgot.

(2) It conflicts with the newcomer's reception.

(3) Tomorrow is the day of my college alumni reunion.

(4) It's almost time to go home already.

(5) I should stop by a watch repair shop when I go home.

(6) Don't you think it might be that the battery is worn out?

3.

(1) 천구백구십칠년 칠월 십육일 chon-gu-baek-gu-sip-chil-lyeon chil-wol sim-nyug-il

(2) 오후 열두시 삼십분 o-hu yeol-ttu-si sam-sip-bun

(3) 천구백육십오년 유월 삼십일 cheon-gu-baek-yuk-sip-o-nyeon yu-wol sam-sib-il

(4) 오후 세시 사십오분 o-hu se-si sa-sib-o-bun

(5) 이천사년 팔월 칠일 i-cheon-sa-nyeon pal-wol chil-il

(6) 오전 일곱시 십오분 o-jeon il-gop-si sib-o-bun

(7) 이천년 시월 이십구일 i-cheon-nyeon si-wol i-sip-gu-il

(8) 오전 아홉시 이십분 o-jeon a-hop-si i-sip-bun

(9) 이천육년 십이월 이십오일 i-cheon-nyung-nyeon sib-i-wol i-sib-o-il

(10) 오전 열시 사십분 o-jeon yeol-ssi sa-sip-bun

Lesson 5

2.

(1) Please say to call back to the office as soon as she gets the message.

(2) Everyone knows there is a staff meeting tomorrow at 4:00, right?

(3) I contacted everyone yesterday, but I couldn't get a hold of one person.

(4) I urgently need to contact him, but I don't have his phone number.

(5) I am sorry for calling you so late at night.

3.

(1) 수신자 부담으로 전화를 좀 걸고 싶은데요.
    su-sin-ja bu-dam-eu-ro jeon-hwa-reul jon geol-go sip-eun-de-yo.

(2) 죄송합니다. 전화를 잘 못 건 것 같아요.

  joe-song-ham-ni-da jeon-hwa-reul jal mot geon geot gat-a-yo.

(3) 자동 응답기에 메모를 남겨 주십시오.

  ja-dong eung-dap-gi-e me-mo-reul nam-gyeo ju-sip-si-o.

(4) 신호는 가는데 전화를 안 받아요.

  sin-ho-neun ga-neun-de jeon-hwa-reul an bad-a-yo.

(5) 전화가 고장난 것 같아요.

  jeon-hwa-ga go-jang-nan geot gat-a-yo.

Lesson 6

2.

(1) It is showing unusually high temperatures not only in Korea but all around the world these days.

(2) It's worse in Korea because it's so humid in the summer.

(3) It's so hot and humid that I don't want to go out.

(4) Actually I had a plan to go to see a movie tomorrow with my friend.

(5) It's a new spy movie and supposed to be really good.

3.

(1) 저는 주말동안 텔레비전 보는 것을 좋아하는데 이번 주말에는 너무 바빴어요.

  jeo-neun ju-mal-ttong-an tel-le-bi-jeon bo-neun geos-eul jo-a-ha-neun-de i-beon ju-mal-e-neun neo-mu ba-ppass-eo-yo.

(2) 제 취미는 그림 그리기이고, 제 남동생 취미는 피아노 치기입니다.

  je chwi-mi-neun geu-rim geu-ri-gi-i-go, je nam-dong-saeng chwi-mi-neun pi-a-no chi-gi-im-ni-da.

(3) 한국의 겨울 날씨는 아주 춥고 바람이 많이 붑니다.

  han-gug-e gyeo-ul nal-ssi-neun a-ju chup-go ba-ram-i man-i bum-ni-da.

(4) 시간이 있을 때 저는 박물관이나 미술관에 가는 것을 좋아
합니다.
si-gan-i iss-eul-ttae jeo-neun bang-mul-gwan-i-na mi-sul-gwan-
e ga-neun geos-eul jo-a-ham-ni-da.

(5) 내일 샌디에고에는 비가 많이 오겠습니다.
nae-il saen-di-e-go-e-neun bi-ga man-i o-get-seum-ni-da.

Lesson 7

2.
(1) This design sells the most these days.
(2) Doesn't this need to be dry-cleaned?
(3) We got a lot of dress pants that don't need to be dry-cleaned
these days.
(4) The regular price is 100,000 won, but there's a sale now so it
will be discounted 25%.
(5) Elderly people like plain colors less than young people do
these days.
(6) I think this dark yellow dress shirt and the striped tie would
match well.
(7) A plain-color one that matches well with any clothes would
be great.

3.
(1) 안겨요. an-gyeo-yo.
(2) 보여요. bo-yeo-yo.
(3) 막혀요. ma-keo-yo.
(4) 물렸어요. mul-lyeoss-eo-yo.
(5) 뺏겼어요. ppaet-gyeoss-eo-yo.

4.
(1) 입고 ip-go   (2) 매고 mae-go   (3) 신고 sin-kko
(4) 끼고 kki-go   (5) 쓰고 sseu-go   (6) 벗고 beot-go
(7) 풀고 pul-go   (8) 벗고 beot-go   (9) 빼고 ppae-go
(10) 벗고 beot-go

Lesson 8

2.
(1) The time seems to be going by so fast today.
(2) All the foods are relatively good there. The restaurant is clean also.
(3) It's my treat today. (or I will treat you today.)
(4) I brought a guest with me today, so please be especially nice.
(5) Please give us some cold water and wet towels, too.
(6) That's why I am a regular customer at this place, you know?

3.
(1) 여기 모두 얼마입니까? yeo-gi mo-du eol-ma-im-ni-kka?
(2) 많이 파세요. man-i pa-se-yo.
(3) 덕분에 잘 먹었습니다. deok-bun-e jal meog-eoss-eum-ni-da.
(4) 다음 번엔 제가 사지요. da-eum beon-en je-ga sa-ji-yo.
(5) 장사 잘 되시지요? jang-sa jal doe-si-ji-yo?
(6) 일찍 나오셨네요. il-jjik na-o-syeon-ne-yo.

4.
(1) 책상 위에 컴퓨터가 없어요. chaek-sang wi-e keom-pu-teo-ga eops-eo-yo.
(2) 우리 아버지는 선생님이 아니세요. u-ri a-beo-ji-neun seon-saeng-nim-i a-ni-se-yo.
(3) 저는 한국어를 잘 몰라요. jeo-neun han-gug-eo-reul jal mol-la-yo.
(4) 저는 한국음식을 안 좋아해요. jeo-neun han-gug-eum-sig-eul an jo-a-hae-yo.
(5) 제 여자친구는 별로 안 예뻐요. je yeo-ja-chin-gu-neun byeol-lo an ye-ppeo-yo.

Lesson 9

2.
(1) Would you like to look at these magazines while you are waiting?
(2) Your hair is pretty thick so without the layering, it will look stuffy.
(3) Since your hair is so dark, try tinting your hair.
(4) Don't change the shape of the hair and just trim it a little shorter, please.
(5) I guess my hair grows faster than other people's.

3.
(1) 태웠어요. tae-woss-eo-yo
(2) 끓여요. kkeul-yeo-yo
(3) 울려요. ul-lyeo-yo
(4) 벗겨요. beot-geo-yo
(5) 입혀요. i-pyeo-yo
(6) 낮춰 주세요. nat-chwo ju-se-yo
(7) 재워요. jae-wo-yo

4.
(1) 그래서 geu-rae-seo
(2) 그런데 geu-reon-de
(3) 그리고 geu-ri-go
(4) 그런데 geu-reon-de
(5) 그래서 geu-rae-seo
(6) 그러면 geu-reo-myeon
(7) 그렇지만 geu-reo-chi-man

Lesson 10

2.
(1) Don't you think traffic is a lot smoother during the weekdays rather than the weekends?

(2) May I have your passport and plane ticket?

(3) If it leaves at 12:30, what time can I expect it to arrive in Pusan?

(4) Since this train will directly take you to Pusan, you will not need to change trains.

(5) The gate number is 38 and your seat number is 27A.

3.

(1) 길이 많이 막히네요. gil-i man-i ma-ki-ne-yo.

(2) 기차 타는 데가 어디죠? gi-cha ta-neun de-ga eo-di-jyo?

(3) 부산행 1시(한 시)표 두장만 주세요. bu-san-haeng han-si-pyo du-jang-man ju-se-yo.

(4) 저기 육교 밑에 세워 주세요. jeo-gi yuk-gyo mit-e se-wo ju-se-yo.

(5) 잔돈은 그냥 가지세요. jan-don-eun geu-nyang ga-ji-se-yo.

Lesson 11

2.

(1) My passort can be used as an ID, right? And I don't have a stamp.

(2) Please write your name, address, and pin number on this application form.

(3) Please give me everything in checks and only the change in cash.

(4) Express mail will take three days, but it's a little expensive. Are you in a hurry?

(5) If you send it as air-mail, it will take about a week.

(6) Because of the price increase last week, you will probably need to use 230-won stamps now.

3.

(1) 통장을 하나 만들려고 하는데요.
tong-jang-eul ha-na man-deul-lyeo-go ha-neun-de-yo.

(2) 신분증하고 도장 좀 주시겠습니까?
sin-bun-jjeung-ha-go do-jang jom ju-si-get-seum-ni-kka?
(3) 현금카드도 필요하시지요?
hyeon-geum-ka-deu-do pil-yo-ha-si-ji-yo?
(4) 오늘 환율이 어떻게 되나요?
o-neul hwan-nyul-i eo-tteo-ke doe-na-yo?
(5) 수수료 5000(오천)원 공제하고 드렸습니다.
su-su-ryo o-cheon-won gong-je-ha-go deu-ryeot-seum-ni-da.

4.
(1) to withdraw money
(2) to earn money
(3) to send money
(4) to win money
(5) to need money

5.
(1) 이백오십원 i-baeg-o-sib-won
(2) 칠만팔천삼백오십원 chil-man-pal-cheon-sam-baeg-o-sib-won
(3) 사십육만구천칠백원
sa-sim-nyung-man-gu-cheonchil-baeg-won
(4) 백이십오만칠천팔백원
baeg-i-sib-o-man-chil-cheon-pal-baeg-won
(5) 삼천사백오십만원 sam-cheon-sa-baeg-o-sim-man-won

Lesson 12

2.
(1) I feel like I have a cold; I am dizzy and have no energy.
(2) I am cold and sweating, and I am coughing frequently.
(3) I have had diarrhea and was throwing up all night yesterday.
(4) I feel so dizzy that I cannot sit down.
(5) I will see the details after tests, but I think you have enteritis.
(6) Because there are lots of good medicines these days, you don't
    need to worry too much.

3.
(1) 잇몸이 자주 붓고 양치질할 때 잇몸에서 자꾸 피가 나요.
(2) 양치질할 때 꼭 치주염 예방용 치약을 사용하세요.
(3) 이 알약은 하루에 3번(세 번)씩 식후에 2알(두 알)씩 드세요.
(4) 치주염 예방용 치약하고 플로스랑 마우스워시도 하나
    주세요.
(5) 양치질 한 다음에 플로스하고 마우스워시 꼭 하시고요.

4.
(1) to feel bored
(2) to be bored to death
(3) to be tired
(4) to be excited
(5) to be scared/afraid

5.
(1) 내과 nae-kkwa
(2) 안과 na-kkwa
(3) 치과 chi-kkwa
(4) 소아과 so-a-kkwa
(5) 외과 oe-kkwa

◇◇◇◇◇◇◇◇

Appendix 1: A Brief Korean Grammar

1. WORD ORDER

Korean is a predicate-final language. All sentences end with the predicate, i.e. the verb or adjective. All other elements in the sentence, such as the subject or object, appear before the predicate. Korean particles, the equivalent of English prepositions (e.g. *from, in, with*, or *to*), always appear after the noun or pronoun to which they're related. The elements before the predicate can be placed in any order as long as the sentence ends with the predicate, a tendency that has led to Korean being called a "free word order" language.

Consider this English sentence: *Michael eats breakfast at a restaurant in the morning.* Let's break it down into its component parts:

Michael <subject>
    eats <predicate>
        breakfast <object>
            at a restaurant <location> (*at* is the preposition/particle)
                in the morning <time> (*in* is the preposition/particle)

Now let's convert this to a Korean structural pattern:

Michael (+ subject marker) <subject>
    the morning + in <time + time particle>
        a restaurant + at <location + location particle>
            breakfast (+ object marker) <object>
                eats <predicate>

So, in Korean, this would be:

마이클이	아침에	식당에서	밥을	먹는다.
(ma-i-keul-i)	(a-chim-e)	(sik-dang-e-seo)	(bab-eul)	(meong-neun-da)
Michael	*the morning-in*	*a restaurant-at*	*breakfast*	*eats.*

Other possibilities include:

식당에서	아침에	마이클이	밥을	먹는다.
(sik-dang-e-seo)	(a-chim-e)	(ma-i-keul-i)	(bab-eul)	(meong-neun-da)
a restaurant-at	*the morning-in*	*Michael*	*breakfast*	*eats.*

아침에	마이클이	식당에서	밥을	먹는다.
(a-chim-e)	(ma-i-keul-i)	(sik-dang-e-seo)	(bab-eul)	(meong-neun-da)
the morning-in	*Michael*	*a restaurant-at*	*breakfast*	*eats.*

As can be seen, the sentence elements can be arranged in any order as long as the sentence ends with the predicate.

2. SPEECH LEVELS

Korean has four speech levels that indicate the speaker's interpersonal relationship with the hearer. These speech levels are indicated by sentence-final suffixes attached to predicates. These suffixes are illustrated below.

	Statement	Question	Request	Suggestion
deferential	-습/ㅂ니다 (-seum/-m-ni-da)	-습/ㅂ니까? (-seum/-m-ni-kka)	-(으)십시오 ([-eu]-sip-si-o)	N/A
polite	-아/어요 (-a/eo-yo)	-아/어요? (-a/eo-yo)	-아/어요 (-a/eo-yo)	-아/어요 (-a/eo-yo)
intimate	-아/어 (-a/eo)	-아/어? (-a/eo)	-아/어 (-a/eo)	-아/어 (-a/eo)
plain	-은/는/ㄴ다 (-eun/neun/n-da)	-니? (-ni)	-아/어라 (-a/eo-ra)	-자 (-ja)

For example, 먹습니다 (meok-seum-ni-da), 먹어요 (meog-eo-yo), 먹어 (meog-eo), and 먹는다 (meong-neun-da) all mean *[someone] eats*, expressed in different speech levels.

The most common level used to an adult is the polite one. While the deferential level is used mostly by male speakers in formal situations such as news reports or public lectures, the polite level is widely used by both males and females in daily conversation.

The intimate level and the plain level are used by an old person when speaking to a younger one, by a child to his or her siblings, or between close friends whose friendship began in childhood or adolescence.

3. PRONOUNS

Personal Pronouns

Singular	*Plain*	*Honorific*	*Humble*
1st person (I, me, myself)	나 / 내 *na / nae*	---	저 / 제 *jeo / je*
2nd person (you)	너 *neo*	---	---
3rd person (for a person) (he, she, it, etc.)	이/그/저사람 *i/geu/jeo-sa-ram*	이/그/저분 *i/geu/jeo-bun*	---
	이/그/저것 (for a thing) *i/geu/jeo-geot*	---	---

The use of personal pronouns is not common in Korean, except for the first person pronoun. With the second and third person, usually either the name or title is used.

Plural	*Plain*	*Honorific*	*Humble*
1st person (we)	우리(들) *u-ri-(deul)*	---	저희(들) *jeo-hui-(deul)*
2nd person (you all)	너희(들) *neo-hui-(deul)*	---	---
3rd person (they)	이/그/저사람들 *i/geu/jeo-sa-ram-deul*	이/그/저분들 *i/geu/jeo-bun-deul*	---
	이/그/저것들 *i/geu/jeo-geot-deul*	---	---

Possessive Pronouns

Singular	*Plain*	*Honorific*	*Humble*
1st person (my)	내 *nae*	---	제 *je*
2nd person (your)	네 *ne*	---	---
3rd person (his/hers/its)	이/그/저 사람(의) *i/geu/jeo-sa-ram-deul-(ui)*	이/그/저분(의) *i/geu/jeo-bun-deul-(ui)*	---

Plural	*Plain*	*Honorific*	*Humble*
1st person (our)	우리(들)(의) *u-ri-(deul)-(ui)*	---	저희(들)(의) *jeo-hui-(deul)-(ui)*
2nd person (your)	너희(들)(의) *neo-hui-(deul)-(ui)*	---	---
3rd person (their)	이/그/저 사람들(의) *i/geu/jeo-sa-ram-deul-(ui)*	이/그/저분들(의) *i/geu/jeo-bun-deul-(ui)*	---
	이/그/저것들(의) *i/geu/jeo-geot-deul-(ui)*	---	---

Plural nouns in English use a plural suffix, e.g. the "s" in "fields". In Korean, the plural suffix –다(-ta, -da) is optional and rarely used.

4. DEMONSTRATIVES

For the topic markers, subject markers and object markers, please see the
section on particles below.

이 (i)
this (*near speaker*)

이것/이거	이건 (*topic*)	이게 (*subj.*)	이걸 (*obj.*)
i-geot/i-geo	*i-geon*	*i-ge*	*i-geol*

여기 (*place*)	이쪽 (*direction*)	이사람 (*person*)	이분 (*person, hon.*)
yeo-gi	*i-jjok*	*i-sa-ram*	*i-bun*

그 (geu)
that (*near listener*)

그것/그거	그건 (*topic*)	그게 (*subj.*)	그걸 (*obj.*)
geu-geot/geu-geo	*geu-geon*	*geu-ge*	*geu-geol*

거기 (*place*)	그쪽 (*direction*)	그사람 (*person*)	그분 (*person, hon.*)
geo-gi	*geu-jjok*	*geu-sa-ram*	*geu-bun*

저(jeo)
that over there (*away from both speaker and listener*)

저것/저거	저건 (*topic*)	저게 (*subj.*)	저걸 (*obj.*)
jeo-geot/jeo-geo	*jeo-geon*	*jeo-ge*	*jeo-geol*

저기 (*place*)	저쪽 (*direction*)	저사람 (*person*)	저분 (*person, hon.*)
jeo-gi	*jeo-jjok*	*jeo-sa-ram*	*jeo-bun*

5. PARTICLES

Particles are words that indicate the context in which one is to understand
the noun, phrase, or sentence to which they are attached. They are usually
short, often no more than a syllable, and some have functions similar to such
English prepositions as *in, to, at,* and *with*. Others are used as markers for
the subject and object nouns in a sentence. Remember that particles always

come after the sentence elements they modify. Occasionally, different particles are used depending on whether the word to which they are attached ends with a consonant or a vowel.

Subject

-이 (-i)	(*used after a consonant*)	학생이 (hak-saeng-i) *student* (+ subject marker [*subj.*])
-가 (-ga)	(*used after a vowel*)	의사가 (ui-sa-ga) *doctor* (+ *subj.*)
-께서 (-kke-seo)	(*honorific*)	아버지께서 (a-beo-ji-kke-seo) *father* (+ *subj.*)

Object

-을 (-eul)	(*used after a consonant*)	책상을 (chaek-sang-eul) *desk* (+ object marker [*obj.*])
-를 (-reul)	(*used after a vowel*)	의자를 (ui-ja-reul) *chair* (+ *obj.*)

Topic

-은 (-eun)	(*used after a consonant*)	한국말은 (han-gung-mal-eun) *Korean language* (+ topic marker [*top.*])
-는 (-nuen)	(*used after a vowel*)	한국어는 (han-gug-eo-neun) *Korean language* (+ *top.*)

Dative (Indirect Object)

-에게 (-e-ge)		친구<u>에게</u> (chin-gu-<u>e-ge</u>) *to my friend*
-한테 (-han-te)	*(colloquial)*	친구<u>한테</u> (chin-gu-<u>han-te</u>) *to my friend*
-께 (-kke)	*(honorific)*	아버지<u>께</u> (a-beo-ji-<u>kke</u>) *to my father*

Source

-에게서 (-e-ge-seo)		친구<u>에게서</u> (chin-gu-<u>e-ge-seo</u>) *from my friend*
-한테서 (-han-te-seo)	*(colloquial)*	친구<u>한테서</u> (chin-gu-<u>han-te-seo</u>) *from my friend*

Location

-에 (-e)	*(current)*	학교<u>에</u> 있어요. (hak-gyo-<u>e</u> iss-eo-yo.) *I am in school.*
	(destination)	학교<u>에</u> 가요. (hak-gyo-<u>e</u> ga-yo.) *I go to school.*
-에서 (-e-seo)	*(place of action)*	학교<u>에서</u> 공부해요. (hak-gyo-<u>e-seo</u> gong-bu-hae-yo.) *I study at school.*

	(*starting point of action*)	학교<u>에서</u> 왔어요. (hak-gyo-<u>e-seo</u> wass-eo-yo.) *I came from the school.*
-(으)로 ([-eu]-ro)	(*direction of action*)	서울<u>로</u> 가요. (seo-<u>ul-lo</u> ga-yo.) *I go to Seoul.*
-에서 . . . -까지 (from . . . to . . .) (-e-seo ... -kka-ji)		미국<u>에서</u> 한국<u>까지</u> (mi-gug-<u>e-seo</u> han-guk-<u>kka-ji</u>) *from America to Korea*

Time

-에 (-e)	아침<u>에</u> (a-chim-<u>e</u>) *in the morning*
-부터 . . . -까지 (from . . . until . . .) (-bu-teo ... -kka-ji)	아침<u>부터</u> 저녁<u>까지</u> (a-chim-<u>bu-teo</u> jeo-nyeok-<u>kka-ji</u>) *from morning until evening*

Purpose

-(으)러 ([-eu]-reo)	(in order to)	친구 만나<u>러</u> (chin-gu man-na-<u>reo</u>) *in order to meet my friend*
-(으)려고 ([-eu]-ryeo-go)	(in order to)	서울에 가<u>려고</u> (seo-ul-e ga-<u>ryeo-go</u>) *in order to go to Seoul*

Miscellaneous

-(으)로 ([-eu]-ro)	(by means of)	비행기<u>로</u> (bi-haeng-gi-<u>ro</u>) *(transportation)*

		볼펜으로 (bol-pen-<u>eu-ro</u>) *(instrument)*
-도 (-do)	(also)	나도 가고 싶어요. (na-<u>do</u> ga-go sip-eo-yo.) *I also want to go.*
-만 (-man)	(only; just)	콜라만 주세요. (col-la-<u>man</u> ju-se-yo) *Please just give me a Coke.*
-(이)나 ([-i]-na)	(or something; just)	오늘 집에서 잠이나 잘래요. (o-neul jib-e-seo jam-<u>i-na</u> jal-lae-yo.) *I'll just stay home and sleep today.*
	(as many as; already)	오늘 커피를 세잔이나 마셨 어요. (o-neul keo-pi-reul se-jan-<u>i-</u> <u>na</u> ma-syeoss-eo-yo.) *I already drank three cups of coffee today.*
-밖에 (-bakk-e)	(nothing but, only)	다섯 사람밖에 안 왔어요. (da-seot sa-ram-<u>bakk-e</u> an wass-eo-yo.) *Only five people came.*

(-밖에 always accompanies a negative verb. [Verbs are discussed below in
Numbers 6, 7, and 8.])

-에 (-e)	(per, for)	한 상자에 2000원이에요. (han sang-ja-<u>e</u> i-cheon-won- i-<u>e</u>-yo.) *It's 2000 won [Korean currency] per box.*

6. QUESTION WORDS

누가
(nu-ga)
who (*subject*)

누가 간호원이세요?
(<u>nu-ga</u> gan-ho-won-i-se-yo?)
Who's the nurse?

누구
(nu-gu)
who

누구를 찾으세요?
(<u>nu-gu</u>-reul chaj-eu-se-yo?)
Who are you looking for?

무슨
(mu-seun)

what kind of; what

무슨 일을 하세요?
(<u>mu-seun</u> il-eul ha-se-yo?)

What kind of work do you do?
What do you do for a living?

무엇
(mu-eot)
what

무엇을 좋아하세요?
<u>mu-eos</u>-eul jo-a-ha-se-yo?
What do you like?

뭐
(mwo)
what (*colloquial*)

뭐가 제일 어려우세요?
(<u>mwo</u>-ga je-il eo-ryeo-u-se-yo?)
What is the most difficult thing for you?

어느
(eo-neu)
which

어느 나라 사람이세요?
(<u>eo-neu</u> na-ra sa-ram-i-se-yo?)
Which country are you from?

어디
(eo-di)
where

어디 사세요?
(<u>eo-di</u> sa-se-yo?)
Where do you live?

어떻게
(eo-tteo-ke)
how

부산에 어떻게 가요?
(bu-san-e <u>eo-tteo-ke</u> ga-yo?)
How can I get to Pusan?

어떤
(eo-tteon)
what kind of

어떤 사람을 좋아하세요?
(<u>eo-tteon</u> sa-ram-eul jo-a-ha-se-yo?)
What kind of people do you like?

언제   <u>언제</u> 한국에 가세요?
(eon-je)   (<u>eon-je</u> han-gug-e ga-se-yo?)
when   *When are you leaving for Korea?*

얼마나   한국에 <u>얼마나</u> 계실 거예요?
(eol-ma-na)   (han-gug-e <u>eol-ma-na</u> gye-sil geo-ye-yo?)
how long/many/much   *How long are you staying in Korea?*

왜   <u>왜</u> 한국에 가세요?
(wae)   (<u>wae</u> han-gug-e ga-se-yo?)
why   *Why are you going to Korea?*

7. INDEFINITE PRONOUNS

누가   <u>누가</u> 왔어요.
(nu-ga)   (<u>nu-ga</u> wass-eo-yo.)
someone/anyone   *There is someone.*

누구   <u>누구</u>를 데리고 올 거예요.
(nu-gu)   (<u>nu-gu</u>-reul de-ri-go ol geo-ye-yo.)
someone/anyone   *I am bringing someone.*

무슨   <u>무슨</u> 냄새가 나요.
(mu-seun)   (<u>mu-seun</u> naem-sae-ga na-yo.)
some kind of   *I smell something.*

뭐   <u>뭐</u> 좀 샀어요.
(mwo)   (<u>mwo</u> jom sass-eo-yo.)
something/anything   *I bought something.*

무엇   (original form of 뭐 *mwo*)
(mu-eot)
something/anything

어느   <u>어느</u> 날 갑자기 귀가 잘 안 들렸어요.
(eo-neu)   (<u>eo-neu</u>-nal gap-ja-gi gwi-ga jal an
                          deul-lyeoss-eo-yo.)
one   *One day, all of a sudden, I couldn't hear.*

어디
(eo-di)
somewhere/anywhere

<u>어디</u> 좀 가고 싶어요.
(<u>eo-di</u> jom ga-go sip-eo-yo.)
I want to go somewhere.

어떻게
(eo-tteo-ke)
somehow

<u>어떻게</u> 좀 해 보세요.
(<u>eo-tteo-ke</u> jom hae bo-se-yo)
Please do something.

어떤
(eo-tteon)
some

<u>어떤</u> 사람이 집에 왔어요.
(<u>eo-tteon</u> sa-ram-i jib-e wass-eo-yo.)
Somebody came to our house.

언제
(eon-je)
sometime/anytime

<u>언제</u> 한번 만날까요?
(<u>eon-je</u> han-beon man-nal-kka-yo?)
Should we meet sometime?

누구든지
(nu-gu-deun-ji)
whoever/whomever

<u>누구든지</u> 안젤라를 좋아해요.
(<u>nu-gu-deun-ji</u> an-jel-la-reul jo-a-hae-yo.)
Whomever you ask, they all like Angela.

뭐든지
(mwo-deun-ji)
whatever; anything

저는 <u>뭐든지</u> 다잘 먹어요.
(jeo-neun <u>mwo-deun-ji</u> da jal meog-eo-yo.)
Whatever the food is, I will eat very well.

어느 것이든지
(eo-neu geos-i-deun-ji)

whichever

한국음식은 <u>어느 것이든지</u> 다 좋아해요.
(han-gug-eum-sig-eun <u>eo-neu geos-i-deun-ji</u> da
jo-a-hae-yo.)
I like all Korean food, whichever dish it may be.

어디든지
(eo-di-deun-ji)

wherever

주말에는 <u>어디든지</u> 여행을 가고 싶어요.
(ju-mal-e-neun <u>eo-di-deun-ji</u> yeo-haeng-eul
ga-go sip-eo-yo.)
*Wherever the destination may be, I want to
travel on weekends.*

어떻게든지
(eo-tteo-ke-deun-ji)

whatsoever, no matter
what

<u>어떻게든지</u> 외국에 한번 가고 싶어요.
(<u>eo-tteo-ke-deun-ji</u> oe-gug-e han-beon ga-go
sip-eo-yo.)
No matter what, I want to go abroad once.

어떤 것이든지 (eo-tteon geos-i-deun-ji) whichever/whatever	저는 영화는 <u>어떤 것이든지</u> 다 봐요. (jeo-neun yeong-hwa-neun <u>eo-tteon geos-i- deun-ji</u> da bwa-yo.) *I like all movies, whatever kind you might think of.*
언제든지 (eon-je-deun-ji) whenever	<u>언제든지</u> 우리 집에 놀러 오세요. (<u>eon-je-deun-ji</u> u-ri-jib-e nol-leo o-se-yo.) *Come to my house whenever you like.*

8. WORD FORMATION

Noun Formation

To form nouns from a verb, add -기 (-gi) or -는 것 (-neun-geot) after the verb stem.

Verb	*Noun*
걷다 (geot-da) *walk*	걷기 / 걷는 것 (geot-gi)/ (geon-neun geot) *walking*
노래하다 (no-rae-ha-da) *sing*	노래하기 / 노래하는 것 (no-rae-ha-gi) / (no-rae-ha-neun geot) *singing*
쇼핑가다 (syo-ping-ga-da) *shop*	쇼핑가기 / 쇼핑가는 것 (syo-ping-ga-gi) / (syo-ping-ga-neun geot) *shopping*
자다 (ja-da) *sleep*	자기 / 자는 것 (ja-gi) / (ja-neun geot) *sleeping*

Verb Formation

To form verbs from a noun, add -하다 (-ha-da) to the noun.

Noun	*Verb*
일	일하다
(il)	(il-ha-da)
work	*to work*
공부	공부하다
(gong-bu)	(gong-bu-ha-da)
study	*to study*
생각	생각하다
(saeng-gak)	(saeng-ga-ka-da)
thinking	*to think*
수영	수영하다
(su-yeong)	(su-yeong-ha-da)
swimming	*to swim*

Noun Modifier Formation

A construction consisting of a clause with either ~는 or (으)ㄴ before a noun is called a relative clause. It is a type of noun-modifying construction. An example would be [hangul/romanization/English]. The key thing to remember about relative clauses in Korean is that they always precede the noun they modify. Korean differs from English in that the clauses are not accompanied by such relative pronouns as *who*, *that*, and *which*.

	Active Verb: 읽다 / 가다 (ilk-da/ga-da) *to read, to go*	**Descriptive:** 좋다 / 싸다 (jo-ta/ssa-da) *to be good,* *to be cheap*	있다/없다 (it-da/eop-da) *to exist, to not exist*	이다 (i-da) *to be*
Past / **Retrospective** **(Imperfect)**	-던 읽던 / 가던 (ilk-deon/ga-deon) *was reading,* *was going*	-던 좋던 / 싸던 (jo-teon/ssa-deon) *was good,* *was cheap*	-던 있던 / 없던 (it-deon/eop-deon) *was, wasn't*	-던 이던 (i-deon) *was*
Past / **Completed**	-(으)ㄴ 읽은 / 간 (ilg-eun/gan) *read, went*			
Present / **Ongoing**	-는 읽는 / 가는 (ilk-neun/ga-neun) *is reading, is going*	-(으)ㄴ 좋은 / 싼 (jo-eun/ssan) *is good, is cheap*	-는 있는 / 없는 (in-neun/eom-neun) *is, isn't*	-ㄴ 인 (in) *is*
Future / **Unrealized**	-(으)ㄹ 읽을 / 갈 (ilg-eul/gal) *will read, will go*	-(으)ㄹ 좋을 / 쌀 (jo-eul/ssal) *will be good,* *will be cheap*	-(으)ㄹ 있을/ 없을 (iss-eul/eops-eul) *will exist, won't exist*	-ㄹ 일 (il) *will be*

Adverb Formation

To form an adverb from a descriptive verb, add -게 (-ge) after the descriptive verb's stem.

Descriptive Verb	*Adverb*
재미있다	재미있게
(jae-mi-it-da)	(jae-mi-it-ge)
interesting	*interestingly*
늦다	늦게
(neut-da)	(neut-ge)
late	*lately*
바쁘다	바쁘게
(ba-ppeu-da)	(ba-ppeu-ge)
busy	busily
시끄럽다	시끄럽게
(si-kkeu-reop-da)	(si-kkeu-reop-ge)
loud	*loudly*

9. TENSES

Korean verbs have three tenses: present, past, and future. The rules for conjugating them into the tenses appear below. Please note that verbs are conjugated by tense only and not by person.

Present:

verb stem + -아/어요

(-a/eo-yo)

지금 한국에 가요.
(ji-geum han-gug-e ga-yo.)
I am leaving for Korea now.

Past:

> verb stem + -았/었어요
> (-ass/eoss-eo-yo)

> 작년에 한국에 갔어요.
> (jang-nyeon-e han-gug-e gass-eo-yo.)
> *I went to Korea last year.*

Future (probability in the future):

> verb stem + -(으)ㄹ 거예요
> (-[eu]l kkeo-ye-yo)

> 내년에 한국에 갈 거예요.
> (nae-nyeon-e han-gug-e gal kkeo-ye-yo.)
> *I will go to Korea next year.*

10. NEGATION OF VERBS

Short-form Negation

안-	안 먹어요.
(an-)	(an meog-eo-yo.)
don't	*I don't eat.*
	공부 안 해요.
	(gong-bu an hae-yo.)
	I don't study.
못-	못 먹어요.
(mot-)	(mot meog-eo-yo.)
can't	*I can't eat.*
	공부 못해요.
	(Gong-bu mo-tae-yo.)
	I can't study.

Long-form Negation

-지 않다
(-ji anta)

먹지 않아요.
(meok-ji an-a-yo.)
I don't eat.

-지 못하다
(ji mo-ta-da)

먹지 못해요.
(meok-ji mo-tae-yo.)
I can't eat.

-지 말다 (request only)
(-ji mal-da)

먹지 마세요.
(meok-ji ma-se-yo)
Please don't eat it.

Special Negation Words

있다 (it-da) versus 없다 (eop-ta)

있어요
(iss-eo-yo)
there is . . .

없어요
(eops-eo-yo)
there is not . . .

이다 (i-da) versus 아니다 (a-ni-da)

이에요.
(i-e-yo)
it is . . .

아니에요.
(a-ni-e-yo)
it is not . . .

알다 (al-da) versus 모르다 (mo-reu-da)

> 알아요 . . .
> (al-a-yo . . .)
> *I know . . .*

> 몰라요 . . .
> (mol-la-yo . . .)
> *I don't know . . .*

좋다 (jo-ta) versus 싫다 (sil-ta)

> 좋아요 . . .
> (jo-a-yo . . .)
> *I like . . .*

> 싫어요 . . .
> (sil-eo-yo . . .)
> *I don't like . . .*

좋아하다 (jo-a-ha-da) vs. 싫어하다 (sil-eo-ha-da)

> 좋아해요 . . .
> (jo-a-hae-yo . . .)
> *s/he likes . . .*

> 싫어해요
> (sil-eo-hae-yo . . .)
> *s/he doesn't like . . .*

11. HONORIFIC EXPRESSIONS

Korean is a language whose honorific patterns are highly systematic.
Honorific forms appear in hierarchical address/reference terms and titles,
some commonly used nouns and verbs, the pronoun system, particles, and
verb suffixes. Sentences in Korean cannot be formed without knowledge
of one's social relationships to the listener or to the one referenced in terms
of age, kinship, and social status. Honorific forms are used when a social
or familial superior, a distant peer, or a stranger must be referred or spoken
to with respect.

Nouns

	Plain	*Honorific*	*Humble*
age	나이 (na-)	연세 (yeon-se)	
name	이름 (i-reum)	성함 (seong-ham)	
birthday	생일 (saeng-il)	생신 (saeng-sin)	
word	말 (mal)	말씀 (mal-sseum)	말씀 (mal-ssum)
house	집 (jip)	댁 (daek)	
meal	밥 (bap)	진지 (jin-ji)	
counter	사람/명 (sa-ram/myeong)	분 (bun)	

Pronouns

	Plain	Honorific	Humble
he/she	이/그/저사람 (i/geu/jeo-sa-ram)	이/그/저분 (i/geu/jeo-bun)	
I	나는/내가 (na-neun/nae-ga)		저는/제가 (jeo-neun/je-ga)
my	내 (nae)		제 (je)
we	우리 (u-ri)		저희 (jeo-hui)

Verbs

	Plain	Honorific	Humble
see/meet	보다/만나다 (bo-da/man-na-da)	보시다/만나시다 bo-si-da/man-na-si-da	뵙다 bwoep-da
be/exist/stay	있다 (it-da)	계시다 (gye-si-da)	
die	죽다 (juk-da)	돌아가시다 (dol-a-ga-si-da)	
be well/fine	잘 있다 (jal it-da)	안녕하시다 (an-nyeong-ha-si-da)	
sleep	자다 (ja-da)	주무시다 (ju-mu-si-da)	
eat	먹다 (meok-da)	드시다/잡수시다 deu-si-da/jap-su-si-da	
give	주다 (ju-da)	주시다 (ju-si-da)	드리다 deu-ri-da
speak	말하다 (mal-ha-da)	말씀하시다 (mal-sseum-ha-si-da)	말씀드리다 (mal-sseum-deu-ri-da)

ask	물어보다	물어보시다	여쭈어보다
	(mul-eo-bo-da)	(mul-eo-bo-si-da)	(yeo-jju-eo-bo-da)

Particles

subject	-이/가	-께서
	(-I)/(-ga)	(-kke-seo)
topic	-은/는	-께서는
	(-eun)/(neun)	(-kke-seo-neun)
goal	-한테/에게	-께
	(-han-te)/(e-ge)	(-kke)

12. IRREGULAR VERBS

In Korean, there are verbs that change their final sound before a suffix that begins with a certain sound. These verbs are commonly called irregular and are nine types, as shown below.

ㄷ-Irregular Verbs

ㄷ-irregular verbs are those whose stem-final ㄷ becomes ㄹ before a vowel, as in 듣는다 (deut-neun-da) *to listen*, which becomes 들어요 (deul-eo-yo). Other examples:

to ask: 묻는다 (mut-neun-da) → 물어요(mul-eo-yo)
to walk: 걷는다 (geot-neun-da) → 걸어요 (geol-eo-yo)

ㅂ-Irregular Verbs

ㅂ-irregular verbs are those whose final ㅂ sound becomes 우 before a vowel, as in 가깝다 (ga-kkap-da) *to be close*, which becomes 가까워요 (ga-kka-wo-yo). Other examples:

to be cold: 춥다 (chup-da) → 추워요 (chu-wo-yo)
to be difficult: 어렵다 (eo-reop-da) → 어려워요 (eo-ryeo-wo-yo)
to be easy: 쉽다 (swip-da) → 쉬워요 (swi-wo-yo)

to be heavy: 무겁다 (mu-geop-da)   →   무거워요 (mu-geo-wo-yo)
to be hot: 덥다 (deop-da)   →   더워요 (deo-wo-yo)

ㅅ-Irregular Verbs

ㅅ-irregular verbs are those whose final ㅅ is deleted before a vowel, such as 짓는다 (jit-neun-da) vs. 지어요 (ji-eo-yo) "to build," 붓는다 (but-neun-da) vs. 부어요 (bu-eo-yo) "to pour," 젓는다 (jeot-neun-da) vs. 저어요 (jeo-eo-yo) "to stir," and 잇는다 (it-neun-da) vs. 이어요 (i-eo-yo) "to connect."

으-Irregular Verbs

으-irregular verbs are those whose final 으 is deleted before another vowel. All 으 final verbs follow this pattern, such as 쓰다 (sseu-da) vs. 써요 (sseo-yo) "to write," 바쁘다 (ba-ppeu-da) vs. 바빠요 (ba-ppa-yo) "to be busy," 크다 (keu-da) vs. 커요 (keo-yo) "to be big," 예쁘다 (ye-ppeu-da) vs. 예뻐요 (ye-ppeo-yo) "to be pretty," 나쁘다 (na-ppeu-da) vs. 나빠요 (na-ppa-yo) "to be bad," and 아프다 (a-peu-da) vs. 아파요 (a-pa-yo) "to be sick."

ㄹ-Irregular Verbs

ㄹ-irregular verbs are those whose stem-final ㄹ is deleted before the consonants ㄴ, ㅂ, or ㅅ, such as 알아요 (al-a-yo) vs. 아세요 (a-se-yo) "to know," 놀아요 (nol-a-yo) vs. 놉니다 (nop-ni-da) "to play," and 돌아요 (dol-a-yo) vs. 도니까 (do-ni-kka) "to turn." All ㄹ final verbs follow this pattern.

르-Irregular Verbs

르-irregular verbs are those whose final 르 becomes ㄹㄹ before a suffix beginning with –eo or –a, as in 부르다 (bu-reu-da) vs. 불러요 (bul-leo-yo) "to call," 모르다 (mo-reu-da) vs. 몰라요 (mol-la-yo) " to not know," and 빠르다 (ppa-reu-da) vs. 빨라요 (ppal-la-yo) "to be fast."

러-Irregular Verbs

러-irregular verbs are those that undergo ㄹ insertion before a suffix beginning with –eo or –a, such as 푸르다 (pu-reu-da) "to be blue" vs. 푸르러서 (pu-reu-reo-seo) "since it is blue." 이르다 (i-reu-da) and 누르다 (nu-reu-da) also follow this pattern.

여-Irregular Verbs

여-irregular verbs are those that undergo vowel change (from ㅏ to ㅐ) before a suffix beginning with –eo or –a, such as 하다 (ha-da) "to do" vs. 해서 (hae-seo) "because someone does something." All verbs with ~하다, such as좋아하다 (jo-a-ha-da), 싫어하다 (sil-eo-ha-da), 여행하다 (yeo-haeng-ha-da), and 수영하다 (su-yeong-ha-da) follow this pattern.

ㅎin Irregular Verbs

ㅎ irregular verbs are those whose final ㅎ is deleted before a nasal consonant (ㄴ, ㄹ, or ㅁ) and a vowel. They may undergo further phonological change with the following vowel, such as 빨갛다 (ppal-ga-ta) "to be red" vs. 빨간 ppal-gan "red," 하얗다 (ha-ya-ta) "to be white" vs. 하야니까 (ha-ya-ni-kka) "because it is white," and 파랗다 (pa-ra-ta) "to be blue" vs. 파라면 (pa-ra-myeon) "if it is blue." The verbs 노랗다 (no-ra-ta), 까맣다 (kka-ma-ta), 이렇다 (i-reo-ta), 그렇다 (geu-reo-ta), and 저렇다 (jeo-reo-ta), and 어떻다 (eo-tteo-ta) also follow this pattern.

13. PASSIVE VERBS

Active	*Passive*	*Example*
보다	보이다	저기 신호등이 보여요.
(bo-da)	(bo-i-da)	(jeo-gi sin-ho-deung-i bo-yeo-yo.)
to see	*to be seen*	*I see the traffic light over there.*
쓰다	쓰이다	이 약이 감기에 잘 쓰여요.
(sseu-da)	(sseu-i-da)	(i-yag-i gam-gi-e jal sseu-yeo-yo.)
to use	*to be used*	*This medicine is often used for colds.*
닫다	닫히다	바람에 문이 닫혔어요.
(dat-da)	(da-chi-da)	(ba-ram-e mun-i da-chyeoss-eo-yo.)
to close	*to be closed*	*The door was closed by the wind.*

막다
(mak-da)

to block

막히다
(ma-ki-da)

to be blocked

차가 많아서 길이 막혀요.
(cha-ga man-a-seo
  gil-i ma-kyeo-yo.)
*The street is blocked due to
  many cars.*

잡다
(jap-da)

to catch

잡히다
(ja-pi-da)

to be caught

도둑이 경찰한테 잡혔어요.
do-dug-i gyeong-chal-han-te
  ja-pyess-eo-yo.)
*The thief was caught by the
  policeman.*

물다
(mul-da)

to bite

물리다
(mul-li-da)

to be bitten

우체부가 개한테 물렸어요.
(u-che-bu-ga gae-han-te mul-
  lyeoss-eo-yo.)
*The mailman was bitten by
  a dog.*

열다
(yeol-da)

to open

열리다
(yeol-li-da)

to be open

가게문이 열렸어요.
(ga-ge-mun-i yeol-lyeoss-eo-
  yo.)
The store door is open.

듣다
(deut-da)

to hear

들리다
(deul-li-da)

to be heard

음악 소리가 들려요.
(eum-ak so-ri-ga
  deul-lyeo-yo.)
Music is heard by me.

팔다
(pal-da)

to sell

팔리다
(pal-li-da)

to be sold

요즘 집이 잘 팔려요.
(yo-jeum jib-i jal
  pal-lyeo-yo.)
*Houses are sold quickly
  these days.*

뺏다
(ppaet-da)

to take away

뺏기다
(ppaet-gi-da)

to be taken away

개한테 사과를 뺏겼어요.
(gae-han-te sa-gwa-reul
  ppaet-gyeoss-eo-yo.)
*My apple was taken away by
  the dog.*

안다
(an-tta)
to hold

안기다
(an-gi-da)
to be held

아이가 엄마한테 안겼어요.
(a-i-ga eom-ma-ha-te an-gyeoss-eo-yo.)
The baby was being held by the mother.

쫓다
(jjot-da)
to chase

쫓기다
(jjot-gi-da)
to be chased

쥐가 고양이한테 쫓겨요.
(jwi-ga go-yang-i han-te jjot-gyeo-yo.)
A mouse is being chased by a cat.

14. CAUSATIVE VERBS

Plain	*Causative*	*Example*
먹다	먹이다	엄마가 아기한테 우유를 먹여요.
(meok-da)	(meog-i-da)	(eom-ma-ga a-gi-han-te u-yu-reul meog-yeo-yo.)
to eat	to feed someone	*The mother is feeding the baby.*
죽다	죽이다	제가 파리를 죽였어요.
(juk-da)	(jug-i-da)	(je-ga pa-ri-reul jug-yeoss-eo-yo.)
to die	to kill someone	*I killed the fly.*
끓다	끓이다	라면을 먹으려고 물을 끓여요.
(kkeul-ta)	(kkeul-i-da)	(ra-myeon-eul meog-eu-ryeo-go mul-eul kkeul-yeo-yo.)
to boil	to boil something	*I'm boiling water to cook ramen.*
입다	입히다	엄마가 아기한테 옷을 입혀요.
(ip-da)	(i-pi-da)	(eom-ma-ga a-gi-han-te os-eul i-pyeo-yo.)
to wear	to dress someone	*The mother is dressing the baby.*

눕다	눕히다	엄마가 아기를 침대에 눕혀요.
(nup-da)	(nu-pi-da)	(eom-ma-ga a-gi-reul chim-dae-e nu-pyeo-yo.)
to lie down	*to lay someone down*	*The mother is laying the baby down on the bed.*

앉다	앉히다	엄마가 아기를 의자에 앉혀요.
(an-tta)	(an-chi-da)	(eom-ma-ga a-gi-reul ui-ja-e an-chyeo-yo.)
to sit	*to seat someone*	*The mother is seating the baby on the chair.*

울다	울리다	형이 동생을 울려요.
(ul-da)	(ul-li-da)	(hyeong-i dong-saeng-eul ul-lyeo-yo.)
to cry	*to make someone cry*	*The older brother makes his younger sibling cry.*

얼다	얼리다	물을 얼려서 얼음을 만들어요.
(eol-da)	(eol-li-da)	(mul-eul eol-lyeo-seo eol-eum-eul man-deul-eo-yo.)
to freeze	*to freeze something*	*You can freeze water to make ice.*

벗다	벗기다	엄마가 아기 옷을 벗겨요.
(beot-da)	(beot-gi-da)	(eom-ma-ga a-gi os-eul beot-geo-yo.)
to take off	*to undress someone*	*The mother is undressing the baby.*

웃다	웃기다	형이 동생을 웃겨요.
(ut-da)	(ut-gi-da)	(hyeong-i dong-saeng-eul ut-gyeo-yo.)
to laugh	*to make someone laugh*	*The older brother makes his younger sibling laugh.*

신다	신기다	엄마가 아기한테 신발을 신겨요.
(sin-tta)	(sin-gi-da)	(eom-ma-ga a-gi-han-te sin-bal-eul sin-gyeo-yo.)
to wear	*to put shoes on someone*	*The mother is putting shoes on the baby.*

자다	재우다	엄마가 아기를 침대에 재워요.
(ja-da)	(jae-u-da)	(eom-ma-ga a-gi-reul chim-dae-e jae-wo-yo.)
to sleep	*to put someone to sleep*	*The mother is putting the baby to sleep on the bed.*

타다	태우다	실수로 생선을 태웠어요.
(ta-da)	(tae-u-da)	(sil-su-ro saeng-seon-eul tae-woss-eo-yo.)
to burn	*to burn something*	*I burned the fish by mistake.*

깨다	깨우다	엄마가 아침에 아이를 깨워요.
(kkae-da)	(kkae-u-da)	(eom-ma-ga a-chim-e a-i-reul kkae-wo-yo.)
to wake	*to wake someone up*	*The mother wakes up the baby in the morning.*

15. CONNECTIVES

Noun Connectives

때문에
(ttae-mun-e)
because of

차 사고 때문에 길이 막혔어요.
(cha sa-go ttae-mun-e gil-i ma-kyeoss-eo-yo.)
There's traffic because of the accident.

-만에
(-man-e)
in

대학교 때 친구를 5년만에 우연히 만났어.
(dae-hak-gyo ttae chin-gu-reul o-nyeon-man-e u-yeon-hi man-nass-eo.)
I ran into my college friend, whom I had not seen in five years.

-만큼   동생이 형만큼 키가 커요.
(-man-keum)   (dong-saeng-i hyeong-man-keum ki-ga
                                  keo-yo.)

as much as   *The younger sibling is as tall as the
                                  older brother.*

-말고   육개장 말고 불고기를 드세요.
(-mal-go)   (yuk-gae-jang mal-go bul-go-gi-reul
                                  deu-se-yo.)

not [X]; instead   *Eat bulgogi instead of yuk-gae-jang.*

과   (*used after a consonant*)   책상과 의자를 샀어요.
(-gwa)   (chaek-sang-gwa ui-ja-reul
                                  sass-eo-yo.)

with, and   *I bought a desk and a chair.*

-와   (*used after a vowel*)   의자와 책상을 샀어요.
(-wa)   (ui-ja-wa chaek-sang-eul sass-eo-yo.)
with, and   *I bought a chair and a desk.*

-이나   (*used after a consonant*)   신문이나 책을 읽어요.
(-i-na)   (sin-mun-i-na chaeg-eul ilg-eo-yo.)
                               I read a newspaper or a book.

—나   (*used after a vowel*)   커피나 차를 마셔요.
(-na)   (keo-pi-na cha-reul ma-syeo-yo.)
or   *I drink a coffee or a tea.*

-이랑   (*used after a consonant*)   책상이랑 의자를 샀어요.
(-i-rang)   (chaek-sang-i-rang ui-ja-reul
                                  sass-eo-yo.)

with, and (colloquial)   *I bought a desk and a chair.*

-랑   (*used after a vowel*)   친구랑 음악을 들어요.
(-na)   (chin-gu-rang eum-ag-eul deul-eo-yo.)
with, and (colloquial)   *I listen to music with my friend.*

-하고
(-ha-go)

with, and (colloquial)

책상하고 의자를 샀어요.
(chaek-sang-ha-go ui-ja-reul
    sass-eo-yo.)
I bought a desk and a chair.

Clausal Connectives

-거나
(-geo-na)

or

주말에 영화를 보거나 쇼핑을 해요.
(ju-mal-e yeong-hwa-reul
    bo-geo-na syo-ping-eul hae-yo.)
*I usually watch a movie or go
    shopping on weekends.*

-게
(-ge)

in order that; to

사진 좀 찍게 사진기 좀 빌려 주세요.
(sa-jin jom jjik-ge sa-jin-gi jom
    bil-lyeo ju-se-yo.)
*Can I borrow your camera to take
    some pictures?*

-고
(-go)

and

아파트가 조용하고 깨끗해요.
(a-pa-teu-ga jo-yong-ha-go
    kkae-kkeu-tae-yo.)
The apartment is quiet and clean.

-고 나서
(-go na-seo)

after

점심 먹고 나서 공원에 갔어요.
(jeom-sim meok-go na-seo
    gong-won-e gass-eo-yo.)
We went to a park after we ate lunch.

-기 때문에

(-gi ttae-mun-e)

because

날씨가 나쁘기 때문에 밖에 안 나갔
    어요.
(nal-ssi-ga na-ppeu-gi ttae-mun-e
    bakk-e an na-gass-eo-yo.)
*We didn't go outside because the
    weather was bad.*

-기 위해서	한국어를 배우기 위해서 한국에 왔어요.
(-gi wi-hae-seo)	(ha-gug-eo-reul bae-u-gi wi-hae-seo han-gug-e wass-eo-yo.)
in order to	*I came to Korea to learn Korean.*
-기 전에	점심 먹기 전에 공원에 갔어요.
(-gi jeon-e)	(jeom-sim meok-gi jeon-e gong-won-e gass-eo-yo.)
before	*I went to the park before lunch.*
-느라고	인터넷 하느라고 텔레비전을 못 봤어요.
(-neu-ra-go)	(in-teo-net ha-neu-ra-go tel-le-bi-jeon-eul mot bwass-eo-yo.)
as a result of . . . ing; because of	*Because of the Internet, I did not watch TV.*
-는 길에	우체국에 가는 길에 시장에도 갔어요.
(-neun gil-e)	(u-che-gug-e ga-neun gil-e si-jang-e-do gass-eo-yo.)
on one's way	*On my way to the post office, I stopped by the market.*
-는 동안	빨래를 하는 동안 신문을 읽어요.
(-neun dong-an)	(ppal-lae-reul ha-neun dong-an sin-mun-eul ilg-eo-yo.)
during; while	*While I do laundry I read the newspaper.*
-는 바람에	넘어지는 바람에 다쳤어요.
(-neun ba-ram-e)	(neom-e-ji-neun ba-ram-e da-cheoss-eo-yo.)
as a result of; because	*Because I fell, I hurt myself.*
-는데(에)	김치찌개 끓이는데 뭐가 필요해요?
(-neun-de-[e])	(gim-chi-jji-gae kkeul-i-neun-de mwo-ga pil-yo-hae-yo?)
in/for . . . -ing	*What do you need in order to make kimchi-jii-gae [Korean dish]?*

-다가
(-da-ga)
while doing something

뛰다가 넘어졌어요.
(ttwi-da-ga neom-eo-jeoss-eo-yo.)
I fell while I was running.

-아/어 가지고

(-a/eo ga-ji-go)

1) because

냉장고가 작아가지고 너무
불편해요.
(naeng-jang-go-ga jag-a ga-ji-go neo-
mu bul-pyeon-hae-yo.)
*Because the refrigerator is so small, it
is inconvenient.*

-아/어 가지고

(-a/eo ga-ji-go)

2) by doing

한국어 배워가지고 한국에서 일할
거예요.
(han-gug-eo-reul bae-wo ga-ji-go han-
gug-e-seo il-hal kkeo-yeo-yo.)
*By learning Korean, I will be able to
work in Korea.*

-아/어서
(-a/-eo-seo)

since

아파트가 멀어서 버스 타고 와요.
(a-pa-teu-ga meol-eo-seo beo-seu ta-
go wa-yo.)
*I take the bus since the apartment is
far away.*

-았/-었다가

(-at/-eot-da-ga)

speaker's past experience

지하철 탔다가 사람이 많아서 혼났
어요.
(ji-ha-cheol-eul tat-da-ga sa-ram-i
man-a-seo hon-nass-eo-yo.)
*I had a hard time because there were
so many people in the subway.*

-았/-었더니

-at/-eot-deo-ni

speaker's past experience

버스를 탔더니 사람이 너무
많았어요.
(beo-seu-reul tat-deo-ni sa-ram-i neo-
mu man-ass-eo-yo.)
*There were many people in the bus
when I rode it.*

-(으)니까
([-eu]-ni-kka)

1) because; since

지금 시간 없으니까 택시 타세요.
(ji-geum si-gan-i eops-eu-ni-kka taek-si ta-se-to.)
Take a taxi because there isn't enough time.

-(으)니까
([-eu]-ni-kka)

2) logical sequence

전화 하니까 친구가 집에 없었어요.
(jeon-hwa ha-ni-kka chin-gu-ga jib-e eops-eoss-eo-yo.)
I called my friend but he/she was not home.

-(으)러
([-eu]-reo)
in order to

옷을 사러 백화점에 가요.
(os-eul sa-reo ba-kwa-jeom-e ga-yo.)
I am going to the mall to buy clothes.

-(으)려고
([-eu]-ryeo-go)

intending to

여행 가려고 준비했어요.
(yeo-haeng ga-ryeo-go jun-bi-haess-eo-yo.)
I prepared to take a trip.

-(으)려다가
([-eu]-ryeo-da-ga)

about to do, but

뭔가 말하려다가 그만뒀어요.
mwon-ga mal-ha-ryeo-da-ga geu-man-dwoss-eo-yo.
I was going to say something but I stopped.

-(으)려면
([-eu]-ryeo-myeon)

if one intends to

편지 부치려면 우체국에 가세요.
(pyeon-ji bu-chi-ryeo-myeon u-che-gug-e ga-se-yo.)
If you want to mail your letter go to the post office.

-(으)면
([-eu]-myeon)

if

돈이 많으면 뭐 할 거예요?
(don-i man-eu-myeon mwo hal kkeo-ye-yo?)
If you had a lot of money, what would you do?

-(으)면 . . . -(으)ㄹ수록

([-eu]-myeon . . . eul-su-rok)

the more . . . the more. . .

이 영화는 보면 볼수록 더
재미있어요.

(i yeong-hwa-neun bo-myeon bol-su-
rok deo jae-mi-iss-eo-yo.)

*The more you see of this movie, the
more you will like it.*

-(으)면서
([-eu]-myeon-seo)

1) while

아침 먹으면서 신문을 읽어요.
(a-chim meog-eu-myeon-seo sin-mun-
eul ilg-eo-yo.)

*While I eat breakfast I read the
newspaper.*

-(으)면서

([-eu]-myeon-seo)

2) even though

돈도 없으면서 비싼 차를 타고
다녀요.

(don-do eops-eu-myeon-seo bi-ssan
cha-reul ta-go da-nyeo-yo.)

*He/she is driving an expensive car
even though he/she does not have
money.*

-은 후/다음에
(-eun hu/da-eum-e)

after

점심 먹은 후에 공원에 갔어요.
(jeom-sim meog-eun hu-e gong-won-e
gass-eo-yo.)

I went to the park after I had lunch.

-은/는/을지

(-eun)/(-neun)/(eul-jji)

indirect questions

이 신발이 동생한테 잘 맞을지 잘 모
르겠어요.

(sin-bal-i dong-saeng-han-te jal maj-
eul-jji jal mo-reu-gess-eo-yo.)

*I am not sure if these shoes will fit my
younger brother/sister.*

-은/-는데
(-eun)/(-neun-de)

but

아파트가 조용한데 안 깨끗해요.
(a-pa-teu-ga jo-yong-han-de an kkae-
kkeu-tae-yo.)

The apartment is quiet but not clean.

-은/-는데도	음식을 많이 먹었는데도 아직도 배가 고파요.
(-eun)/(-neun-de-do)	(eum-sig-eul man-i meog-eon-neun-de-do a-jik-do bae-ga go-pa-yo.)
despite; although	*Although I ate a lot I am still hungry.*
-을 때	시간 있을 때 텔레비전을 봐요.
(-eul ttae)	(sin-gan iss-eul ttae tel-le-bi-jeon-eul bwa-yo.)
when	*Watch TV when you have time.*
-을까봐	한국 날씨가 너무 추울까봐 걱정이에요.
(-eul-kka-bwa)	(han-guk nal-ssi-ga neo-mu chu-ul-kka-bwa geok-geong-i-e-yo.)
for fear that; worry that	*I am afraid the weather in Korea is too cold.*
-을 만큼	음식은 먹을 만큼만 가지고 오세요.
(-eul man-keum)	(eum-sig-eun meog-eul man-keum-man ga-ji-go o-se-yo.)
to the extent/as much as	*Please bring only as much food as you can finish.*
-을 테니까	내일 갈 테니까 맛있는 음식 많이 준비하세요.
(-eul-te-ni-kka)	(nae-il gal te-ni-kka mas-in-neun eum-sik man-i jun-bi-ha-se-yo.)
because one will . . . ; so	*I will be there tomorrow, so please prepare enough food.*
-이/가 아니라	화가 난 게 아니라 아픈 거예요.
(-i/-ga a-ni-ra)	(hwa-ga nan ge a-ni-ra a-peun geo-yeo-yo.)
it is not . . . but . . .	*I am not angry but sick.*

-이라면

(-i-ra-myeon)

if it is . . .

내가 만일 부자라면 좋은 차를
사겠다.

(nae-ga man-il bu-ja-ra-myeon jo-eun
cha-reul sa-get-da.)

If I were rich I would buy a good car.

-이라서

(-i-ra-seo)

because; since

오늘은 일요일이라서 학교에
안 가요.

(o-neul-eun il-yo-il-i-ra-seo hak-gyo-e
an ga-yo.)

*I am not going to school today since it
is Sunday.*

-자마자

(-ja-ma-ja)

as soon as

아침에 일어나자마자 화장실에
가요.

(a-chim-e il-eo-na-ja-ma-ja hwa-jang-
sil-e ga-yo.)

*I go to the bathroom as soon as I get
up in the morning.*

-지만
(-ji-man)

but

아파트가 조용하지만 안 깨끗해요.

(a-pa-teu-ga jo-yong-ha-ji-man an
kkae-kkeu-tae-yo.)

The apartment is quiet but not clean.

아무 . . . -(이)나
(a-mu . . . [-i]-na)

any

저는 아무 음식이나 다 잘 먹어요.

(jeo-neun a-mu eum-sig-i-na da jal
meog-eo-yo.)

I can eat any kind of food.

아무리 . . . -아/어도
(a-mu-ri . . . -a/-eo-do)

no matter how

아무리 기다려도 택시가 안 와요.

(a-mu-ri gi-da-ryeo-do taek-si-ga an
wa-yo.)

*No matter how long I wait for the taxi,
it's not coming.*

얼마나 . . . -은/는지

(eol-ma-na . . . –eun)/(-neun-ji)

so . . . that . . .

서울에 사람이 얼마나 많은지 깜짝 놀랐어요.

(seo-ul-e sa-ram-i eol-ma-na man-eun-ji kkam-jjak nol-lass-eo-yo.)

I was so surprised that there are so many people in Seoul.

하나도 안/못 . . .

(ha-na-do an/mot . . .)

not at all

바빠서 영화도 하나도 못 봐요.

(ba-ppa-seo yeong-hwa-do ha-na-do mot bwa-yo.)

I cannot watch movies at all because I am so busy.

Sentence Connectives

그리고

(geu-ri-go)

and

아파트가 조용해요. 그리고 깨끗해요.

(a-pa-teu-ga jo-yong-hae-yo geu-ri-go kkae-kkeu-tae-yo.)

The apartment is quiet and clean.

그래서

(geu-rae-seo)

so

아파트가 멀어요. 그래서 버스 타고 와요.

(a-pa-teu-ga meol-eo-yo geu-rae-seo beo-seu ta-go wa-yo.)

The apartment is far away so I took the bus.

그런데

(geu-reon-de)

but (spoken form)

아파트가 조용해요. 그런데 안 깨끗해요.

(a-pa-teu-ga jo-yong-hae-yo geu-reon-de an kkae-kkeu-tae-yo.)

The apartment is quiet but not clean.

그렇지만

(geu-reo-chi-man)

but (written form)

아파트가 조용해요. 그렇지만 안 깨끗해요.

(a-pa-teu-ga jo-yong-hae-yo geu-reo-chi-man an kkae-kkeu-tae-yo.)

The apartment is quiet. However, it is not clean.

16. SENTENCE ENDINGS & HELPING VERBS

-거든요
(-geo-deun-yo)

you see, because . . .

지난 주에 비자를 받았거든요.
(ji-nan ju-e bi-ja-reul
    bad-at-geo-deun-yo.)
You see, I got my visa last week.

-게 되다
(-ge doe-da)

a change of events

한국을 좋아하게 됐어요.
(han-gug-eul jo-a-ha-ge
    dwaess-eo-yo.)
I came to like Korea.

-게 하다

(-ge ha-da)

make someone/something

아이들이 방에 못 들어오게 해
    주세요.
(a-i-deul-i bang-e mot deul-eo-o-ge
    hae ju-se-yo.)
*Please make the children stay out of
    the room.*

-게요
(-ge-yo)
intend to

지금 청소하게요.
(ji-geum cheong-so-ha-ge-yo.)
I am going to clean now.

-겠습니다
(-get-seum-ni-da)

announcement

오늘의 날씨를 말씀 드리겠습니다.
(o-neul-ui nal-ssi-reul mal-sseum deu-
    ri-get-seum-ni-da).
I will tell you today's weather.

-고 싶다/싶어하다

(-go sip-da/sip-eo-ha-da)
want to

갈비를 먹고 싶어요. (-고 싶다 [first
    person only])
(gal-bi-reul meok-go sip-eo-yo.)
I want to eat galbi [Korean dish].

-고 있다/-계시다

(-go it-da)/(-gye-si-da)
progressive

지금 밥 먹고 있어요. (-고 계시다
    [*honorific*])
(ji-geum bap meok-go iss-eo-yo.)
S/he is eating right now.

-군요
(-gun-yo)
exclamation

아직 집에 계셨군요!
(a-jik jib-e gye-syeot-gun-yo!)
You are still home!

-기 시작하다
(-gi si-ja-ka-da)

begin to

한국어를 배우기 시작했어요.
(han-gug-eo-reul bae-u-gi si-ga-kaess-
  eo-yo.)
I began to learn Korean.

-기 싫다
(-gi sil-ta)
I don't want to

버스 타기 싫어요.
(beo-seu ta-gi sil-eo-yo.)
I don't want to ride the bus.

-기가 불편하다
-gi-ga bul-pyeon-ha-da
it is inconvenient to

버스 타기가 불편해요.
beo-seu ta-gi-ga bul-pyeon-hae-yo.
It is inconvenient to ride the bus.

-기가 쉽다
(-gi-ga swip-da)
it is easy to

버스 타기가 쉬워요.
(beo-seu ta-gi-ga swi-wo-yo.)
It is easy to ride the bus.

-기가 어렵다
(-gi-ga eo-ryeop-da)
it is difficult to

버스 타기가 어려워요.
(beo-seu ta-gi-ga eo-ryeo-wo-yo.)
It is difficult to ride the bus.

-기가 편하다
(-gi-ga pyeon-ha-da)
it is convenient to

버스 타기가 편해요.
(beo-seu ta-gi-ga pyeon-hae-yo)
It is convenient to ride the bus.

-기는 하다
(-gi-neun ha-da)

as for. . . -ing, I did. But . . .

많이 자기는 했는데 아직도 졸려요.
(man-i ja-gi-neun han-neun-de a-jik-
  do jol-lyeo-yo.)
I slept a lot, but I am still sleepy.

-기는요?
(-gi-neun-yo?)

no way

한국말을 잘하기는요? 잘 못해요.
(han-gung-mal-eul jal-ha-gi-neun-yo?
  jal mo-tae-yo.)
*No way do I speak Korean well! I
  can't speak well.*

-기도 하다

(-gi-do ha-da)

they also did

시간 있으면 가끔 볼링을 치기도
해요.

(si-gan iss-eo-myeon ga-kkeum bol-
ling-eul chi-gi-do hae-yo.)

*I sometimes go bowling when I have
time, as they also did.*

-기로 하다
(-gi-ro ha-da)

decide/plan to

여름에 한국에 가기로 했어요.

(yeo-reum-e han-gug-e ga-gi-ro
haess-eo-yo.)

We/I plan to go Korea this summer.

-내요
(-nyae-yo)
indirect speech (question)

동물원에 가내요.

(dong-mul-won-e ga-nyae-yo.)

*Someone asked if I am going to
the zoo.*

-네요
 (-ne-yo)
surprise/admiration/sympathy

미국에서 오래 살았네요.

(mi-gug-e-seo o-rae sal-an-ne-yo.)

*My goodness, you lived in America for
a long time.*

-는 길이다
(-neun gil-i-da)

be on one's way

지금 우체국에 가는 길이에요.

(ji-geum u-che-gug-e ga-neun
gil-i-e-yo.)

I am on my way to the post office.

-는 중이다
(-neun jung-i-da)

in the process of

지금 청소하는 중이에요.

(ji-geum cheong-so-ha-neun
jung-i-e-yo.)

I am in the middle of cleaning up.

-다/-라면서요?
(-da)/(-ra-myeon-seo-yo?)
confirming information

한국에 간다면서요?

(han-gug-e gan-da-myeon-seo-yo?)

I heard you are going to Korea.

-대요/(-이)래요
(-dae-yo)/([-i]-rae-yo)
indirect speech (statement)

동물원에 간대요.

(dong-mul-won-e gan-dae-yo.)

I heard s/he is going to the zoo.

-더라고(요)

마이클 조던이 정말 농구를 잘 하더
라고.

(-deo-ra-go-yo)

(ma-i-keul jo-deon-i jeong-mal nong-
gu-reul jal ha-deo-ra-go.)

speaker's experience

*Michael Jordan plays basketball very
well, in my experience.*

-던데요
(-deon-de-yo)

호텔 식당 음식이 아주 맛있던데요.
(ho-tel sik-dang eum-sig-i a-ju mas-it-
deon-de-yo.)

speaker's experience

*The food at the hotel restaurant was
delicious, in my experience.*

-래요
(-rae-yo)
indirect speech (request)

동물원에 가래요.
(dong-mul-won-e ga-rae-yo.)
Somebody told me to go to the zoo.

-만 . . . -으면 되다
(-man . . . -eu-myeon doe-da)

이젠 비행기표만 사면 돼요.
(i-jen bi-haeng-gi-pyo-man sa-myeon
dwae-yo.)

all one needs is . . .

All I need to buy is an airplane ticket.

-아/어 버리다

남은 스파게티를 동생이 다 먹어 버
렸어요.

(-a)/(-eo beo-ri-da)

(nam-eun seu-pa-ge-ti-reul dong-
saeng-i meog-eo-beo-ryeoss-eo-
yo.)

to get done/finish

*My younger brother/sister finished the
leftover spaghetti.*

-아/어 보다
(-a)/(-eo bo-da)
try doing

김치 먹어 봤어요?
(gim-chi meog-eo bwass-eo-yo?)
Have you tried kimchi [Korean dish]?

-아/어 보이다
-a/-eo bo-i-da
someone/something looks

케이크가 맛있어 보여요.
ke-i-keu-ga mas-iss-eo bo-yeo-yo.
The cake looks delicious.

-아/어 본 적이 없다
(-a)/(-eo bon jeog-i eop-da)
there has been no occasion of

스키 타 본 적이 없어요.
(seu-ki ta bon jeog-i eops-eo-yo.)
I have never skied before.

-아/어 본 적이 있다
(a)/(-eo bon jeog-i it-da)
there has been an occasion of

스키 타 본 적이 있어요.
(seu-ki ta bon jeog-i iss-eo-yo.)
I have skied before.

-아/어 있다
(-a)/(-eo it-da)

be . . . -ing (state)

한 상자에 사과가 10개 들어 있어요.
(han sang-ja-e sa-gwa-ga yeol-kkae
deul-eo iss-eo-yo.)
There are ten apples in a box.

-아/어 주다/드리다

(-a)/(-eo ju-da)/(deu-ri-da)
benefactive

다시 설명해 주세요. (-아/어 드리다
[*humble*])
(da-si seol-myeong-hae ju-se-yo.)
Please explain to me again.

-아/어도 되다
(-a)/(-eo-do doe-da)
permission

이 케이크 먹어도 돼요?
(i ke-i-keu meog-eo-do dwae-yo.)
May I eat this cake?

-아/어야 되다/하다
(-a)/(-eo-ya doe-da)/(ha-da)
necessity

매일 운동해야 돼요.
(mae-il un-dong-hae-ya dwae-yo.)
One needs to exercise every day.

-아/어야지요
(-a)/(-eo-ya-ji-yo)
surely have to/ should

피곤한데 일찍 자야지요.
(pi-gon-han-de il-jjik ja-ya-ji-yo.)
*You must be tired. You should go to
sleep early.*

-아/어야할지 모르겠다
(-a)/(-eo-ya-hal-jji mo-reu-get-da)

don't know-[Qword] to

뭘 사야할지 모르겠어요.
(mwol sa-ya-hal-jji
mo-reu-gess-eo-yo.)
I don't know what to buy.

-아/어지다
(-a)/(-eo-ji-da)
become, get to be

날씨가 추워졌어요.
(nal-ssi-ga chu-wo-jeoss-eo-yo.)
The weather became cold.

-아/어하다

(-a)/(-eo-ha-da)

feeling of the third person

어머니가 케이크를 아주 좋아하세요.
(eo-meo-ni-ga ke-i-keu-reul a-ju jo-a-ha-se-yo.)
My mother really likes cake.

-았/었으면 하다
(-ass)/(-eoss-eu-myeon ha-da)

wish

앞으로 한국에서 살았으면 해요.
(a-peu-ro han-gug-e-seo sal-ass-eu-myeon hae-yo.)
I wish to live in Korea in the future.

-(으)면 좋겠다
([-eu]-myeon jo-ket-da)

speaker's wish; want

피곤해서 잤으면 좋겠어요.
(pi-gon-hae-seo jass-eu-myeon jo-kess-eo-yo.)
I am tired. I want to sleep.

-(으)려고 하다
([-eu]-ryeo-go ha-da)

intend to

너무 피곤해서 자려고 해요.
(neo-mu pi-gon-hae-seo ja-ryeo-go hae-yo.)
I am so tired, I am going to sleep.

-(으)면 안 되다
([-eu]-myeon an doe-da)
prohibition

아니오, 먹으면 안 돼요.
(a-ni-o meog-eu-myeon an dwae-yo.)
No, please don't eat.

-은/는 거예요
(-eun)/(-neun geo-ye-yo)

the fact is

잇몸 때문에 이가 아픈 거예요.
(in-mom ttae-mun-e i-ga a-peun geo-ye-yo.)
My teeth hurt a lot because of the chewing gum.

-은/는 줄 알다
(-eun)/(-neun jul al-da)
I thought. . . .

미국사람인줄 알았어요.
(mi-guk-sa-ram-in-jul al-ass-eo-yo.)
I thought you were American.

-은/는 척하다
(-eun)/(-neun cheo-ka-da)

to pretend to

친구가 내 말을 못 들은 척했어요.
(chin-gu-ga nae mal-eul mot deul-eun cheo-kaess-eo-yo.)
My friend pretended not to listen.

-은/는 편이다
(-eun)/(-neun pyeon-i-da)

relatively

우리 부모님은 건강하신 편이에요.
(u-ri bu-mo-nim-eun geon-gang-ha-sin
pyeon-i-e-yo.)
My parents are relatively healthy.

-은/는/을 것 같다
(-eun)/(-neun)/(-eul geot gat-da)
it seems/looks like

어제 비가 온 것 같아요.
(eo-je bi-ga on-geot gat-a-yo.)
It looks like it rained yesterday.

지금 비가 오는 것 같아요.
(ji-geum bi-ga o-neun-geot gat-a-yo.)
It looks like it's raining now.

내일 비가 올 것 같아요.
(nae-il bi-ga ol-kkeot gat-a-yo.)
*It looks like it's going to rain
tomorrow.*

-은/는/을 모양이다
(-eun)/(-neun)/(-eul mo-yang-i-da)
it appears

기분이 좋은 모양이에요.
(gi-bun-i jo-eun mo-yang-i-e-yo.)
You appear to be in a good mood.

-은/는/을 줄 모르다
(-eun)/(-neun)/(-eul jul mo-reu-da)

don't know

한국음식이 이렇게 맛있는 줄 몰랐
어요.
(han-gug-eum-sig-i i-reo-ke mas-in-
neun jul mol-lass-eo-yo.)
*I didn't know that Korean food was so
delicious.*

-은/는/을 줄 알다
(-eun)/(-neun)/(-eul jul al-da)

know; thought

음식이 아직 많은 줄 알았어요.
(eum-sig-i a-jik man-eun-jul
al-ass-eo-yo.)
I thought there was plenty of food left.

-은/는데요
(-eun)/(-neun-de-yo)

마이클씨 지금 집에 없는데요.
(ma-i-keul-ssi ji-geum jib-e eom-
neun-de-yo.)
Michael is not home right now.

-은/는지 . . . 되다
(-eun)/(-neun-ji . . . doe-da)

It has been [TIME] since

한국에 온지 일년 됐어요.
(han-gug-e on-ji il-lyeon dwaess-eo-yo.)

It has been one year since I came to Korea.

-은/는지 모르다
(-eun)/(-neun-ji mo-reu-da)
don't know that . . .

우체국이 어디 있는지 몰라요.
u-che-gug-i eo-di in-neun-ji mol-la-yo.

I don't know where the post office is.

-은/는지 알다
(-eun)/(-neun-ji al-da)
know that . . .

우체국이 어디 있는지 아세요?
(u-che-gug-i eo-di in-neun-ji a-se-yo?)

Do you know where the post office is?

-은가/는가/나보다
(-eun-ga)/(-neun-ga)/(na-bo-da)
it seems that . . . /I guess

오늘 기분이 좋은가봐요.
(o-neul gi-bun-i jo-eun-ga-bwa-yo.)

I guess you are in a good mood today.

-은/는요?

(-eun/-neun-yo)

what about. . . ?

저는 집이 좀 멀어요. 마이클씨는 요?

(jeo-neun jib-i jom meol-eo-yo. ma-i-keul-ssi-neun-yo.)

My house is pretty far away. What about yours, Michael?

-(으)ㄹ 뻔하다
(-eul ppeon-ha-da)

almost, nearly

지갑을 잃어버릴 뻔했어요.
(ji-gab-eul il-eo-beo-ril ppeon-haess-eo-yo.)

I almost lost my wallet.

-(으)ㄹ 수 있다/없다
(-eul ssu it-da)/(-eop-da)
potential

내일 갈 수 없어요.
(nae-il gal-ssu eops-eo-yo.)

I cannot go tomorrow.

-(으)ㄹ 줄 모르다
(-eul jjul mo-reu-da)
not know how to

테니스 칠 줄 몰라요.
(te-ni-seu chil jjul mol-la-yo.)

I don't know how to play tennis.

-(으)ㄹ 줄 알다
(-eul jjul al-da)
know how to

테니스 칠 줄 알아요.
(te-ni-seu chil jjul al-a-yo.)
I know how to play tennis.

-(으)ㄹ 걸 그랬다
(-eul kkeol geu-raet-da)

regret for a past action

우산을 가지고 나올 걸 그랬어요.
(u-san-eul ga-ji-go na-ol kkeol geu-raess-eo-yo.)
I should have brought my umbrella.

-(으)ㄹ게요
(-eul-kke-yo)
willingness

이따가 다시 올게요.
(i-tta-ga da-si ol-kke-yo)
I will come back later.

-(으)ㄹ까 생각하다
(-eul-kka saeng-ga-ka-da)

think about

선물로 뭘 살까 생각하고 있어요.
(seon-mul-lo mwol sal-kka saeng-ga-ka-go iss-eo-yo.)
I am thinking about what to buy for a gift.

-(으)ㄹ까 하다
(-eul-kka ha-da)

thinking of –ing

주말에 영화 보러 갈까 해요.
(ju-mal-e yeong-hwa bo-reo gal-kka hae-yo.)
I am thinking of going to the movies this weekend.

-(으)ㄹ까요?
(-eul-kka-yo)
1) Shall I/we. . . ?

한국어로 말할까요?
(han-gug-eo-ro mal-hal-kka-yo?)
Should I speak in Korean?

-(으)ㄹ까요?
(-eul-kka-yo?)
2) Do you think ....?

내일 날씨가 좋을까요?
(nae-il nal-ssi-ga jo-eul-kka-yo?)
Do you think tomorrow's weather will be nice?

-(으)ㄹ래요.
(-eul-lae-yo.)
intention

영화 보러 갈래요.
(yeong-hwa bo-reo gal-lae-yo.)
I will go to see a movie.

-잖아요
(-jan-a-yo)
you know

밖에 비가 오잖아요.
(bakk-e bi-ga o-jan-a-yo.)
It's raining outside.

-재요
(-jae-yo)
indirect speech (suggestion)

동물원에 가재요.
(dong-mul-won-e ga-jae-yo.)
H/she asked me to go to the zoo.

-지요
(-ji-yo)

suggestion

길이 많이 막히는데 지하철 타고 가지요.
(gil-i man-i ma-ki-neun-de ji-ha-cheol ta-go ga-ji-yo.)
We should take the subway since there is heavy traffic.

-지요?/-죠?
(-ji-yo?)/(-jyo?)
seeking agreement

오늘 날씨가 참 좋지요?
(o-neul nal-ssi-ga cham jo-chi-yo?)
Isn't today's weather really nice?

(마치) -은/-는/-을 것 같다
([ma-chi] -eun/-neun/-eul geot gat-da)

as if

두 사람이 마치 형제인 것 같이 닮았어요.
(du sa-ram-i ma-chi hyeong-je-in geot ga-chi dalm-ass-eo-yo.)
The two people look alike as if they were brothers.

(차라리) . . . 이/가 더 낫다
([cha-ra-ri] . . . i/ga deo nat-da)

had better

차라리 혼자 사는 게 더 낫겠어요.
(cha-ra-ri hon-ja sa-neun ge deo nat-gess-eo-yo.)
It is better to live alone.

17. INDIRECT QUOTATION

Standard Form (Colloquial Form)

Statement:
-는/-ㄴ다고 해요 (-는/-ㄴ대요)
(-neun/-n-da-go hae-yo [-neun/-n-dae-yo])

> 밥을 먹는다고 해요. / 밥을 먹는대요.
> (bab-eul meong-neun-da-go hae-yo.) / (bab-eul meong-neun-dae-yo.)
> *Someone said (he/she) is eating.*

-라고 해요 (-래요)
(-ra-go hae-yo [-rae-yo])

> 의사라고 해요. / 의사래요.
> (ui-sa-ra-go hae-yo.) / (ui-sa-rae-yo.)
> *Someone said (he/she) is a doctor.*

Question:
-냐고 해요 (-내요)
(-nya-go-hae-yo [nyae-yo])

> 밥을 먹냐고 해요. / 밥을 먹내요.
> (bab-eul meong-nya-go hae-yo.) / (bab-eul meong-nyae-yo.)
> *Someone asked if (he/she) is eating.*

Proposal:
-자고 해요 (-재요)
(-ja-go hae-yo [-jae-yo])

> 밥을 먹자고 해요. / 밥을 먹재요.
> (bab-eul meok-ja-go hae-yo.) / (bab-eul meok-jae-yo.)
> *Someone said let's eat.*

Request:

-(으)라고 해요 /-(으)래요
([eu]-ra-go hae-yo)/([eu]-rae-yo)

밥을 먹으라고 해요. / 밥을 먹으래요.
(bab-eul meog-eu-ra-go hae-yo.) / (bab-eul meog-eu-rae-yo.)
Someone told me to eat.

◇◇◇◇◇◇◇◇

Appendix 2:
Korean-English Vocabulary

ㄱ

가게 ga-ge	store, shop, convenient store
가격 ga-gyeok	price
가깝다 ga-kkap-da	to be close
가는 머리 ga-neun meo-ri	thin hair
가다 ga-da	to go
가루약 ga-ru-yak	powdered medicine
가수 ga-su	singer
가슴 ga-seum	chest/breast
가운데 ga-un-de	middle
가을 ga-eul	fall, autumn
가족 ga-jok	family, family members (formal)
가지고 오다 ga-ji-go o-da	to bring something
가지고 타다 ga-ji-go ta-da	to ride having something
가지다 ga-ji-da	to have
간호사 gan-ho-sa	nurse
간호원 gan-ho-won	nurse
갈색 gal-saek	light brown
갈아타는 곳 gal-a-ta-neun got	subway transfer place
갈아타다 gal-a-ta-da	to transfer
감기 gam-gi	cold
감기에 걸리다 gam-gi-e geol-li-da	to have a cold
감사하다 gam-sa-ha-da	to thank
갖다 드리다 gat-da deu-ri-da	to bring or take something (hon.)
갖다 주다 gat-da ju-da	to bring or take something
같다 gat-da	to be same
같이 ga-chi	together
개 gae	items
거기 geo-gi	there
거스름돈 geo-seu-reum-tton	change
거의 geo-ui	almost
걱정하다 geok-jeong-ha-da	to worry
건너다 geon-neo-da	to cross (a street)

건너편 geon-neo-pyeon — across the street
건물 geon-mul — building
건축학 geon-chuk-hak — architecture
걷다 geot-da — to walk
걸리다 geol-li-da — to take time
걸어서 geol-eo-seo — on foot, by walking
검사를 하다 geom-sa-reul ha-da — to get an exam
게이트 ge-i-teu — gate
겨울 geo-wul — winter
겨자색 gyeo-ja-saek — dark yellow, mustard color

결혼하다 gyeol-hon-ha-da — to get married
겹치다 gyeop-chi-da — to be overlapped
경영학 gyeong-yeong-hak — business management

경제학 gyeong-je-hak — economics
경찰 gyeong-chal — police
경찰서 gyeong-chal-sseo — police department, police station

계산서 gye-san-seo — check, bill
계시다 gye-si-da — to exist, to be, to stay (*hon.*)

고등학교 go-deung-hak-go — high school
고등학생 go-deung-hak-saeng — high school student
고맙다 go-map-da — to thank
고모 go-mo — aunt (father's sister)
고모부 go-mo-bu — uncle (고모's husband)

고생 go-saeng — hard work
고속버스 go-sok-beo-seu — express bus
고장나다 go-jang-na-da — to be broken
골프를 치다 gol-peu-reul chi-da — to play golf
곱슬머리 gop-seul meo-ri — curly hair
공과대학 (공대) gong-kkwa-dae-hak (gong-dae) — engineering school
공무원 gong-mu-won — civil servant
공복에 gong-bog-e — on an empty stomach

공사 중 gong-sa-jung — on the construction site

공제하다 gong-je-ha-da — to deduct
공학 gong-hak — engineering

공항 gong-hang — airport
과 gwa — number of lessons, lessons in order

과목 gwa-mok — courses
과장님 gwa-jang-nim — department manager
괜찮다 gwaen-chan-ta — to be OK, to be good
괜찮아 보이다 gwaen-chan-a bo-i-da — to look good
교수 gyo-su — professor
교육학 gyo-yuk-hak — education study
교환해 드리다 gyo-hwan-hae deu-ri-da — to exchange (hon.)
구 gu — nine
구경하다 gu-gyeong-ha-da — to just look around
구급차 gu-geup-cha — ambulance
구름이 끼다 gu-reum-i kki-da — to get cloudy
구월 gu-wol — September
국 guk — soup
국내선 gung-nae-seon — domestic airlines
국물 gung-mul — soup
국제선 guk-je-seon — international airlines
군인 gun-in — military personnel
굵은 머리 gulg-eun meo-ri — thick hair
굵은 파마 gulg-eun pa-ma — perm with large rolls
권 gwon — volumes
권투를 하다 gwon-tu-reul ha-da — to play boxing
귀 gwi — ear
그 geu — that
그 동안 geu-dong-an — during the time
그 쪽 geu jjok — that side
그걸로 geu-geol-lo — that one
그냥 geu-nyang — just, only
그래도 geu-rae-do — even it is true, although, even though

그래서 geu-rae-so-eo — so
그러다 geu-reo-da — to do so
그러면 geu-reo-myeon — if
그러세요? geu-reo-se-yo — really?
그러자 geu-reo-ja — let's do that
그런데 geu-reon-de — but, by the way (when changing topic)

그럼 geu-reom — then
그럼요 geu-reom-yo — of course
그렇게 geu-reo-ke — like that
그렇구나 geu-reo-ku-na — that's right
그렇다 geu-reo-ta — to be so
그렇지만 geu-reo-chi-man — but
그리고 geu-ri-go — and
그림을 그리다 geu-rim-eul geu-ri-da — to draw a picture
그저께 geu-jeo-kke — the day before yesterday
그제 geu-je — the day before yesterday
근무하다 geun-mu-ha-da — to work at (company name)
근처 geun-cheo — near, nearby
금년 geum-nyeon — this year
금방 geum-bang — soon
금요일 geum-yo-il — Friday
급하다 geu-pa-da — to be hurry
급히 geu-pi — in a hurry
기다리다 gi-da-ri-da — to wait
기쁘다 gi-ppeu-da — to be happy
기사 gi-sa — driver
기온이 낮다 gi-on-i nat-da — the temperature is low
기온이 높다 gi-on-i nop-da — the temperature is high
기운이 없다 gi-un-i eop-da — to be lacking in energy
기운이 없다 gi-un-i eop-da — to have no energy
기자 gi-ja — journalist
기차 gi-cha — train
기침을 하다 gi-chim-eul ha-da — to cough
기타 gi-ta-reul chi-da — to play guitar
긴 머리 gin meo-ri — long hair
길 gil — street, road
길다 gil-da — to be long
길이 gil-i — length
김치 gim-chi — kimchi
까만 kka-man — black

까만색 kka-man-saek — black color
까맣다 kka-ma-ta — to be black
깎다 kkak-da — to have a haircut
깜빡 kkam-ppak — completely
깨끗하다 kkae-kkeu-ta-da — to be clean
깨다 kkae-da — to wake
깨우다 kkae-u-da — to wake someone up
꼭 kkok — for sure
꽂다 kkot-da — to wear (a pin)
꽃무늬 kkon-mu-ni — flower pattern
꽃집 kkot-jip — flower shop
끄르다 kkeu-reu-da — to untie, to loose
끈끈하다 kkeun-kkeun-ha-da — to be humid, sticky, muggy
끓다 kkeul-ta — to boil
끓이다 kkeul-i-da — to boil something
끼다 kki-da — to wear (a ring, gloves, etc.)

ㄴ

나 na — I, me
나가는 곳 na-ga-neun got — exit
나가다 na-ga-da — to go out
나오다 na-o-da — to come out
나이 na-I — age
나이가 많다 na-i-ga man-ta — to be old (*person*)
나이드신 분들 na-i-deu-sin bun-deul — old people
나중에 na-jung-e — later
나타나다 na-ta-na-da — to appear
나흘 na-heul — 4 days
낚시를 가다/하다 nak-si-reul ga-da/ha-da — to go fishing
날 nal — day, date
날씨 nal-ssi — weather, climate
날씨가 나쁘다 nal-ssi-ga na-ppeu-da — the weather is bad
날씨가 좋다 nal-ssi-ga jo-ta — the weather is good
낡다 nalk-da — to be old (*object*)
남기다 nam-gi-da — to leave
남동생 nam-dong-saeng — younger brother
남들 nam-deul — other people
남방 nam-bang — tennis/golf shirt

남자 nam-ja — man
남편 nam-pyeon — husband
낫다 nat-da — to be better
낮 nat — day
낮다 nat-da — to be low
낮추다 nat-chu-da — to make something low

내 nae — my
내과 nae-kkwa — internal department
내년 nae-nyeon — next year
내려가다 nae-ryeo-ga-da — to go down
내려오다 nae-ryeo-o-da — to come down
내일 nae-il — tomorrow
내후년 nea-hu-nyeon — the year after next year

냉면 naeng-myeon — cold noodle
냉수 naeng-su — ice water
냉커피 naeng-keo-pi — ice coffee
너무 neo-mu — too, too much
넘다 neom-tta — to go over
넣다 neo-ta — to put inside
넣어 주다 neo-eo ju-da — to put on something (for someone)

네 ne — yes
넥타이 nek-ta-i — necktie
넷 net — four
년 nyeon — year
노란 no-ran — yellow
노란색 no-ran-saek — yellow color
노랗다 no-ra-ta — to be yellow
노래를 부르다 no-rae-reul bu-reu-da — to sing a song
노래방에 가다 no-rae-bang-e ga-da — to go to a karaoke room

노래하다 no-rae-ha-da — to sing
노인용 no-in-yong — things for old people
놀아주다 nol-a-ju-da — to play for someone's benefit

농구를 하다 nong-gu-reul ha-da — to play basketball
높다 nop-da — to be high
누가 nu-ga — someone/anyone, who (*subject*)

누구 nu-gu — someone/anyone, who

누나 nu-na — man's older sister
눈 nun — snow, eye
눈이 오다 nun-i o-da — to snow
눕다 nup-da — to lay down
눕히다 nu-pi-da — to lay someone down

뉴질랜드 nyu-jil-laen-deu — New Zealand
뉴질랜드 사람 nyu-jil-laen-deu sa-ram — New Zealand (*adj.*)
뉴질랜드인 nyu-jil-laen-deu-in — New Zealander
늙다 neulk-da — to be old (*person or animal*)

늦게 nut-ge — late
늦다 neut-da — to be late
늦어도 nuj-eo-do — at latest

ㄷ

다 da — all
다 같이 da ga-chi — all together
다 되다 da doe-da — to be all done, to worn out, to be all done

다니다 da-ni-da — to attend
다들 da-deul — everyone, all
다듬어 주다 da-deum-eo ju-da — to trim
다른 데 da-reun de — other places
다리 da-ri — leg
다림질하다 da-rim-jil-ha-da — to iron
다방 da-bang, — café, coffee shop
다섯 da-seot — five
다시 da-si — again
다음 달 da-eum-ttal — next month
다음 번 da-eum-beon — next time
다음 주 da-eum-jju — next week
다음에 da-eum-e — next time
다치다 da-chi-da — to get injured
다행이다 da-haeng-i-da — to be lucky
단골 dan-gol — regular customer
단골이 되다 dan-gol-i doe-da — to become a regular customer

단발머리 dan-bal meo-ri — shoulder-length hair
단지 dan-ji — apartment complex
닫다 dat-da — to close
닫히다 da-chi-da — to be closed
달 dal — months
달다 dal-da — to be sweet
달러 dal-leo — dollars
달러당 dal-leo-dang — per dollar
닭고기 dak-go-gi — chicken
답답해 보이다 dap-dap-hae bo-i-da — to look heavy
답장을 쓰다 dap-jang-eul sseu-da — to write a reply
닷새 tat-sae — 5 days
대머리 dae-meo-ri — bald
대충 dae-chung — roughly
대학 dae-hak — college
대학교 dae-hak-gyo — college, university
대학로 dae-hang-no — university street
대학생 dae-hak-saeng — college student
대학원 dae-hag-won — graduate school
대학원생 dae-hag-won-saeng — graduate student
대한은행 dae-han-eun-haeng — Dae-Han Bank
댁 daek — home, house (*hon.*)
더 deo — more
더운 날 deo-un nal — hot day
더워지다 deo-wo-ji-da — to become hot, to get hot

덕분에 deok-bun-e — thanks to (you)
덥다 deop-da — to be hot
데리고 오다/가다 de-ri-go o-da/ga-da — to bring/take (someone)

도와 드리다 do-wa deu-ri-da — to help (*hon.*)
도와주다 do-wa-ju-da — to help for someone's benefit

도장 do-jang — stamp, seal
도착하다 do-cha-ka-da — to arrive
독일 dog-il — Germany
독일 사람 dog-il-ssa-ram — German
독일어 dog-il-eo — German language
독일인 dog-il-in — German
독하다 do-ka-da — to be strong, to be severe

돈 don — money
돈을 따다 don-eul tta-da — to win money
돈을 맞기다 don-eul mat-gi-da — to save money
돈을 받다 don-eul bat-da — to receive money
돈을 벌다 don-eul beol-da — to earn money
돈을 부치다 don-eul bu-chi-da — to send money
돈을 쓰다 don-eul sseu-da — to spend money
돈을 잃다 don-eul il-ta — to lose money
돈을 잃어버리다 don-eul il-eo-beo-ri-da — to misplace money
돈을 주다 don-eul ju-da — to give money
돈을 줍다 don-eul jup-da — to find money
돈을 찾다 don-eul chat-da — to withdraw money
돈이 들다 don-i deul-da — to need money
돌리다 dol-li-da — to turn
돌아가시다 dol-a-ga-si-da — to pass away
동갑 dong-gap — same age
동그라미 dong-geu-ra-mi — round
동네 dong-ne — village, town
동생 dong-saeng — younger sibling
동양학 dong-yang-hak — Asian studies
동창회 dong-chang-hoe — alumni assembly
돼지고기 dwae-ji-go-gi — pork
되다 doe-da — to become
되돌아 가다 doe-dol-a ga-da — to go back
두르다 du-reu-da — to wear a (scarf)
둘 dul — two
뒤 dwi — back, behind
뒷머리 dwin-meo-ri — back hair
드라이 deu-ra-i — dry cleaning, blow dry
드라이하다 deu-ra-i-ha-da — to have a blow dry, to dry clean
드럼 deu-reom-eul chi-da — to play drum
드리다 deu-ri-da — to give (*hon.*)
드시다 deu-si-da — to eat (*hon.*)
듣다 deut-da — to hear
들다 deul-da — to take, to eat (*hon.*)
들러 보다 deul-leo-bo-da — to stop by
들리다 deul-li-da — to be heard
들어가다 deul-eo-ga-da — to enter

들어오다 deul-eo-o-da — to enter
등 deung — back
등기우편 deung-gi-u-pyeon — registered mail
등산을 하다/가다 deung-san-eul ha-da/ga-da — to climb a mountain
디자이너 di-ja-i-neo — designer
디자인 di-ja-in — design
따뜻하다 tta-tteu-ta-da — to be warm
따라오다 tta-ra-o-da — to follow
따르릉 tta-reu-reung — ring ring…. (*telephone*)

딸 ttal — daughter
땀이 나다 ttam-i na-da — to sweat
또 tto — again
똑 같다 ttok gat-da — to be same
똑바로 ttok-ba-ro — straight
똑바로 가다 ttok-ba-ro ga-da — to go straight
뛰어서 ttwi-eo-seo — by running

ㄹ

러시아 reo-si-a — Russia
러시아 사람 reo-si-a sa-ram — Russian
러시아어 reo-si-a-eo — Russian language
러시아인 reo-si-a-in — Russian
레슬링을 하다 re-seul-ling-eul ha-da — to play wrestling
레이어 le-i-eo — layer
레이어를 주다 le-i-eo-reul ju-da — to layer
렌트카 ren-teu-ka — rental car
린스 하다 rin-seu ha-da — to rinse out, to wash out

ㅁ

마리 ma-ri — counter for animals
마실 것 ma-sil kkeot — something to drink
마우스워시 ma-u-seu-wo-si — mouthwash
마음에 들다 ma-eum-e deul-da — to like, to fit someone's taste
마음에 안 들다 ma-eum-e an deul-da — to not like
마일 ma-il — mile
마일리지 ma-il-li-ji — mileage

마지막으로 ma-ji-mag-eu-ro — at last
마침 ma-chim — just in time
마흔 ma-heun — forty
막다 mak-da — to block
막히다 ma-ki-da — to be blocked, to be jammed

만 man — 10 thousand
만나 뵙다 man-na-boep-da — to meet (*hon.*)
만나다 man-na-da — to meet
만들다 man-deul-da — to make
많다 man-ta — to be many
많이 man-i — a lot
말 mal — word, language
말리다 mal-li-da — to dry
말씀 mal-sseum — word (*hon.*)
말씀 드리다 mal-sseum deu-ri-da — to talk to (someone) (*hon.*)
말씀하시다 mal-sseum-ha-si-da — to speak (*hon.*)
말하다 mal-ha-da — to speak
맑아지다 malg-a-ji-da — to become clean
맛이 없다 mas-i eop-da — to not be delicious
맛이 있다 mas-i it-da — to be delicious
맛있게 mas-it-ge — tastily
맛있다 mass-it-da — to be tasty
맞다 mat-da — to be correct, to fit
맞추다 mat-chu-da — to fit, to set, to adjust, to make something fit

매년 mae-nyeon — every year
매다 mae-da — to tie
매월 mae-wol — every month
매일 mae-il — every day
매주 mae-ju — every week
맥주 maek-ju — bear
맵다 maep-da — to be spicy/hot
맵지 않게 maep-ji an-ke — to not be hot
머리 meo-ri — head, hair
머리 감다 meo-ri gam-tta — to wash hair
머리 결 meo-ri kkyeol — quality of hair
머리 숱 meo-ri sut — volume of hair

머리가 아프다 meo-ri-ga a-peu-da	to have headache
머리를 감다 meo-ri-reul gam-tta	to wash one's hair, to shampoo
머리를 깎다 meo-ri-reul kkak-da	to have a haircut (*man*)
머리를 다듬다 meo-ri-reul da-deum-tta	to trim hair
머리를 말리다 meo-ri-reul mal-li-da	to have a towel dry
머리를 빗다 meo-ri-reul bit-da	to brush hair
머리를 자르다 meo-ri-reul ja-reu-da	to have a haircut (*woman*)
머리를 헹구다 meo-ri-reul heng-gu-da	to rinse out, to wash out
머리색깔 meo-ri-saek-kkal	hair color
머리핀 meo-ri-pin	hairpin
먹는 약 meong-neun nyak	pills
먹다 meok-da	to eat
먹어 보다 meog-eo bo-da	to try to eat
먹이다 meog-i-da	to feed someone
먼저 meon-jeo	ahead, first
멀다 meol-da	to be far
메뉴 me-nyu	menu
메시지 me-se-ji	message
멕시코 mek-si-ko	Mexico
멕시코 사람 mek-si-ko sa-ram	Mexican
멕시코인 mek-si-ko-in	Mexican
며느리 myeo-neu-ri	daughter-in-law
며칠 myeo-chil	several days, what date?
명 myeong	persons
몇 myeot	what
몇 가지 myeot ga-ji	a couple of, several
몇 개 myeot-gae	how many items?
몇 년생 myeon-nyeon-saeng	which year of being born?
몇 번째 myeot-beon-jjae	what is the order [of something]?
몇 시 myeot-si	what time?
몇 시쯤 myeot-si-jjeum	approximately what time?

몇 회 myeo-toe — what is the version/ episode/sequence of something?

몇 째 myeot-jjae — what is the order of something.
(*used when asked about the order among siblings*)

모두 mo-du — all

모레 mo-re — the day after tomorrow

모르다 mo-reu-da — not to know

모셔다 드리다 mo-syeo-da deu-ri-da — to take someone (*hon.*)

모시고 가다 mo-si-go ga-da — to bring someone (*hon.*)

모시고 오다 mo-si-go o-da — to bring someone (*hon.*)

모시다 mo-si-da — to take care (*hon.*)

모양 mo-yang — shape

모자 mo-ja — hat

목 mok — throat, neck

목감기에 걸리다 mok-gam-gi-e geol-li-da — to have a sore throat

목도리 mok-do-ri — muffler/scarf

목사 mok-sa — pastor

목요일 mog-yo-il — Thursday

목욕을 하다 mog-yog-eul ha-da — to take a bath

목이 마르다 mog-i ma-reu-da — to be thirsty

목이 붓다 mog-i but-da — to have a sore throat

못 보다 mot bo-da — not to see

무난하다 mu-nan-ha-da — to be decent

무단횡단을 하다 mu-dan hoeng-dan-eul ha-da to — jaywalk

무릎 mu-reup — knee

무섭다 mu-seop-da — to be scared/afraid

무스/젤리를 바르다 mu-sseu/jel-li-reul ba-reu-da — to put on hair mousse/gel

무슨 mu-seun — some kind of, what kind of; what

무슨 날 mu-seun nal — special day

무슨 요일 mu-seun yo-il — what day?

무엇 nu-eot — something/anything, what

문학 mun-hak — literature

물 mul — water
물냉면 mul-laeng-myeon — cold noodle soup
물다 mul-da — to bite
물리다 mul-li-da — to be bitten
물리학 mul-li-hak — physics
물수건 mul-ssu-geon — wet towel
물약 mul-lyak — liquid medicine
물어보다 mul-eo-bo-da — to ask
뭐 mwo — what, something
미국 mi-guk — United States of America
미국 사람 mi-guk-sa-ram — American
미국시민 mi-guk-si-min — American citizen
미국인 mi-gug-in — American
미술 mi-sul — fine arts
미술관에 가다 mi-sul-gwan-e ga-da — to go to an art gallery
미술대학 (미대) mi-sul-dae-hak (mi-dae) — art school
미시간 mi-si-gan — Michigan
미식축구를 하다 mi-sik-chuk-gu-reul ha-da — to play football
미용사 mi-yong-sa — hairstylist
밑 mit — under, beneath, underneath

ㅂ

바깥 ba-kkat — out, outside
바꾸다 ba-kku-da — to change, to switch
바꾸러 오다 ba-kku-reo o-da — to come to exchange
바꿔주다 ba-kkwo-ju-da — to change, to switch (*telephones*)
바다 쪽 ba-da jjok — sea side
바람이 불다 ba-ram-i bul-da — the wind blows
바로 ba-ro — as soon as possible (a.s.a.p.)
바로 가다 ba-ro ga-da — to go directly
바로 뒤 ba-ro dwi — right behind
바르는 약 ba-reu-neun nyak — ointment
바쁘게 ba-ppeu-ge — busily
바쁘다 ba-ppeu-da — to be busy

바이올린을 켜다 va-i-ol-in-eul kyeo-da — to play violin
바지 ba-ji — pants
박물관에 가다 bang-mul-gwan-e ga-da — to go to a museum
밖 bak — outside
반갑다 ban-gap-da — to be glad
반지 ban-ji — ring
반찬 ban-chan — side dishes
받는 사람 ban-neun sa-ram — recipient
받다 bat-da — to receive
받으실 분 bad-eu-sil bun — receiver
발 bal — foot
발가락 bal-kka-rak — toe
발라 주다 bal-la ju-da — to put on
밝다 balk-da — to be bright
밤 bam — night
밤새도록 bam-sae-do-rok — for all night
밥 bap — cooked rice
방학 bang-hak — (school) vacation
배 bae — boat, ship, belly
배가 고프다 bae-ga go-peu-da — to be hungry
배가 부르다 bae-ga bu-reu-da — to be full
배가 아프다 bae-ga a-peu-da — to have stomach pain

배구를 하다 bae-gu-reul ha-da — to play volleyball
배터리 bae-teo-ri — battery
백 baek — hundred
백화점 bae-kwa-jeom — department store
버스 beo-seu — bus
번 beon — number, times
벌 beol — one pair
벌써 beol-sseo — already
법과대학 (법대) beop-gwa-dae-hak (beop-dae) — law school
법학 beo-pak — law study
벗기다 beot-gi-da — to undress someone
벗다 beot-da — to take off
벨트 bel-teu — belt
벽 byeok — wall
변호사 byeon-ho-sa — lawyer
별로 byeol-lo — not particularly
병 byeong — bottles

병원 byeong-won	hospital, clinic
보내는 사람 bo-nae-neun sa-ram	sender
보내다 bo-nae-da	to send
보다 bo-da	to see
보딩패스 bo-ding-pae-sseu	boarding pass
보라색 bo-ra-saek	purple (*color*)
보름 bo-reum	15 days
보여 주다 bo-yeo ju-da	to show
보이다 bo-i-da	to be seen
보통 bo-tong	in general, medium
보통 우편 bo-tong u-pyeon	regular mail
보험카드 bo-heom-ka-deu	insurance card
복잡하다 bok-ja-pa-da	to be busy, to be crowded
봄 bom	spring
뵙다 boep-da	to meet, to see (*hon.*)
부드러운 머리 bu-deu-reo-un meo-ri	soft hair
부드러워 보이다 bu-deu-reo-wo bo-i-da	to look soft
부드럽다 bu-deu-reop-da	to be soft
부모 bu-mo	parents
부산 bu-san	Pusan
부산행 bu-san-haeng	going to Pusan
부치다 bu-chi-da	to send
부탁하다 bu-ta-ka-da	to request
분 bun	minutes, persons (*hon.*)
분홍색 bun-hong-saek	pink color
불 bul	dollars
붓다 but-da	to be swollen
붙다 but-da	to attach, to be attached
블라우스 beul-la-u-seu	blouse
비 bi	rain
비가 오다 bi-ga o-da	to rain
비교적 bi-gyo-jeok	relatively
비디오를 보다 vi-di-o-reul bo-da	to watch a videotape
비밀번호 bi-mil-beon-ho	PIN number
비빔냉면 bi-bim-naeng-myeon	cold noodle with hot paste

비빔밥 bi-bim-ppap	rice with mixed vegetables
비서 bi-seo	secretary
비슷하다 bi-seu-ta-da	to be similar
비싸다 bi-ssa-da	to be expensive
비올라 vi-ol-la-reul kyeo-da	viola
비자 bi-ja	visa
비행기 bi-haeng-gi	airplane
비행기표 bi-haeng-gi-pyo	airplane ticket
비행장 bi-haeng-jang	airport
빌려주다 bil-lyeo-ju-da	to lend for someone's benefit
빠른 우편 ppa-reun u-pyeon	express mail
빨간 ppal-gan	red
빨간색 ppal-gan-saek	red (color)
빨갛다 ppal-ga-ta	to be red
빨래를 하다 ppal-lae-reul ha-da	to do laundry
빨리 ppal-li	fast
빵집 ppang-jjip	bakery
빼다 ppae-da	to pull out, to take off (rings, gloves, etc.)
뺏기다 ppaet-gi-da	to be taken away
뺏다 ppaet-da	to take away
뻣뻣한 머리 ppeot-ppeo-tan meo-ri	thick hair

ㅅ

사 sa	four
사각형 sa-ga-kyeong	square
사거리 sa-geo-ri	four-way intersection
사다 sa-da	to buy
사람 sa-ram	persons, people
사무실 sa-mu-sil	office
사범대학 (사대) sa-beom-dae-hak (sa-dae)	teacher education school
사실은 sa-sil-eun	in fact
사업가 sa-eop-ga	businessman
사용하다 sa-yong-ha-da	to use

사월 sa-wol — April
사위 sa-wi — son-in-law
사이다 sa-i-da — 7-up
사이즈 sa-i-jeu — size
사인 sa-in — signature
사장 sa-jang — president of a company

사진관 sa-jin-gwan — photograph developing shop

사진을 찍다 sa-jin-eul jjik-da — to take a picture
사촌 sa-chon — cousin
사촌동생 sa-chon-dong-saeng — younger cousin
사회학 sa-hoe-hak — sociology
사흘 sa-heul — 3 days
산 san — mountain
산 쪽 san jjok — mountainside
산뜻하다 san-tteu-ta-da — to be neat and fresh
산책을 하다 san-chaeg-eul ha-da — to go for a walk
살다 sal-da — to live
삼 sam — three
삼각형 sam-ga-kyeong — triangle
삼월 sam-wol — March
삼촌 sam-chon — uncle (*father's brothers in general*)

상가 sang-ga — mall
상경대학 (상대) sang-gyeong-dae-hak (sang-dae) — business school
상관없다 sang-gwan-eop-da — to be all right, to not matter

상상이 안 되다 sang-sang-i an-doe-da — to be unable to imagine

상자 sang-ja — box
상처가 나다 sang-cheo-ga na-da — to get hurt
상태 sang-tae — condition
상하다 sang-ha-da — to be damaged
새로 sae-ro — newly
새로 나오다 sae-ro na-o-da — to be newly released
새벽 sae-byeok — dawn
색깔 saek-kkal — color
색상 saek-sang — color and shape

샌디에이고 saen-di-e-i-go — San Diego
생기다 saeng-gi-da — to form, to open
생리하다 saeng-ri-ha-da — to menstruate, to be having one's period

생물학 saeng-mul-hak — biology
생선 saeng-seon — fish
생신 saeng-sin — birthday (*hon.*)
생일 saeng-il — birthday
샤워를 하다 sya-wo-reul ha-da — to take a shower
샴푸하다 syam-pu-ha-da — to shampoo
서다 seo-da — to stop
서른 seo-reun — thirty
서비스 sseo-bi-sseu — service
서울 seo-ul — Seoul
서점 seo-jeom — bookstore
섞다 seok-da — to mix
선물하다 seon-mul-ha-da — to give a present
선생 seon-saeng — teacher
선풍기 seon-pung-gi — fan
설거지를 하다 seol-geo-ji-reul ha-da — to wash dishes
설사하다 seol-ssa-ha-da — to have diarrhea
섭씨 seop-ssi — Celsius
성명 seong-myeong — name (*formal*)
성함 seong-ham — name (*hon.*)
세수를 하다 se-su-reul ha-da — to wash one's face
세워 드리다 se-wo deu-ri-da — to stop (*hon.*)
세워 주다 se-wo ju-da — to stop
세일기간 se-il-gi-gan — sale period
세일해 드리다 se-il-hae deu-ri-da — to discount (*hon.*)
세탁기 se-tak-gi — washing machine
센트 sen-teu — cents
셋 set — three
셔츠 syeo-cheu — shirt
소고기 so-go-gi — beef
소방서 so-bang-seo — fire department, fire station

소방차 so-bang-cha — fire truck
소아과 so-a-kkwa — pediatrics
소주 so-ju — soju

소포 so-po — package
소화가 안 되다 so-hwa-ga an-doe-da — to have indigestion
속 sok — in, inside
속달우편 sok-dal-u-pyeon — express mail
속옷 sog-ot — underwear
손 son — hand
손/발을 씻다 son/bal-eul ssit-da — to wash one's hands/ feet
손가락 son-kka-rak — finger
손녀 son-nyeo — granddaughter
손님 son-nim — guest, visitor, customer
손자 son-ja — grandson
손주 son-ju — grandchildren
손질하다 son-jil-ha-da — to take care
쇼핑가다 syo-ping-ga-da — to go shopping
수건 su-geon — towel
수고하다 su-go-ha-da — to work hard
수박 su-bak — watermelon
수수료 su-su-ryo — fee, charge
수영을 하다 su-yeong-eul ha-da — to swim
수영장 su-yeong-jang — swimming pool
수요일 su-yo-il — Wednesday
수원 su-won — Su-won, Korea
수표 supyo — check
수학 su-hak — mathematics
숨쉬기가 힘들다 sum-swi-gi-ga him-deul-da — to have difficulty breathing
숨을 쉬다 sum-eul swi-da — to breath
쉰 swin — fifty
슈퍼마켓 syu-peo-ma-ket — supermarket
스무날 seu-mu-nal — 20 days
스물 seu-mul — twenty
스웨터 seu-we-teo — sweater
스카프 seu-ka-peu — scarf
스케이트를 타다 seu-ke-i-teu-reul ta-da — to skate
스키를 타다 seu-ki-reul ta-da — to ski
스타킹 seu-ta-king — panty hose
스트레스가 많다/쌓이다 seu-teu-re-sseu-ga man-ta /ssa-i-da — to be stressed

스트레스가 풀리다 seu-teu-re-sseu-ga pul-li-da	to relieve stress
스트레이트 파마 seu-teu-re-i-teu pa-ma	straight permanent (*hairstyle*)
스페인 seu-pe-in	Spain
스페인 사람 seu-pe-in sa-ram	Spanish
스페인어 seu-pe-in-eo	Spanish language
스페인인 seu-pe-in-in	Spanish
스프레이를 하다 seu-peu-re-i-reul ha-da	to put on hairspray
슬프다 seul-peu-da	to be sad
습도 seup-do	humidity
시 si	o'clock
시간 si-gan	time, hour
시간(이) 있다 si-gan(-i) it-da	to have the time
시계 si-ge	watch, clock
시계 방 si-ge ppang	watch repair store
시끄럽게 si-kkeu-reop-ge	loudly
시끄럽다 si-kkeu-reop-da	to be loud
시내 si-nae	downtown
시다 si-da	to be sour
시아버님 si-a-beo-nim	father-in-law (*female speaker*)
시어머님 si-eo-meo-nim	mother-in-law (*female speaker*)
시원하다 si-won-ha-da	to be cool
시월 si-wol	October
시작하다 si-ja-ka-da	to start
시키다 si-ki-da	to order
식구 sik-gu	family, family members (*casual*)
식사 후 sik-sa hu	after a meal
식전(에) sik-jeon-(e)	before a meal
식후(에) si-ku-(e)	after a meal
신기다 sin-gi-da	to put shoes on someone
신나다 sin-na-da	to be excited
신다 sin-tta	to wear
신발 sin-bal	shoes
신발가게 sin-bal-kka-ge	shoe store
신분증 sin-bun-jjeung	ID card
신청서 sin-cheong-seo	application

신호 sin-ho — signal
신호등 sin-ho-deung — traffic signal
실내 수영장 sil-lae su-yeong-jang — indoor swimming pool

실례 sil-lye — bad manners
실례지만 sil-lye-ji-man — Excuse me....
싫다 sil-ta — to not be likable
싫어하다 sil-eo-ha-da — to dislike
심리학 sim-ni-hak — psychology
심심하다 sim-sim-ha-da — to feel bored
심하다 sim-ha-da — to be serious, to be severe

십 sip — ten
십이월 sib-i-wol — December
십일월 sib-il-wol — November
싱겁다 sing-geop-da — to be blend
쌀쌀하다 ssal-ssal-ha-da — to be chilly
써 있다 sseo it-da — to be written
써 주다 sseo ju-da — to write
쓰다 sseu-da — to write, to use, to be tart

쓰이다 sseu-i-da — to be used

ㅇ

아 a — ah
'아' 하다 a-ha-da — to say "ah"
아내 a-nae — wife
아니다 a-ni-da — not to be
아니면 a-ni-myeon — or, if not ~
아니오 a-ni-o — no
아들 a-deul — son
아래 a-rae — under, below, down
아무 a-mu — any
아무 분 a-mu bun — anyone
아버지 a-beo-ji — father
아이 a-i — child, kid
아이구 a-i-gu — oh
아주 a-ju — very, very much
아주머니 a-ju-meo-ni — middle-aged woman
아직 a-jik — yet, still

아직도 a-jik-do — yet
아참 a-cham — oh,
아침 a-chim — morning, breakfast
아침을 먹다 a-chim-eul meok-da — to have a breakfast
아파트 a-pa-teu — apartment
아프다 a-peu-da — to be hurt, to be sick
아홉 a-hop — nine
아흐레 a-heu-re — 9 days
아흔 a-heun — ninety
안 an — inside, not
안경 an-gyeong — glasses
안과 an-kkwa — opthalmology
안기다 an-gi-da — to be held
안녕하다 an-nyeong-ha-da — to be well
안녕히 an-nyeong-hi — safely, peacefully
안다 an-tta — to hold
앉다 an-tta — to sit
앉아 있다 anj-a it-da — to be sitting
앉히다 an-chi-da — to seat someone
알다 al-da — to know
알아서 al-a-seo — in a way that one thinks is right without getting permisson or confirmation from others
알아서 하다 al-a-seo ha-da — to do something in a way that one thinks is right without asking permission or receiving confirmation from another person
알약 al-lyak — pill, tablet
앞 ap — front
앞머리 am-meo-ri — front hair
앞으로 ap-eu-ro — from now on
앰뷸런스 aem-byul-leon-seu — ambulance

야구를 하다 ya-gu-reul ha-da — to play baseball
약국 yak-guk — drugstore
약방 yak-bang — drugstore
약사 yak-sa — pharmacist
약속시간 yak-sok-si-gan — appointment time
약을 먹다 yag-eul meok-da — to take a medication
약하다 ya-ka-da — to be weak
약학대학 (약대) yak-hak-dae-hak (yak-dae) — college of pharmacy
양말 yang-mal — socks
양식 yang-sik — Western food
양식당 yang-sik-dang — Western restaurant
양주 yang-ju — Western liquors
양치질하다 yang-chi-jil-ha-da — to brush one's teeth
양화점 yang-hwa-jeom — shoe store
어깨 eo-kkae — shoulder
어느 eo-neu — some, which
어느 분 eo-neu-bun — which person
어느 쪽 eo-neu jjok — which way
어디 eo-di — where, somewhere/anywhere
어떠세요? eo-tteo-se-yo — How about ~?, How is it?
어떤 eo-tteon — which, a certain, what kind of
어떤 거 eo-tteon geo — which one
어떻게 eo-tteo-ke — how, somehow
어떻다 eo-tteo-ta — to be how
어렸을 때 eo-reoss-eul ttae — when (someone was) young
어머 eo-meo — uh uh
어머니 eo-meo-ni — mother
어서 eo-seo — quickly, please
어울리게 eo-ul-li-ge — match well
어울리다 eo-ul-li-da — to match well
어제 eo-je — yesterday
어지럽다 eo-ji-reop-da — to be dizzy
어휴 eo-hu — alas, wow…
억 eok — hundred million
언니 eon-ni — woman's older sister
언어학 eon-eo-hak — linguistics

언제 eon-je — sometime/anytime, when?

언제나 eon-je-na — whenever, always
언제든지 eon-je-deun-ji — whenever
얼굴 eol-gul — face
얼다 eol-da — to freeze
얼리다 eol-li-da — to freeze something
얼마 eol-ma — how much?
얼마 전 eol-ma jeon — a while ago
얼마나 eol-ma-na — how long/much/many?

얼음이 얼다 eol-eum-i eol-da — the ice freezes
없다 eop-da — not to exist, not to have

엉덩이 eong-deong-i — buttocks, hip
에어컨 e-eo-keon — air conditioner
엔지니어 en-ji-ni-eo — engineer
여권 yeo-kkwon — passport
여기 yeo-gi — here
여덟 yeo-deol — eight
여동생 yeo-dong-saeng — younger sister
여드레 yeo-deu-re — 8 days
여든 yeo-deun — eighty
여름 yeo-reum — summer
여섯 yeo-seot — six
여자 yeo-ja — woman
여쭈어 보다 yeo-jju-eo bo-da — to ask (*hum.*)
여행 yeo-haeng — travel
여행을 하다/가다 yeo-haeng-eul ha-da/ga-da — to travel
역사학 yeok-sa-hak — history
연극 구경을 가다/하다 yeon-geuk gu-gyeong-eul ga-da/ha-da — to go to watch a play
연노란색 yeon-no-ran-saek — light yellow (*color*)
연노랑색 yeon-no-rang-saek — light yellow (*color*)
연두색 yeon-du-saek — light green (*color*)
연락 yeol-lak — contact
연락 드리다 yeol-lak deu-ri-da — to contact (*hum.*)
연락하다 yeol-la-ka-da — to contact
연말 yeon-mal — end of the year
연세 yeon-se — age (*hon.*)

연세가 많으시다 yeon-se-ga man-eu-si-da — to be old (*hon.*)
연하다 yeon-ha-da — to be light, to be tender
연한 노란색 yeon-han no-ran-saek — light yellow (*color*)
열 yeol — ten
열다 yeol-da — to open
열리다 yeol-li-da — to be open
열이 나다 yeol-i na-da — to have fever
열흘 yeol-heul — 10 days
염색 yeom-saek — dyeing
염색하다 yeom-sae-ka-da — to dye
엽서 yeop-seo — postcard
엿새 yeot-sae — 6 days
영국 yeong-guk — England
영국 사람 yeong-guk sa-ram — British
영국인 yeong-gug-in — British
영상 yeong-sang — above zero
영수증 yeong-su-jeung — receipt
영어 yeong-eo — English
영하 yeong-ha — below zero
영화 구경을 가다/하다 yeong-hwa gu-gyeong-eul ga-da/ha-da — to go to watch a movie
영화(를) 보다 yeong-hwa(-reul) bo-da — to watch a movie
옆 yeop — beside, side, nearby
옆머리 yeom-meo-ri — side hair
예 ye — yes, OK
예금하다 ye-geum-ha-da — to save money, to deposit
예방용 ye-bang-nyong — for prevention
예쁘게 ye-ppeu-ge — pretty, beautifully
예쁘다 ye-ppeu-da — to be pretty
예순 ye-sun — sixty
오 o — five
오늘 o-neul — today
오다 o-da — to come
오래간만에 o-rae-gan-man-e — after a long time
오래간만이다 o-rae-gan-man-i-da — long time no see
오래되다 o-rae-doe-da — to be old (*object*)
오른쪽 o-reun-jjok — right side

오른쪽으로 가다 o-reun-jjog-eu-ro ga-da — to turn right
오바 o-ba — coat
오빠 o-ppa — woman's older brother

오월 o-wol — May
오전 o-jeon — A.M.
오토바이 o-to-ba-i — motorcycle
오후 o-hu — P.M.
온도 on-do — temperature
올라가다 ol-la-ga-da — to go up
올라오다 ol-la-o-da — to come up
올해 ol-hae — this year
옷 ot — clothes
옷가게 ot-ga-ge — clothing store
와 wa — wow
와이셔츠 wa-i-syeo-cheu — dress shirts
왜 wae — why
외과 oe-kkwa — external department
외사촌 oe-sa-chon — cousin (*maternal*)
외삼촌 oe-sam-chon — uncle (*maternal*)
외숙모 oe-sung-mo — aunt (외삼촌's wife)
왼쪽 oen-jjok — left
왼쪽으로 가다 oen-jjog-eu-ro ga-da — to turn left
요금 yo-geum — fare
요즘 yo-jeum — these days
우리 u-ri — we, us, our
우체국 u-che-guk — post office
우체국 직원 u-che-guk jig-won — post office employee
우체부 u-che-bu — postman
우체통 u-che-tong — mailbox
우편번호 u-pyeon-beon-ho — zip code
우편요금 u-pyeon-yo-geum — postage, postal charge

우표 u-pyo — stamp
우표를 붙이다 u-pyo-reul bu-chi-da — to put on a stamp
우표를 사다 u-pyo-reul sa-da — to buy a stamp
우회전하다 u-hoe-jeon-ha-da, — to make a right turn
운동선수 un-dong-seon-su — sportsman
운전기사 un-jeon-gi-sa — driver
운전하다 un-jeon-ha-da — to drive

운전해서 un-jeon-hae-seo	by driving
울다 ul-da	to cry
울리다 ul-li-da	to make someone cry
웃기다 ut-gi-da	to make someone laugh
웃다 ut-da	to laugh
원 won	Korean won
원피스 won-pi-seu	dress
원형 won-hyeong	round
월 wol	month
월말 wol-mal	end of the month
월요일 wol-yo-il	Monday
웬일 wen-il	what thing?
위 wi	top, above, up
유월 yu-wol	June
유치원 yu-chi-won	kindergarten
유치원생 yu-chi-won-saeng	kindergarten student
육 yuk	six
육교 yuk-gyo	overpass
은행 eun-haeng	bank
은행거래신청서 eun-haeng-geo-rae-sin-cheong-seo	bank account application
음료수 eum-nyo-su	drink, beverage
음식 eum-sik	food
음악 eum-ak	music
음악대학 (음대) eum-ak-dae-hak (eum-dae)	music school
음악을 듣다 eum-ag-eul deut-da	to listen to music
음악회에 가다 eum-a-koe-e ga-da	to go to a concert
의과대학 (의대) ui-kkwa-dae-hak (ui-dae)	medical school
의료보험카드 ui-ryo-bo-heom-ka-deu	health insurance card
의사 ui-sa	doctor
의사 선생님 ui-sa seon-saeng-nim	doctor
의학 ui-hak	medical study
이 i	two
이/그/저 분 i/geu/jeo bun	this/that person (*hon.*)
이/그/저 사람 i/geu/jeo sa-ram	this/that person
이/그/저 i/geu/jeo	this/that

이/그/저 거 i/geu/jeo-geo — this/that one
이가 아프다 i-ga a-peu-da — to have a toothache
이것 저것 i-geot jeo-geot — this and that
이다 i-da — to be
이렇게 i-reo-ke — like this
이레 i-re — 7 days
이를 닦다 i-reul dak-da — to brush one's teeth
이름 i-reum — name
이리 i-ri — this way
이모 i-mo — aunt (*maternal*)
이모부 i-mo-bu — uncle (이모's husband)

이발사 i-bal-ssa — man's hairdresser
이번 달 i-beon-ttal — this month
이번 주 i-beon-jju — this week
이사 i-sa — moving
이사하다 i-sa-ha-da — to move
이상기온 현상 i-sang-gi-on hyeon-sang — abnormal (*temperature*)

이상하다 i-sang-ha-da — to be strange, to be unusual

이월 i-wol — February
이제 i-je — now
이쪽 i-jjok — this side, this way
이틀 han i-teul jeon — 2 days
인류학 il-lyu-hak — anthropology
인문대학 (인문대) in-mun-dae-hak (in-mun-dae) — school of the humanities
인상 in-sang — facial impression
인상되다 in-sang-doe-da — to be increased
인연 in-yeon — destiny
일 il — one, date, things, work, job

일곱 il-gop — seven
일기예보 il-gi-ye-bo — weather forecast
일반우편 il-ban u-pyeon — regular mail, ground mail

일본 il-bon — Japan
일본 사람 il-bon sa-ram — Japanese
일본어 il-bon-eo — Japanese language
일본인 il-bon-in — Japanese

일식 il-ssik — Japanese food
일식당 il-ssik-dang — Japanese restaurant
일어나다 il-eo-na-da — to get up, to wake up
일요일 il-yo-il — Sunday
일월 il-wol — January
일주일 han il-jju-il — a week
일찍 il-jjik — early
일흔 il-heun — seventy
읽어주다 ilg-eo-ju-da — to read for someone's benefit

입 ip — mouth
입금표 ip-geum-pyo — deposit slip
입다 ip-da — to wear
입어 보다 ib-eo-bo-da — to try on (clothes), to wear

입에 맞다 ib-e mat-da — to fit someone's taste
입원하다 ib-won-ha-da — to hospitalize
입히다 i-pi-da — to dress someone
잇몸 in-mom — gum
있다 it-da — to exist, to have
잊어버리다 ij-eo-beo-ri-da — to forget

ㅈ

자가용 ja-ga-yong — car, automobile (*personal*)

자기앞수표 ja-gi-ap su-pyo — official check
자꾸 ja-kku — again and again
자다 ja-da — to sleep
자동 응답기 ja-dong eung-dap-gi — answering machine
자동차 ja-dong-cha — car, automobile (*in general*)

자라다 ja-ra-da — to grow
자르다 ja-reu-da — to have a cut, to cut
자리 ja-ri — seat
자연대학 (자연대) ja-yeon-dae-hak (ja-yeon-dae) — school of sciences

자전거 ja-jeon-geo — bike
자전거를 타다 ja-jeon-geo-reul ta-da — to ride a bicycle
자주 ja-ju — often
자켓 ja-ket — jacket

자판기 ja-pan-gi — banding machine
작가 jak-ga — writer
작년 jang-nyeon — last year
작은 아버지 jag-eun a-beo-ji — uncle (*father's younger brother*)
작은 어머니 jag-eun eo-meo-ni — aunt (작은 아버지's wife)
잔 jan — cups, glasses
잔돈 jan-don — change
잘 jal — well
잘 되다 jal doe-da — to have done well, to be going well
잘 맞다 jal mat-da — to fit well
잘 먹다 jal meok-da — to eat well
잘 있다 jal it-da — to be well
잘 해 주다 jal hae ju-da — to give special care
잘라 드리다 jal-la deu-ri-da — to cut something for someone (*hum.*)
잠깐만 jam-kkan-man — for a minute
잠시 후 jam-si-hu — after a while
잠을 자다 jam-eul ja-da — to sleep
잡다 jap-da — to catch
잡수시다 jap-su-si-da — to eat (*hon.*)
잡지 jap-ji — magazine
잡히다 ja-pi-da — to be caught
장 jang — sheets
장갑 jang-gap — glove
장난감 가게 jang-nan-kkam ga-ge — toy store
장모님 jang-mo-nim — mother-in-law (*male speaker*)
장사 jang-sa — business
장염에 걸리다 jang-yeom-e geol-li-da — to have an intestinal problem
장인어른 jang-in-eo-reun — father-in-law (*male speaker*)
재미있게 jae-mi-it-ge — interestingly
재미있다 jae-mi-it-da — to be fun, to be interesting
재우다 jae-u-da — to make someone sleep

재작년 jae-jang-nyeon — the year before last year

저 jeo — I (*hum.*)

저금하다 jeo-geum-ha-da — to save money, to deposit (money)

저기 jeo-gi — there

저녁 jeo-nyeok — evening, dinner

저녁을 먹다 jeo-nyeog-eul meok-da — to have dinner

저쪽 jeo-jjok — that side

저희 jeo-hi — our (*hum.*)

전 세계적으로 jeon se-gye-jeog-eu-ro — worldwide

전부 jeon-bu — all

전화 jeon-hwa — telephone

전화 걸다 jeon-hwa geol-da — to make a telephone call

전화 드리다 jeon-hwa deu-ri-da — to make a telephone call (*hum.*)

전화번호 jeon-hwa-beon-ho — telephone number

전화하다 jeon-hwa-ha-da — to make a telephone call

점심 jeom-sim — afternoon, lunch

점심 먹다 jeom-sim meok-da — to eat lunch

점심시간 jeom-sim-si-gan — lunch time

점원 jeom-won — salesperson

점잖다 jeom-jan-ta — to be decent

점잖은 것 jeom-jan-eun geot — plain item

점점 jeom-jeom — gradually

정가 jeong-kka — original price

정리하다 jeong-ri-ha-da — to organize

정말 jeong-mal — really, so

정사각형 jeong-sa-ga-kyeong — square

정삼각형 jeong-sam-ga-kyeong — triangle

정장 jeong-jang — suit

정장 바지 jeong-jang ba-ji — dress pants

정치학 jeong-chi-hak — political science

제 je — my

제가 보기에는 je-ga bo-gi-e-neun — in my opinion

제과점 je-gwa-jeom — bakery

제일 je-il — the most, the first

제일빌딩 je-il-bil-ding — Je-Il Building

제품 je-pum — product
조 jo — trillion
조금 jo-geum — a little
조금만 jo-geum-man — a little
조깅을 하다 jo-ging-eul ha-da — to jog
조카 jo-ka — nephew, niece
좀 jom — a little, please
종업원 jong-eob-won — waiter, waitress, employee

종합검사를 하다/받다 jong-hap-geom-sa-reul ha-da/bat-da — to get a general examination
좋다 jo-ta — to like, to be likable, to be good

좋아하다 jo-a-ha-da — to like
좋은 아침 jo-eun a-chim — good morning
좋은 약 jo-eun yak — good medicine
좌석 jwa-seok — seat
좌석번호 jwa-seok-beon-ho — seat number
좌회전하다 jwa-hoe-jeon-ha-da — to make a left turn
죄송하다 joe-song-ha-da — to be sorry
주다 ju-da — to give
주말 ju-mal — weekend
주무시다 ju-mu-si-da — to sleep (hon.)
주문하다 ju-mun-ha-da, — to order
주사를 맞다 ju-sa-reul mat-da — to get injected
주소 ju-so — address
주소를 쓰다 ju-so-reul sseu-da — to write an address
주스 ju-seu — juice
주인 ju-in — owner
주중 ju-jung — weekdays
주황색 ju-hwang-saek — orange (color)
죽다 juk-da — to die
죽이다 jug-i-da — to kill someone
줄무늬 jul-mu-ni — stripe pattern
중간에 jung-gan-e — in the middle, on the way ~

중국 jung-guk — China
중국 사람 jung-guk sa-ram — Chinese
중국어 jung-gug-eo — Chinese language
중국인 jung-gug-in — Chinese

중식 jung-sik — Chinese food
중식당 jung-sik-dang — Chinese restaurant
중앙우체국 jung-ang-u-che-guk — central post office
중학교 jung-hak-gyo — junior high school
중학생 jung-hak-saeng — junior high student
즐겁다 jeul-geop-da — to be happy
증상 jeung-sang — symptom
지금 ji-geum — now
지금도 ji-geum-do — even now
지난 달 ji-nan dal — last month
지난 주 ji-nan ju — last week
지내다 ji-nae-da — to spend time, to live
지루하다 ji-ru-ha-da — to be bored to death
지하 ji-ha — basement
지하도 ji-ha-do — underpass
지하철 ji-ha-cheol — subway
직사각형 jik-sa-ga-kyeong — rectangle
직원 jig-won — employee
직원회의 jig-won-hoe-ui — staff meeting
직진하다 jik-jin-ha-da — to go straight
직행 jik-haeng — non-stop, direct
진노란색 jin-no-ran-saek — dark yellow (*color*)
진노랑색 jin-no-rang-saek — dark yellow (*color*)
진지 jin-ji — meal (*hon.*)
진찰을 하다/받다 jin-chal-eul ha-da/bat-da — to examine (in a hospital)

진한 노란색 jin-han no-ran-saek — dark yellow (*color*)
짐 jim — baggage
집 jip — house
집사람 jip-sa-ram — (my) wife
짓다 jit-da — to build
짙다 jit-da — to be dark
짜다 jja-da — to be salty
짧게 jjalp-ge — short, shortly
짧다 jjalp-da — to be short
짧은 머리 jjalb-eun meo-ri — short hair
쫓기다 jjot-gi-da — to be chased
쫓다 jjot-da — to chase
쭉 jjuk — straight

ㅊ

차 타는 곳 cha ta-neun got — ground transportation

차다 cha-da — to be cold
찬물 chan-mul — cold water
참 cham — really, oh
참다 cham-tta — to be patient
창측 chang-cheuk — window side
찾다 chat-da — to look for, to find
찾아 보다 chaj-a-bo-da — to look for
찾아 오다 chaj-a o-da — to come to see
책방 chaek-bang — bookstore
책을 읽다 chaeg-eul ilk-da — to read a book
처방전 cheo-bang-jeon — prescription
처음 cheo-eum — for the first time
천 cheon — thousand
첩보영화 cheop-bo-yeong-hwa — spy movie
첫번째 cheot-beon-jjae — first
청색 cheong-saek — navy blue (color)
체육대학 (체대) che-yuk-dae-hak (che-dae) — college of physical education

체크무늬 che-keu-mu-nui, che-keu-mu-ni — checkered pattern
첼로 chel-lo-reul kyeo-da — cello
초등학교 cho-deung-hak-gyo — elementary school
초등학생 cho-deung-hak-saeng — elementary student
초록색 cho-rok-saek — green (color)
추워지다 chu-wo-ji-da — to get cold
축구를 하다 chuk-gu-reul ha-da — to play soccer
출금표 ip-chul-geum-pyo — withdrawal slip
출발하는 곳 chul-bal-ha-neun got — departure
출발하다 chul-bal-ha-da — to depart
춤을 추다 chum-eul chu-da — to dance
춥다 chup-da — to feel cold, to be cold

층 cheung — layer, story, floor
치과 chi-kkwa — dentistry
치과대학 (치대) chi-kkwa-dae-hak (chi-dae) — dental school
치료를 하다 chi-ryo-reul ha-da — to give medical treatment

치마 chi-ma — skirt

치실 chi-sil — floss

치약 chi-yak — toothpaste

치주염 chi-ju-yeom — gum disease

칠 chil — seven

칠월 chil-wol — July

ㅋ

카드 ka-deu — card, credit card

카드놀이를 하다 ka-deu nol-i-reul ha-da — to play a card game

카페 ka-pe — café, coffee shop

캐나다 kae-na-da — Canada

캐나다 사람 kae-na-da sa-ram — Canadian

캐나다인 kae-na-da-in — Canadian

캐주얼 kae-ju-eol — casual

커트 하다 keo-teu-ha-da — to have a haircut

커피 keo-pi — coffee

커피숍 keo-pi-syop — coffee shop

컴퓨터 keom-pu-teo — computer

컴퓨터 게임을 하다 keom-pyu-teo ge-im-eul ha-da — to play a computer game

코 ko — nose

코가 막히다 ko-ga ma-ki-da — to have nasal congestion

코트 co-teu — coat

콜라 kol-la — cola

콧물이 나다 kon-mul-i na-da — to have a runny nose

크게 keu-ge — widely, big, loudly

큰아버지 keun-a-beo-ji — uncle (*father's older brother*)

큰어머니 keun-eo-meo-ni — aunt (큰아버지's wife)

큰일 나다 keun-il na-da — to have trouble

클라리넷 keul-la-ri-net-eul bul-da — to play clarinet

ㅌ

타기 ta-gi — riding

타는 데 ta-neun de — place to ride

타다 ta-da — to ride, to burn

타원형 ta-won-hyeong — oval

타일 ta-il — tile

탁구를 치다 tak-gu-reul chi-da — to play ping-pong
탈의실 tal-ui-sil — fitting room
태어나다 tae-eo-na-da — to be born
태우다 tae-u-da — to burn something
택시 taek-si — taxi
턱 teok — chin
털다 teol-da — to shake off
테니스를 치다 te-ni-seu-reul chi-da — to play tennis
텔레비전을 보다 tel-le-bi-jeon-eul bo-da — to watch TV
토요일 to-yo-il — Saturday
토하다 to-ha-da — to vomit
통장 tong-jang — deposit and withdrawal record, bank account

통장 만들기 tong-jang man-deul-gi — opening a bank account

퇴근시간 toe-geun-si-gan — time to leave the office

퇴원하다 toe-won-ha-da — to release (from a hospital)

트럼펫 teu-reom-pes-eul bul-da — to play trumpet
트럼프를 치다 teu-reom-peu-reul chi-da — to play a card game

특별히 teuk-byeol-hi — especially
틀어 놓다 teul-eo no-ta — to turn on

ㅍ

파란 pa-ran — blue
파란색 pa-ran-saek — blue (*color*)
파랗다 pa-ra-ta — to be blue
파마머리 pa-ma meo-ri — permanent-waved hair

파마하다 pa-ma-ha-da — to have a permanent
파운드 pa-un-deu — pounds
파전 pa-jeon — scallion pancake
팔 pal — eight, arm
팔다 pal-da — to sell
팔리다 pal-li-da — to be sold
팔월 pal-wol — August

편리하다 pyeol-li-ha-da	to be convenient
편의점 pyeon-ui-jeom	convenient store
편지 pyeon-ji	letter
편지 부치기 pyeon-ji bu-chi-gi	sending a mail
편지/소포를 받다 pyeon-ji/so-po-reul bat-da	to receive a letter/ package
편지/소포를 부치다 pyeon-ji/so-po-reul bu-chi-da	to send a letter/ package
편지를 쓰다 pyeon-ji-reul sseu-da	to write a letter
편지봉투 pyeon-ji-bong-tu	envelope
편지지 pyeon-ji-ji	letter paper
포도주 po-do-ju	wine
표 pyo	ticket
풀다 pul-da	to untie
프랑스 peu-rang-sseu	France
프랑스 사람 peu-rang-sseu sa-ram	French
프랑스어 peu-rang-sseu-eo	French language
프랑스인 peu-rang-sseu-in	French
플랫폼 peul-laet-pom	platform
플로스 peul-lo-seu	floss
플룻을 불다 peul-lus-eul bul-da	to play flute
피가 나다 pi-ga na-da	to bleed
피곤하다 pi-gon-ha-da	to be tired
피아노를 치다 pi-a-no-reul chi-da	to play piano
필요하다 pil-yo-ha-da	to need
필요한 것 pil-yo-han geot	things to be needed

ㅎ

하나 ha-na	one
하다 ha-da	to do
하루 ha-ru	1 day
하루에 ha-ru-e	per day
하얀 ha-yan	white
하얀색 ha-yan-saek	white (*color*)
하얗다 ha-ya-ta	to be white
학년 hang-nyeon	school year
학생 hak-saeng	student
한국 han-guk	Korea
한국 분 han-guk-bun	Korean (*hon.*)
한국 사람 han-guk sa-ram	Korean

한국계 han-guk-gye	Korean-, related to Korea
한국어 han-gug-eo	Korean language
한국인 han-gug-in	Korean
한번 han-beon	once
한식 han-sik	Korean food
한식당 han-sik-dang	Korean restaurant
한식집 han-sik-jip	Korean restaurant
한영서점 han-yeong-seo-jeom	Han-Yeong Bookstore
한잔 han jan	one cup
할 수 없다 hal sue op-da	cannot help, there is no other choice
할머니 hal-meo-ni	grandmother
할머니 댁 hal-meo-ni daek	grandmother's house (*hon.*)
할아버지 hal-a-beo-ji	grandfather
합승 하다 hap-seung-ha-da	to share a ride
항공 우편 hang-gong u-pyeon	air mail, first-class mail
항공편으로 hang-gong-pyeon-eu-ro	via airmail
항상 hang-sang	always
해 드리다 hae deu-ri-da	to do (*hum.*)
해 주다 hae ju-da	to do
핸드폰 haen-deu-pon	cellular phone
행복하다 haeng-bo-ka-da	to be happy
행인 haeng-in	passer-by
허리 heo-ri	waist
헤어 디자이너 he-eo di-ja-i-neo	hair dresser
헤어 크림 he-eo keu-rim	hair cream
현금 hyeon-geum	cash
현금지급기 hyeon-geum-gi-geup-gi	ATM machine
현금카드 hyeon-geum-ka-deu	ATM card
형 hyeong	man's older brother
호주 ho-ju	Australia
호주 사람 ho-ju sa-ram	Australian
호주인 ho-ju-in	Australian
혹시 hok-si	by any chance, just in case
혼자 hon-ja	by oneself, alone

화가 나다 hwa-ga na-da	to be angry
화씨 hwa-ssi	Fahrenheit
화요일 hwa-yo-il	Tuesday
화원 hwa-won	florist/flower shop
화학 hwa-hak	chemistry
환영회 hwan-yeong-hoe	welcome party
환율 hwan-nyul	exchange rate
환율이 내리다 hwan-nyul-i nae-ri-da	the exchange rate goes down
환율이 오르다 hwan-nyul-i o-reu-da	the exchange rate goes up
환전을 하다 hwan-jeon-eul-ha-da	to exchange money
환전하기 hwan-jeon-ha-gi	exchanging currency
환전하다 hwan-jeon-ha-da	to exchange money
회사 hoe-sa	company
회사원 hoe-sa-won	office employee
회색 hoe-saek	gray (*color*)
횡단보도 hoeng-dan-bo-do	crosswalk
훨씬 hwol-ssin	much more
흐려지다 heu-ryeo-ji-da	to get cloudy
흠... heum	hmmm...

◇◇◇◇◇◇◇◇

Appendix 3:
English-Korean Vocabulary

A

abnormal weather	이상기온 현상 i-sang-gi-on hyeon-sang
above zero	영상 yeong-sang
above	위 wi
account	구좌 gu-jwaacross, 건너 gon-neo
across the street	건너편 geon-neo-pyeon
address	주소 ju-so
adjust	맞추다 mat-chu-da
afraid	무섭다 mu-seop-da
after a long time	오래간만에 o-rae-gan-man-e
after a meal	식사 후 sik-sa hu, 식후(에) si-ku-(e)
after a while	잠시 후 jam-si-hu
afternoon	점심 jeom-sim
again	다시 da-si, 또 tto
again and again	자꾸 ja-kku
age	연세 yeon-se, 나이 na-i
same age	동갑 dong-gap
ah	아 a
ahead	먼저 meon-jeo
air	공기 gong-gi
air conditioner	에어컨 e-eo-keon
air mail	항공 우편 hang-gong u-pyeon
via airmail	항공편으로 hang-gong-pyeon-eu-ro
airline	
(domestic)	국내선 gung-nae-seon
(international)	국제선 guk-je-seon
airplane	비행기 bi-haeng-gi
airplane ticket	비행기표 bi-haeng-gi-pyo
airport	공항 gong-hang, 비행장 bi-haeng-jang
alas	어휴 eo-hu
all	다 da, 모두 mo-du, 전부 jeon-bu
all done	다 되다 da doe-da
all together	다 같이 da ga-chi
almost	거의 geo-ui
alone	혼자 hon-ja
already	벌써 beol-sseo
although	그래도 geu-rae-do
alumni	동창 dong-chang
alumni assembly	동창회 dong-chang-hoe
always	언제나 eon-je-na, 항상 hang-sang

ambulance	구급차 gu-geup-cha, 앰뷸런스 aem-byul-leon-seu
A.M.	오전 o-jeon
America	미국 mi-guk
American	미국 사람 mi-guk-sa-ram, 미국인 mi-gug-in
American citizen	미국시민 mi-guk-si-min
and	그리고 geu-ri-go
anger	화 hwa
angry	화가 나다 (hwa-ga na-da)
animal	동물 dong-mul
answering machine	자동 응답기 ja-dong eung-dap-gi
anthropology	인류학 il-lyu-hak
any	아무 a-mu, 어느 eo-neu
anyone	아무 분이나 a-mu bun-i-na, 아무나 a-mu-na
apartment	아파트 a-pa-teu
apartment complex	아파트 단지 a-pa-teu dan-ji
appear	나타나다 na-ta-na-da
application	신청서 sin-cheong-seo
appointment	약속 yak-sok
appointment time	약속시간 yak-sok-si-gan
approximately	대략 dae-ryak, 대충 dae-chung
April	사월 sa-wol
architecture	건축학 geon-chuk-hak
arm	팔 pal
arrive	도착하다 do-cha-ka-da
art gallery	미술관 mi-sul-gwan
art school	미술대학 (미대) mi-sul-dae-hak (mi-dae)
as soon as possible (a.s.a.p.)	바로 ba-ro
Asian studies	동양학 dong-yang-hak
ask	물어보다 mul-eo-bo-da, 여쭈어 보다 yeo-jju-eo bo-da
at last	마지막으로 ma-ji-mag-eu-ro
at latest	늦어도 nuj-eo-do
ATM card	현금카드 hyeon-geum-ka-deu
ATM machine	현금지급기 hyeon-geum-gi-geup-gi
attach	붙이다 bu-chi-da
attached	붙다 but-da
attend	다니다 da-ni-da
August	팔월 pal-wol

aunt	고모go-mo, 이모i-mo, 외숙모 oe-sung-mo, 작은 어머니 jag-eun eo-meo-ni, 큰어머니 keun-eo-meo-ni
Australia	호주 ho-ju
Australian	호주 사람 ho-ju sa-ram, 호주인 ho-ju-in
automobile	자가용 ja-ga-yong, 자동차 ja-dong-cha
autumn	가을 ga-eul

B

back	등 deung, 뒤 dwi
bad	나쁘다na-ppeu-da
baggage	짐 jim
bakery	빵집 ppang-jjip, 제과점 je-gwa-jeom
bald	대머리 dae-meo-ri
banding machine	자판기 ja-pan-gi
bank	은행 eun-haeng
bank account	통장 tong-jang, 은행구좌 eun-haeng-gu-jwa
bank account application	은행거래신청서 eun-haeng-geo-rae-sin-cheong-seo
barber	이발사 i-bal-ssa
baseball	야구 ya-gu
play baseball	야구를 하다 ya-gu-reul ha-da
basement	지하 ji-ha, 지하실 ji-ha-sil
basketball	농구 nong-gu
play basketball	농구를 하다 nong-gu-reul ha-da
bath	목욕 mog-yok
take a bath	목욕을 하다 mog-yog-eul ha-da
battery	배터리 bae-teo-ri
be	이다 i-da, 있다 it-da, 계시다 gye-si-da
(to) not be	아니다 a-ni-da
beautifully	예쁘게 ye-ppeu-ge
become	되다 doe-da
beef	소고기 so-go-gi
beer	맥주 maek-ju
before a meal	식전(에) sik-jeon-(e)
behind	뒤 dwi
belly	배 bae
below	아래 a-rae
below zero	영하 yeong-ha

belt	벨트 bel-teu
beneath	밑 mit
beside	옆 yeop
better	낫다 nat-da
beverage	음료수 eum-nyo-su
bicycle	자전거 ja-jeon-geo
big	크다 keu-da, 크게 keu-ge
bill	계산서 gye-san-seo
biology	생물학 saeng-mul-hak
birthday	생신 saeng-sin, 생일 saeng-il
bite	물다 mul-da
bitten	물리다 mul-li-da
black	까만색 kka-man-saek, 까만 kka-man, 까맣다 kka-ma-ta
bleed	피가 나다 pi-ga na-da, 피를 흘리다 pi-reul heul-li-da
blend	싱겁다 sing-geop-da
block	막다 mak-da
blocked	막히다 ma-ki-da
blouse	블라우스 beul-la-u-seu
blow	불다 bul-da
blow-dry	드라이 deu-ra-i
(have a) blow-dry	드라이하다 deu-ra-i-ha-da
blue	파란색 pa-ran-saek, 파란 pa-ran, 파랗다 pa-ra-ta
navy blue	청색 cheong-saek
boarding pass	보딩패스 bo-ding-pae-sseu
boat	배 bae
boil	끓다 kkeul-ta
boil something	끓이다 kkeul-i-da
book	책 chaek
bookstore	서점 seo-jeom, 책방 chaek-bang
bored	지루하다 ji-ru-ha-da, 심심하다 sim-sim-ha-da
born	태어나다 tae-eo-na-da
bottle	병 byeong
box	상자 sang-ja
(to) box	권투를 하다 gwon-tu-reul ha-da
boxing	권투 gweon-tu
breakfast	아침 a-chim

(have) breakfast		아침을 먹다 a-chim-eul meok-da
breast		가슴 ga-seum
breath		숨을 쉬다 sum-eul swi-da
breathing		호흡 ho-heum, 숨쉬기 sum-swi-gi
(have difficulty) breathing		숨쉬기가 힘들다 sum-swi-gi-ga him-deul-da
bright		밝다 balk-da
bring someone		모시고 오다 mo-si-go o-da, 데리고 오다 de-ri-go o-da
bring something		가지고 오다 ga-ji-go o-da
British		영국 사람 yeong-guk sa-ram, 영국인 yeong-gug-in
broken		고장나다 go-jang-na-da, 깨지다 kkae-ji-da
brother		
	older	오빠 o-ppa, 형 hyeong
	younger	남동생 nam-dong-saeng
brown		
	light brown	갈색 gal-saek
brush		빗다 bit-da, 닦다 dak-da
brush hair		머리를 빗다 meo-ri-reul bit-da
brush teeth		이를 닦다 i-reul dak-da, 양치질하다 yang-chi-jil-ha-da
build		짓다 jit-da
building		건물 geon-mul
burn		타다 ta-da
burn something		태우다 tae-u-da
bus		버스 beo-sseu
(express) bus		고속버스 go-sok-beo-seu
busily		바쁘게 ba-ppeu-ge
business		장사 jang-sa, 사업 sa-eop
business management		경영학 gyeong-yeong-hak
business school		상경대학 (상대) sang-gyeong-dae-hak (sang-dae)
businessman		사업가 sa-eop-ga
busy		바쁘다 ba-ppeu-da, 복잡하다 bok-ja-pa-da
but		그렇지만 geu-reo-chi-man, 그런데 geu-reon-de
buttocks		엉덩이 eong-deong-i
buy		사다 sa-da

C

café	다방 da-bang, 카페 ka-pe
Canada	캐나다 kae-na-da
Canadian	캐나다 사람 kae-na-da sa-ram,
	캐나다인 kae-na-da-in
car	자가용 ja-ga-yong, 자동차 ja-dong-cha
rental car	렌트카 ren-teu-ka
card	카드 ka-deu
card game	
play a card game	카드놀이를 하다 ka-deu nol-i-reul ha-da,
	트럼프를 치다 teu-reom-peu-reul chi-da
cash	현금 hyeon-geum
casual	캐주얼 kae-ju-eol
catch	잡다 jap-da
caught	잡히다 ja-pi-da
cello	첼로 chel-lo-reul kyeo-da
cellular phone	핸드폰 haen-deu-pon
Celsius	섭씨 seop-ssi
cent	센트 sen-teu
central	중앙 jung-ang
certain	어떤 eo-tteon
(by any) chance	혹시 hok-si
change	거스름돈 geo-seu-reum-tton, 잔돈 jan-don,
chapter	과 gwa
charge	수수료 su-su-ryo
chase	쫓다 jjot-da
chased	쫓기다 jjot-gi-da
check	계산서 gye-san-seo, 수표 supyo
official check	자기앞수표 ja-gi-ap su-pyo
checkered pattern	체크무늬 che-keu-mu-nui, che-keu-mu-ni
chemistry	화학 hwa-hak
chest	가슴 ga-seum
chicken	닭고기 dak-go-gi
child	아이 a-i
chilly	쌀쌀하다 ssal-ssal-ha-da
chin	턱 teok
China	중국 jung-guk
Chinese	중국 사람 jung-guk sa-ram,
	중국인 jung-gug-in
Chinese food	중국음식 jung-gug-eum-sik

Chinese language	중국어 jung-gug-eo
Chinese restaurant	중국식당 jung-guk-sik-dang
civil servant	공무원 gong-mu-won
clarinet	클라리넷 keul-la-ri-net
play clarinet	클라리넷을 불다 keul-la-ri-nes-eul bul-da
clean	깨끗하다 kkae-kkeu-ta-da
(become) clean	맑아지다 malg-a-ji-da,
	깨끗해지다 kkae-kkeu-ta-ji-da
climate	날씨 nal-ssi
climb	올라가다 ol-la-ga-da
climb a mountain	등산을 하다/가다 deung-san-eul ha-da/ga-da
clinic	병원 byeong-won
clock	시계 si-ge
close	가깝다 ga-kkap-da, 닫다 dat-da
closed	닫히다 da-chi-da
clothes	옷 ot
clothing store	옷가게 ot-ga-ge
cloudy	구름이 끼다 gu-reum-i kki-da,
	흐려지다 heu-ryeo-ji-da
coat	오바 o-ba, 코트 co-teu
coffee shop	다방 da-bang, 카페 ka-pe, 커피숍 keo-pi-syop
coffee	커피 keo-pi
cola	콜라 kol-la
cold (*noun*)	감기 gam-gi
have a cold	감기에 걸리다 gam-gi-e geol-li-da
cold (*adjective*)	차다 cha-da, 차갑다 cha-gap-da, 춥다 chup-da
get cold	추워지다 chu-wo-ji-da
cold noodle	냉면 naeng-myeon
cold noodle soup	물냉면 mul-laeng-myeon
cold noodle with	비빔냉면 bi-bim-naeng-myeon
hot paste	
cold water	찬물 chan-mul, 냉수 naeng-su
college of pharmacy	약학대학 (약대) yak-hak-dae-hak (yak-dae)
college of physical	체육대학 (체대) che-yuk-dae-hak (che-dae)
education	
college	대학 dae-hak, 대학교 dae-hak-gyo
college student	대학생 dae-hak-saeng
color	색깔 saek-kkal
color and shape	색상 saek-sang
come	오다 o-da

come down	내려오다	nae-ryeo-o-da
come out	나오다	na-o-da
come to see	찾아 오다	chaj-a o-da,
	만나러 오다	man-na-reo o-da
come up	올라오다	ol-la-o-da
company	회사	hoe-sa
completely	깜빡	kkam-ppak, 완전히 wan-jeon-hi
computer	컴퓨터	keom-pu-teo
play a		
computer game	컴퓨터 게임을 하다	keom-pyu-teo
		ge-im-eul ha-da
concert	음악회	eum-a-koe
condition	상태	sang-tae
congestion	막힘	ma-kim
(have nasal) congestion	코가 막히다	ko-ga ma-ki-da
construction	공사	gong-sa
on the con-		
struction site	공사 중	gong-sa-jung
contact	연락	yeol-lak, 연락하다 yeol-la-ka-da
convenience store	가게	ga-ge, 편의점 pyeon-ui-jeom
convenient	편리하다	pyeol-li-ha-da
cook	음식을 만들다	eum-sig-eul man-deul-da
cooked rice	밥	bap
cool	시원하다	si-won-ha-da
correct	맞다	mat-da
cough	기침	gi-chim, 기침을 하다 gi-chim-eul ha-da
couple of	몇 가지	myeot ga-ji
course	과목	gwa-mok
cousin	사촌	sa-chon, 외사촌 oe-sa-chon
cousin (younger)	사촌동생	sa-chon-dong-saeng
credit card	신용카드	sin-yong-ka-deu
cross	건너다	geon-neo-da
crosswalk	횡단보도	hoeng-dan-bo-do
crowd	복잡하다	bok-ja-pa-da
cry	울다	ul-da
(make someone) cry	울리다	ul-li-da
cup	잔	jan
curly	곱슬곱슬한	gop-seul-gop-seul-han
curly hair	곱슬머리	gop-seul meo-ri

customer   손님 son-nim
        regular customer   단골 dan-gol
cut   자르다 ja-reu-da

D

damaged   상하다 sang-ha-da
dance   춤을 추다 chum-eul chu-da
dark   진하다 jin-ha-da, 어둡다 eo-dup-da,
                            짙다 jit-da
date   날 nal, 날짜 nal-jja, 일 il
daughter   딸 ttal
daughter-in-law   며느리 myeo-neu-ri
dawn   새벽 sae-byeok
day   낮 nat, 날 nal
        per day   하루에 ha-ru-e
December   십이월 sib-i-wol
decent   무난하다 mu-nan-ha-da, 점잖다 jeom-jan-ta
deduct   공제하다 gong-je-ha-da
delicious   맛이 있다 mas-i it-da
dental school   치과대학 (치대) chi-kkwa-dae-hak (chi-dae)
dentistry   치과 chi-kkwa
depart   출발하다 chul-bal-ha-da
department manager   과장님 gwa-jang-nim
department store   백화점 bae-kwa-jeom
departure   출발하는 곳 chul-bal-ha-neun got
deposit   저금하다 jeo-geum-ha-da,
                            예금하다 ye-geum-ha-da
deposit slip   입금표 ip-geum-pyo
deposit/withdrawal record   통장 tong-jang
design   디자인 di-ja-in
designer   디자이너 di-ja-i-neo
destiny   인연 in-yeon, 운명 un-myeong
diarrhea   설사 seol-ssa
(have) diarrhea   설사하다 seol-ssa-ha-da
die   죽다 juk-da
difficult   어렵다 eo-ryeop-da
dinner   저녁 jeo-nyeok
(have) dinner   저녁을 먹다 jeo-nyeog-eul meok-da
direct   직행 jik-haeng
directly   직접 jik-jeop

discount		깎아주다 kkakk-a-ju-da
disease		병 byeong, 질병 jil-byeong
dislike		싫다 sil-ta, 싫어하다 sil-eo-ha-da
dizzy		어지럽다 eo-ji-reop-da
do		하다 ha-da
doctor		의사 ui-sa, 의사 선생님 ui-sa seon-saeng-nim
dollar		달라 dal-la, 불 bul
	per dollar	달러당 dal-leo-dang
down		아래 a-rae
	go down	내려가다 nae-ryeo-ga-da, 내리다 nae-ri-da
downtown		시내 si-nae
draw a picture		그림을 그리다 geu-rim-eul geu-ri-da
dress		원피스 won-pi-seu, 입다 ip-da
	dress someone	입히다 i-pi-da
drink		음료수 eum-nyo-su, 마시다 ma-si-da
	something	
	to drink	마실 것 ma-sil kkeot
drive		운전하다 un-jeon-ha-da
driver		기사 gi-sa, 운전기사 un-jeon-gi-sa
(by) driving		운전해서 un-jeon-hae-seo
drugstore		약국 yak-guk, 약방 yak-bang
drum		드럼 deu-reom
	play drums	드럼을 치다 deu-reom-eul chi-da
dry		말리다 mal-li-da
dry-clean		드라이하다 deu-ra-i-ha-da
dry cleaning		드라이 deu-ra-i,
		드라이클리닝 deu-ra-i-keul-li-ning
during the time		그 동안 geu-dong-an
dye		염색하다 yeom-sae-ka-da
dyeing		염색 yeom-saek

E

ear		귀 gwi
early		일찍 il-jjik
earn money		돈을 벌다 don-eul beol-da
eat		먹다 meok-da, 드시다 deu-si-da,
		잡수시다 jap-su-si-da
	try to eat	먹어 보다 meog-eo bo-da
economics		경제학 gyeong-je-hak
education study		교육학 gyo-yuk-hak

eight days   여드레 yeo-deu-re
eight   여덟 yeo-deol, 팔 pal
eighty   여든 yeo-deun
elementary school   초등학교 cho-deung-hak-gyo
elementary school
   student   초등학생 cho-deung-hak-saeng
employee   종업원 jong-eob-won, 직원 jig-won
end   끝 kkeut
end of the month   월말 wol-mal
end of the year   연말 yeon-mal
energy   기운 gi-un, 힘 him
(have no) energy   기운이 없다 gi-un-i eop-da
(lacking in) energy   기운이 없다 gi-un-i eop-da
engineer   엔지니어 en-ji-ni-eo, 기술자 gi-sul-jja
engineering   공학 gong-hak
engineering school   공과대학 (공대) gong-kkwa-dae-hak
          (gong-dae)

England   영국 yeong-guk
English   영어 yeong-eo
enter   들어가다 deul-eo-ga-da,
          들어오다 deul-eo-o-da
entrance   입구 ip-gu
envelope   편지봉투 pyeon-ji-bong-tu
especially   특별히 teuk-byeol-hi
even if it is true   그래도 geu-rae-do
even now   지금도 ji-geum-do
even though   그래도 geu-rae-do
evening   저녁 jeo-nyeok
every day   매일 mae-il
every month   매월 mae-wol
every week   매주 mae-ju
every year   매년 mae-nyeon
everyone   다들 da-deul
(general) examination   종합검사 jong-hap-geom-sa
get an examination   검사를 하다/받다 geom-sa-reul ha-da/bat-da
(get a general)
     examination   종합검사를 하다/받다 jong-hap-geom-sa-reul
          ha-da/bat-da
examine (in a hospital)   진찰을 하다/받다 jin-chal-eul ha-da/bat-da

exchange	교환하다 gyo-hwan-ha-da, 바꾸다 ba-kku-da, 바꾸다 ba-kku-da, 바꿔주다 ba-kkwo-ju-da
exchange money	환전하다 hwan-jeon-ha-da
exchange rate	환율 hwan-nyul
exchanging currency	환전하기 hwan-jeon-ha-gi
excited	신나다 sin-na-da
Excuse me....	실례지만 sil-lye-ji-man
exist	있다 it-da, 계시다 gye-si-da
exit	나가는 곳 na-ga-neun got, 출구 chul-gu
expensive	비싸다 bi-ssa-da
express mail	빠른 우편 ppa-reun u-pyeon, 속달우편 sok-dal-u-pyeon
external department	외과 oe-kkwa
eye	눈 nun

F

face	얼굴 eol-gul
facial impression	인상 in-sang
(in) fact	사실은 sa-sil-eun
Fahrenheit	화씨 hwa-ssi
fall	가을 ga-eul
family	식구 sik-gu, 가족 ga-jok
family members	식구 sik-gu, 가족 ga-jok
fan	선풍기 seon-pung-gi
far	멀다 meol-da
fare	요금 yo-geum
fast	빠르다 ppa-reu-da, 빨리 ppal-li
father	아버지 a-beo-ji
father-in-law	장인어른 jang-in-eo-reun, 시아버님 si-a-beo-nim
February	이월 i-wol
fee	수수료 su-su-ryo
feed	먹이다 meog-i-da
fever	열 yeol
(have a) fever	열이 나다 yeol-i na-da
fifteen days	보름 bo-reum
fifty	쉰 swin
find	찾다 chat-da
find money	돈을 줍다 don-eul jup-da

fine arts   미술 mi-sul
finger   손가락 son-kka-rak
fire   불 bul
fire station   소방서 so-bang-seo
fire truck   소방차 so-bang-cha
first   먼저 meon-jeo, 첫번째 cheot-beon-jjae
        the first   제일 je-il
first-class mail   항공 우편 hang-gong u-pyeon
(for the) first time   처음 cheo-eum
fish   생선 saeng-seon, 물고기 mul-kko-gi
fishing   낚시 nak-si
        go fishing   낚시를 가다/하다 nak-si-reul ga-da/ha-da
fit   맞다 mat-da
        make
        something fit   맞추다 mat-chu-da
fit someone's taste   마음에 들다 ma-eum-e deul-da,
                             입에 맞다 ib-e mat-da
fitting room   탈의실 tal-ui-sil
five   다섯 da-seot, 오 o
five days   닷새 tat-sae
floor   층 cheung
florist   화원 hwa-won
floss   치실 chi-sil, 플로스 peul-lo-seu
flower pattern   꽃무늬 kkon-mu-ni
flower shop   화원 hwa-won, 꽃집 kkot-jip
flute   플룻 peul-lut
        play flute   플룻을 불다 peul-lus-eul bul-da
follow   따라오다 tta-ra-o-da
food   음식 eum-sik
foot   발 bal
        on foot   걸어서 geol-eo-seo
football   미식축구 mi-sik-chuk-gu, 풋볼 put-bol
        play football   미식축구를 하다 mi-sik-chuk-gu-reul ha-da
forget   잊어버리다 ij-eo-beo-ri-da
form   생기다 saeng-gi-da
forty   마흔 ma-heun
four   넷 net, 사 sa
four days   나흘 na-heul
four-way intersection   사거리 sa-geo-ri
France   프랑스 peu-rang-sseu

freeze	얼다 eol-da, 얼음이 얼다 eol-eum-i eol-da
freeze something	얼리다 eol-li-da
French	프랑스 사람 peu-rang-sseu sa-ram,
	프랑스인 peu-rang-sseu-in
French language	프랑스어 peu-rang-sseu-eo
Friday	금요일 geum-yo-il
front	앞 ap
full	배가 부르다 bae-ga bu-reu-da,
	가득차다 ga-deuk-cha-da
fun	재미있다 jae-mi-it-da

G

game	게임 ge-im, 놀이 nol-i
gate	게이트 ge-i-teu
(in) general	보통 bo-tong
German	독일 사람 dog-il-ssa-ram, 독일인 dog-il-in
German language	독일어 dog-il-eo
Germany	독일 dog-il
get off	내리다 nae-ri-da
get up	일어나다 il-eo-na-da
give	주다 ju-da, 드리다 deu-ri-da
give a present	선물하다 seon-mul-ha-da
give money	돈을 주다 don-eul ju-da
glad	반갑다 ban-gap-da
glass	잔 jan
glasses	안경 an-gyeong
gloves	장갑 jang-gap
go	가다 ga-da
go back	되돌아 가다 doe-dol-a ga-da
go directly	바로 가다 ba-ro ga-da
go out	나가다 na-ga-da
go over	넘다 neom-tta
go straight	똑바로 가다 ttok-ba-ro ga-da,
	직진하다 jik-jin-ha-da
going on well	잘 되다 jal doe-da
golf	골프 gol-peu
play golf	골프를 치다 gol-peu-reul chi-da
good	좋다 jo-ta, 괜찮다 gwaen-chan-ta
gradually	점점 jeom-jeom
graduate school	대학원 dae-hag-won

graduate student		대학원생 dae-hag-won-saeng
grandchildren		손주 son-ju
granddaughter		손녀 son-nyeo
grandfather		할아버지 hal-a-beo-ji
grandmother		할머니 hal-meo-ni
grandson		손자 son-ja
gray		회색 hoe-saek
green		초록색 cho-rok-saek
	(light) green	연두색 yeon-du-saek
ground mail		일반우편 il-ban u-pyeon
ground transportation		차 타는 곳 cha ta-neun got
ground		땅 ttang
grow		자라다 ja-ra-da
guest		손님 son-nim
guitar		기타 gi-ta
	play guitar	기타를 치다 gi-ta-reul chi-da
gum		잇몸 in-mom
gum disease		치주염 chi-ju-yeom

H

hair		머리 meo-ri
	(back of head)	뒷머리 dwin-meo-ri
	(front of head)	앞머리 am-meo-ri
	(side of head)	옆머리 yeom-meo-ri
	long hair	긴 머리 gin meo-ri
	short hair	짧은 머리 jjalb-eun meo-ri
	shoulder-length hair	단발머리 dan-bal meo-ri
	soft hair	부드러운 머리 bu-deu-reo-un meo-ri
	thick hair	뻣뻣한 머리 ppeot-ppeo-tan meo-ri
	volume of hair	머리 숱 meo-ri sut
hair color		머리색깔 meo-ri-saek-kkal
hair cream		헤어 크림 he-eo keu-rim
hair mousse/gel		무스/젤리 mu-sseu/jel-li
	put on hair mousse/gel	무스/젤리를 바르다 mu-sseu/jel-li-reul ba-reu-da
hair quality		머리 결 meo-ri kkyeol
hair spray		
	put on hair spray	스프레이를 하다 seu-peu-re-i-reul ha-da
hair straightening		스트레이트 파마 seu-teu-re-i-teu pa-ma

hairstylist 미용사 mi-yong-sa,
헤어 디자이너 he-eo di-ja-i-neo

(get a) haircut 머리를 깎다/자르다 meo-ri-reul
kkak-da/ja-reu-da, 커트 하다 keo-teu-ha-da

hairpin 머리핀 meo-ri-pin

hand 손 son

happy 기쁘다 gi-ppeu-da, 즐겁다 jeul-geop-da,
행복하다

hard 힘들다 him-deul-da, 딱딱하다 ttak-tta-ka-da

hard work 고생 go-saeng

hat 모자 mo-ja

have 있다 it-da, 가지다 ga-ji-da

       (to) not have 없다 eop-da

head 머리 meo-ri

headache 두통 du-tong

(have a) headache 머리가 아프다 meo-ri-ga a-peu-da

health 건강 geon-gang

health insurance 건강보험 geon-gang-bo-heom

health insurance card 의료보험카드 ui-ryo-bo-heom-ka-deu

hear 듣다 deut-da

heard 들리다 deul-li-da

heavy 무겁다 mu-geop-da

held 안기다 an-gi-da

help 도와주다 do-wa-ju-da,
도와 드리다 do-wa deu-ri-da

      cannot help 할 수 없다 hal sue op-da

here 여기 yeo-gi

high 높다 nop-da

high school 고등학교 go-deung-hak-go

high school student 고등학생 go-deung-hak-saeng

hip 엉덩이 eong-deong-i

history 역사학 yeok-sa-hak

hold 안다 an-tta

home 댁 daek (*hon.*), 집 jip

hospital 병원 byeong-won

hospitalized 입원하다 ib-won-ha-da

hot 덥다 deop-da, 맵다 maep-da

      become hot 더워지다 deo-wo-ji-da

      get hot 더워지다 deo-wo-ji-da

hot day 더운 날 deo-un nal

hour 시간 si-gan
house 댁 daek (*hon.*), 집 jip
how 어떻게 eo-tteo-ke
How about ~ 어떠세요? eo-tteo-se-yo
How is it? 어떠세요? eo-tteo-se-yo
how long/much/many? 얼마나 eol-ma-na
how many items? 몇 개 myeot-gae
how much? 얼마 eol-ma
humanities, school of 인문대학 (인문대) in-mun-dae-hak
　　　　　　　　　　(in-mun-dae)
humid 끈끈하다 kkeun-kkeun-ha-da
humidity 습도 seup-do
hundred 백 baek
hundred million 억 eok
hungry 배가 고프다 bae-ga go-peu-da
hurry 급하다 geu-pa-da, 서두르다 seoo-du-reu-da
　　　　in a hurry 급히 geu-pi
hurt 다치다 da-ch-da, 아프다 a-peu-da
husband 남편 nam-pyeon

I

I 나 na, 저 jeo (*hum.*)
ice 얼음 eol-eum
ice coffee 냉커피 naeng-keo-pi
ice water 냉수 naeng-su, 찬물 can-mul
ID card 신분증 sin-bun-jjeung
if 그러면 geu-reo-myeon
if not 아니면 a-ni-myeon
imagine, unable to 상상이 안 되다 sang-sang-i an-doe-da
in 속 sok, 안 an
increase 인상하다 in-sang-ha-da
increased 인상되다 in-sang-doe-da
indigestion 소화불량 so-hwa-bul-lyang
　　　　have indigestion 소화가 안 되다 so-hwa-ga an-doe-da
indoor 실내 sil-lae
(get) injected 주사를 맞다 ju-sa-reul mat-da
injured 다치다 da-chi-da
inside 속 sok, 안 an
　　　　put inside 넣다 neo-ta
insurance card 보험카드 bo-heom-ka-deu

interesting	재미있다 jae-mi-it-da
interestingly	재미있게 jae-mi-it-ge
internal department	내과 nae-kkwa
intestine	장 jang
(have) intestinal trouble	장염에 걸리다 jang-yeom-e geol-li-da
iron	다리미 da-ri-mi, 다림질하다 da-rim-jil-ha-da
item	항목 hang-mok, 개 gae

J

jacket	자켓 ja-ket
jammed	막히다 ma-ki-da
January	일월 il-wol
Japan	일본 il-bon
Japanese	일본 사람 il-bon sa-ram, 일본인 il-bon-in
Japanese food	일식 il-ssik, 일본음식 il-bon-eum-sik
Japanese language	일본어 il-bon-eo
Japanese restaurant	일식당 il-ssik-dang, 일본식당 il-bon-sik-dang
jaywalk	무단횡단을 하다 mu-dan hoeng-dan-eul ha-da
job	일 il, 직업 jig-eop
jog	조깅을 하다 jo-ging-eul ha-da
jogging	조깅 jo-ging
journalist	기자 gi-ja
juice	주스 ju-seu
July	칠월 chil-wol
June	유월 yu-wol
junior high school	중학교 jung-hak-gyo
junior high school student	중학생 jung-hak-saeng
just	그냥 geu-nyang
just in case	혹시 hok-si
just in time	마침 ma-chim

K

karaoke room	노래방 no-rae-bang
kid	아이 a-i
kill	죽이다 jug-i-da
kimchi	김치 gim-chi
kindergarten	유치원 yu-chi-won
kindergarten student	유치원생 yu-chi-won-saeng
knee	무릎 mu-reup

know	알다 al-da
(to) not know	모르다 mo-reu-da
Korea	한국 han-guk
Korean	한국 사람 han-guk sa-ram, 한국인 han-gug-in
Korean-	한국계 han-guk-gye
Korean food	한식 han-sik, 한국음식 han-gug-eum-sik
Korean language	한국어 han-gug-eo
Korean restaurant	한식당 han-sik-dang, 한식집 han-sik-jip
Korean won	원 won

L

language	말 mal, 언어 eon-eo
late	늦다 neut-da, 늦게 nut-ge
later	나중에 na-jung-e
laugh	웃다 ut-da
(make someone) laugh	웃기다 ut-gi-da
laundry	빨래 ppal-lae
law school	법과대학 (법대) beop-gwa-dae-hak (beop-dae)
law study	법학 beo-pak
lawyer	변호사 byeon-ho-sa
lay down	눕다 nup-da
lay someone down	눕히다 nu-pi-da
layer	층 cheung, 레이어 le-i-eo, 레이어를 주다 le-i-eo-reul ju-da
leave	남기다 nam-gi-da, 떠나다 tteo-na-da
left	왼쪽 oen-jjok
left turn	좌회전 jwa-hoe-jeon
leg	다리 da-ri
lend	빌려주다 bil-lyeo-ju-da
length	길이 gil-i
let's do that	그러자 geu-reo-ja
letter	편지 pyeon-ji
letter paper	편지지 pyeon-ji-ji
light	가볍다 ga-byeop-da, 밝다 balk-da, 연하다 yeon-ha-da
like	좋다 jo-ta, 좋아하다 jo-a-ha-da, 마음에 들다 ma-eum-e deul-da
(to) not like	마음에 안 들다 ma-eum-e an deul-da
like that	그렇게 geu-reo-ke
like this	이렇게 i-reo-ke

linguistics	언어학 eon-eo-hak
listen	듣다 deut-da
literature	문학 mun-hak
little	조금 jo-geum, 조금만 jo-geum-man, 좀 jom
live	살다 sal-da
long	길다 gil-da
long time no see	오래간만이다 o-rae-gan-man-i-da
look around	구경하다 gu-gyeong-ha-da
look for	찾아 보다 chaj-a-bo-da, 찾다 chat-da
look good	괜찮아 보이다 gwaen-chan-a bo-i-da
look heavy	답답해 보이다 dap-dap-hae bo-i-da
look soft	부드러워 보이다 bu-deu-reo-wo bo-i-da
loose	풀다 pul-da, 끄르다 kkeu-reu-da
lose	잃다 il-ta, 지다 ji-da
lose money	돈을 잃다 don-eul il-ta
(a) lot	많이 man-i
loud	시끄럽다 si-kkeu-reop-da
loudly	시끄럽게 si-kkeu-reop-ge, 크게 keu-ge
low	낮다 nat-da
(make something) low	낮추다 nat-chu-da
lucky	다행이다 da-haeng-i-da
lunch	점심 jeom-sim
lunch time	점심시간 jeom-sim-si-gan

M

magazine	잡지 jap-ji
mail	우편물 u-pyeon-mul
registered mail	등기우편 deung-gi-u-pyeon
regular mail	보통 우편 bo-tong u-pyeon, 일반우편 il-ban u-pyeon
mailbox	우체통 u-che-tong
make	만들다 man-deul-da
mall	상가 sang-ga
man	남자 nam-ja
manner	예의 ye-ui
many	많다 man-ta
March	삼월 sam-wol
marry	결혼하다 gyeol-hon-ha-da
match well	어울리다 eo-ul-li-da
mathematics	수학 su-hak

(does not) matter		상관없다 sang-gwan-eop-da
May		오월 o-wol
me		나na, 저 jeo (*hum.*)
meal		밥 bap, 식사 sik-sa, 진지 jin-ji
medical school		의과대학 (의대) ui-kkwa-dae-hak (ui-dae)
medical study		의학 ui-hak
medical treatment		치료 chi-ryo
medicine		약 yak
	(liquid)	물약 mul-lyak
	(powdered)	가루약 ga-ru-yak
	take medicine	약을 먹다 yag-eul meok-da
medium		보통 bo-tong
meet		만나다 man-na-da, 뵙다 boep-da, 만나 뵙다 man-na-boep-da
	staff meeting	직원회의 jig-won-hoe-ui
menu		메뉴 me-nyu
message		메시지 me-se-ji
Mexican		멕시코 사람 mek-si-ko sa-ram, 멕시코인 mek-si-ko-in
Mexico		멕시코 mek-si-ko
Michigan		미시간 mi-si-gan
middle		가운데 ga-un-de
(in the) middle		중간에 jung-gan-e
middle age		중년 jung-nyeon
mile		마일 ma-il
mileage		마일리지 ma-il-li-ji
military personnel		군인 gun-in
minute		분 bun
(for a) minute		잠깐만 jam-kkan-man
misplace money		돈을 잃어버리다 don-eul il-eo-beo-ri-da
mix		섞다 seok-da
Monday		월요일 wol-yo-il
money		돈 don
month		월 wol, 달 dal
	last month	지난 달 ji-nan dal
	next month	다음 달 da-eum-ttal
	this month	이번 달 i-beon-ttal
more		더 deo
(much) more		훨씬 hwol-ssin
morning		아침 a-chim

most, the	제일 je-il	
mother	어머니 eo-meo-ni	
mother-in-law	장모님 jang-mo-nim, 시어머님 si-eo-meo-nim	
motorcycle	오토바이 o-to-ba-i	
mountain	산 san	
mountain side	산 쪽 san jjok	
mouth	입 ip	
mouthwash	마우스워시 ma-u-seu-wo-si	
move	이사하다 i-sa-ha-da	
movie	영화 yeong-hwa	
moving	이사 i-sa	
muffler	목도리 mok-do-ri	
muggy	끈끈하다 kkeun-kkeun-ha-da	
museum	박물관 bang-mul-gwan	
music	음악 eum-ak	
music school	음악대학 (음대) eum-ak-dae-hak (eum-dae)	
my	내 nae, 제 je	

N

name	성명 seong-myeong, 성함 seong-ham, 이름 i-reum	
near	근처 geun-cheo	
nearby	근처 geun-cheo, 옆 yeop	
neat and fresh	산뜻하다 san-tteu-ta-da	
neck	목 mok	
necktie	넥타이 nek-ta-i	
need	필요하다 pil-yo-ha-da	
need money	돈이 들다 don-i deul-da	
nephew	남자조카 nam-ja-jo-ka	
New Zealand	뉴질랜드 nyu-jil-laen-deu	
New Zealander	뉴질랜드인 nyu-jil-laen-deu-in, 뉴질랜드 사람 nyu-jil-laen-deu sa-ram	
newly	새로 sae-ro	
newly released	새로 나오다 sae-ro na-o-da	
niece	여자조카 yeo-ja-jo-ka	
night	밤 bam	
	for all night	밤새도록 bam-sae-do-rok
nine	구 gu, 아홉 a-hop	
	nine days	아흐레 a-heu-re
ninety	아흔 a-heun	

no		아니오 a-ni-o
	no other choice	할 수 없다 hal sue op-da
non-stop		직행 jik-haeng
nose		코 ko
not		안 an
November		십일월 sib-il-wol
now		이제 i-je, 지금 ji-geum
	from now on	앞으로 ap-eu-ro
number		번 beon, 번호 beon-ho
nurse		간호사 gan-ho-sa, 간호원 gan-ho-won

O

o'clock		시 si
October		시월 si-wol
of course		그럼요 geu-reom-yo
office		사무실 sa-mu-sil
	office employee	회사원 hoe-sa-won
often		자주 ja-ju
oh		아이구 a-i-gu, 아참 a-cham
ointment		바르는 약 ba-reu-neun nyak, 연고 yeon-go
OK		괜찮다 gwaen-chan-ta, 좋다 jo-ta
old		늙다 neulk-da,
		연세가 많으시다 yeon-se-ga man-eu-si-da,
		낡다 nalk-da, 오래되다 o-rae-doe-da,
		나이가 많다 na-i-ga man-ta
	old people	나이드신 분들 na-i-deu-sin bun-deul,
		노인들 no-in-deul
once		한번 han-beon
one		하나 ha-na, 일 il
	one cup	한잔 han jan
	one day	하루 ha-ru
	one pair	한벌 han-beol
(by) oneself		혼자 hon-ja
only		그냥 geu-nyang
open		열다 yeol-da
opened		열리다 yeol-li-da
opening a bank account		통장 만들기 tong-jang man-deul-gi
(in my) opinion		제가 보기에는 je-ga bo-gi-e-neun
opthalmology		안과 an-kkwa

or	아니면 a-ni-myeon
orange	주황색 ju-hwang-saek, 오렌지 o-ren-ji
order	시키다 si-ki-da, 주문하다 ju-mun-ha-da,
organize	정리하다 jeong-ri-ha-da
other people	남들 nam-deul
our	우리 u-ri, 저희 jeo-hi
out	바깥 ba-kkat, 밖 bak
outside	바깥 ba-kkat, 밖 bak
oval	타원형 ta-won-hyeong
overlapped	겹치다 gyeop-chi-da
overpass	육교 yuk-gyo
owner	주인 ju-in

P

package	소포 so-po
pants	바지 ba-ji
dress pants	정장 바지 jeong-jang ba-ji
panty hose	스타킹 seu-ta-king
parents	부모 bu-mo, 부모님 bu-mo-nim
particularly	특별히 teuk-byeol-hi
not particularly	별로 byeol-lo
pass away	돌아가시다 dol-a-ga-si-da
passer-by	행인 haeng-in
passport	여권 yeo-kkwon
pastor	목사 mok-sa, 목사님 mok-sa-nim
patient	참다 cham-tta, 환자 hwan-ja
peacefully	안녕히 an-nyeong-hi
pediatrics	소아과 so-a-kkwa
be in a period	생리하다 saeng-ri-ha-da
permanent	파마 pa-ma
permanent wave (hair)	파마머리 pa-ma meo-ri
get a permanent	파마하다 pa-ma-ha-da
person	분 bun, 사람 sa-ram, 명 myeong
pharmacist	약사 yak-sa
photo developing shop	사진관 sa-jin-gwan
physics	물리학 mul-li-hak
piano	피아노 pi-a-no
play piano	피아노를 치다 pi-a-no-reul chi-da

picture		그림 geu-rim, 사진 sa-jin
	take a picture	사진을 찍다 sa-jin-eul jjik-da
pill		알약 al-lyak
PIN number		비밀번호 bi-mil-beon-ho
ping-pong		탁구 tak-gu
	play ping-pong	탁구를 치다 tak-gu-reul chi-da
pink		분홍색 bun-hong-saek
place		장소 jang-so
	other places	다른 데 da-reun de
platform		플랫폼 peul-laet-pom
play		놀다 nol-da, 연극 yeon-geuk
play for someone's benefit		놀아주다 nol-a-ju-da
please		어서 eo-seo, 좀 jom
P.M.		오후 o-hu
police		경찰 gyeong-chal
police station		경찰서 gyeong-chal-sseo
political science		정치학 jeong-chi-hak
pork		돼지고기 dwae-ji-go-gi
post office		우체국 u-che-guk
post office employee		우체국 직원 u-che-guk jig-won
postage		우편요금 u-pyeon-yo-geum
postal charge		우편요금 u-pyeon-yo-geum
postcard		엽서 yeop-seo
postman		우체부 u-che-bu
pound		파운드 pa-un-deu
powder		가루 ga-ru
prescription		처방전 cheo-bang-jeon
present		선물 seon-mul
president (of a company)		사장 sa-jang
pretty		예쁘다 ye-ppeu-da
(for) prevention		예방용 ye-bang-nyong
price		가격 ga-gyeok, 값 gap
	original price	정가 jeong-kka
product		제품 je-pum
professor		교수 gyo-su
psychology		심리학 sim-ni-hak
pull out		뽑다 ppop-da
purple		보라색 bo-ra-saek

Pusan	부산 bu-san
(going to) Pusan	부산행 bu-san-haeng
put on	넣다 neo-ta, 발라 주다 bal-la ju-da, 바르다 ba-reu-da

Q

quickly	어서 eo-seo, 빨리 ppal-li

R

rain	비 bi, 비가 오다 bi-ga o-da
read	읽다 ilk-da, 읽어주다 ilg-eo-ju-da
really	정말 jeong-mal, 참 cham
receipt	영수증 yeong-su-jeung
receive	받다 bat-da
receiver	받으실 분 bad-eu-sil bun, 받는 사람 ban-neun sa-ram
recipient	받는 사람 ban-neun sa-ram
rectangle	직사각형 jik-sa-ga-kyeong
red	빨간색 ppal-gan-saek, 빨간 ppal-gan, 빨갛다 ppal-ga-ta
relatively	비교적 bi-gyo-jeok
release	나오다 na-o-da
released (from a hospital)	퇴원하다 toe-won-ha-da
relieved	풀리다 pul-li-da
request	부탁하다 bu-ta-ka-da
rice	쌀 ssal, 밥 bap
rice with mixed vegetables	비빔밥 bi-bim-ppap
ride	타다 ta-da
place to ride	타는 데 ta-neun de
riding	타기 ta-gi
right	오른쪽 o-reun-jjok
right behind	바로 뒤 ba-ro dwi
right side	오른쪽 o-reun-jjok
right turn	우회전 u-hoe-jeon
ring	반지 ban-ji
ring ring....	따르릉 tta-reu-reung
rinse out	린스 하다 rin-seu ha-da, 헹구다 heng-gu-da
road	길 gil
roughly	대충 dae-chung

round	동그라미 dong-geu-ra-mi, 원형 won-hyeong
(by) running	뛰어서 ttwi-eo-seo
runny nose	콧물 kon-mul
have a runny nose	콧물이 나다 kon-mul-i na-da
Russia	러시아 reo-si-a
Russian	러시아 사람 reo-si-a sa-ram, 러시아인 reo-si-a-in
Russian language	러시아어 reo-si-a-eo

S

sad	슬프다 seul-peu-da
safely	안녕히 an-nyeong-hi, 안전하게 (an-jeon-ha-ge)
sale period	세일기간 se-il-gi-gan
salesperson	점원 jeom-won
salty	짜다 jja-da
same	같다 gat-da, 똑 같다 ttok gat-da
San Diego	샌디에이고 saen-di-e-i-go
Saturday	토요일 to-yo-il
save money	돈을 맞기다 don-eul mat-gi-da, 저금하다 jeo-geum-ha-da, 예금하다 ye-geum-ha-da
scallion	파 pa
scallion pancake	파전 pa-jeon
scared	무섭다 mu-seop-da
scarf	목도리 mok-do-ri, 스카프 seu-ka-peu
school year	학년 hang-nyeon
sciences, school of	자연대학 (자연대) ja-yeon-dae-hak (ja-yeon-dae)
sea	바다 ba-da
seaside	바다 쪽 ba-da jjok
seal	도장 do-jang
seat	자리 ja-ri, 좌석 jwa-seok
seat number	좌석번호 jwa-seok-beon-ho
seat someone	앉히다 an-chi-da
secretary	비서 bi-seo
see	보다 bo-da, 뵙다 boep-da
seen	보이다 bo-i-da
sell	팔다 pal-da

send		부치다 bu-chi-da, 보내다 bo-nae-da
sender		보내는 사람 bo-nae-neun sa-ram
sending mail		편지 부치기 pyeon-ji bu-chi-gi
Seoul		서울 seo-ul
September		구월 gu-wol
serious		심하다 sim-ha-da
service		서비스 sseo-bi-sseu
set		맞추다 mat-chu-da
seven		일곱 il-gop, 칠 chil
	seven days	이레 i-re
seventy		일흔 il-heun
7-up (beverage)		사이다 sa-i-da
several		몇 가지 myeot ga-ji, 몇 myeot
	several days	며칠 myeo-chil
severe		독하다 do-ka-da, 심하다 sim-ha-da
shake		흔들다 heun-deul-da
shake off		털다 teol-da
shampoo		머리를 감다 meo-ri-reul gam-tta, 샴푸하다 syam-pu-ha-da
shape		모양 mo-yang
share		함께 쓰다 ham-kke sseu-da, 같이 쓰다 ga-chi sseu-da
	share a ride	합승 하다 hap-seung-ha-da
sheet		장 jang
ship		배 bae
shirt		셔츠 syeo-cheu
	dress shirt	와이셔츠 wa-i-syeo-cheu
	tennis/golf shirt	남방 nam-bang
shoe store		신발가게 sin-bal-kka-ge, 양화점 yang-hwa-jeom
shoes		신발 sin-bal
	put on shoes	신기다 sin-gi-da
shop		가게 ga-ge
shopping		쇼핑 syo-ping
	go shopping	쇼핑가다 syo-ping-ga-da
short		짧다 jjalp-da
shortly		짧게 jjalp-ge
shoulder		어깨 eo-kkae
show		보여 주다 bo-yeo ju-da

shower		샤워 sya-wo
	take a shower	샤워를 하다 sya-wo-reul ha-da
sibling (younger)		동생 dong-saeng
sick		아프다 a-peu-da
side		옆 yeop
	this side	이쪽 i-jjok
side dishe		반찬 ban-chan
signal		신호 sin-ho
signature		사인 sa-in
similar		비슷하다 bi-seu-ta-da
sing		노래하다 no-rae-ha-da
sing a song		노래를 부르다 no-rae-reul bu-reu-da
singer		가수 ga-su
sister		
	older	누나 nu-na, 언니 eon-ni
	younger	여동생 yeo-dong-saeng
sit		앉다 an-tta
six		여섯 yeo-seot, 육 yuk
	six days	엿새 yeot-sae
sixty		예순 ye-sun
size		사이즈 sa-i-jeu
skate		스케이트 seu-ke-i-teu
ski		스키 seu-ki
skirt		치마 chi-ma
sleep		주무시다 ju-mu-si-da, 자다 ja-da, 잠을 자다 jam-eul ja-da
	make someone sleep	재우다 jae-u-da
snow		눈 nun, 눈이 오다 nun-i o-da
so		정말 jeong-mal, 그래서 geu-rae-seo
soccer		축구 chuk-gu
	play soccer	축구를 하다 chuk-gu-reul ha-da
sociology		사회학 sa-hoe-hak
socks		양말 yang-mal
soft		부드럽다 bu-deu-reop-da
soju		소주 so-ju
sold		팔리다 pal-li-da
some kind of		무슨 mu-seun
somehow		어떻게 eo-tteo-ke

someone	누구 nu-gu, 누가 nu-ga
something	무엇 nu-eot, 뭐 mwo
sometime	언제 eon-je
somewhere	어디 eo-di
son	아들 a-deul
song	노래 no-rae
son-in-law	사위 sa-wi
soon	금방 geum-bang, 곧 got
sore throat, have a	목감기에 걸리다 mok-gam-gi-e geol-li-da, 목이 붓다 mog-i but-da
sorry	죄송하다 joe-song-ha-da, 미안하다 mi-an-ha-da
soup	국 guk, 국물 gung-mul
sour	시다 si-da
Spain	스페인 seu-pe-in
Spanish	스페인 사람 seu-pe-in sa-ram, 스페인인 seu-pe-in-in
Spanish language	스페인어 seu-pe-in-eo
speak	말하다 mal-ha-da, 말씀하시다 mal-sseum-ha-si-da,
special	특별한 teuk-byeol-han
special care	특별대우 teuk-byeol-dae-u
special day	무슨 날 mu-seun nal, 특별한 날 teuk-byeol-han nal
spend	쓰다 sseu-da, 사용하다 sa-yong-ha-da
spend money	돈을 쓰다 don-eul sseu-da
spend time	지내다 ji-nae-da
spicy	맵다 maep-da
sports	운동 un-dong
sportsman	운동선수 un-dong-seon-su
spring	봄 bom
spy movie	첩보영화 cheop-bo-yeong-hwa
square	정사각형 jeong-sa-ga-kyeong
stamp	우표 u-pyo, 도장 do-jang
put on a stamp	우표를 붙이다 u-pyo-reul bu-chi-da
start	시작하다 si-ja-ka-da
stay	계시다 gye-si-da
sticky	끈끈하다 kkeun-kkeun-ha-da
still	아직 a-jik

stomach	배 bae
have stomach pain	배가 아프다 bae-ga a-peu-da
on an empty stomach	공복에 gong-bog-e
stop	서다 seo-da, 세워 주다 se-wo ju-da, 세워 드리다 se-wo deu-ri-da,
stop by	들러 보다 deul-leo-bo-da
store	가게 ga-ge
story	층 cheung
straight	똑바로 ttok-ba-ro, 쭉 jjuk
strange	이상하다 i-sang-ha-da
street	길 gil
stressed	스트레스가 많다/쌓이다 seu-teu-re-sseu-ga man-ta /ssa-i-da
stripe pattern	줄무늬 jul-mu-ni
strong	강하다 gang-ha-da, 힘이 세다 him-i se-da, 독하다 do-ka-da
student	학생 hak-saeng
subway	지하철 ji-ha-cheol
suit	정장 jeong-jang
summer	여름 yeo-reum
Sunday	일요일 il-yo-il
supermarket	슈퍼마켓 syu-peo-ma-ket
sure, for	꼭 kkok, 확실히 hawk-sil-hi
Su-won	수원 su-won
sweat	땀 ttam, 땀이 나다 ttam-i na-da
sweater	스웨터 seu-we-teo
sweet	달다 dal-da
swim	수영을 하다 su-yeong-eul ha-da
swimming	수영 su-yeong
swimming pool	수영장 su-yeong-jang
switch	바꾸다 ba-kku-da, 바꿔주다 ba-kkwo-ju-da
swollen	붓다 but-da
symptom	증상 jeung-sang

T

tablet	알약 al-lyak
take away	뺏다 ppaet-da
take care	모시다 mo-si-da, 손질하다 son-jil-ha-da

take off	벗다 beot-da, 빼다 ppae-da, 풀다 pul-da
take someone	모셔다 드리다 mo-syeo-da deu-ri-da,
	모시고 가다 mo-si-go ga-da,
	데리고 가다 de-ri-go ga-da
take something	가지고 가다 ga-ji-go ga-da
taken away	뺏기다 ppaet-gi-da
talk	말하다 mal-ha-da, 말씀 드리다 mal-sseum
deu-ri-da	
tart	쓰다 sseu-da
tastily	맛있게 mas-it-ge
tasty	맛있다 mass-it-da
taxi	택시 taek-si
teacher	선생 seon-saeng, 선생님 seon-saeng-nim
teacher education school	사범대학 (사대) sa-beom-dae-hak (sa-dae)
telephone	전화 jeon-hwa
make a	
telephone call	전화하다 jeon-hwa-ha-da,
	전화 걸다 jeon-hwa geol-da
telephone number	전화번호 jeon-hwa-beon-ho
television (TV)	텔레비전 tel-le-bi-jeon
temperature	온도 on-do, 기온 gi-on
ten	십 sip, 열 yeol
ten days	열흘 yeol-heul
ten thousand	만 man
tender	연하다 yeon-ha-da
tennis	테니스 te-ni-sseu
play tennis	테니스를 치다 te-ni-sseu-reul chi-da
thank	감사하다 gam-sa-ha-da, 고맙다 go-map-da
thanks to (you)	덕분에 deok-bun-e
that	그 geu
that one	그걸로 geu-geol-lo
that over there	저 jeo
that side	그 쪽 geu jjok
that side over there	저 쪽 jeo-jjok
that's right	그렇구나 geu-reo-ku-na, 맞아요 maj-a-yo
then	그럼 geu-reom
there	거기 geo-gi
over there	저기 jeo-gi
these days	요즘 yo-jeum

thick	굵다	gulk-da
thin	가늘다	ga-neul-da
things	물건	mul-geon
things for elderly people	노인용	no-in-yong
things that are needed	필요한 것	pil-yo-han geot
thirsty	목이 마르다	mog-i ma-reu-da
thirty	서른	seo-reun
this	이	i
this and that	이것 저것	i-geot jeo-geot
thousand	천	cheon
three	삼 sam, 셋 set	
three days	사흘	sa-heul
throat	목	mok
Thursday	목요일	mog-yo-il
ticket	표	pyo
tie	매다	mae-da
tile	타일	ta-il
time	시간	si-gan
have time	시간(이) 있다	si-gan(-i) it-da
next time	다음 번 da-eum-beon, 다음에 da-eum-e	
take time	걸리다	geol-li-da
time to leave the office	퇴근시간	toe-geun-si-gan
times	번	beon
tired	피곤하다	pi-gon-ha-da
today	오늘	o-neul
toe	발가락	bal-kka-rak
together	같이	ga-chi
tomorrow	내일	nae-il
day after tomorrow	모레	mo-re
too	너무	neo-mu
tooth	이	i
toothache, have a	이가 아프다	i-ga a-peu-da
toothpaste	치약	chi-yak
top	위	wi
tough	뻣뻣하다	ppeot-ppeo-ta-da
towel	수건	su-geon
have a towel-dry	머리를 말리다	meo-ri-reul mal-li-da
town	동네	dong-ne
toy	장난감	jang-nan-kkam

toy store		장난감 가게 jang-nan-kkam ga-ge
traffic signal		신호등 sin-ho-deung
train		기차 gi-cha
transfer		갈아타다 gal-a-ta-da
place to transfer		갈아타는 곳 gal-a-ta-neun got
travel		여행 yeo-haeng, 여행을 하다/가다
		yeo-haeng-eul ha-da/ga-da
triangle		정삼각형 jeong-sam-ga-kyeong
trillion		조 jo
trim		다듬다 da-deum-tta,
		다듬어 주다 da-deum-eo ju-da
trouble		문제 mun-je
	have trouble	큰일 나다 keun-il na-da
trumpet		트럼펫 teu-reom-pet
	play trumpet	트럼펫을 불다 teu-reom-pes-eul bul-da
try		해 보다 hae bo-da
try on (clothes)		입어 보다 ib-eo-bo-da
Tuesday		화요일 hwa-yo-il
turn		돌리다 dol-li-da
	make a left turn	좌회전하다 jwa-hoe-jeon-ha-da
	make a right turn	우회전하다 u-hoe-jeon-ha-da,
	turn left	왼쪽으로 가다 oen-jjog-eu-ro ga-da
	turn on	틀어 놓다 teul-eo no-ta
	turn right	오른쪽으로 가다 o-reun-jjog-eu-ro ga-da
twenty		스물 seu-mul
	twenty days	스무날 seu-mu-nal
two		둘 dul, 이 i
	two days	이틀 han i-teul jeon

U

uh uh (no)		어머 eo-meo
uncle		삼촌 sam-chon, 큰아버지 keun-a-beo-ji,
		작은 아버지 jag-eun a-beo-ji,
		외삼촌 oe-sam-chon, 고모부 go-mo-bu,
		이모부 i-mo-bu
under		아래 a-rae, 밑 mit
underneath		밑 mit
underpass		지하도 ji-ha-do
underwear		속옷 sog-ot
undress		벗다 beot-da

undress someone	벗기다 beot-gi-da
university	대학교 dae-hak-gyo
university street	대학로 dae-hang-no
untie	풀다 pul-da, 끄르다 kkeu-reu-da
unusual	이상하다 i-sang-ha-da
up	위 wi
go up	올라가다 ol-la-ga-da, 오르다 o-reu-da
us	우리 u-ri, 저희 jeo-hi
use	사용하다 sa-yong-ha-da, 쓰다 sseu-da
used	쓰이다 sseu-i-da

V

vacation	방학 bang-hak, 휴가 hyu-ga
very	아주 a-ju
videotape	비디오 bi-di-o
village	동네 dong-ne
viola	비올라 vi-ol-la-reul kyeo-da
violin	바이올린 va-i-ol-in
play violin	바이올린을 켜다 va-i-ol-in-eul kyeo-da
visa	비자 bi-ja
visitor	손님 son-nim
volleyball	배구 bae-gu
play volleyball	배구를 하다 bae-gu-reul ha-da
volume	권 gwon
vomit	토하다 to-ha-da

W

waist	허리 heo-ri
wait	기다리다 gi-da-ri-da
waiter	종업원 jong-eob-won
waitress	여종업원 yeo-jong-eob-won
wake someone up	깨우다 kkae-u-da
wake up	일어나다 il-eo-na-da, 깨다 kkae-da
walk	걷다 geot-da
by walking	걸어서 geol-eo-seo
go for a walk	산책을 하다 san-chaeg-eul ha-da
wall	벽 byeok
warm	따뜻하다 tta-tteu-ta-da
wash	씻다 ssit-da, 빨다 ppal-da
wash dishes	설거지를 하다 seol-geo-ji-reul ha-da

wash hair	머리 감다 meo-ri gam-tta
wash one's face	세수를 하다 se-su-reul ha-da
wash one's hands/feet	손/발을 씻다 son/bal-eul ssit-da
wash out	린스 하다 rin-seu ha-da, 헹구다 heng-gu-da
washing machine	세탁기 se-tak-gi
watch (*noun*)	시계 si-ge
watch (*verb*)	보다 bo-da
watch a movie	영화 보다 yeong-hwa bo-da
watch a videotape	비디오를 보다 vi-di-o-reul bo-da
watch repair store	시계 방 si-ge ppang
watch TV	텔레비전을 보다 tel-le-bi-jeon-eul bo-da
water	물 mul
watermelon	수박 su-bak
way	
by the way	그런데 geu-reon-de
on the way	중간에 jung-gan-e, 도중에 do-jung-e
this way	이리 i-ri
we	우리 u-ri, 저희 jeo-hi
weak	약하다 ya-ka-da
wear	입다 ip-da, 입어 보다 ib-eo-bo-da, 꼽다 kkop-da, 끼다 kki-da, 두르다 du-reu-da, 신다 sin-tta
weather	날씨 nal-ssi
weather forecast	일기예보 il-gi-ye-bo
Wednesday	수요일 su-yo-il
week	주 ju
last week	지난 주 ji-nan ju
next week	다음 주 da-eum-jju
this week	이번 주 i-beon-jju
weekday	주중 ju-jung
weekend	주말 ju-mal
welcome party	환영회 hwan-yeong-hoe
well	안녕하다 an-nyeong-ha-da, 잘 있다 jal it-da, 잘 jal
done well	잘 되다 jal doe-da
Western food	양식 yang-sik
Western liquor	양주 yang-ju
Western restaurant	양식당 yang-sik-dang
wet	젖다 jeot-da
wet towel	물수건 mul-ssu-geon

what	무엇 nu-eot, 뭐 mwo
what date	며칠 myeo-chil(noun)
what day	무슨 요일 mu-seun yo-il
what kind of	무슨 mu-seun, 어떤 eo-tteon
what thing	웬일 wen-il
what time	몇 시 myeot-si
when	언제 eon-je
whenever	언제든지 eon-je-deun-ji, 언제나 eon-je-na
where	어디 eo-di
which	어느 eo-neu, 어떤 eo-tteon
which one	어떤 거 eo-tteon geo
which person	어느 분 eo-neu-bun
which way	어느 쪽 eo-neu jjok
which year born	몇 년생 myeon-nyeon-saeng
(a) while ago	얼마 전 eol-ma jeon
white	하얀색 ha-yan-saek, 하얀 ha-yan, 하얗다 ha-ya-ta
who	누구 nu-gu, 누가 nu-ga
why	왜 wae
widely	크게 keu-ge
wife	아내 a-nae, 집사람 jip-sa-ram, 부인 bu-in
win	이기다 i-gi-da
win money	돈을 따다 don-eul tta-da
wind	바람 ba-ram
window side	창측 chang-cheuk
wine	포도주 po-do-ju
winter	겨울 geo-wul
withdraw money	돈을 찾다 don-eul chat-da
withdrawal slip	출금표 chul-geum-pyo
woman	여자 yeo-ja
middle-aged woman	아주머니 a-ju-meo-ni
word	말씀 mal-sseum, 말 mal, 단어 dan-eo
work (*noun*)	일 il
work (*verb*)	일하다 il-ha-da, 근무하다 geun-mu-ha-da
work hard	수고하다 su-go-ha-da
worldwide	전 세계적으로 jeon se-gye-jeog-eu-ro
worn out	다 되다 da doe-da, 닳다 dal-ta
worry	걱정하다 geok-jeong-ha-da
wow	와 wa, 어휴 eo-hu

wrestle (*verb*)		레슬링을 하다 re-seul-ling-eul ha-da
wrestling		레슬링 re-seul-ling
write		쓰다 sseu-da, 써 주다 sseo ju-da
write a reply		답장을 쓰다 dap-jang-eul sseu-da
writer		작가 jak-ga
written		써 있다 sseo it-da

Y

year		년 nyeon
	last year	작년 jang-nyeon
	next year	내년 nae-nyeon
	this year	금년 geum-nyeon, 올해 ol-hae
	year after	
	next year	내후년 nea-hu-nyeon
	year before	
	last year	재작년 jae-jang-nyeon
yellow		노란색 no-ran-saek, 노란 no-ran, 노랗다 no-ra-ta
	(light) yellow	겨자색 gyeo-ja-saek
yes		네 ne, 예 ye
yesterday		어제 eo-je
	day before	
	yesterday	그저께 geu-jeo-kke, 그제 geu-je
yet		아직도 a-jik-do, 아직 a-jik
young		어리다 eo-ri-da, 젊다 jeom-tta

Z

zero		공 gong, 영 yeong
zip code		우편번호 u-pyeon-beon-ho

AUDIO TRACK LIST

 Audio files available for download at:
http://www.hippocrenebooks.com/beginners-online-audio.html

FOLDER ONE

. Alphabet and Pronunciation Guide
. Lesson 1: Patterns
. Lesson 1: Model Conversations 1
. Lesson 1: Model Conversations 2
. Lesson 1: Model Conversations 3
. Lesson 1: Vocabulary

. Lesson 2: Patterns
. Lesson 2: Model Conversations 1
. Lesson 2: Model Conversations 2
). Lesson 2: Model Conversations 3
. Lesson 2: Model Conversations 4
2. Lesson 2: Vocabulary

. Lesson 3: Patterns
. Lesson 3: Model Conversations 1
. Lesson 3: Model Conversations 2
. Lesson 3: Model Conversations 3
. Lesson 3: Vocabulary

. Lesson 4: Patterns
. Lesson 4: Model Conversations 1
. Lesson 4: Model Conversations 2
. Lesson 4: Model Conversations 3
. Lesson 4: Vocabulary

. Lesson 5: Patterns
. Lesson 5: Model Conversations 1
. Lesson 5: Model Conversations 2
. Lesson 5: Model Conversations 3
. Lesson 5: Vocabulary

. Lesson 6: Patterns
. Lesson 6: Model Conversations 1
. Lesson 6: Model Conversations 2
. Lesson 6: Model Conversations 3
. Lesson 6: Vocabulary

33. Lesson 7: Patterns
34. Lesson 7: Model Conversations 1
35. Lesson 7: Model Conversations 2
36. Lesson 7: Model Conversations 3
37. Lesson 7: Vocabulary

FOLDER TWO

1. Lesson 8: Patterns
2. Lesson 8: Model Conversations 1
3. Lesson 8: Model Conversations 2
4. Lesson 8: Model Conversations 3
5. Lesson 8: Model Conversations 4
6. Lesson 8: Vocabulary

7. Lesson 9: Patterns
8. Lesson 9: Model Conversations 1
9. Lesson 9: Model Conversations 2
10. Lesson 9: Model Conversations 3
11. Lesson 9: Vocabulary

12. Lesson 10: Patterns
13. Lesson 10: Model Conversations 1
14. Lesson 10: Model Conversations 2
15. Lesson 10: Model Conversations 3
16. Lesson 10: Vocabulary

17. Lesson 11: Patterns
18. Lesson 11: Model Conversations 1
19. Lesson 11: Model Conversations 2
20. Lesson 11: Model Conversations 3
21. Lesson 11: Vocabulary

22. Lesson 12: Patterns
23. Lesson 12: Model Conversations 1
24. Lesson 12: Model Conversations 2
25. Lesson 12: Model Conversations 3
26. Lesson 12: Vocabulary

CPSIA information can be obtained
at www.ICGtesting.com
Printed in the USA
LVHW010849100119
603376LV00001B/1/P

9 780781 813778